Prentice Hall

Biology

Reading and Study Workbook A

PEARSON
Prentice Hall

Upper Saddle River, New Jersey
Boston, Massachusetts

Pearson Prentice Hall™ is a trademark of Pearson Education, Inc.
Pearson® is a registered trademark of Pearson plc.
Prentice Hall® is a registered trademark of Pearson Education, Inc.

ISBN 0-13-166257-0

23 V001 15 14

How to Use the *Reading and Study Workbook A*

Did you know that learning to study more effectively can make a real difference in your performance at school? Students who master study skills are more confident and have more fun learning. This book, the *Reading and Study Workbook* for *Prentice Hall Biology*, is designed to help you acquire the skills that will allow you to study biology more effectively. Your active participation in class and use of this book can go a long way toward helping you achieve success in biology.

The *Reading and Study Workbook* can be used to
- preview a chapter,
- learn key vocabulary terms,
- master difficult concepts, and
- review for chapter and unit tests.

The *Reading and Study Workbook* concentrates on the key concepts presented in each chapter of the textbook. Each chapter in the *Reading and Study Workbook* is divided into the same numbered sections as in the textbook. By completing each section after you have read the section in the textbook, you will be better able to understand and remember the important points made in the chapter. In addition, your ability to tie information together in order to see the "big picture" in biology will be greatly improved.

Each chapter in the *Reading and Study Workbook* begins with a two-page chapter summary. This review material stresses the key concepts and facts you should focus on in that particular chapter. As you read the chapter review, try to relate the material you have read in the chapter to the material stressed in the summary. If parts of the summary are not clear to you, go back to that part of the section in the textbook and read it again.

An alternate way of using the chapter summary is to read it before you read the chapter in the textbook. In that way you will be alerted to the important facts contained in the chapter. Used in this manner, the summary can be a prereading guide to the chapter material.

Following the chapter summary, you will find specific workbook activities designed to help you read and understand the textbook. Completing these worksheets will help you master the key concepts and vocabulary in each section.

Each lesson in the *Reading and Study Workbook* provides questions to help you understand the content found under each of the main headings in the textbook. Diagrams, charts, and word puzzles provide a variety of formats to help you master key terms.

An activity that focuses on a particular reading strategy for each chapter is also provided. These activities will help improve your reading skills. Strategies include
- outlining,
- sequencing information,
- identifying cause and effect, and
- identifying main ideas and supporting details.

The final part of each chapter consists of Vocabulary Reviews. The Vocabulary Reviews take a variety of formats including flowcharts, crossword puzzles, labeling diagrams, multiple-choice questions, and matching exercises.

Contents

Chapter 21 Fungi

Chapter 22 Plant Diversity

Chapter 23 Roots, Stems, and Leaves

Chapter 24 Reproduction of Seed Plants

Chapter 25 Plant Responses and Adaptations

Chapter 26 Sponges and Cnidarians

Chapter 27 Worms and Mollusks

Chapter 28 Arthropods and Echinoderms

Chapter 29 Comparing Invertebrates

Chapter 30 Nonvertebrate Chordates, Fishes, and Amphibians

Chapter 31 Reptiles and Birds

Chapter 32 Mammals

Chapter 33 Comparing Chordates

Chapter 34 Animal Behavior

Chapter 35 Nervous System

Chapter 36 Skeletal, Muscular, and Integumentary Systems

Chapter 37 Circulatory and Respiratory Systems

Chapter 38 Digestive and Excretory Systems

Chapter 39 Endocrine and Reproductive Systems

Chapter 40 The Immune System and Disease

Chapter 1   The Science of Biology

Summary

1–1 What Is Science?

Science is an organized way of using evidence to learn about the natural world. Scientific thinking usually begins with observation, which is the process of gathering information about events or processes in a careful, orderly way. The information gathered from observations is called data. Quantitative data are expressed as numbers, obtained by counting or measuring. Qualitative data are descriptive and involve characteristics that can't usually be counted. Scientists use data to make inferences. An inference is a logical interpretation based on prior knowledge or experience.

After making first observations, a researcher will propose one or more hypotheses. A hypothesis is a proposed scientific explanation for a set of observations. Scientists generate hypotheses using prior knowledge, logical inference, and informed, creative imagination. Scientific hypotheses must be proposed in a way that enables them to be tested. Some hypotheses are tested by performing controlled experiments. Other hypotheses are tested by gathering more data. The conclusions researchers draw from experiments or data must be valid. To be valid, a conclusion must be based on logical interpretation of reliable data.

1–2 How Scientists Work

Conducting a scientific investigation involves a series of steps. The first step is asking a question. The second step involves forming a hypothesis. The third step in conducting a scientific investigation is setting up a controlled experiment. Whenever possible, a hypothesis should be tested by an experiment in which only one variable is changed at a time. All other variables should be kept unchanged. This type of experiment is called a controlled experiment. The variable that is deliberately changed is called the manipulated variable. The variable that is observed and

that changes in response to the manipulated variable is called the responding variable.

The fourth step in conducting a scientific investigation is recording and analyzing results. The fifth step is drawing a conclusion. A key assumption in science is that experimental results can be reproduced.

Sometimes, controlled experiments are not possible. When researchers design alternative investigations, they try to maintain the rigorous thinking associated with a controlled experiment. As evidence from numerous investigations builds up, a particular hypothesis may become so well supported that scientists consider it a theory. In science, a theory is a well-tested explanation that unifies a broad range of observations.

1–3 Studying Life

Although living things vary greatly, all living things share eight characteristics:

1. Living things are made up of units called cells. A cell is a collection of living matter enclosed by a barrier that separates the cell from its surroundings. Cells are the smallest units of an organism that can be considered alive.

2. Living things reproduce. In sexual reproduction, cells from two different parents unite to produce the first cell of the new organism. In asexual reproduction, a single-celled organism divides in half to form two new organisms.

3. Living things are based on a universal genetic code. The directions for inheritance are carried by a molecule called DNA.

4. Living things grow and develop. Multicellular organisms typically go through a process called development. As cells divide, they change in shape and structure in a process called differentiation.

5. Living things obtain and use materials and energy. The combination of chemical reactions through which an organism builds up or breaks down materials as it carries out its life processes is called metabolism.

6. Living things respond to their environment. Organisms detect and respond to stimuli from their environment. A stimulus is a signal to which an organism responds.

7. Living things maintain a stable internal environment. The process by which they do this is called homeostasis.

8. Taken as a group, living things change over time. Change over time in living things is called evolution.

Biology is divided into different fields of study. Some fields focus on the study of living systems at different levels. These levels include, from smallest to largest: molecules, cells, groups of cells, organisms, populations, communities, ecosystems, and the biosphere.

1–4 Tools and Procedures

Most scientists use the metric system when collecting data. The metric system is a decimal system of measurement whose units are based on certain physical standards and are scaled on multiples of 10. A revised version of the original metric system is called the International System of Units, or SI.

The simplest way to find out whether factors in an experiment changed or remained the same is to record data in a table and then make a graph.

A microscope is a device that produces magnified images of structures that are too small to see with the unaided eye. Light microscopes produce magnified images by focusing visible light rays. Compound light microscopes allow light to pass through the specimen and use two lenses to form an image. Electron microscopes use beams of electrons to produce magnified images. Biologists use two main types: the transmission electron microscope (TEM) and the scanning electron microscope (SEM).

A cell culture is a group of cells that develops from a single cell placed in a dish containing a nutrient solution. Cell fractionation is a technique in which cells are broken into pieces and different cell parts are separated for study.

Whenever you work in your biology laboratory, it's important for you to follow safe practices. The single most important rule for your safety is simple: Always follow your teacher's instructions and the textbook directions exactly. Because you may be in contact with organisms you cannot see, it is essential that you wash your hands thoroughly after every scientific activity.

Chapter 1 The Science of Biology

Section 1–1 What Is Science? (pages 3–7)

🔑 **Key Concept**
- What is the goal of science?

What Science Is and Is Not (page 3)

1. What is the goal of science? _____
_____
_____

2. What is science? _____
_____

Thinking Like a Scientist (page 4)

3. What is observation? _____
_____
_____

4. The information gathered from observation is called _____.

5. Complete the table about types of data.

TYPES OF DATA

Type	Data Involves . . .	Example
	Numbers	
	Characteristics that cannot be easily measured or counted	

6. What is an inference? _____
_____

Explaining and Interpreting Evidence (page 5)

7. What is a hypothesis? _____

   _____

8. In science, a hypothesis is useful only if it can be _____.

9. Is the following sentence true or false? A hypothesis should be stated in such a way
   that it can never be proved wrong. _____

10. What are three sources from which hypotheses may arise?

   a. _____

   b. _____

   c. _____

11. Circle the letter of each of the following that may be an outcome of testing a hypothesis.

   a. The hypothesis is partly true but needs to be revised.

   b. The hypothesis is wrong.

   c. The hypothesis is supported.

   d. The hypothesis is of no value.

Science as a Way of Knowing (page 6)

12. What do scientists assume about the universe?

   _____

   _____

13. What are some qualities that are desirable in a scientist? _____

   _____

   _____

Science and Human Values (page 7)

14. Is the following sentence true or false? A community must use its shared values to
   make decisions about scientific issues. _____

Section 1–2 How Scientists Work (pages 8–15)

🔑 **Key Concepts**
- How do scientists test hypotheses?
- How does a scientific theory develop?

Designing an Experiment (pages 8–10)

1. The idea that life can arise from nonliving matter is called

   _____ .

2. What was Francesco Redi's hypothesis about the appearance of maggots?

   _____

3. What are variables in an experiment? _____

4. Ideally, how many variables should an experiment test at a time? _____

   _____

5. What is a controlled experiment? _____

   _____

   _____

6. The illustration below shows the beginning of Redi's experiment. Complete the
   illustration by showing the outcome.

Redi's Experiment on Spontaneous Generation

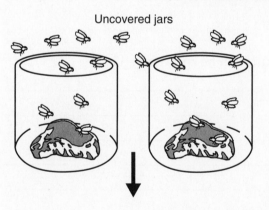

Uncovered jars

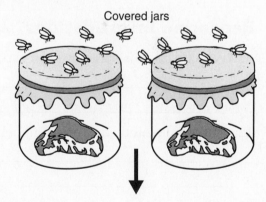

Covered jars

Several
days pass.

7. Complete the table about variables.

VARIABLES

Type of Variable	Definition
Manipulated variable	
Responding variable	

8. In Redi's experiment, what were the manipulated variable and the responding variable?

_____

_____

_____

9. For what do scientists use the data from a controlled experiment? _____

_____

10. When scientists look for explanations for specific observations, what do they assume

about nature? _____

_____

Repeating Investigations (pages 10–13)

11. Why do scientists assume that experimental results can be reproduced?

_____

_____

12. What did Anton van Leeuwenhoek discover? _____

_____

_____

13. What did John Needham conclude from his test of Redi's findings? _____

_____

14. What did Spallanzani do to improve upon Redi's and Needham's work? _____

_____

_____

15. How did Pasteur settle the spontaneous generation argument? _____

_____

_____

When Experiments Are Not Possible (page 14)

16. In animal field studies, why do scientists usually try to work without making the animals aware that humans are present? _____

_____

17. When a controlled experiment is not possible, why do scientists try to identify as many relevant variables as possible? _____

_____

How a Theory Develops (pages 14–15)

18. In science, what is a theory? _____

_____

19. Is the following sentence true or false? A theory may be revised or replaced by a more useful explanation. _____

Reading Skill Practice

A flowchart can help you remember the order in which a set of events has occurred or should occur. On a separate sheet of paper, create a flowchart that represents the process that Redi carried out in his investigation of spontaneous generation. This process is explained under the heading Designing an Experiment on pages 8–10. For more information about flowcharts, see Organizing Information in Appendix A of your textbook.

Section 1–3 Studying Life (pages 16–22)

Key Concepts

- What are some characteristics of living things?
- How can life be studied at different levels?

Introduction (page 16)

1. What is biology? _____

_____

Characteristics of Living Things (pages 16–20)

2. What is a cell? _____

_____

_____

3. Circle the letter of each sentence that is true about cells.

   a. A cell is the smallest unit of an organism that can be considered alive.

   b. A multicellular organism may contain trillions of cells.

   c. A living thing that consists of a single cell is a multicellular organism.

   d. Organisms are made up of cells.

4. What are two types of asexual reproduction?

   a. _____

   b. _____

5. Living things are based on a universal _____.

6. Circle the letter of each sentence that is true about living things.

   a. The life cycle of many organisms involves development.

   b. For bacteria, growth is mostly a simple increase in size.

   c. Each type of organism has a distinctive life cycle.

   d. Cells may change in number but never differentiate.

7. Why does an organism need energy and a constant supply of materials?

_____

_____

8. What is metabolism? _____

_____

_____

_____

9. Is the following sentence true or false? All organisms respond to the environment in exactly the same ways. _____

10. What is homeostasis? _____
_____
_____

11. A group of organisms that changes over time is said to _____.

Branches of Biology (pages 20–21)

Match the different kinds of biologists with the focus of their study.

Kinds of Biologists	Focus of Study
_____ 12. Zoologist	**a.** Plants
_____ 13. Botanist	**b.** Ancient life
_____ 14. Paleontologist	**c.** Animals

15. Label each of the illustrations below according to the level of study represented.

_____   _____   _____

16. The largest level of biological study is the _____.

Biology in Everyday Life (page 22)

17. What kinds of information can the study of biology provide about matters affecting human society? _____
_____
_____

Section 1–4 Tools and Procedures (pages 24–28)

Key Concepts

- What measurement system do most scientists use?
- How are light microscopes and electron microscopes similar? How are they different?

A Common Measurement System (page 24)

1. Why do scientists need a common system of measurement? _____
_____
_____

2. When collecting data and doing experiments, what system of measurement do most scientists use? _____

3. What is the metric system? _____
_____
_____

4. Complete each equation by writing the correct number or metric unit.

   a. 1000 meters = 1 _____

   b. 1 liter = _____ milliliters

   c. 1 gram = _____ milligrams

   d. 1000 kilograms = 1 _____

Analyzing Biological Data (page 25)

5. When scientists collect data, what are they often trying to find out? _____
_____
_____

6. What does a graph of data make easier to recognize and understand than a table of data? _____

Microscopes (pages 25–26)

7. What are microscopes? _____
_____

8. What are compound light microscopes? _____
_____
_____

9. How do chemical stains make light microscopes more useful? _____
_____

10. What are the two main types of electron microscopes?

    a. _____

    b. _____

11. Compare how a TEM and an SEM produce images. _____

_____

_____

_____

12. How must samples be prepared for observation by an electron microscope?

_____

Laboratory Techniques (page 27)

13. A group of cells grown in a nutrient solution from a single original cell is called a(an)

    _____.

14. What technique do biologists use to separate one part of a cell from the rest of the cell?

    _____

Working Safely in Biology (page 28)

15. What is the single most important rule for your safety while working in a laboratory?

_____

_____

Vocabulary Review

Completion   *Fill in the blanks with terms from Chapter 1.*

1. The process of gathering information about events or processes in a careful, orderly way is called _____.

2. The information gathered from observations is called _____.

3. A(An) _____ is a logical interpretation based on prior knowledge or experience.

4. A(An) _____ is a proposed scientific explanation for a set of observations.

5. In a(an) _____ experiment, only one variable is changed at a time, while all other variables are kept unchanged.

6. The variable that is deliberately changed in a controlled experiment is called the _____ variable.

7. A(An) _____ is a well-tested explanation that unifies a broad range of observations.

8. In _____ reproduction, the new organism has a single parent.

9. A(An) _____ is a signal to which an organism responds.

10. The _____ system is a decimal system of measurement whose units are based on certain physical standards and are scaled on multiples of 10.

Matching   *In the space provided, write the letter of the definition that best matches each term.*

_____ 11. biology

_____ 12. microscope

_____ 13. cell

_____ 14. cell fractionation

_____ 15. homeostasis

_____ 16. metabolism

_____ 17. cell culture

a. a collection of living matter enclosed by a barrier that separates it from its environment

b. combination of chemical reactions through which an organism builds up or breaks down materials

c. a laboratory technique in which a group of cells develops from a single cell

d. process of keeping an organism's internal conditions constant

e. a device that produces magnified images of structures that are too small to see with the unaided eye

f. a laboratory technique in which cells are separated into cell parts

g. the science that seeks to understand the living world

Chapter 2   The Chemistry of Life

Summary

2–1 The Nature of Matter

The basic unit of matter is the atom. The subatomic particles that make up atoms are protons, neutrons, and electrons. Protons and neutrons have about the same mass. Protons are positively charged particles (+), and neutrons carry no charge. Protons and neutrons together form the nucleus, at the center of the atom. The electron is a negatively charged particle (–). Atoms have equal numbers of electrons and protons, and therefore atoms do not have a charge.

A chemical element is a pure substance that consists entirely of one type of atom. The number of protons in an atom of an element is the element's atomic number. Atoms of an element can have different numbers of neutrons. Atoms of the same element that differ in the number of neutrons they contain are known as isotopes. Because all the isotopes of an element have the same number of electrons, they all have the same chemical properties.

A chemical compound is a substance formed by the chemical combination of two or more elements in definite proportions. Atoms in compounds are held together by chemical bonds. An ionic bond is formed when one or more electrons are transferred from one atom to another. A covalent bond forms when electrons are shared between atoms. The structure that results when atoms are joined together by covalent bonds is called a molecule. Unequal sharing of electrons creates regions of positive and negative charges in molecules. Slight attraction can develop between the oppositely charged regions of nearby molecules. Such intermolecular forces of attraction are called van der Waals forces.

2–2 Properties of Water

The water molecule (H_2O) is neutral. Yet, the oxygen end of the molecule has a slight positive charge, and the hydrogen end has a slight negative charge.

A molecule in which the charges are unevenly distributed is called a polar molecule. Polar molecules can attract each other. The attraction between the hydrogen atom on one water molecule and the oxygen atom on another water molecule is called a hydrogen bond. Cohesion is an attraction between molecules of the same substance. Adhesion is an attraction between molecules of different substances.

A mixture is a material composed of two or more elements or compounds that are physically mixed together—the substances are not chemically combined. A solution is a mixture in which all the components are evenly distributed throughout the mixture. In a solution, the substance that is dissolved is called the solute. The substance in which the solute dissolves is called the solvent. Water is the greatest solvent on Earth.

A water molecule can react to form ions. A water molecule (H_2O) can form a hydrogen ion (H^+) and a hydroxide ion (OH^-). The pH scale indicates the concentration of H^+ ions in a solution. Pure water has a pH of 7. An acid is any compound that forms H^+ ions in solution. Acidic solutions contain higher concentrations of H^+ ions than pure water. A base is a compound that produces OH^- ions in solution. Basic, or alkaline, solutions contain lower concentrations of H^+ ions than pure water and have pH values above 7.

2–3 Carbon Compounds

Organic chemistry is the study of all compounds that contain bonds between carbon atoms. Carbon compounds are also called organic compounds. Many of the molecules in living things are so large that they are known as macromolecules. Macromolecules are formed in a process called polymerization. Smaller units, called monomers, join together to form macromolecules, or polymers.

Four groups of organic compounds found in living things are carbohydrates, lipids, nucleic acids, and proteins. Carbohydrates are compounds made up of carbon, hydrogen, and oxygen atoms. Living things use carbohydrates as their main source of energy. Plants and some animals use carbohydrates in structures. Starches and sugars are examples of carbohydrates.

Lipids are made mostly from carbon and hydrogen atoms. Fats, oils, and waxes are lipids. Lipids are used in living things to store energy. Some lipids are important parts of biological membranes and waterproof coverings. Lipid molecules are made up of compounds called fatty acids and glycerol.

Nucleic acids contain hydrogen, oxygen, nitrogen, carbon, and phosphorus. Nucleotides are the monomers that make up nucleic acids. Each nucleotide consists of a 5-carbon sugar, a phosphate group, and a nitrogenous base. Nucleic acids store and transmit hereditary, or genetic, information. There are two kinds of nucleic acids: ribonucleic acid (RNA) and deoxyribonucleic acid (DNA).

Proteins contain nitrogen as well as carbon, hydrogen, and oxygen. Proteins are polymers of molecules called amino acids. Some proteins control the rate of reactions and regulate cell processes. Some are used to form bones and muscles. Others transport substances into or out of cells or help to fight disease.

2–4 Chemical Reactions and Enzymes

A chemical reaction is a process that changes one set of chemicals (reactants) into another set of chemicals (products). Chemical reactions always involve the breaking of bonds in reactants and the formation of new bonds in products.

Some chemical reactions release energy, and other reactions absorb energy. Chemical reactions that release energy often occur spontaneously. Every chemical reaction needs energy to get started, and that starting energy is called activation energy.

A catalyst is a substance that speeds up the rate of a chemical reaction. Catalysts work by lowering a reaction's activation energy. Enzymes are proteins that act as biological catalysts. Enzymes speed up chemical reactions by lowering activation energies. In an enzyme-catalyzed reaction, the reactants are known as substrates. The substrates bind to a site on the enzyme called the active site.

Chapter 2 The Chemistry of Life

Section 2–1 The Nature of Matter (pages 35–39)

⚷ Key Concepts
- What three subatomic particles make up atoms?
- How are all of the isotopes of an element similar?
- What are the two main types of chemical bonds?

Atoms (page 35)

1. The basic unit of matter is called a(an) _____.

2. Describe the nucleus of an atom. _____

_____

3. Complete the table about subatomic particles.

SUBATOMIC PARTICLES

Particle	Charge	Location in Atom
	Positive	
	Neutral	
	Negative	

4. Why are atoms neutral despite having charged particles? _____

_____

Elements and Isotopes (page 36)

5. What is a chemical element? _____

_____

6. What does an element's atomic number represent? _____

_____

7. Atoms of the same element that differ in the number of neutrons they contain are

   known as _____.

8. How are isotopes identified? _____

9. Why do all isotopes of an element have the same chemical properties? _____

_____

_____

Chemical Compounds (page 37)

10. What is a chemical compound? _____

_____

_____

11. What does the formula for table salt indicate about that compound?

_____

_____

_____

_____

Chemical Bonds (pages 38–39)

12. What holds atoms in compounds together? _____

13. Complete the table about the main types of chemical bonds.

CHEMICAL BONDS

Type	Formed when . . .
Covalent bond	
Ionic bond	

14. What is an ion? _____

_____

_____

15. Is the following sentence true or false? An atom that loses electrons has a negative charge. _____

16. The structure that results when atoms are joined together by covalent bonds is called a(an) _____.

17. Circle the letter of each sentence that is true about covalent bonds.

   a. When atoms share two electrons, it is called a double bond.

   b. In a water molecule, each hydrogen atom forms a single covalent bond.

   c. Atoms can share six electrons and form a triple bond.

   d. In a covalent bond, atoms share electrons.

18. The slight attractions that develop between oppositely charged regions of nearby molecules are called _____.

Section 2–2 Properties of Water (pages 40–43)

⊷ **Key Concepts**
- Why are water molecules polar?
- What are acidic solutions? What are basic solutions?

The Water Molecule (pages 40–41)

1. Is the following sentence true or false? A water molecule is neutral. _____

2. Why is a water molecule polar? _____

_____

_____

3. Circle the letter of each sentence that is true about hydrogen bonds.

   a. A hydrogen bond is stronger than an ionic bond.

   b. The attraction between the hydrogen atom on one water molecule and the oxygen atom on another water molecule is an example.

   c. A hydrogen bond is stronger than a covalent bond.

   d. They are the strongest bonds that form between molecules.

4. Complete the table about forms of attraction.

FORMS OF ATTRACTION

Form of Attraction	Definition
Cohesion	
Adhesion	

Solutions and Suspensions (pages 41–42)

5. What is a mixture? _____

_____

_____

6. A mixture of two or more substances in which the molecules of the substances are evenly mixed is called a(an) _____.

7. The greatest solvent in the world is _____.

8. What is a suspension? _____

_____

9. Complete the table about substances in solutions.

SUBSTANCES IN SOLUTIONS

Substance	Definition	Saltwater Solution
Solute		
		Water

Acids, Bases, and pH (pages 42–43)

10. Why is water neutral despite the production of hydrogen ions and hydroxide ions?

_____

_____

_____

11. What does the pH scale indicate? _____

_____

12. On the pH scale below, indicate which direction is increasingly acidic and which is increasingly basic.

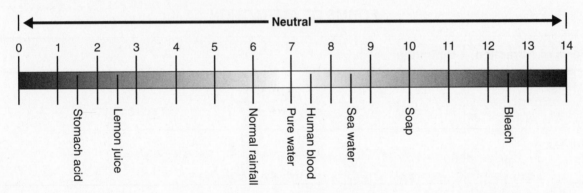

13. How many more H⁺ ions does a solution with a pH of 4 have than a solution with a pH of 5? _____

14. What is an acid? _____

15. Is the following sentence true or false? Strong bases have pH values ranging from 11 to 14. _____

16. What are buffers? _____

_____

_____

Section 2–3 Carbon Compounds (pages 44–48)

Key Concept
- What are the functions of each group of organic compounds?

The Chemistry of Carbon (page 44)

1. How many valence electrons does each carbon atom have? _____
   _____

2. What gives carbon the ability to form chains that are almost unlimited in length?
   _____
   _____

Macromolecules (page 45)

3. Many of the molecules in living cells are so large that they are known as
   _____ .

4. What is the process called by which macromolecules are formed? _____

5. When monomers join together, what do they form? _____

6. What are four groups of organic compounds found in living things?

   a. _____

   b. _____

   c. _____

   d. _____

Carbohydrates (pages 45–46)

7. What atoms make up carbohydrates? _____
   _____

8. Circle the letter of each sentence that is true about carbohydrates.

   a. Starches and sugars are examples of carbohydrates.

   b. Living things use them as their main source of energy.

   c. The monomers in sugar polymers are starch molecules.

   d. Plants and some animals use them for strength and rigidity.

9. Single sugar molecules are also called _____ .

10. Circle the letter of each monosaccharide.

    a. galactose   c. glucose

    b. glycogen   d. fructose

11. What are polysaccharides? _____

_____

12. How do plants and animals store excess sugar? _____

_____

Lipids (pages 46–47)

13. What kinds of atoms are lipids mostly made of? _____

_____

_____

14. What are three common categories of lipids?

a. _____ b. _____ c. _____

15. Many lipids are formed when a glycerol molecule combines with compounds

called _____.

16. Circle the letter of each way that fats are used in living things.

a. As parts of biological membranes

b. To store energy

c. To give plants rigidity

d. As chemical messengers

17. Complete the table about lipids.

LIPIDS

Kind of Lipid	Description
	Each carbon atom in a lipid's fatty acid chain is joined to another carbon atom by a single bond.
Unsaturated	
	A lipid's fatty acids contain more than one double bond.

Nucleic Acids (page 47)

18. Nucleic acids contain what kinds of atoms? _____

_____

19. The monomers that make up nucleic acids are known as _____.

20. A nucleotide consists of what three parts? _____

_____

_____

21. What is the function of nucleic acids in living things? _____

_____

_____

22. What are two kinds of nucleic acids?

a. _____

b. _____

Proteins (pages 47–48)

23. Proteins contain what kinds of atoms? _____

_____

_____

24. Proteins are polymers of molecules called _____.

25. What are four roles that proteins play in living things?

a. _____

b. _____

c. _____

d. _____

Reading Skill Practice

You can often increase your understanding of what you've read by making comparisons. A compare-and-contrast table helps you to do this. On a separate sheet of paper, make a table to compare the four groups of organic compounds you read about in Section 2–3. You might use the heads Elements, Functions, and Examples for your table. For more information about compare-and-contrast tables, see Organizing Information in Appendix A.

Section 2–4 Chemical Reactions and Enzymes (pages 49–53)

Key Concepts
- What happens to chemical bonds during chemical reactions?
- How do energy changes affect whether a chemical reaction will occur?
- Why are enzymes important to living things?

Chemical Reactions (page 49)

1. What is a chemical reaction? _____

_____

2. Complete the table about chemicals in a chemical reaction.

CHEMICALS IN A CHEMICAL REACTION

Chemicals	Definition
Reactants	
Products	

3. Chemical reactions always involve changes in chemical _____.

Energy in Reactions (page 50)

4. What is released or absorbed whenever chemical bonds form or are broken?

_____

5. What do chemical reactions that absorb energy need to occur? _____

_____

6. Chemists call the energy needed to get a reaction started the _____.

7. Complete the graph of an energy-releasing reaction by adding labels to show the energy of the reactants, the energy of the products, and the activation energy.

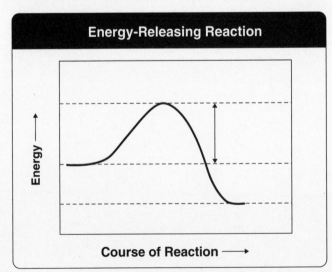

© Pearson Education, Inc., publishing as Pearson Prentice Hall.

Enzymes (pages 51–52)

8. What is a catalyst? _____

_____

9. Proteins that act as biological catalysts are called _____.

10. What do enzymes do? _____

_____

11. From what is part of an enzyme's name usually derived? _____

_____

_____

Enzyme Action (pages 52–53)

12. The reactants of enzyme-catalyzed reactions are known as _____.

13. Why are the active site and the substrates in an enzyme-catalyzed

reaction often compared to a lock and key? _____

_____

_____

14. The binding together of an enzyme and a substrate forms a(an)

_____.

15. How do most cells regulate the activity of enzymes? _____

_____

_____

_____

Chapter 2   The Chemistry of Life

Vocabulary Review

Crossword Puzzle   *Use the clues below to fill in the spaces in the puzzle with the correct words.*

Across

1. element or compound that enters into a chemical reaction
4. process that changes one set of chemicals into another
7. positively charged subatomic particle
8. substance formed by the chemical combination of two or more elements in definite proportions
11. positively or negatively charged atom
12. carbon compound that stores and transmits genetic information
14. the center of an atom
16. bond formed when electrons are shared between atoms
17. macromolecule formed when monomers join together

Down

2. negatively charged subatomic particle
3. compound that produces hydroxide ions in solution
5. bond formed when one or more electrons are transferred from one atom to another
6. monomer of nucleic acid
9. monomer of protein
10. compound that forms hydrogen ions in solution
13. atom of same element that differs in number of neutrons compared with other atoms of the element
15. basic unit of matter

© Pearson Education, Inc., publishing as Pearson Prentice Hall.

Summary

3–1 What Is Ecology?

Ecology is the scientific study of interactions among organisms and between organisms and their environment. Earth's organisms live in the biosphere. The biosphere consists of the parts of the planet in which all life exists. It includes land; water; and air, or atmosphere.

Ecology includes the study of all the different levels of life, ranging from the individual organism to the biosphere. Above the level of the individual organism is the species. A species is a group of organisms so similar to one another that they can breed together and produce fertile offspring. A group of individuals that belong to the same species and live in the same area is called a population. A collection of different populations that live together in an area is referred to as a community. An ecosystem includes all the organisms that live in a particular place, together with their physical environment. A group of ecosystems that have the same climate and similar dominant communities is called a biome.

Ecologists use three basic methods of research: observing, experimenting, and modeling. Observing often leads to questions and hypotheses. Experimenting can be used to test hypotheses. Experimenting may be done in a laboratory or in the natural world. Modeling helps ecologists understand complex processes.

3–2 Energy Flow

All organisms need to obtain energy from their environment to power life processes. Sunlight is the main energy source for life on Earth. Organisms that can capture energy from sunlight or chemicals and use that energy to produce food are called autotrophs, or producers. Only plants, some algae, and certain bacteria are producers. On land, plants are the main autotrophs.

The process in which autotrophs use light energy to make food is called photosynthesis. In photosynthesis, light provides the energy needed to turn carbon dioxide and water into oxygen and carbohydrates. The process in which autotrophs use chemical energy to produce carbohydrates is called chemosynthesis. Chemosynthesis is performed by only certain types of bacteria.

Organisms that rely on other organisms for their energy and food are called heterotrophs. Heterotrophs are also referred to as consumers. There are many different types of heterotrophs. Herbivores, such as cows, obtain energy by eating only plants. Carnivores, such as snakes, eat only animals. Omnivores, such as humans, eat both plants and animals. Detritivores, such as earthworms, feed on plant and animal remains and other dead matter. Decomposers, such as fungi, break down organic matter.

Energy flows through an ecosystem in one direction. It flows from the sun or from inorganic compounds, first to autotrophs and then to heterotrophs. A food chain is a series of steps in which organisms transfer energy by eating and being eaten. A food web links together all the food chains in an ecosystem. Each step in a food chain or food web is called a trophic level. Producers make up the first trophic level. Consumers make up higher trophic levels. Each consumer depends on the trophic level below it for energy.

An ecological pyramid is a diagram that shows the relative amounts of energy or matter contained within each trophic level in a food chain or food web. Types of ecological pyramids are energy pyramids, biomass pyramids, and pyramids of numbers. Energy pyramids show how much energy is available within each trophic level. Only about 10 percent of the energy available within one trophic level is transferred to organisms at the next trophic level.

Biomass pyramids show the biomass, or total amount of living tissue, within each trophic level. A pyramid of numbers shows the relative number of individual organisms at each trophic level.

3–3 Cycles of Matter

Matter, unlike energy, is recycled within and between ecosystems. Matter is passed from one organism to another and from one part of the biosphere to another through biogeochemical cycles. These cycles connect biological, geological, and chemical processes. Matter can cycle through the biosphere because biological systems do not use up matter; they only change it.

All living things require water to survive. Water cycles between the ocean, atmosphere, and land. Several different processes are involved in the water cycle, including evaporation and transpiration. Evaporation is the process in which water changes from a liquid to a gas. Transpiration is the process in which water evaporates from the leaves of plants.

All the chemical substances that an organism needs to survive are called nutrients. Like water, nutrients cycle within and between ecosystems.

The three most important nutrient cycles are the carbon, nitrogen, and phosphorus cycles. Carbon is a key ingredient of living tissue. Processes involved in the carbon cycle include photosynthesis and human activities such as burning. Nitrogen is needed by all organisms to build proteins. Processes involved in the nitrogen cycle include nitrogen fixation and denitrification. In nitrogen fixation, certain bacteria convert nitrogen gas into ammonia. In denitrification, other bacteria convert nitrogen compounds called nitrates back into nitrogen gas. Phosphorus is needed for molecules such as DNA and RNA. Most of the phosphorus in the biosphere is stored in rocks and ocean sediments. Stored phosphorus is gradually released into water and soil, where it is used by organisms.

The primary productivity of an ecosystem is the rate at which organic matter is created by producers. One factor that controls primary productivity is the amount of available nutrients. When an ecosystem is limited by a single nutrient that is scarce or cycles very slowly, this substance is called a limiting nutrient. If an aquatic ecosystem receives a large quantity of a limiting nutrient, there may be a sudden increase in the amount of algae, called an algal bloom.

Chapter 3 The Biosphere

Section 3–1 What Is Ecology? (pages 63–65)

Key Concepts
- What different levels of organization do ecologists study?
- What methods are used to study ecology?

Interactions and Interdependence (page 63)

1. What is ecology? _____

_____

_____

2. What does the biosphere contain? _____

_____

_____

Levels of Organization (page 64)

3. Why do ecologists ask questions about events and organisms that range in complexity from an individual to the biosphere? _____

_____

_____

4. Complete the table about levels of organization.

LEVELS OF ORGANIZATION

Level	Definition
Species	
	A group of individuals that belong to the same species and live in the same area
Community	
Ecosystem	
	A group of ecosystems that have the same climate and dominant communities

5. What is the highest level of organization that ecologists study? _____

_____

Ecological Methods (page 65)

6. What are the three basic approaches scientists use to conduct modern ecological research?

   a. _____ b. _____ c. _____

7. Why might an ecologist set up an artificial environment in a laboratory?

_____

_____

_____

8. Why are many ecological phenomena difficult to study? _____

_____

_____

9. Why do ecologists make models? _____

_____

_____

10. Is the following sentence true or false? An ecological model may consist of a

    mathematical formula. _____

Section 3–2 Energy Flow (pages 67–73)

🔷 Key Concepts
- Where does the energy for life processes come from?
- How does energy flow through living systems?
- How efficient is the transfer of energy among organisms in an ecosystem?

Producers (pages 67–68)

1. What is at the core of every organism's interaction with the environment?

_____

2. What source of energy do organisms use if they don't use the sun's energy?

_____

_____

3. What are autotrophs? _____

_____

_____

4. Why are autotrophs also called producers? _____

5. What do autotrophs do during photosynthesis? _____

_____

_____

_____

6. For each of the following, write which kind of autotroph is the main producer.
   a. Land: _____
   b. Upper layers of ocean: _____
   c. Tidal flats and salt marshes: _____

7. What is chemosynthesis? _____

_____

_____

8. Where do bacteria that carry out chemosynthesis live? _____

_____

_____

_____

Consumers (pages 68–69)

9. Heterotrophs are also called _____.

10. Plant and animal remains and other dead matter are collectively called

_____.

11. Complete the table about types of heterotrophs.

TYPES OF HETEROTROPHS

Type	Definition	Examples
Herbivore		Cows, rabbits
	Heterotroph that eats animals	
Omnivore		Humans, bears, crows
Detritivore		
Decomposer		

Feeding Relationships (pages 69–71)

12. How does energy flow through an ecosystem? _____

_____

_____

13. Complete the table about feeding relationships.

FEEDING RELATIONSHIPS

Relationship	Description
Food Chain	
Food Web	

14. What does a food web link together? _____

15. What is a trophic level? _____

16. In a food web, what organisms make up the first trophic level? _____

17. What does a consumer in a food chain depend on for energy? _____

_____

Ecological Pyramids (pages 72–73)

18. What is an ecological pyramid? _____

_____

19. Why is it that only part of the energy stored in one trophic level is passed on to the next level? _____

_____

20. Complete the energy pyramid by writing the source of the energy for the food web and how much energy is available to first-, second-, and third-level consumers.

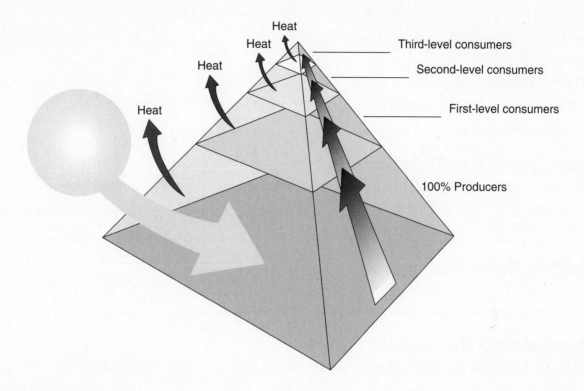

Heat

Heat

Heat

Heat

Heat

_____ Third-level consumers

_____ Second-level consumers

_____ First-level consumers

100% Producers

21. What is biomass? _____

_____

22. What does a biomass pyramid represent? _____

_____

23. What does a pyramid of numbers show? _____

_____

24. Why can each trophic level support only about one tenth the amount of living tissue of the level below it? _____

_____

Reading Skill Practice

When you read about complex topics, writing an outline can help you organize and understand the material. Outline Section 3–2 by using the headings and sub-headings as topics and subtopics and then writing the most important details under each topic. Do your work on a separate sheet of paper.

Section 3–3 Cycles of Matter (pages 74–80)

Key Concepts
- How does matter move among the living and nonliving parts of an ecosystem?
- How are nutrients important in living systems?

Introduction (page 74)

1. What are the four elements that make up over 95 percent of the body in most

   organisms? _____

Recycling in the Biosphere (page 74)

2. How is the movement of matter through the biosphere different from the flow

   of energy? _____

   _____

3. Matter moves through an ecosystem in _____.

4. What do biogeochemical cycles connect? _____

   _____

The Water Cycle (page 75)

5. Water can enter the atmosphere by evaporating from the leaves of plants in the

   process of _____.

6. Circle the letter of each process involved in the water cycle.

   a. precipitation **b.** evaporation **c.** runoff **d.** fertilization

Nutrient Cycles (pages 76–79)

7. What are nutrients? _____

   _____

8. What are the three nutrient cycles that play especially prominent roles in the biosphere?

   a. _____

   b. _____

   c. _____

9. Why is carbon especially important to living systems? _____

   _____

10. What are three large reservoirs where carbon is found in the biosphere?

    a. As carbon dioxide gas in the _____

    b. As dissolved carbon dioxide in the _____

    c. As coal, petroleum, and calcium carbonate rock found _____

11. In what process do plants use carbon dioxide? _____

12. Why do all organisms require nitrogen? _____

_____

13. What is nitrogen fixation? _____

_____

14. What is denitrification? _____

_____

15. What role does denitrification play in the nitrogen cycle? _____

_____

16. Circle the letter of each sentence that is true about the phosphorus cycle.

    a. Phosphate is released as rocks and sediments wear down.

    b. Plants absorb phosphate from the soil or from water.

    c. Phosphorus is abundant in the atmosphere.

    d. Organic phosphate cannot move through food webs.

17. Why is phosphorus essential to living things? _____

_____

_____

Nutrient Limitation (page 80)

18. What is the primary productivity of an ecosystem? _____

_____

19. If a nutrient is in short supply in an ecosystem, how will it affect an organism?

_____

20. When is a substance called a limiting nutrient? _____

_____

_____

21. Why do algal blooms occur? _____

_____

_____

Chapter 3   The Biosphere

Vocabulary Review

Matching   *In the space provided, write the letter of the definition that best matches each term.*

_____ 1. biosphere

_____ 2. community

_____ 3. autotroph

_____ 4. chemosynthesis

_____ 5. detritivore

_____ 6. biomass

_____ 7. transpiration

_____ 8. denitrification

_____ 9. biome

_____ 10. trophic level

a. collection of different populations that live together in an area

b. consumer that feeds on plant and animal remains and other dead matter

c. process in which water evaporates from the leaves of plants

d. combined parts of the planet in which all life exists

e. each step in a food chain or food web

f. total amount of living tissue within a trophic level

g. organism that can capture energy and use it to produce food

h. group of ecosystems that have the same climate and similar dominant communities

i. process in which organisms use chemical energy to produce carbohydrates

j. process in which bacteria convert nitrates into nitrogen gas

True or False   *Determine whether each statement is true or false. If it is true, write* true *in the space provided. If the statement is false, change the underlined word or words to make the statement true.*

_____ 11. A(An) <u>species</u> is a collection of all the organisms that live in a particular place, together with their physical environment.

_____ 12. The process in which autotrophs use light energy to make carbohydrates is called <u>nitrogen fixation</u>.

_____ 13. Heterotrophs that eat both plants and animals are referred to as <u>carnivores</u>.

_____ 14. A(An) <u>food web</u> links together all the food chains in an ecosystem.

_____ 15. The rate at which organic matter is created by producers is called the <u>limiting nutrient</u> of an ecosystem.

_____ 16. <u>Ecology</u> is the scientific study of interactions among organisms and between organisms and their environment.

_____ 17. A(An) <u>community</u> is a group of individuals that belong to the same species and live in the same area.

_____ 18. Autotrophs are also called <u>consumers</u>.

_____ 19. Organisms that break down organic matter are called <u>herbivores</u>.

_____ 20. The process in which water changes from a liquid to a gas is called <u>evaporation</u>.

Summary

4–1 The Role of Climate

Weather is the condition of Earth's atmosphere at a particular time and place. Climate is the average yearly condition of temperature and precipitation in a region. Climate is caused by latitude, winds, ocean currents, and the shape and height of landmasses. Climate affects ecosystems, because all organisms have certain needs for temperature and other aspects of climate.

Temperature on Earth stays within a range suitable for life due to the greenhouse effect. The greenhouse effect is the trapping of heat by gases in the atmosphere.

Differences in latitude determine the angle of sunlight striking Earth. This angle determines how much of the surface is heated. Differences in heating result in three main climate zones: polar, temperate, and tropical. Unequal heating of Earth's surface also causes winds and ocean currents. Winds and currents move heat through the biosphere.

4–2 What Shapes an Ecosystem?

Organisms in ecosystems are influenced by both biological, or biotic, and physical, or abiotic, factors. Biotic factors include all the living things with which organisms interact. Abiotic factors include temperature, soil type, and other nonliving factors. The area where an organism lives is called its habitat. A habitat includes both biotic and abiotic factors.

A niche consists of all the physical and biological conditions in which an organism lives and the way in which the organism uses those conditions. For example, a niche includes what an organism eats and how it gets its food.

Organisms in communities may interact in one of three ways: competition, predation, or symbiosis. Competition occurs when organisms try to use the same resources, or necessities of life. Competition often results in one organism dying out.

This is the basis of the competitive exclusion principle. This principle states that no two species can occupy the same niche in the same habitat at the same time. Predation occurs when one organism (the predator) captures and eats another (the prey). Symbiosis occurs when two species live closely together in one of three ways: mutualism, commensalism, or parasitism. In mutualism, both species benefit from the relationship. In commensalism, one species benefits and the other is neither helped nor harmed. In parasitism, one species benefits by living in or on the other and the other is harmed.

As an ecosystem ages, older inhabitants gradually die out and new organisms move in. The series of predictable changes that occurs in a community over time is called ecological succession. Primary succession occurs on bare rock surfaces where no soil exists. The first species to live in an area of primary succession are called pioneer species. Secondary succession occurs when a disturbance changes a community without removing the soil.

4–3 Biomes

A biome is a group of communities on land that covers a large area and is characterized by certain soil and climate. Within a biome, there may be microclimates. A microclimate is the climate of a small area that differs from the climate around it. Species may be found over a large or small area, depending on their tolerance. Tolerance is the ability to survive and reproduce under difficult conditions.

There are ten major biomes: tropical rain forest, tropical dry forest, tropical savanna, desert, temperate grassland, temperate woodland and shrubland, temperate forest, northwestern coniferous forest, boreal forest (or taiga), and tundra. Each biome has a unique set of abiotic factors and a characteristic collection of organisms.

In tropical rain forests, the tops of tall trees form a covering, called the canopy. Shorter trees and vines form another layer, called the understory. In other forests, trees may be deciduous, meaning they shed their leaves during a particular season each year. Coniferous forests have trees called conifers that produce seed cones. Temperate forests have soils rich in humus, which forms from decaying leaves and makes soil fertile. Tundra is characterized by permafrost, a layer of permanently frozen subsoil. Some areas, such as mountains and polar ice caps, do not fall neatly into the major biomes.

4–4 Aquatic Ecosystems

Aquatic ecosystems are determined mainly by the depth, flow, temperature, and chemistry of the water. In many aquatic ecosystems, tiny organisms called plankton are common. Plankton consist of phytoplankton and zooplankton. Phytoplankton are single-celled algae that use nutrients in water to produce food. They form the base of many aquatic food webs. Zooplankton are animals that feed on phytoplankton.

Freshwater ecosystems include flowing-water ecosystems (rivers and streams), standing-water ecosystems (lakes and ponds), and freshwater wetlands (bogs and swamps). In wetlands, water either covers the soil or is present at or near the surface for at least part of the year.

Estuaries are wetlands formed where rivers meet the sea. They contain a mixture of fresh and salt water. Most of the food produced in estuaries enters food webs as tiny pieces of organic matter, or detritus. Salt marshes are temperate estuaries. Mangrove swamps are tropical estuaries.

Marine ecosystems are found in the ocean. The ocean can be divided into zones based on how much light penetrates the water. The photic zone is the well-lit upper layer of water where photosynthesis can occur. The aphotic zone is the permanently dark lower layer of water where only chemosynthesis can occur.

The ocean also can be divided into three zones based on depth and distance from shore: the intertidal zone, coastal ocean, and open ocean. The intertidal zone is exposed to the rise and fall of tides each day. This may lead to zonation, or horizontal distribution of different types of organisms. Coastal ocean is the relatively shallow border of water that surrounds the continents. Kelp forests and coral reefs are found in coastal ocean. Open ocean consists of the rest of the ocean. Nutrients are scarce in open ocean, and fish are the dominant animals. The ocean floor is the benthic zone. Organisms that live on the ocean floor are called benthos.

Chapter 4 Ecosystems and Communities

Section 4–1 The Role of Climate (pages 87–89)

🔑 Key Concepts

- How does the greenhouse effect maintain the biosphere's temperature range?
- What are Earth's three main climate zones?

What Is Climate? (page 87)

1. How is weather different from climate? _____

_____

_____

_____

_____

2. What factors cause climate? _____

_____

_____

_____

_____

The Greenhouse Effect (pages 87–88)

3. Circle the letter of the world's insulating blanket.

    a. oxygen   **b.** the atmosphere   **c.** the oceans   **d.** solar energy

4. Complete the illustration of the greenhouse effect by showing in arrows and words what happens to the sunlight that hits Earth's surface.

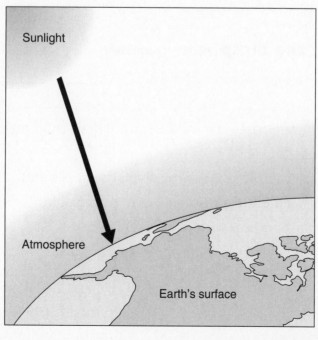

Name_____ Class_____ Date_____

5. What effect do carbon dioxide, methane, and a few other atmospheric gases have on Earth's temperature? _____

6. What is the greenhouse effect? _____
_____

The Effect of Latitude on Climate (page 88)

7. Why does solar radiation strike different parts of Earth's surface at an angle that varies throughout the year? _____
_____

8. Circle the letter of where the sun is almost directly overhead at noon all year.

   a. the North Pole   b. China   c. the equator   d. the South Pole

9. Why does Earth have different climate zones? _____
_____
_____

10. Complete the table about Earth's three main climate zones.

MAIN CLIMATE ZONES

Climate Zone	Location	Climate Characteristics
	Areas around North and South poles	
	Between the polar zones and the tropics	
	Near the equator	

Heat Transport in the Biosphere (page 89)

11. What force drives winds and ocean currents? _____
_____

12. The process in which water rises toward the surface in warmer regions is called
_____.

13. Circle the letter of each sentence that is true about ocean currents.

   a. Patterns of heating and cooling result in ocean currents.

   b. Ocean currents transport heat within the biosphere.

   c. Surface water moved by winds results in ocean currents.

   d. Ocean currents have no effect on the climate of landmasses.

Section 4–2 What Shapes an Ecosystem? (pages 90–97)

🔑 Key Concepts
- How do biotic and abiotic factors influence an ecosystem?
- What interactions occur within communities?
- What is ecological succession?

Biotic and Abiotic Factors (page 90)

1. Complete the table about factors that influence ecosystems.

FACTORS THAT INFLUENCE ECOSYSTEMS

Type of Factor	Definition	Examples
Biotic factors		
Abiotic factors		

2. What do the biotic and abiotic factors together determine? _____

_____

_____

The Niche (pages 91–92)

3. What is a niche? _____

_____

4. In what ways is food part of an organism's niche? _____

_____

5. Circle the letter of each sentence that is true about niches.

   a. Different species can share the same niche in the same habitat.

   b. No two species can share the same niche in the same habitat.

   c. Two species in the same habitat have to share a niche to survive.

   d. Different species can occupy niches that are very similar.

Community Interactions (pages 92–93)

6. When does competition occur? _____

_____

7. What is a resource? _____

8. What is often the result of direct competition in nature? _____

_____

9. What is the competitive exclusion principle? _____

_____

10. What is predation? _____

_____

11. When predation occurs, what is the organism called that does the killing and eating, and what is the food organism called? _____

_____

12. What is symbiosis? _____

_____

13. Complete the table about main classes of symbiotic relationships.

MAIN CLASSES OF SYMBIOTIC RELATIONSHIPS

Class	Description of Relationship
Mutualism	
Commensalism	
Parasitism	

14. The organism from which a parasite obtains nutritional needs is called a(an)

_____ .

15. Circle the letter of each sentence that is true of parasites.
   a. They generally weaken but do not kill their host.
   b. They obtain all or part of their nutritional needs from the host.
   c. They neither help nor harm the host.
   d. They are usually smaller than the host.

Ecological Succession (pages 94–97)

16. What is ecological succession? _____

_____

17. What is primary succession? _____

_____

18. The first species to populate an area when primary succession begins are called

_____ .

19. When a disturbance changes a community without removing the soil, what follows?

_____

20. An area that was once referred to as a climax community may appear to be permanent, but what might cause it to undergo change? _____

_____

_____

Section 4–3 Biomes (pages 98–105)

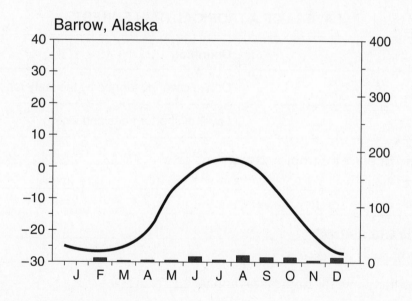

Key Concept
- What are the unique characteristics of the world's major biomes?

Introduction (page 98)

1. What is a biome? _____

_____

_____

Biomes and Climate (page 98)

2. What does a climate diagram summarize? _____

_____

_____

3. Complete the climate diagram by adding labels to the bottom and both sides of the graph to show what the responding variables are.

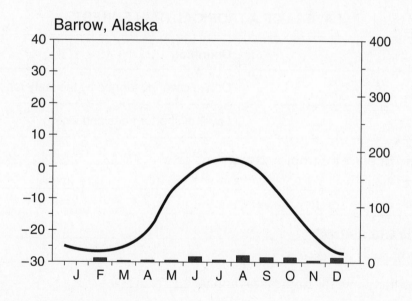

4. On a climate diagram, what does the line plot, and what do the vertical bars show?

_____

_____

_____

5. What is a microclimate? _____

_____

_____

The Major Biomes (pages 99–104)

6. Circle the letter of each sentence that is true about how each of the world's major biomes is defined.

    a. Each is defined by a unique set of abiotic factors.

    b. Each has a characteristic ecological community.

    c. Each is defined by the country it is in.

    d. Each is particularly defined by climate.

Use the map in Figure 4–11 on page 99 of your textbook to match the biome with its geographic distribution.

Biome	Geographic Distribution
_____ **7.** Tropical rain forest	**a.** Forest biome that occurs almost exclusively in the Northern Hemisphere
_____ **8.** Tundra	**b.** Biome that occurs on or near the equator
_____ **9.** Boreal forest	**c.** Biome that occurs near or above 60°N latitude

10. Complete the table about layers of a tropical rain forest.

LAYERS OF A TROPICAL RAIN FOREST

Layer	Definition
	Dense covering formed by the leafy tops of tall trees
	Layer of shorter trees and vines

11. In what kind of place do tropical dry forests grow? _____

_____

_____

12. What is a deciduous tree? _____

_____

13. What is another name for tropical savannas? _____

14. Is the following sentence true or false? Savannas are found in large parts of eastern

    Africa. _____

15. Circle the letter of each sentence that is true about deserts.

    a. They are hot, day and night.

    b. The soils are rich in minerals but poor in organic material.

    c. Cactuses and other succulents are dominant plants.

    d. Reptiles are the only wildlife.

16. What amount of annual precipitation defines a desert biome? _____

_____

_____

17. What factors maintain the characteristic plant community of temperate grasslands?

_____

_____

_____

18. Why is fire a constant threat in temperate woodland and shrubland? _____

_____

_____

19. Communities that are dominated by shrubs are also known as _____.

20. What kinds of trees do temperate forests contain? _____

_____

21. What is a coniferous tree? _____

_____

22. What is humus? _____

_____

23. What is the geographic distribution of the northwestern coniferous forest?

_____

_____

24. Boreal forests are also called _____.

25. What are the seasons like in a boreal forest? _____

_____

_____

26. Circle the letter of each sentence that is true about boreal forests.

    a. Dominant plants include spruce and fir.

    b. They have very high precipitation.

    c. They have soils that are rich in humus.

    d. Dominant wildlife includes moose and other large herbivores.

27. What is permafrost? _____

_____

28. What happens to the ground in tundra during the summer? _____

_____

_____

29. Why are tundra plants small and stunted? _____

_____

_____

_____

Other Land Areas (page 105)

30. When are the polar regions cold? _____

_____

31. What plants and algae can be found in the polar ice regions? _____

_____

32. In the north polar region, what are the dominant animals? _____

_____

33. The abiotic and biotic conditions of mountain ranges vary with _____.

34. Number the sequence of conditions you would find as you moved from the base to the summit of a mountain. Number the conditions at the base *1*.

_____ **a.** Stunted vegetation like that in tundra

_____ **b.** Grassland

_____ **c.** Forest of spruce and other conifers

_____ **d.** Open woodland of pines

Reading Skill Practice

You can often increase your understanding of what you've read by making comparisons. A compare-and-contrast table helps you to do this. On a separate sheet of paper, make a table to compare the major land biomes you read about in Section 4–3. The characteristics that you might use to form the basis of your comparison could include a general description, abiotic factors, dominant plants, dominant wildlife, and geographic distribution. For more information about compare-and-contrast tables, see Organizing Information in Appendix A of your textbook.

Section 4–4 Aquatic Ecosystems (pages 106–112)

Key Concepts

- What are the main factors that govern aquatic ecosystems?
- What are the two types of freshwater ecosystems?
- What are the characteristics of the different marine zones?

Introduction (page 106)

1. Aquatic ecosystems are primarily determined by what characteristics of the overlying water?

   a. _____   c. _____

   b. _____   d. _____

2. What does the depth of the water determine? _____

_____

3. What does water chemistry primarily refer to? _____

_____

_____

Freshwater Ecosystems (pages 106–107)

4. What are the two main types of freshwater ecosystems?

   a. _____   b. _____

5. Where do flowing-water ecosystems originate? _____

_____

_____

6. How does the circulating water in a standing-water ecosystem affect the ecosystem?

_____

7. What is plankton? _____

_____

_____

8. Complete the table about kinds of plankton.

KINDS OF PLANKTON

Kind	Organisms	How Nutrition Obtained
	Unicellular algae	
	Planktonic animals	

9. What is a wetland? _____

_____

_____

10. What is brackish water? _____

11. What are three main types of freshwater wetlands?

    a. _____ b. _____ c. _____

12. What distinguishes a marsh from a swamp? _____

    _____

    _____

Estuaries (page 108)

13. What are estuaries? _____

    _____

14. Tiny pieces of decaying plants and animals make up the _____ that provides food for organisms at the base of an estuary's food web.

15. Circle the letter of each sentence that is true about estuaries.

    a. Most primary production is consumed by herbivores.

    b. They contain a mixture of fresh water and salt water.

    c. Sunlight can't reach the bottom to power photosynthesis.

    d. They are affected by the rise and fall of ocean tides.

16. What are salt marshes? _____

    _____

    _____

17. What are mangrove swamps, and where are they found? _____

    _____

    _____

Marine Ecosystems (pages 109–112)

18. What is the photic zone of the ocean? _____

    _____

19. The permanently dark zone below the photic zone is called the

    _____.

20. What are the three main vertical divisions of the ocean based on the depth and distance from the shore?

    a. _____

    b. _____

    c. _____

21. Circle the letter of each sentence that is true about the intertidal zone.

    a. Organisms there are exposed to extreme changes in their surroundings.

    b. The rocky intertidal zones exist in temperate regions.

    c. Organisms are battered by currents but not by waves.

    d. Competition among organisms often leads to zonation.

22. What is zonation? _____

_____

23. What are the boundaries of the coastal ocean? _____

_____

_____

24. Why is the coastal ocean often rich in plankton and many other organisms?

_____

_____

_____

25. A huge forest of giant brown algae in the coastal ocean is a(an)

_____.

26. Circle the letter of each sentence that is true about coral reefs.

    a. The coasts of Florida and Hawaii have coral reefs.

    b. The primary structure of coral reefs is made of the skeletons of coral animals.

    c. Almost all growth in a coral reef occurs within 40 meters of the surface.

    d. Only a few organisms are able to live near coral reefs.

27. What are the boundaries of the open ocean? _____

_____

_____

28. The benthic zone covers the ocean _____.

29. What are the boundaries of the benthic zone? _____

_____

_____

30. Organisms that live attached to or near the bottom of the ocean are called

_____.

Vocabulary Review

Multiple Choice   *In the space provided, write the letter of the answer that best completes each sentence.*

_____ 1. The situation in which atmospheric gases trap the sun's heat and keep Earth's surface warm is called
   a. weather.
   c. climate.
   b. greenhouse effect.
   d. primary succession.

_____ 2. Earth's three main climate zones are the result of
   a. latitude and angle of heating.
   c. winds and ocean currents.
   b. precipitation and temperature.
   d. air masses and mountains.

_____ 3. An example of a biotic factor is
   a. air temperature.
   c. soil type.
   b. availability of water.
   d. soil organisms.

_____ 4. The type of community interaction that involves one species living in or on another organism and harming the other organism is called
   a. commensalism.
   c. competition.
   b. parasitism.
   d. mutualism.

_____ 5. A group of communities on land that covers a large area and is characterized by certain soil and climate is referred to as a(an)
   a. niche.
   c. biome.
   b. wetland.
   d. habitat.

Completion   *Fill in the blanks with terms from Chapter 4.*

6. The average yearly condition of temperature and precipitation in a region is called

   _____.

7. A physical factor that influences an ecosystem is called a(an) _____.

8. When one organism captures and eats another it is referred to as

   _____.

9. The first species to live in an area of primary succession are called

   _____.

10. The area where an organism lives is its _____.

11. The ability of organisms to survive and reproduce under less than optimal conditions is

    called _____.

12. The well-lit upper layer of ocean water is known as the _____.

13. Kelp forests are found in the ocean zone called _____.

14. Organisms that live on the ocean floor are referred to as _____.

15. Zonation occurs in the ocean zone called the _____.

Chapter 5   Populations

Summary

5–1 How Populations Grow

Important characteristics of a population are its geographic distribution, density, growth rate, and age structure. Geographic distribution, or range, is the area a population inhabits. Density is the number of individuals per unit area, such as number of people per square kilometer.

Population growth rate refers to how quickly a population is increasing or decreasing in size. Growth rate depends on how many individuals are added to the population or removed from it. Individuals are added to a population through births and immigration, or movement of individuals into an area. Individuals are removed from a population through deaths and emigration, or movement of individuals out of an area.

If a population has unlimited resources and limited predators and disease, it will grow exponentially. Exponential growth is a pattern of growth represented by a J-shaped curve. Exponential growth occurs when the individuals in a population reproduce at a constant rate. As the population grows, the number of individuals who are reproducing keeps increasing. This causes the population to grow faster and faster.

Exponential growth does not continue in natural populations for very long. Resources eventually are used up, and population growth slows or stops. When population growth slows or stops following a period of exponential growth, the pattern of growth is called logistic growth. Logistic growth is represented by an S-shaped curve. The population size when the growth rate stops is called the carrying capacity. Carrying capacity is defined as the number of individuals of a particular species that a given environment can support.

5–2 Limits to Growth

A factor that causes population growth to decrease is referred to as a limiting factor. Limiting factors can be either density dependent or density independent.

Density-dependent limiting factors depend on population size. They operate most strongly when a population is large and dense. Density-dependent limiting factors include competition, predation, parasitism, and disease. When populations become crowded, organisms compete, or struggle, with one another for food, water, space, sunlight, and other life essentials. The more individuals in an area, the sooner they use up the available resources. In nature, populations are often controlled by predation. Just about every species serves as food for some other species. In a predator-prey relationship, a decrease in the prey population will be followed, sooner or later, by a decrease in the predator population. Parasites can also limit the size of a population because they live off their hosts, weakening them and causing disease. Like predators, parasites work most effectively if hosts are present in large numbers.

Density-independent limiting factors do not depend on population size. They include unusual weather, natural disasters, seasonal cycles, and human activities such as damming rivers. In response to such factors, many species have a rapid drop in population size.

5–3 Human Population Growth

Like the populations of many other organisms, the human population tends to increase with time. For most of human existence, the population grew slowly. Limiting factors such as scarce food kept population sizes low. About 500 years ago, the human population began growing faster. First agriculture and later industry increased the food supply and made life easier and safer. Improved sanitation and medicine reduced death rates. However, birthrates remained high in most places. This led to exponential growth of the human population. Exponential growth continues today in the human population as a whole.

The human population cannot keep growing exponentially forever, because Earth and its resources are limited. Factors such as war, starvation, and disease limit some human populations. Scientists also have identified a variety of social and economic factors that can affect human populations. The scientific study of human populations is called demography. Demographers study characteristics of human populations and try to predict how the populations will change over time.

Over the past century, population growth in the United States, Japan, and much of Europe slowed dramatically. Demographers call this shift in population growth rates the demographic transition. In the transition, first death rates fell, causing a temporary increase in population growth. Then, birthrates fell, causing population growth to slow. Most people live in countries that have not yet completed the demographic transition.

To help predict future population growth, demographers use models called age-structure diagrams. An age-structure diagram is a bar graph of the number of people in each age group in the population. To predict how the world's human population will grow, demographers also must consider factors such as the number of people with fatal diseases, including AIDS.

Section 5–1 How Populations Grow (pages 119–123)

🔑 Key Concepts
- What characteristics are used to describe a population?
- What factors affect population size?
- What are exponential growth and logistic growth?

Characteristics of Populations (page 119)

1. What are the four main characteristics of a population?

a. _____   c. _____

b. _____   d. _____

2. What is a population's geographic distribution? _____

_____

3. Another term for geographic distribution is _____.

4. What is population density? _____

_____

Population Growth (page 120)

5. Circle the letter of each sentence that is true about populations.

a. They can grow rapidly.

b. They can decrease in size.

c. They may stay the same size from year to year.

d. They stay the same size until they disappear.

6. What three factors can affect population size?

a. _____

b. _____

c. _____

7. If more individuals are born than die in any period of time, how will the population change? _____

8. Complete the table about changes in population.

CHANGES IN POPULATION

Type of Change	Definition	Resulting Change in Size
Immigration		
Emigration		

9. What are two possible reasons individuals may immigrate into an area? _____

_____

Exponential Growth (page 121)

10. How will a population change if there is abundant space and food and if the population is protected from predators and disease? _____

_____

11. When does exponential growth occur? _____

_____

12. What are three ways that a growth rate may be stated, or expressed? _____

_____

_____

13. Under ideal conditions with unlimited resources, how will a population grow?

_____

14. Complete the graph by drawing the characteristic shape of exponential population growth.

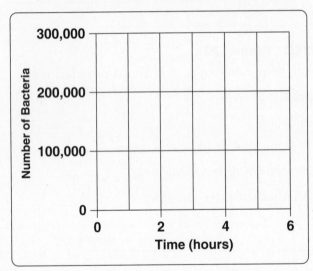

Exponential Growth of Bacterial Population

15. Is the following sentence true or false? Elephants never grow exponentially because their rate of reproduction is so slow. _____

Logistic Growth (pages 122–123)

16. Circle each sentence that is true about exponential growth.

   a. It continues until the organism covers the planet.

   b. It continues at the same rate as resources become less available.

   c. It does not continue in natural populations for very long.

   d. It continues in natural populations until the birthrate increases.

17. When resources become less available, how does population growth change?

_____

18. When does logistic growth occur? _____

_____

19. Circle the letter of each instance when a population's growth will slow down.

    a. The birthrate and death rate are the same.

    b. The birthrate is greater than the death rate.

    c. The rate of immigration is equal to the rate of emigration.

    d. The rate of emigration is less than the rate of immigration.

20. What is the carrying capacity of the environment for a particular species?

_____

_____

21. Complete the graph by drawing the characteristic shape of logistic population growth.

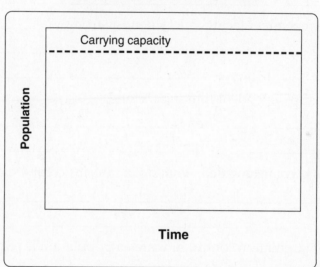

Logistic Growth of a Population

Section 5–2 Limits to Growth (pages 124–127)

⬤⇄ **Key Concept**
- What factors limit population growth?

Limiting Factors (pages 124–125)

1. What is a limiting factor? _____

   _____

2. A limiting nutrient is an example of a _____.

Density-Dependent Factors (pages 125–126)

3. What is a density-dependent limiting factor? _____

   _____

   _____

4. When do density-dependent factors become limiting? _____

   _____

   _____

5. When do density-dependent factors operate most strongly? _____

   _____

   _____

6. What are four density-dependent limiting factors?

   a. _____   c. _____

   b. _____   d. _____

7. When populations become crowded, what do organisms compete with one another for?

   _____

   _____

8. The mechanism of population control in which a population is regulated by predation is called a(an) _____.

9. What are the prey and what are the predators in the predator-prey relationship on Isle Royale? _____

   _____

10. Why does the wolf population on Isle Royale decline following a decline in the moose population? _____

   _____

11. How are parasites like predators? _____

   _____

   _____

Density-Independent Factors (page 127)

12. A limiting factor that affects all populations in similar ways, regardless of population size, is called a(an) _____.

13. What are examples of density-independent limiting factors? _____

_____

_____

14. Circle the letter of each sentence that is true about changes caused by density-independent factors.

    a. Most populations can adapt to a certain amount of change.

    b. Periodic droughts can affect entire populations of grasses.

    c. Populations never build up again after a crash in population size.

    d. Major upsets in an ecosystem can lead to long-term declines in certain populations.

15. What is the characteristic response in the population size of many species to a density-independent limiting factor? _____

_____

Reading Skill Practice

A graph can help you understand comparisons of data at a glance. By looking carefully at a graph in a textbook, you can help yourself understand better what you have read. Look carefully at the graph in Figure 5–7 on page 126. What important concept does this graph communicate?

Section 5–3 Human Population Growth
(pages 129–132)

🔑 **Key Concepts**
- How has the size of the human population changed over time?
- Why do population growth rates differ in countries throughout the world?

Historical Overview (page 129)

1. How does the size of the human population change with time? _____
_____

2. Why did the population grow slowly for most of human existence? _____
_____
_____

3. Circle the letter of each reason why the human population began to grow more rapidly about 500 years ago.
   a. Improved sanitation and health care reduced the death rate.
   b. Industry made life easier and safer.
   c. The world's food supply became more reliable.
   d. Birthrates in most places remained low.

Patterns of Population Growth (pages 130–131)

4. Why can't the human population keep growing exponentially forever? _____
_____

5. What is demography? _____
_____

6. What factors help predict why the populations of some countries grow faster than others? _____
_____

7. The hypothesis that explains why population growth has slowed dramatically in the United States, Japan, and much of Europe is called the _____.

8. Throughout much of human history, what have been the levels of birthrates and death rates in human societies? _____
_____
_____

9. What factors lower the death rate? _____
_____
_____

10. Is the following sentence true or false? Population growth depends, in part, on how many people of different ages make up a given population. _____

11. Complete the flowchart about the demographic transition.

```
┌──────────────────────────────────────────────────────────────────────────┐
│ Changes brought about by modernization lower the _____ rate.      │
└──────────────────────────────────────────────────────────────────────────┘
                                    ↓
┌──────────────────────────────────────────────────────────────────────────┐
│ Births greatly exceed deaths, resulting in rapid population _____.   │
└──────────────────────────────────────────────────────────────────────────┘
                                    ↓
┌──────────────────────────────────────────────────────────────────────────┐
│ As modernization continues, the birthrate _____ and population growth  │
│ _____.                                                               │
└──────────────────────────────────────────────────────────────────────────┘
                                    ↓
┌──────────────────────────────────────────────────────────────────────────┐
│ The birthrate falls to meet the death rate, and population growth           │
│ _____.                                                             │
└──────────────────────────────────────────────────────────────────────────┘
```

12. Circle the letter of each sentence that is true about human population growth.

    a. The demographic transition is complete in China and India.

    b. The worldwide human population is still growing exponentially.

    c. Most people live in countries that have not yet completed the demographic transition.

    d. The demographic transition has happened in the United States.

13. What do age-structure diagrams graph? _____

_____

14. What do the age structures of the United States and of Rwanda predict about the population growth of each country? _____

_____

_____

_____

Future Population Growth (page 132)

15. What may cause the growth rate of the world population to level off or even slow down? _____

_____

16. What do many ecologists suggest will happen if the growth in human population does not slow down? _____

_____

Name_____ Class_____ Date_____

Chapter 5 Populations

Vocabulary Review

Labeling Diagrams *Label the diagrams of population growth.*

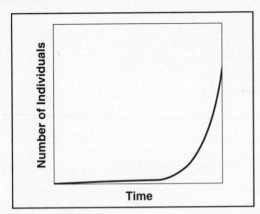

Pattern of Growth: 1. _____   Pattern of Growth: 2. _____

True or False *Determine whether each statement is true or false. If it is true, write* true *in the space provided. If the statement is false, change the underlined word or words to make the statement true.*

_____ 4. Population density is the number of individuals per unit area.

_____ 5. Emigration causes population size to increase.

_____ 6. The movement of individuals out of an area is called immigration.

_____ 7. A(An) population profile is any factor that causes population growth to decrease.

_____ 8. Density-independent limiting factors include competition and parasitism.

_____ 9. A predator-prey relationship is a(an) density-dependent limiting factor.

_____10. The scientific study of human populations is called demography.

Answering Questions *Write one or more sentences to answer each question.*

11. How do birth and death rates change when a population goes through the demographic transition? _____

_____

_____

12. What do demographers try to predict using age-structure diagrams? _____

_____

13. What does the term *geographic distribution* mean? _____

_____

14. When does exponential growth occur? _____

_____

15. Which countries have completed the demographic transition? _____

_____

58 Chapter 5

Chapter 6   Humans in the Biosphere

Summary

6–1 A Changing Landscape

All organisms on Earth share limited resources. They also depend on ecological processes, such as the water cycle, that sustain the resources. To protect these resources and processes, we must know how humans interact with the biosphere. Humans have become the most important source of environmental change. They affect the biosphere through hunting and gathering, agriculture, industry, and urban development.

Prehistoric hunters and gatherers changed their environments by hunting some species of animals to extinction. When humans began the practice of farming, or agriculture, they could produce more food. More food enabled the development of cities, and cities produced wastes. Advances in agriculture occurred later. These advances included the development of pesticides and monoculture—the planting of large fields with the same crop year after year. Advances such as these dramatically increased the world's food supply, an event called the green revolution. Agricultural advances also created problems, such as pollution from pesticides. After the Industrial Revolution, machines and factories increased the human impact on the biosphere. Industry used more resources and produced more pollution than ever before.

6–2 Renewable and Nonrenewable Resources

Environmental resources may be renewable or nonrenewable. Renewable resources, such as forests or water, can regrow if they are alive or be replaced by biochemical cycles if they are nonliving. Nonrenewable resources, such as fossil fuels, cannot be replaced by natural processes. Environmental resources are threatened by human activities. Sustainable development of renewable resources means using the resources without using them up.

Plowing removes roots that hold soil in place. This causes soil erosion. Soil erosion is the wearing away of surface soil by water and wind. In some areas, plowing and other factors have turned good soils into deserts. This process is called desertification. Sustainable development of soils includes contour plowing, which reduces soil erosion.

Forests provide wood, oxygen, and other important resources. Forests are being used up rapidly. Loss of forests is called deforestation. Sustainable development of forests includes planting trees to replace those that are cut down. Fish populations are declining because of overfishing. Aquaculture is the raising of aquatic animals for food. It is helping to sustain fish resources.

Smog is a mixture of chemicals that forms a gray-brown haze in the air. It is caused mostly by car exhausts and industrial emissions. Smog is considered a pollutant. A pollutant is a harmful material that can enter the biosphere through land, air, or water. Burning fossil fuels also releases compounds that combine with water vapor in air and produce acid rain. Acid rain kills plants and causes other damage. Emission controls have improved air quality and reduced acid rain.

Water supplies can be polluted by sewage or discarded chemicals. Sustainable development of water includes protecting the water cycle. Wetlands play an important role in the water cycle. Thus, protecting wetlands is one way to sustain water resources.

6–3 Biodiversity

Biological diversity, or biodiversity, is the sum of the genetically based variety of all organisms in the biosphere. Ecosystem diversity is the variety of habitats, communities, and ecological processes in ecosystems. Species diversity is the number of different species in the biosphere.

Genetic diversity refers to all the different forms of genetic information carried by all organisms living on Earth today. Biodiversity is one of Earth's greatest natural resources. Diverse species have provided humans with foods, industrial products, and medicines.

Humans reduce biodiversity by destroying habitats, hunting species to extinction, introducing toxic compounds into food webs, and introducing foreign species into new environments. Extinction occurs when a species disappears from all or part of its range. An endangered species is a species whose population size is declining in a way that places it in danger of extinction. As humans destroy habitats, the species that once lived in the habitats die out. Development often splits habitats into separate pieces. This process is called habitat fragmentation. The smaller the pieces of habitat, the less likely that their species will be able to survive.

Pollution can seriously threaten biodiversity. Toxic compounds build up in the tissues of organisms. Concentrations of toxins increase in organisms at higher trophic levels in a food chain or food web. This is called biological magnification.

Plants and animals introduced from other areas are an important threat to biodiversity. Introduced organisms often become invasive species. Invasive species increase rapidly because their new habitat lacks the parasites and predators that control their population "back home."

Conservation is the wise management of natural resources. Conservation focuses on protecting entire ecosystems as well as single species. Protecting entire ecosystems ensures that many species are preserved.

6–4 Charting a Course for the Future

The ozone layer is an area of relatively great concentration of ozone gas high in the atmosphere. The layer protects Earth from harmful radiation. The ozone layer has been damaged by compounds in certain products. The compounds have now been banned.

Global warming refers to the increase in average temperature of the biosphere. It is mainly due to humans burning fossil fuels. Burning adds gases to the atmosphere, causing the atmosphere to retain more heat. Continued global warming may lead to rising sea levels and coastal flooding, among other environmental changes.

People can help maintain the health of the biosphere by conserving resources. For example, they can avoid using more water than necessary. They can also reuse or recycle trash.

Section 6–1 A Changing Landscape (pages 139–143)

Key Concept
- What types of human activities can affect the biosphere?

Earth as an Island (page 139)

1. Increasing demands on what resources come with a growing human population?

_____

_____

Human Activities (page 140)

2. Is the following sentence true or false? Human activity uses as much energy as all of Earth's other multicellular species combined. _____

3. What four human activities have transformed the biosphere?

    a. _____

    b. _____

    c. _____

    d. _____

Hunting and Gathering (page 140)

4. How did prehistoric hunters and gatherers change the environment? _____

_____

_____

Agriculture (pages 141–142)

5. What is agriculture? _____

6. Why was the spread of agriculture an important event in human history?

_____

_____

_____

7. What social changes came with the cultivation of both plants and animals?

_____

_____

_____

8. What changes in agriculture occurred in the 1800s as a result of advancements in science and technology? _____

_____

_____

9. What was the green revolution? _____

_____

_____

_____

10. What is the farming method called monoculture? _____

_____

_____

11. Circle the letter of each benefit of the green revolution to human society.
a. It helped prevent food shortages.
b. China and India depleted water supplies.
c. It increased food production.
d. Global food production was cut in half.

Industrial Growth and Urban Development (page 143)

12. What occurred during the Industrial Revolution of the 1800s? _____

_____

13. From what resources do we obtain most of the energy to produce and power the machines we use? _____

_____

14. The continued spread of suburban communities across the American landscape is referred to as _____.

15. How does suburban growth place stress on plant and animal populations?

_____

Section 6–2 Renewable and Nonrenewable Resources (pages 144–149)

Key Concepts
- How are environmental resources classified?
- What effects do human activities have on natural resources?

Introduction (page 144)

1. How were the commons in an old English village destroyed? _____
_____
_____
_____

2. What is meant by the phrase the "tragedy of the commons"? _____
_____
_____

Classifying Resources (page 144)

3. Complete the table about types of environmental resources.

TYPES OF ENVIRONMENTAL RESOURCES

Type of Resource	Definition	Examples
Renewable resources		
Nonrenewable resources		

Sustainable Development (page 145)

4. What is sustainable development? _____
_____

5. How do human activities affect renewable resources? _____
_____
_____

6. What are five characteristics of sustainable use?

    a. _____

    b. _____

    c. _____

    d. _____

    e. _____

Land Resources (page 145)

7. What is fertile soil? _____

8. The uppermost layer of soil is called _____.

9. What is soil erosion? _____

10. How does plowing the land increase the rate of soil erosion? _____

_____

11. The conversion of a previously soil-rich, productive area into a desert is called

_____.

12. What can cause desertification? _____

_____

Forest Resources (page 146)

13. Why have forests been called the "lungs of the Earth"? _____

_____

14. Why are forests in Alaska and the Pacific Northwest called old-growth forests?

_____

15. What is deforestation, and how does it affect soil? _____

_____

Fishery Resources (page 147)

16. For what resources are Earth's oceans particularly valuable? _____

_____

17. The practice of harvesting fish faster than they can reproduce is called

_____.

18. What is one approach to sustainable development of fisheries? _____

_____

19. What is aquaculture? _____

Air Resources (page 148)

20. What is smog? _____

_____

21. What is a pollutant? _____

_____

22. How does the burning of fossil fuels affect air quality? _____

_____

_____

23. Microscopic particles of ash and dust in the air that can cause health problems are
called _____.

24. What does acid rain contain that kills plants and harms soil? _____

_____

25. Complete the illustration by writing the names of the processes that lead to the formation of acid rain.

Freshwater Resources (page 149)

26. Why are protecting water supplies from pollution and managing demand for water
major priorities? _____

_____

27. What is domestic sewage, and how does it threaten water supplies? _____

_____

_____

_____

28. How can protecting forests ensure sustainable use of water resources?

_____

_____

29. Why can conservation in agriculture save large amounts of water? _____

_____

_____

Section 6–3 Biodiversity (pages 150–156)

⬤ Key Concepts
- What is the value of biodiversity?
- What are the current threats to biodiversity?
- What is the goal of conservation biology?

The Value of Biodiversity (page 150)

1. What is biodiversity? _____

_____

2. Complete the table about diversity.

DIVERSITY IN THE BIOSPHERE

Type of Diversity	Definition
Ecosystem diversity	
Species diversity	
Genetic diversity	

3. Why is biodiversity one of Earth's greatest natural resources? _____

_____

_____

Threats to Biodiversity (page 151)

4. What are four ways that human activity can reduce biodiversity?

a. _____

b. _____

c. _____

d. _____

5. When does extinction occur? _____

_____

6. A species whose population size is declining in a way that places it in danger of extinction is called a(an) _____.

7. Why does a declining population make a species more vulnerable to extinction?

_____

_____

Habitat Alteration (page 151)

8. The process of splitting a habitat into small pieces is called _____.

9. What is the relationship between biological "island" size and the number of species that can live there? _____

_____

_____

_____

_____

Demand for Wildlife Products (page 151)

10. Why are species hunted? _____

_____

_____

Pollution (page 152)

11. What is DDT? _____

12. What two properties of DDT make it hazardous over the long term? _____

_____

_____

13. What is biological magnification? _____

_____

_____

Introduced Species (page 153)

14. Plants and animals that have migrated to places where they are not native are called

_____.

15. Why do invasive species reproduce rapidly and increase their populations?

_____

_____

Conserving Biodiversity (pages 154–156)

16. What is conservation? _____

_____

_____

17. What is the purpose of conservation biology? _____

_____

18. What does protecting an ecosystem ensure? _____

_____

_____

19. What are some of the challenges that conservationists face? _____

_____

_____

Reading Skill Practice

Writing a summary can help you remember the information you have read. When you write a summary, write only the important points. Write a summary of the information in Section 6–3. Your summary should be shorter than the text on which it is based.

Section 6–4 Charting a Course for the Future
(pages 157–160)

🔑 **Key Concept**
- What are two types of global change of concern to biologists?

Ozone Depletion (pages 157–158)

1. Where is ozone concentrated in the atmosphere? _____
_____
_____

2. What is causing the problem of ozone depletion? _____
_____
_____
_____

Global Climate Change (page 159)

3. What is global warming? _____
_____

4. What is the most widely accepted hypothesis about the cause of global warming?
_____
_____
_____

5. If global warming continues at the current rate, how might sea level be affected?
_____
_____

The Value of a Healthy Biosphere (page 160)

6. What goods and services does a healthy biosphere provide to us? _____
_____
_____

7. What is the first step in charting a course that will improve living conditions without harming the environment? _____
_____

Vocabulary Review

Matching   *In the space provided, write the letter of the definition that best matches each term.*

_____ **1.** monoculture

_____ **2.** green revolution

_____ **3.** renewable resource

_____ **4.** soil erosion

_____ **5.** smog

_____ **6.** acid rain

_____ **7.** sustainable development

_____ **8.** endangered species

_____ **9.** habitat fragmentation

_____ **10.** global warming

a. wearing away of surface soil by water and wind

b. way of using resources without using them up

c. practice in which large fields are planted with a single crop year after year

d. splitting of a habitat into pieces

e. dramatic increase in the world's food supply due to agricultural advances

f. increase in the average temperature of the biosphere

g. resource that can regenerate or be replenished

h. mixture of chemicals that occurs as a gray-brown haze in the atmosphere

i. species in danger of extinction

j. rain that forms from pollutants and kills plants

Completion   *Fill in the blanks with terms from Chapter 6.*

11. The raising of aquatic animals for human food is called _____.

12. The loss of forests is referred to as _____.

13. A harmful material that can enter the biosphere through the land, air, or water is a(an)

_____.

14. The process in which good soils are turned into deserts is called

_____.

15. When a species disappears from all or part of its range, _____ has occurred.

16. The wise management of natural resources is called _____.

Writing Descriptions   *Describe each type of diversity in the space provided.*

17. biological diversity _____

_____

18. ecosystem diversity _____

_____

19. species diversity _____

_____

20. genetic diversity _____

_____

Summary

7–1 Life Is Cellular

Since the 1600s, scientists have made many discoveries that have showed how important cells are in living things. Such discoveries are summarized in the cell theory. The cell theory states:

- All living things are composed of cells.
- Cells are the basic units of structure and function in living things.
- New cells are produced from existing cells.

All cells have two characteristics in common. They are surrounded by a barrier called a cell membrane, and they contain the molecule that carries biological information—DNA.

Cells fall into two broad categories, depending on whether they contain a nucleus. The nucleus is a large membrane-enclosed structure that contains the cell's genetic material in the form of DNA. The nucleus controls many of the cell's activities. Prokaryotic cells have genetic material that is not contained in a nucleus. Bacteria are prokaryotes. Eukaryotic cells contain a nucleus in which their genetic material is separated from the rest of the cell. Plants, animals, fungi, and protists are eukaryotes.

7–2 Eukaryotic Cell Structure

Cell biologists divide the eukaryotic cell into two major parts: the nucleus and the cytoplasm. The cytoplasm is the portion of the cell outside the nucleus. Eukaryotic cells contain structures known as organelles.

The nucleus contains nearly all the cell's DNA and with it the coded instructions for making proteins. The nucleus is surrounded by a nuclear envelope composed of two membranes. Inside the nucleus is granular material called chromatin. Most nuclei also contain a small, dense region known as the nucleolus.

Ribosomes are small particles of RNA and protein found throughout the cytoplasm. Proteins are assembled on ribosomes. Eukaryotic cells contain an internal membrane system known as the endoplasmic reticulum, or ER. The ER is where lipid components of the cell membrane are assembled, along with proteins and other materials that are exported from the cell. The portion of the ER involved in the synthesis of proteins is called rough ER. Smooth ER, which does not contain ribosomes, is involved in the making of lipids. The function of the Golgi apparatus is to modify, sort, and package proteins and other materials from the ER for storage in the cell or secretion outside the cell.

Other organelles include lysosomes, vacuoles, mitochondria, and chloroplasts. Mitochondria are organelles that convert the chemical energy stored in food into compounds that are more convenient for the cell to use. Chloroplasts are organelles that capture the energy from sunlight and convert it into chemical energy.

Eukaryotic cells have a structure called the cytoskeleton that helps support the cell. The cytoskeleton is a network of protein filaments that helps the cell to maintain its shape. The cytoskeleton is also involved in movement.

7–3 Cell Boundaries

All cells are surrounded by a thin, flexible barrier known as the cell membrane. The cell membrane regulates what enters and leaves the cell and also provides protection and support. The composition of nearly all cell membranes is a double-layered sheet called a lipid bilayer. Many cells also produce a strong supporting layer around the membrane known as the cell wall. Cell walls are present in plants, algae, fungi, and many prokaryotes. The main function of the cell wall is to provide support and protection for the cell.

One of the most important functions of the cell membrane is to regulate the movement of dissolved molecules from the liquid on one side of the membrane to the liquid on the other side. The cytoplasm of a cell contains a solution of many different substances in water. The concentration of a solution is the mass of solute in a given volume of solution.

In a solution, particles move constantly. Particles tend to move from an area where they are more concentrated to an area where they are less concentrated, a process called diffusion. When the concentration of a solute is the same throughout a solution, the solution has reached equilibrium. Because diffusion depends upon random particle movements, substances diffuse across membranes without requiring the cell to use energy. Water passes quite easily across most membranes. Osmosis is the diffusion of water through a selectively permeable membrane. Many cell membranes have protein channels that allow certain molecules to cross the membranes. In such cases, the cell membrane protein is said to facilitate, or help, the diffusion of the molecules across the membrane. This process is called facilitated diffusion. It does not require use of the cell's energy.

Active transport does require the cell's energy. In active transport, cells move materials from one side of a membrane to the other side against the concentration difference. Types of active transport include endocytosis, phagocytosis, pinocytosis, and exocytosis.

7–4 The Diversity of Cellular Life

An organism that consists of a single cell is called a unicellular organism. Unicellular organisms carry out all the essential functions of life. Organisms that are made up of many cells are called multicellular organisms. Cells throughout a multicellular organism can develop in different ways to perform different tasks. This process is called cell specialization.

The levels of organization in a multicellular organism are individual cells, tissues, organs, and organ systems. Individual cells are the first level. Similar cells are grouped into units called tissues. A tissue is a group of cells that perform a particular function. Groups of tissues that work together form an organ. A group of organs that work together to perform a specific function is called an organ system.

© Pearson Education, Inc., publishing as Pearson Prentice Hall.

Chapter 7 Cell Structure and Function

Section 7–1 Life Is Cellular (pages 169–173)

👄 **Key Concepts**
- What is the cell theory?
- What are the characteristics of prokaryotes and eukaryotes?

Introduction (page 169)

1. What is the structure that makes up every living thing? _____

The Discovery of the Cell (pages 169–170)

2. What was Anton van Leeuwenhoek one of the first to see in the 1600s? _____
_____

3. What did a thin slice of cork seem like to Robert Hooke when he observed it
through a microscope? _____
_____

4. What did the German botanist Matthias Schleiden conclude? _____
_____

5. What did the German biologist Theodor Schwann conclude? _____
_____
_____

6. How did Rudolph Virchow summarize his years of work? _____
_____

7. What are the three concepts that make up the cell theory?

   a. _____

   b. _____

   c. _____

Exploring the Cell (pages 170–172)

8. Why are electron microscopes capable of revealing details much smaller than those
seen through light microscopes? _____
_____
_____

Prokaryotes and Eukaryotes (pages 172–173)

9. Circle the letter of each sentence that is true about prokaryotes.

    a. They grow and reproduce.

    b. Many are large, multicellular organisms.

    c. They are more complex than cells of eukaryotes.

    d. They have cell membranes and cytoplasm.

10. Are all eukaryotes large, multicellular organisms? _____

_____

_____

11. Complete the table about the two categories of cells.

TWO CATEGORIES OF CELLS

Category	Definition	Examples
	Organisms whose cells lack nuclei	
	Organisms whose cells contain nuclei	

Section 7–2 Eukaryotic Cell Structure
(pages 174–181)

Key Concept
- What are the functions of the major cell structures?

Comparing a Cell to a Factory (page 174)

1. What is an organelle? _____
_____

2. Label the structures on the illustrations of the plant and animal cells.

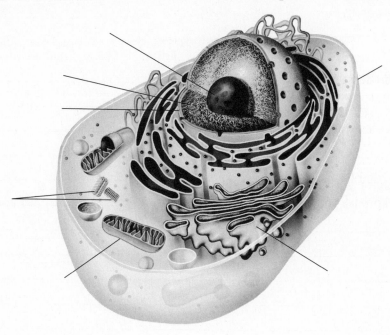

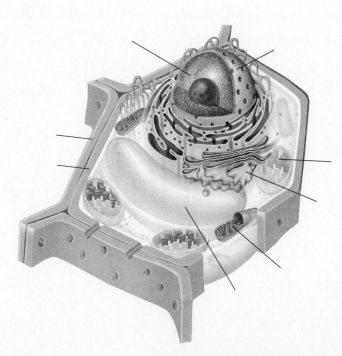

3. Circle the letter of each structure that animal cells contain.

   a. chloroplasts

   b. lysosomes

   c. mitochondria

   d. ER

4. Circle the letter of each structure that plant cells contain.

   a. cell wall

   b. ER

   c. lysosomes

   d. chloroplast

Nucleus (page 176)

5. What is the function of the nucleus? _____

   _____

6. What important molecules does the nucleus contain? _____

   _____

7. The granular material visible within the nucleus is called _____.

8. What does chromatin consist of? _____

   _____

9. What are chromosomes? _____

   _____

   _____

   _____

10. Most nuclei contain a small, dense region known as the _____.

11. What occurs in the nucleolus? _____

   _____

12. What is the nuclear envelope? _____

   _____

Ribosomes (page 177)

13. What are ribosomes? _____

   _____

   _____

© Pearson Education, Inc., publishing as Pearson Prentice Hall.

Endoplasmic Reticulum (pages 177–178)

14. What is the difference between rough ER and smooth ER? _____

_____

_____

Golgi Apparatus (page 178)

15. Using the cell as a factory analogy, describe the role of the Golgi apparatus in the cell.

_____

_____

_____

Lysosomes (page 179)

16. Circle the letter of each sentence that is true about lysosomes.

   a. They contain enzymes that help synthesize lipids.

   b. They break down organelles that have outlived their usefulness.

   c. They produce proteins that are modified by the ER.

   d. They contain enzymes that break down lipids, carbohydrates, and proteins.

Vacuoles (page 179)

17. What are vacuoles? _____

_____

_____

18. What is the role of the central vacuole in plants? _____

_____

_____

19. How does the contractile vacuole in a paramecium help maintain homeostasis?

_____

_____

Mitochondria and Chloroplasts (pages 179–180)

20. Is the following sentence true or false? Both chloroplasts and mitochondria are

enclosed by two membranes. _____

21. Chloroplasts and mitochondria contain their own genetic information in the form of

_____.

22. What are mitochondria? _____

_____

_____

23. Are mitochondria found in plant cells, animal cells, or both? _____

24. Where are chloroplasts found? _____

_____

25. Biologist Lynn Margulis has suggested that mitochondria and chloroplasts are descendants of what kind of organisms? _____

Cytoskeleton (page 181)

26. What is the cytoskeleton? _____

_____

_____

27. Complete the table about structures that make up the cytoskeleton.

STRUCTURES OF THE CYTOSKELETON

Structure	Description	Functions
		Maintain cell shape, help build cilia and flagella, form centrioles in cell division
		Support the cell, help cells move

© Pearson Education, Inc., publishing as Pearson Prentice Hall.

Match the organelle with its description.

Organelle	Description
_____ 28. Ribosome	**a.** Uses energy from sunlight to make energy-rich food
_____ 29. Endoplasmic reticulum	**b.** Stack of membranes in which enzymes attach carbohydrates and lipids to proteins
_____ 30. Golgi apparatus	**c.** Uses energy from food to make high-energy compounds
_____ 31. Lysosome	**d.** An internal membrane system in which components of cell membrane and some proteins are constructed
_____ 32. Vacuole	**e.** Saclike structure that stores materials
_____ 33. Chloroplast	**f.** Small particle of RNA and protein that produces protein following instructions from nucleus
_____ 34. Mitochondrion	**g.** Filled with enzymes used to break down food into particles that can be used

Reading Skill Practice

A flowchart can help you remember the order in which events occur. On a separate sheet of paper, create a flowchart that describes the steps by which proteins are made in the cell. You will find that the steps of this process are explained on pages 176–178. For more information about flowcharts, see Organizing Information in Appendix A in your textbook.

Section 7–3 Cell Boundaries (pages 182–189)

Key Concepts

- What are the main functions of the cell membrane and the cell wall?
- What happens during diffusion?
- What is osmosis?

Cell Membrane (page 182)

1. What are the functions of the cell membrane? _____

_____

2. The core of nearly all cell membranes is a double-layered sheet called a(an)

_____.

3. What is the difference in the function of the proteins and the carbohydrates attached to

a cell membrane? _____

_____

_____

Cell Walls (page 183)

4. In what organisms are cell walls found? _____

_____

5. Is the following sentence true or false? The cell wall lies inside the cell membrane.

_____

6. What is the main function of the cell wall? _____

_____

7. What are plant cell walls mostly made of? _____

_____

Diffusion Through Cell Boundaries (pages 183–184)

8. What is the concentration of a solution? _____

_____

9. What is diffusion? _____

_____

_____

10. What is meant when a system has reached equilibrium? _____

_____

_____

11. The molecules of solute in the illustration are moving through the cell membrane from top to bottom. Indicate with labels which side of the membrane has a high concentration of solute and which has a low concentration.

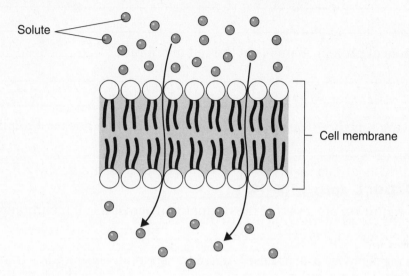

Osmosis (pages 185–186)

12. What does it mean that biological membranes are selectively permeable?

_____

_____

13. What is osmosis? _____

_____

14. Is the following sentence true or false? Water tends to diffuse from a region where it is less concentrated to a region where it is highly concentrated. _____

15. When will water stop moving across a membrane? _____

_____

_____

Match the situation to the description.

Situation	Description
_____ **16.** Two solutions are isotonic.	**a.** The solution is above strength in solute.
_____ **17.** A solution is hypertonic.	**b.** The solutions are the same strength.
_____ **18.** A solution is hypotonic.	**c.** The solution is below strength in solute.

19. On which side of a selectively permeable membrane does osmosis exert a pressure?

_____

_____

Facilitated Diffusion (page 187)

20. What happens during the process of facilitated diffusion? _____

_____

_____

21. What is the role of protein channels in the cell membrane? _____

_____

_____

22. Is the following sentence true or false? Facilitated diffusion does not require the cell to use energy. _____

Active Transport (pages 188–189)

23. The energy-requiring process that moves material across a cell membrane against a concentration difference is called _____.

24. Is the following sentence true or false? Active transport always requires transport proteins during the process. _____

25. Complete the table about types of active transport.

TYPES OF ACTIVE TRANSPORT

Type	Description
Endocytosis	
Phagocytosis	
Exocytosis	

26. During endocytosis, what happens to the pocket in the cell membrane when it breaks loose from the membrane? _____

_____

Section 7–4 The Diversity of Cellular Life
(pages 190–193)

 Key Concepts

- What is cell specialization?
- What are the four levels of organization in multicellular organisms?

Unicellular Organisms (page 190)

1. A single-celled organism is also called a(an) _____ organism.

Multicellular Organisms (pages 190–192)

2. What is cell specialization in a multicellular organism? _____

_____

_____

3. Circle the letter of each sentence that is true about cell specialization.

   a. Specialized cells perform particular functions within the organism.

   b. Only unicellular organisms have specialized cells.

   c. The human body contains many different cell types.

   d. Some cells are specialized to enable movement.

Levels of Organization (pages 192–193)

4. What are four levels of organization in a multicellular organism?

   a. _____

   b. _____

   c. _____

   d. _____

5. What is a tissue? _____

_____

6. What are the four main types of tissue in most animals?

   a. _____

   b. _____

   c. _____

   d. _____

7. Groups of tissues that work together to perform a specific function are called a(an)

   _____.

8. What kinds of tissues can be found within a muscle in your body? _____

_____

_____

9. What is an organ system? _____

_____

Chapter 7   Cell Structure and Function

Vocabulary Review

Matching   *In the space provided, write the letter of the function that best matches each organelle.*

_____ **1.** mitochondrion

_____ **2.** ribosome

_____ **3.** endoplasmic reticulum

_____ **4.** Golgi apparatus

_____ **5.** lysosome

_____ **6.** chloroplast

a. site where lipid components of the cell membrane are assembled

b. captures energy from sunlight and converts it into chemical energy

c. modifies, sorts, and packages proteins

d. site where proteins are assembled

e. converts chemical energy in food into compounds the cell can use

f. acts as the cell's cleanup crew

Completion   *Fill in the blanks with terms from Chapter 7.*

7. Bacteria are examples of _____.

8. Cells that are larger and more complex than prokaryotes are _____ cells.

9. The _____ is the portion of the cell outside of the nucleus.

10. The supporting structure of the cell that is also involved in movement is the _____.

11. All cells are surrounded by a flexible barrier known as the _____.

12. The movement of particles from an area of greater concentration to an area of lower concentration is called _____.

13. When comparing two solutions, the solution with the greater concentration of solutes is called _____, while the solution with the lower concentration of solutes is called _____.

14. The process of taking material into the cell by means of infoldings of the cell membrane is called _____.

15. Amoebas use the process of _____ to take in food and other materials.

16. _____ is the process by which cells in an organization develop in different ways to perform different tasks.

17. In the process of _____, a protein channel helps the diffusion of glucose across a membrane.

18. The diffusion of water through a selectively permeable membrane is called _____.

19. The process that moves materials through a membrane against a concentration difference is known as _____.

Chapter 8   Photosynthesis

Summary

8–1 Energy and Life

Plants and some other types of organisms are able to use light energy from the sun to produce food. Organisms that make their own food are called autotrophs. Other organisms cannot use the sun's energy directly. These organisms, called heterotrophs, obtain energy from the foods they consume.

One of the principal chemical compounds that cells use to store and release energy is adenosine triphosphate, or ATP. ATP consists of adenine, a 5-carbon sugar called ribose, and three phosphate groups. Adenosine diphosphate (ADP) is a similar compound that has only two phosphate groups instead of three. When a cell has energy available, it can store small amounts of energy by adding a third phosphate group to ADP, producing ATP. The energy stored in ATP can be released by breaking the bond between the second and third phosphate groups. Because a cell can subtract this third phosphate group, it can release energy as needed. The characteristics of ATP make it exceptionally useful as the basic energy source of all cells. Cells use energy from ATP to carry out many important activities, including active transport, synthesis of proteins and nucleic acids, and responses to chemical signals at the cell surface. Cells store a small amount of ATP because ATP is easy to regenerate from ADP. When ATP is needed, cells use the energy in foods such as glucose to produce ATP.

8–2 Photosynthesis: An Overview

Research into photosynthesis began centuries ago. In 1643, Jan van Helmont concluded that trees gain most of their mass from water. In 1771, Joseph Priestley determined that plants release oxygen, which can keep a candle burning.

In 1779, Jan Ingenhousz concluded that plants need sunlight to produce oxygen. The experiments performed by van Helmont, Priestley, and Ingenhousz led to work by other scientists who finally discovered that in the presence of light, plants transform carbon dioxide and water into carbohydrates and plants also release oxygen.

The overall equation for photosynthesis can be shown as follows:

$$6CO_2 + 6\,H_2O \overset{light}{\rightarrow} C_6H_{12}O_6 + 6O_2$$

$$\text{carbon dioxide} + \text{water} \overset{light}{\rightarrow} \text{sugars} + \text{oxygen}$$

Photosynthesis uses the energy of sunlight to convert water and carbon dioxide into high-energy sugars and oxygen. Plants use the sugars to produce complex carbohydrates such as starches. Plants obtain the carbon dioxide they need for photosynthesis from the air or from the water in which they grow.

In addition to water and carbon dioxide, photosynthesis requires light and chlorophyll. Plants gather the sun's energy with light-absorbing molecules called pigments. The plants' principal pigment is chlorophyll. There are two main types of chlorophyll: chlorophyll *a* and chlorophyll *b*.

The wavelengths of sunlight you can see make up the visible spectrum, which contains all the colors. Chlorophyll absorbs light in the blue-violet and red regions very well. But it does not absorb light in the green region well. Green light is reflected by leaves, which is why plants look green.

Any compound that absorbs light absorbs the energy in light. When chlorophyll absorbs sunlight, much of the energy of the light is transferred directly to the electrons in the chlorophyll molecule, raising the energy level of the electrons.

8–3 The Reactions of Photosynthesis

In plants and other photosynthetic prokaryotes, photosynthesis takes place inside the chloroplasts. Chloroplasts contain saclike photosynthetic membranes called thylakoids. Thylakoids are arranged in stacks called grana. Proteins in the thylakoid membrane organize chlorophyll and other pigments into clusters known as photosystems. These photosystems are the light-collecting units of chlorophyll. The reactions of photosynthesis occur in two parts: (1) the light-dependent reactions and (2) the light-independent reactions, which are also called the Calvin cycle. The light-dependent reactions take place within the thylakoid membranes. The Calvin cycle takes place in the stroma—the region outside of the thylakoid membranes.

When sunlight excites electrons in chlorophyll, the electrons gain a great deal of energy. A carrier molecule is a compound that can accept a pair of high-energy electrons and transfer them along with most of their energy to another molecule. One of these carrier molecules is $NADP^+$. In the process of photosynthesis, $NADP^+$ accepts and holds 2 high-energy electrons along with a hydrogen ion (H^+). This converts the $NADP^+$ into NADPH.

The light-dependent reactions require light. These reactions use energy from light to produce oxygen gas and convert ADP and $NADP^+$ into the energy carriers ATP and NADPH. Photosynthesis begins when pigments in photosystem II absorb light. A series of reactions follows. The reactants are water, ADP, and $NADP^+$. The products are oxygen gas, ATP, and NADPH. The oxygen gas produced by photosynthesis is the source of nearly all the oxygen in Earth's atmosphere.

The Calvin cycle does not require light. During the Calvin cycle, plants use the energy of ATP and NADPH—products of the light-dependent reactions—to produce high-energy sugars. The Calvin cycle uses carbon dioxide in its series of reactions. As photosynthesis proceeds, the Calvin cycle works steadily, removing carbon dioxide from the atmosphere and turning out energy-rich sugars. Six carbon dioxide molecules are needed to produce a single 6-carbon sugar.

Many factors affect the rate of photosynthesis. Such factors include availability of water, temperature, and intensity of light.

Chapter 8 Photosynthesis

Section 8–1 Energy and Life (pages 201–203)

Key Concepts
- Where do plants get the energy they need to produce food?
- What is the role of ATP in cellular activities?

Autotrophs and Heterotrophs (page 201)

1. Where does the energy of food originally come from? _____

_____

2. Complete the table describing the types of organisms.

TYPES OF ORGANISMS

Type	Description	Examples
	Organisms that make their own food	
	Organisms that obtain energy from the food they eat	

Chemical Energy and ATP (page 202)

3. What is one of the principal chemical compounds that cells use to store energy?

_____

4. How is ATP different from ADP? _____

_____

5. Label each part of the ATP molecule illustrated below.

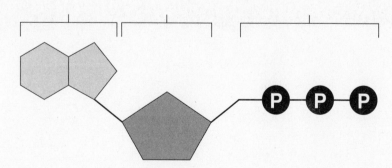

6. When a cell has energy available, how can it store small amounts of that energy?

_____

_____

7. When is the energy stored in ATP released? _____

_____

_____

8. For what purpose do the characteristics of ATP make it exceptionally useful to all types of cells? _____

_____

9. What are two ways in which cells use the energy provided by ATP?

    a. _____

    b. _____

Using Biochemical Energy (pages 202–203)

10. Why is it efficient for cells to keep only a small supply of ATP on hand?

_____

_____

_____

11. Circle the letter of where cells get the energy to regenerate ATP.

    a. ADP

    b. phosphates

    c. foods like glucose

    d. organelles

Section 8–2 Photosynthesis: An Overview (pages 204–207)

⊂▭ Key Concepts

- What did the experiments of van Helmont, Priestley, and Ingenhousz reveal about how plants grow?
- What is the overall equation for photosynthesis?
- What is the role of light and chlorophyll in photosynthesis?

Introduction (page 204)

1. What occurs in the process of photosynthesis? _____

_____

_____

Investigating Photosynthesis (pages 204–206)

2. What did Jan van Helmont conclude from his experiment? _____

_____

_____

3. Circle the letter of the substance produced by the mint plant in Joseph Priestley's experiment.

   a. carbon dioxide

   b. water

   c. air

   d. oxygen

4. What did Jan Ingenhousz show? _____

_____

_____

The Photosynthesis Equation (page 206)

5. Write the overall equation for photosynthesis using words.

_____

6. Photosynthesis uses the energy of sunlight to convert water and

   carbon dioxide into oxygen and high-energy _____.

Light and Pigments (page 207)

7. What does photosynthesis require in addition to water and carbon dioxide?

_____

_____

8. Plants gather the sun's energy with light-absorbing molecules called _____.

9. What is the principal pigment of plants? _____

10. Circle the letters of the regions of the visible spectrum in which chlorophyll absorbs light very well.

    a. blue-violet region

    b. green region

    c. red region

    d. yellow region

Reading Skill Practice

By looking at illustrations in textbooks, you can help yourself remember better what you have read. Look carefully at Figure 8–4 on page 206. What important ideas does this illustration communicate? Do your work on a separate sheet of paper.

Section 8–3 The Reactions of Photosynthesis
(pages 208–214)

Key Concepts
- What happens in the light-dependent reactions?
- What is the Calvin cycle?

Inside a Chloroplast (page 208)

1. Chloroplasts contain saclike photosynthetic membranes called _____.

2. What is a granum? _____

_____

3. The region outside the thylakoid membranes in the chloroplasts is called the

_____.

4. What are the two stages of photosynthesis called?

a. _____

b. _____

5. Complete the illustration of the overview of photosynthesis by writing the products and the reactants of the process, as well as the energy source that excites the electrons.

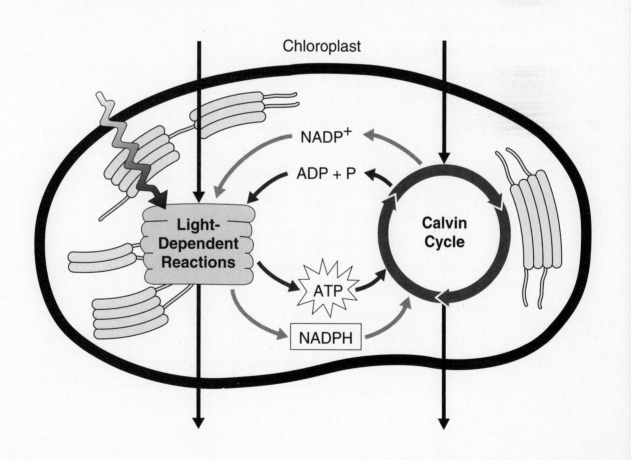

Chloroplast

Electron Carriers (page 209)

6. When sunlight excites electrons in chlorophyll, how do the electrons change?

_____

_____

7. What is a carrier molecule? _____

_____

_____

_____

8. Circle the letter of the carrier molecule involved in photosynthesis.

   a. H_2O c. CO_2

   b. $NADP^+$ d. O_2

9. How does $NADP^+$ become NADPH? _____

_____

_____

Light-Dependent Reactions (pages 210–211)

10. Circle the letter of each sentence that is true about the light-dependent reactions.

    a. They convert ADP into ATP.

    b. They produce oxygen gas.

    c. They convert oxygen into carbon dioxide.

    d. They convert $NADP^+$ into NADPH.

11. Where do the light-dependent reactions take place? _____

_____

12. Circle the letter of each sentence that is true about the light-dependent reactions.

    a. High-energy electrons move through the electron transport chain from photosystem II to photosystem I.

    b. Photosynthesis begins when pigments in photosystem I absorb light.

    c. The difference in charges across the thylakoid membrane provides the energy to make ATP.

    d. Pigments in photosystem I use energy from light to reenergize electrons.

13. How does ATP synthase produce ATP? _____

_____

_____

_____

The Calvin Cycle (pages 212–214)

14. What does the Calvin cycle use to produce high-energy sugars?

_____

_____

15. Why are the reactions of the Calvin cycle also called the light-independent reactions?

_____

16. Circle the letter of each statement that is true about the Calvin cycle.

    a. The main products of the Calvin cycle are six carbon dioxide molecules.

    b. Carbon dioxide molecules enter the Calvin cycle from the atmosphere.

    c. Energy from ATP and high-energy electrons from NADPH are used to convert 3-carbon molecules into higher-energy forms.

    d. The Calvin cycle uses six molecules of carbon dioxide to produce a single 6-carbon sugar molecule.

Factors Affecting Photosynthesis (page 214)

17. What are three factors that affect the rate at which photosynthesis occurs?

    a. _____

    b. _____

    c. _____

18. Is the following sentence true or false? Increasing the intensity of light decreases the rate of photosynthesis. _____

Chapter 8 Photosynthesis

Vocabulary Review

Matching *In the space provided, write the letter of the definition that best matches each term.*

_____ 1. photosynthesis

_____ 2. chlorophyll

_____ 3. pigment

_____ 4. adenosine triphosphate

_____ 5. thylakoid

_____ 6. photosystems

_____ 7. stroma

_____ 8. NADP⁺

_____ 9. Calvin cycle

_____ 10. light-dependent reactions

a. clusters in the thylakoid membrane of chlorophyll and other pigments

b. the region of the chloroplast outside the thylakoid membranes

c. electron carrier

d. process in which plants use the energy of sunlight to make high-energy carbohydrates

e. reactions that use ATP and NADPH to produce high-energy sugars

f. light-absorbing molecules

g. the basic energy source of all cells

h. reactions that produce oxygen gas and convert ADP and NADP⁺ into the energy carriers ATP and NADPH

i. saclike photosynthetic membranes in chloroplasts

j. principal pigment of plants

Answering Questions *In the space provided, write an answer to each question.*

11. What is an organism that obtains energy from the food it consumes? _____

_____

12. What is an organism that is able to make its own food? _____

_____

13. What is released when the chemical bond is broken between the second and third

phosphates of an ATP molecule? _____

_____

14. What are the reactants of the equation for photosynthesis? _____

_____

15. What are the products of the equation for photosynthesis? _____

_____

Summary

9–1 Chemical Pathways

Food serves as the source of energy for cells. Quite a lot of energy is stored in food. For instance, 1 gram of the sugar glucose releases 3811 calories of heat energy when burned in the presence of oxygen. A calorie is the amount of energy needed to raise the temperature of 1 gram of water 1 degree Celsius. Cells don't burn glucose and other food compounds. They gradually release the energy. The process begins with a pathway called glycolysis. In the presence of oxygen, glycolysis is followed by the Krebs cycle and the electron transport chain. Together, these three pathways make up cellular respiration. Cellular respiration is the process that releases energy by breaking down glucose and other food molecules in the presence of oxygen. The equation for cellular respiration is:

$$6O_2 + C_6H_{12}O_6 \rightarrow 6CO_2 + 6H_2O + \text{Energy}$$

$$\text{oxygen} + \text{glucose} \rightarrow \frac{\text{carbon}}{\text{dioxide}} + \text{water} + \text{energy}$$

There are three main stages of cellular respiration: (1) glycolysis, (2) the Krebs cycle, and (3) electron transport.

Glycolysis is the process in which one molecule of glucose is broken in half, producing two molecules of pyruvic acid, a 3-carbon compound. Through glycolysis, the cell gains 2 ATP molecules. In one of the reactions of glycolysis, the electron carrier NAD^+ accepts a pair of high-energy electrons, producing NADH. By doing this, NAD^+ helps pass energy from glucose to other pathways in the cell.

When oxygen is not present, glycolysis is followed by another pathway. This pathway is called fermentation. Fermentation releases energy from food molecules by producing ATP. Because fermentation does not require oxygen, it is said to be anaerobic.

During fermentation, cells convert NADH back into the electron carrier NAD^+, which is needed for glycolysis.

This action allows glycolysis to continue producing a steady supply of ATP. The two main types of fermentation are alcoholic fermentation and lactic acid fermentation. Yeasts and a few other microorganisms carry out alcoholic fermentation. The equation for alcoholic fermentation after glycolysis is:

$$\frac{\text{pyruvic}}{\text{acid}} + \text{NADH} \rightarrow \text{alcohol} + CO_2 + NAD^+$$

Lactic acid fermentation occurs in your muscles during rapid exercise. The equation for lactic acid fermentation after glycolysis is:

$$\text{pyruvic acid} + \text{NADH} \rightarrow \text{lactic acid} + NAD^+$$

9–2 The Krebs Cycle and Electron Transport

When oxygen is available, glycolysis is followed by the Krebs cycle and the electron transport chain. The three pathways together make up the process of cellular respiration. Because the pathways of cellular respiration require oxygen, they are said to be aerobic.

The Krebs cycle is the second stage of cellular respiration. In eukaryotes, the Krebs cycle takes place in the mitochondrion. During the Krebs cycle, pyruvic acid is broken down into carbon dioxide in a series of energy-extracting reactions. The Krebs cycle is also known as the citric acid cycle, because citric acid is one of the first products.

The Krebs cycle begins when pyruvic acid produced by glycolysis enters the mitochondrion. One carbon atom from pyruvic acid becomes part of a molecule of carbon dioxide, which is eventually released into the air. The carbon dioxide released during the Krebs cycle is the source of much of the carbon dioxide in air. The other two carbon atoms from pyruvic acid are used in a series of reactions. During these reactions, two energy carriers accept high-energy electrons. NAD^+ is changed to NADH, and FAD is changed to $FADH_2$. These molecules carry the high-energy electrons to the electron transport chain.

Electron transport is the third stage of cellular respiration. The electron transport chain uses the high-energy electrons from the Krebs cycle to convert ADP into ATP. In eukaryotes, the electron transport chain is composed of a series of carrier proteins located in the inner membrane of the mitochondrion. In prokaryotes, the same chain is in the cell membrane. In this pathway, high-energy electrons move from one carrier protein to the next. Their energy is used to move hydrogen ions across the membrane through a protein sphere called ATP synthase. Each time an ATP synthase spins, a phosphate group is added to an ADP molecule, producing an ATP molecule.

In the absence of oxygen, all the energy that a cell can extract from a single molecule of glucose is 2 ATP molecules—the product of glycolysis.

In the presence of oxygen, though, the cell can extract many more ATP molecules. The Krebs cycle and the electron transport chain enable the cell to produce 34 more ATP molecules per glucose molecule. The total, then, for cellular respiration (glycolysis plus the Krebs cycle plus electron transport) is 36 ATP molecules per glucose molecule.

Human body cells normally contain small amounts of ATP produced during cellular respiration. When the body needs energy in a hurry, muscle cells produce ATP by lactic acid fermentation. For long-term energy needs, the body must use cellular respiration.

The energy flows in photosynthesis and cellular respiration take place in opposite directions. On a global level, photosynthesis and cellular respiration are also opposites. Photosynthesis removes carbon dioxide from the atmosphere and puts back oxygen. Cellular respiration removes oxygen from the atmosphere and puts back carbon dioxide.

Chapter 9   Cellular Respiration

Section 9–1 Chemical Pathways (pages 221–225)

Key Concepts

- What is cellular respiration?
- What happens during the process of glycolysis?
- What are the two main types of fermentation?

Chemical Energy and Food (page 221)

1. What is a calorie? _____

_____

2. How many calories make up 1 Calorie? _____

3. Cellular respiration begins with a pathway called _____.

4. Is the following sentence true or false? Glycolysis releases a great amount of energy.

_____

Overview of Cellular Respiration (page 222)

5. What is cellular respiration? _____

_____

_____

6. What is the equation for cellular respiration, using chemical formulas?

_____

7. Label the three main stages of cellular respiration on the illustration of the complete process.

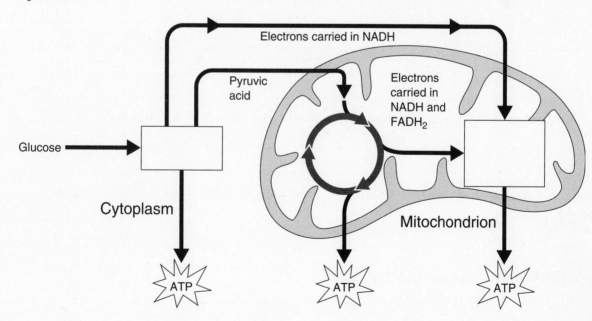

© Pearson Education, Inc., publishing as Pearson Prentice Hall.

Name_____ Class_____ Date _____

8. What would be the problem if cellular respiration took place in just one step?

_____

_____

9. Where does glycolysis take place? _____

_____

10. Where do the Krebs cycle and electron transport take place? _____

_____

Glycolysis (page 223)

11. What is glycolysis? _____

_____

12. How does the cell get glycolysis going? _____

13. If the cell uses 2 ATP molecules at the beginning of glycolysis, how does it end up with a net gain of 2 ATP molecules? _____

_____

_____

14. What is NAD$^+$? _____

_____

15. What is the function of NAD$^+$ in glycolysis? _____

_____

_____

_____

16. Why can glycolysis supply energy to cells when oxygen is not available? ____

_____

_____

17. What problem does a cell have when it generates large amounts of ATP from glycolysis? _____

_____

Fermentation (pages 224–225)

18. What is fermentation? _____

_____

98 Chapter 9

© Pearson Education, Inc., publishing as Pearson Prentice Hall.

19. How does fermentation allow glycolysis to continue? _____

_____

20. Because fermentation does not require oxygen, it is said to be _____.

21. What are the two main types of fermentation?

    a. _____

    b. _____

22. What organisms use alcoholic fermentation? _____

_____

23. What is the equation for alcoholic fermentation after glycolysis?

_____

24. What happens to the small amount of alcohol produced in alcoholic fermentation during the baking of bread? _____

25. What does lactic acid fermentation convert into lactic acid? _____

_____

26. What is the equation for lactic acid fermentation after glycolysis?

_____

27. During rapid exercise, how do your muscle cells produce ATP? _____

_____

_____

Reading Skill Practice

When you read about complex topics, writing an outline can help you organize and understand the material. Outline Section 9–1 by using the headings and subheadings as topics and subtopics and then writing the most important details under each topic. Do your work on a separate sheet of paper.

Section 9–2 The Krebs Cycle and Electron Transport (pages 226–232)

Key Concepts
- What happens during the Krebs cycle?
- How are high-energy electrons used by the electron transport chain?

Introduction (page 226)

1. At the end of glycolysis, how much of the chemical energy in glucose is still unused?

   _____

2. Because the final stages of cellular respiration require oxygen, they are said to be

   _____ .

The Krebs Cycle (pages 226–227)

3. In the presence of oxygen, how is the pyruvic acid produced in glycolysis used?

   _____

   _____

4. What happens to pyruvic acid during the Krebs cycle? _____

   _____

   _____

5. Why is the Krebs cycle also known as the citric acid cycle? _____

   _____

   _____

6. When does the Krebs cycle begin? _____

   _____

7. What happens to each of the 3 carbon atoms in pyruvic acid when it is broken down?

   _____

   _____

   _____

8. What happens to the carbon dioxide produced in breaking down pyruvic acid?

   _____

9. How is citric acid produced? _____

   _____

   _____

10. During the energy extraction part of the Krebs cycle, how many molecules of CO_2 are

    released? _____

11. What is the energy tally from 1 molecule of pyruvic acid during the Krebs cycle?

    _____

12. When electrons join NAD$^+$ and FAD during the Krebs cycle, what do they form? _____

13. Why is the 4-carbon compound generated in the breakdown of citric acid the only permanent compound in the Krebs cycle? _____

_____

_____

Electron Transport (pages 228–229)

14. What is the electron transport chain? _____

_____

15. What does the electron transport chain use the high-energy electrons from the Krebs cycle for? _____

_____

16. How does the location of the electron transport chain differ in eukaryotes and prokaryotes? _____

_____

_____

_____

17. Where does the electron transport chain get the high-energy electrons that are passed down the chain? _____

_____

_____

18. Is the following sentence true or false? Hydrogen serves as the final electron acceptor of the electron transport chain. _____

19. What is the energy of the high-energy electrons used for every time 2 high-energy electrons move down the electron transport chain? _____

_____

20. What causes the H$^+$ ions in the intermembrane space to move through the channels in the membrane and out into the matrix? _____

_____

_____

_____

_____

_____

21. On average, how many ATP molecules are produced as each pair of high-energy electrons moves down the electron transport chain? _____

22. Complete the flowchart about electron transport. (Review Figure 9–7 on page 228 of your textbook.)

> High-energy electrons from NADH and FADH$_2$ are passed into and along the
> _____ .

↓

> The energy from the electrons moving down the chain is used to move H$^+$ ions across the
> _____ .

↓

> H$^+$ ions build up in the _____ space, making it
> _____ charged and making the matrix negatively charged.

↓

> H$^+$ ions move through channels of _____ in the inner membrane.

↓

> The ATP synthase uses the energy from the moving ions to combine ADP and phosphate,
> forming high-energy _____ .

The Totals (page 229)

23. How many ATP molecules are formed during cellular respiration? _____

24. Why is more ATP generated from glucose in the presence of oxygen?

_____

_____

_____

_____

25. What happens to the energy of glucose that is not used to make ATP molecules?

_____

26. What are the final waste products of cellular respiration? _____

Energy and Exercise (pages 230–231)

27. What are three sources of ATP a human body uses at the beginning of a race?

_____

_____

_____

28. When a runner needs quick energy for a short race, what source can supply enough ATP for about 90 seconds? _____

29. Why does a sprinter have an oxygen debt to repay after the race is over? _____

_____

_____

_____

30. A runner needs more energy for a longer race. How does the body generate the necessary ATP? _____

31. Why are aerobic forms of exercise so beneficial for weight control? _____

_____

_____

_____

Comparing Photosynthesis and Cellular Respiration (page 232)

32. If photosynthesis is the process that "deposits" energy in a "savings account," then what is cellular respiration? _____

_____

33. How are photosynthesis and cellular respiration opposite in terms of carbon dioxide?

_____

_____

34. How are photosynthesis and cellular respiration opposite in terms of oxygen?

_____

_____

Vocabulary Review

Matching   *In the space provided, write the letter of the definition that best matches each term.*

_____ **1.** calorie

_____ **2.** glycolysis

_____ **3.** cellular respiration

_____ **4.** NAD⁺

_____ **5.** fermentation

_____ **6.** anaerobic

_____ **7.** aerobic

a. electron carrier

b. pathway that releases energy from food in the absence of oxygen

c. requires oxygen

d. process in which one molecule of glucose is broken in half, producing two molecules of pyruvic acid

e. does not require oxygen

f. amount of energy needed to raise 1 gram of water 1 degree Celsius

g. process that releases energy by breaking down food molecules in the presence of oxygen

Answering Questions   *In the space provided, write an answer to each question.*

8. What is the first stage of cellular respiration? _____

_____

9. What is the second stage of cellular respiration? _____

_____

10. What is the third stage of cellular respiration? _____

_____

11. How many ATP molecules can the cell produce from a single molecule of glucose

through glycolysis? _____

12. How many ATP molecules can the cell produce from a single molecule of glucose

through the complete process of cellular respiration? _____

Completion   *Write an equation for each of the pathways below.*

13. lactic acid fermentation after glycolysis _____

_____

14. alcoholic fermentation after glycolysis _____

_____

15. cellular respiration _____

_____

Summary

10–1 Cell Growth

The larger a cell becomes, the more demands the cell places on its DNA. As a cell increases in size, it usually does not make copies of DNA. If a cell were to grow without limit, an "information crisis" would occur. In addition, as a cell increases in size, the more trouble it has moving enough nutrients (food) and wastes across its cell membrane. The rate at which materials move through the cell membrane depends on the surface area of the cell—the total area of its cell membrane. However, the rate at which food and oxygen are used up and waste products are produced depends on the volume of the cell.

If a cell were a cube, you could determine surface area by multiplying length × width × number of sides. You could determine volume by multiplying length × width × height. You then could determine the cell's ratio of surface area to volume by dividing the surface area by the volume. As a cell grows, its volume increases more rapidly than its surface area. That is, as a cell becomes larger, its ratio of surface area to volume decreases.

Before a cell becomes too large, a growing cell divides, forming two "daughter" cells. The process by which a cell divides into two new daughter cells is called cell division.

10–2 Cell Division

Each cell has only one set of genetic information. For that reason, a cell must first copy its genetic information before cell division begins. Each daughter cell then gets a complete copy of that information. In most prokaryotes, cell division is a simple matter of separating the contents of the cell into two parts. In eukaryotes, cell division occurs in two main stages. The first stage is division of the nucleus, called mitosis. The second stage is division of the cytoplasm, called cytokinesis.

In eukaryotes, genetic information is passed on by chromosomes. Well before cell division, each chromosome is replicated (copied). When copying occurs, each chromosome consists of two identical "sister" chromatids. Each pair of chromatids is attached at an area called a centromere.

The cell cycle is a series of events that cells go through as they grow and divide. During the cell cycle, a cell grows, prepares for division, and divides to form two daughter cells, each of which then begins the cycle again. The cell cycle consists of four phases. The M phase includes mitosis and cytokinesis. The other three phases are sometimes grouped together and called interphase. Interphase is divided into three phases: G_1, S, and G_2. During the G_1 phase, cells increase in size and make new proteins and organelles. During the next phase, the S phase, the replication (copying) of chromosomes takes place. When the S phase is complete, the cell enters the G_2 phase. During the G_2 phase, many of the organelles and molecules required for cell division are produced.

Mitosis consists of four phases: prophase, metaphase, anaphase, and telophase. The first and longest phase is prophase. During prophase, the chromosomes condense and become visible. The centrioles separate and take up positions on opposite sides of the nucleus. Centrioles are two tiny structures located in the cytoplasm near the nuclear envelope. The centrioles lie in a region called the centrosome that helps to organize the spindle, a fanlike microtubule structure that helps separate the chromosomes.

During the second phase, called metaphase, chromosomes line up across the center of the cell. During the third phase, called anaphase, the centromeres that join the sister chromatids split and the sister chromatids become individual chromosomes. The two sets of chromosomes move apart. During the fourth and final phase, called telophase, the chromosomes gather at opposite ends of the cell and lose their distinct shapes. Two new nuclear envelopes form.

Cytokinesis usually occurs at the same time as telophase. In most animal cells, the cell membrane is drawn inward until the cytoplasm is pinched into two nearly equal parts. In plant cells, a structure known as a cell plate forms midway between the divided nuclei. A cell wall then begins to appear in the cell plate.

10–3 Regulating the Cell Cycle

In a multicellular organism, cell growth and cell division are carefully controlled. For instance, when an injury such as a cut in the skin occurs, cells at the edge of the cut will divide rapidly. When the healing process nears completion, the rate of cell division slows down and then returns to normal.

Cyclins—a group of proteins—regulate the timing of the cell cycle in eukaryotic cells. There are two types of these regulatory proteins: internal regulators and external regulators.

Internal regulators are proteins that respond to events inside the cell. They allow the cell cycle to proceed only when certain processes have happened inside the cell. External regulators are proteins that respond to events outside the cell. They direct cells to speed up or slow down the cell cycle. Growth factors are important external regulators. Growth factors stimulate growth and division of cells, such as during the development of the embryo or when a wound is healing.

Cancer is a disorder in which some of the body's own cells lose the ability to control growth. Cancer cells do not respond to the signals that regulate the growth of most cells. As a result, they divide uncontrollably and form masses of cells called tumors. Cancer cells may break lose from tumors and spread throughout the body. Cancer cells damage tissues and disrupt normal activities, causing serious medical problems or even death.

Chapter 10 Cell Growth and Division

Section 10–1 Cell Growth (pages 241–243)

 Key Concept
 • What problems does growth cause for cells?

Limits to Cell Growth (pages 241–243)

1. What are two reasons why cells divide rather than continue to grow indefinitely?

   a. _____

   _____

   b. _____

   _____

   _____

2. Is the following sentence true or false? As a cell increases in size, it usually makes extra copies of its DNA. _____

3. Circle the letter of what determines the rate at which food and oxygen in a cell are used up and waste products produced.

   a. The cell's organelles   c. The cell's location

   b. The cell's volume   d. The cell's DNA

4. How can you obtain a cell's ratio of surface area to volume? _____

   _____

5. If a cell's surface area is 6 cm^3 and its volume is 1 cm^3, then what is its ratio of surface area to volume? _____

6. Is the following sentence true or false? As a cell grows in size, its volume increases much more rapidly than its surface area. _____

7. Circle the letter of what happens to a cell's ratio of surface area to volume as the cell's volume increases more rapidly than its surface area.

   a. The ratio decreases.   c. The ratio remains the same.

   b. The ratio increases.   d. The ratio disappears.

Division of the Cell (page 243)

8. What is cell division? _____

   _____

   _____

9. How does cell division solve the problem of increasing size? _____

   _____

   _____

Section 10–2 Cell Division (pages 244–249)

⊂⊐ **Key Concepts**

- What are the main events of the cell cycle?
- What are the four phases of mitosis?

Chromosomes (pages 244–245)

1. In eukaryotic cells, what are the two main stages of cell division? _____

_____

2. When chromosomes become visible at the beginning of cell division, what does each chromosome consist of? _____

_____

3. Each pair of chromatids is attached at an area called the _____.

The Cell Cycle (page 245)

4. The period of growth in between cell divisions is called _____.

5. What is the cell cycle? _____

_____

_____

6. Complete the diagram of the cell cycle by writing the names of each of the four phases.

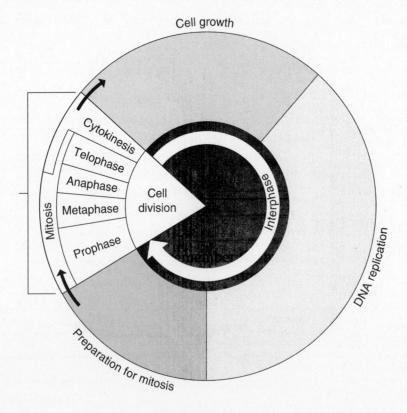

© Pearson Education, Inc., publishing as Pearson Prentice Hall.

7. The division of the cell nucleus during the M phase of the cell cycle is called

_____.

Events of the Cell Cycle (page 245)

8. Interphase is divided into what three phases?

a. _____ b. _____ c. _____

9. What happens during the G₁ phase? _____

_____

_____

10. What happens during the S phase? _____

_____

_____

11. What happens during the G₂ phase? _____

_____

_____

Mitosis (pages 246–248)

12. What are the four phases of mitosis?

a. _____   c. _____

b. _____   d. _____

13. What are the two tiny structures located in the cytoplasm near the nuclear envelope at the beginning of prophase? _____

14. What is the spindle? _____

_____

Match the description of the event with the phase of mitosis it is in. Each phase may be used more than once.

	Event	Phase
_____	**15.** The chromosomes move until they form two groups near the poles of the spindle.	**a.** Prophase
_____	**16.** The chromosomes become visible. The centrioles take up positions on opposite sides of the nucleus.	**b.** Metaphase
_____	**17.** A nuclear envelope re-forms around each cluster of chromosomes. The nucleolus becomes visible in each daughter nucleus.	**c.** Anaphase **d.** Telophase
_____	**18.** The chromosomes line up across the center of the cell.	

19. Identify each of the four phases of mitosis pictured below.

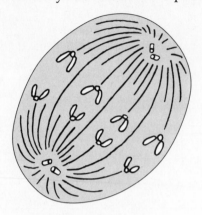

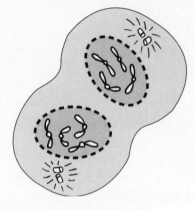

a. _____

c. _____

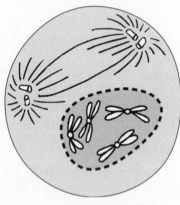

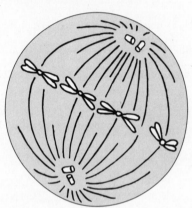

b. _____

d. _____

Cytokinesis (page 248)

20. What is cytokinesis? _____

21. How does cytokinesis occur in most animal cells? _____

_____

22. What forms midway between the divided nucleus during cytokinesis in plant cells?

_____

Reading Skill Practice

You may sometimes forget the meanings of the vocabulary terms that were introduced earlier in the textbook. When this happens, you can check the meanings of the terms in the Glossary, which you can find at the end of the book, preceding the Index. Use the Glossary to review the meanings of all the vocabulary terms listed on page 244. Write their definitions on a separate sheet of paper.

Section 10–3 Regulating the Cell Cycle
(pages 250–252)

Key Concepts

- How is the cell cycle regulated?
- How are cancer cells different from other cells?

Controls on Cell Division (page 250)

1. What happens to the cells at the edges of an injury when a cut in the skin or a break in a bone occurs? _____

2. What happens to the rapidly dividing cells when the healing process nears completion?
_____
_____

Cell Cycle Regulators (page 251)

3. What do cyclins regulate? _____
_____

4. What are internal regulators? _____

5. Circle the letter of each sentence that is true about external regulators.

   a. They direct cells to speed up or slow down the cell cycle.

   b. They prevent the cell from entering anaphase until all its chromosomes are attached to the mitotic spindle.

   c. They include growth factors.

   d. They prevent excessive cell growth and keep the tissues of the body from disrupting one another.

Uncontrolled Cell Growth (page 252)

6. What is cancer? _____
_____

7. Complete the flowchart about cancer.

> Cancer cells don't respond to signals that regulate _____.

⬇

> Cancer cells form masses of cells called _____.

⬇

> Cancer cells break loose and spread throughout the _____.

8. Is the following sentence true or false? Cancer is a disease of the cell cycle.

_____

Vocabulary Review

Completion   *Fill in the blanks with terms from Chapter 10.*

1. The division of a cell's cytoplasm is called _____.

2. The final phase of mitosis is _____.

3. The phase of mitosis in which microtubules connect the centromere of each chromosome to the poles of the spindle is _____.

4. At the beginning of cell division, each chromosome consists of two sister _____.

5. The longest phase of mitosis is _____.

6. The phase of mitosis that ends when the chromosomes stop moving is _____.

7. The process by which a cell divides into two new daughter cells is called _____.

8. A tiny structure located in the cytoplasm near the nuclear envelope is a(an) _____.

9. A disorder in which some of the body's cells lose the ability to control growth is called _____.

10. The area where a pair of chromatids is attached is the _____.

11. The division of the cell nucleus is called _____.

12. A protein that regulates the timing of the cell cycle in eukaryotic cells is _____.

13. The series of events that cells go through as they grow and divide is known as the _____.

14. A fanlike microtubule structure that helps separate the chromosomes is a(an) _____.

15. The time period between cell divisions is called _____.

Summary

11–1 The Work of Gregor Mendel

The scientific study of heredity is called genetics. Gregor Mendel used purebred pea plants in a series of experiments to understand inheritance.

Pea flowers have both male and female parts. Normally, pollen from the male part of the pea flower fertilizes the female egg cells of the same flower. This is called self-pollination. Seeds that come from self-pollination inherit all their characteristics from just one parent.

To carry out his experiments, Mendel had to prevent self-pollination. He did this by cutting away the pollen-bearing male parts and then dusting pollen from another plant on the flower. This process is called cross-pollination. The seeds that come from cross-pollination are the offspring of two different parents.

Mendel decided to study just a few traits, or characteristics, of the pea plants. He studied seven traits: seed shape, seed color, seed coat color, pod shape, pod color, flower position, and plant height.

First, Mendel crossed two plants with different characters, or forms, for the same trait. For example, one plant was tall and the other was short. Mendel used the seeds produced by this cross to grow plants. These plants were hybrids. Hybrids are the offspring of crosses between parents with different traits.

To Mendel's surprise, the hybrid plants looked like only one of the parents. He concluded that each trait was controlled by one gene that occurred in two different forms. The different forms of a gene are called alleles. Mendel formed the theory of dominance. He concluded that some alleles are dominant, while others are recessive. Whenever a living thing inherits a dominant allele, that trait is visible. The effects of a recessive allele are not seen if the dominant allele is present.

Mendel wanted to know what happened to the recessive allele. He allowed his hybrid plants to self-pollinate. Some of the plants that were produced showed the recessive trait. The alleles responsible for the recessive characters had not disappeared. Before, the dominant allele had masked the recessive allele, so it was not visible. Mendel concluded that the alleles for the same trait can be separated. He called this segregation. Alleles segregate when gametes are formed. Each gamete carries only one copy of each gene.

11–2 Probability and Punnett Squares

Mendel used the principles of probability to explain his results. Probability is the likelihood that a particular event will occur. Probability can be used to predict the outcome of genetic crosses because alleles segregate randomly. The gene combinations that might result from a genetic cross can be determined by drawing a Punnett square.

In a Punnett square, alleles are represented by letters. A capital letter represents the dominant allele, and a lowercase letter represents the recessive allele. Organisms that have two identical alleles for a particular trait are called homozygous. Homozygous organisms are true-breeding for a particular trait. Organisms that have two different alleles for a particular trait are called heterozygous. Heterozygous organisms are hybrid for a particular trait.

The physical traits of an organism make up its phenotype (for example, height). The genetic makeup of an organism is its genotype (for example, *TT* or *Tt*).

One important rule of probability is that probabilities predict the average outcome of a large number of events. They cannot predict what will happen in a single event. The more organisms examined, the closer the numbers will get to the expected values.

11–3 Exploring Mendelian Genetics

Mendel wondered whether genes that determine one trait have anything to do with genes that determine another trait. He wanted to know, for example, whether the gene that determines seed shape affects the gene for seed color. To answer this question, he did an experiment. He crossed plants and recorded two traits—seed shape and seed color.

Mendel found that the gene controlling seed shape did not affect the gene controlling seed color. Mendel concluded that genes can segregate independently, or undergo independent assortment, during gamete formation.

Not all genes show simple patterns of dominant and recessive alleles. In incomplete dominance, one allele is not completely dominant over another. In codominance, both alleles contribute to the phenotype. Many genes have more than two alleles and are said to have multiple alleles. Polygenic traits are traits controlled by two or more genes.

The characteristics of any organism are not caused only by its genes. Instead, characteristics are determined by the interaction between the genes and the environment.

11–4 Meiosis

According to Mendel, living things inherit a single copy of each gene from each of their parents. When gametes are formed, these two copies are separated.

Gametes are made during meiosis. In a complex process, the number of chromosomes in each cell is cut in half. The chromosomes are different from one another and from the parent cell.

There are two stages in meiosis. During the first stage, the DNA in special cells in the reproductive organs is copied. The cells then divide. Two cells are formed. These cells are different from each other and different from the parent cell. In the second stage of meiosis, the cells divide again. This time, their DNA is not copied first. Four daughter cells are produced. Each cell contains half the number of chromosomes of the original parent cell.

In male animals, the gametes produced by meiosis are called sperm. Some plants also have sperm cells. In females, meiosis produces one large reproductive cell and three smaller cells. In animals, the larger reproductive cell is called an egg. In some plants, it is called an egg cell. The three smaller cells produced during meiosis are called polar bodies. They do not participate in reproduction.

Meiosis is very different from mitosis. Mitosis makes two cells that are exactly alike. The cells are also exactly like the parent cell. Meiosis, however, produces four cells. Each of the cells has only half the number of chromosomes of the parent cell. The cells are genetically different from one another.

11–5 Linkage and Gene Maps

Some genes are almost always inherited together. These genes belong to the same linkage group. A chromosome is a group of linked genes. It is actually the chromosomes that assort independently during gamete formation, not single genes.

The location of genes can be mapped to a chromosome. The rate of crossover events is used to find the distance between genes on a chromosome. The farther apart two genes are, the more likely they will be separated by a crossover event.

Chapter 11 Introduction to Genetics

Section 11–1 The Work of Gregor Mendel
(pages 263–266)

Key Concepts
- What is the principle of dominance?
- What happens during segregation?

Gregor Mendel's Peas (pages 263–264)

1. The scientific study of heredity is called _____.

2. Circle the letter of each sentence that is true about Gregor Mendel's peas.

   a. The male parts of pea flowers produce eggs.

   b. When pollen fertilizes an egg cell, a seed for a new plant is formed.

   c. Pea plants normally reproduce by self-pollination.

   d. Seeds that are produced by self-pollination inherit their characteristics from two different plants.

3. What does it mean when pea plants are described as being true-breeding?

   _____

   _____

4. To perform his experiments, how did Mendel prevent pea flowers from self-pollinating and control their cross-pollination? _____

   _____

   _____

Genes and Dominance (pages 264–265)

Match the term with its definition.

Terms	Definitions
_____ 5. genes	a. Specific characteristics that vary from one individual to another
_____ 6. hybrids	b. The offspring of crosses between parents with different traits
_____ 7. traits	c. Chemical factors that determine traits
_____ 8. alleles	d. The different forms of a gene

9. State the principle of dominance. _____

   _____

10. Is the following sentence true or false? An organism with a recessive allele for a particular form of a trait will always exhibit that form. _____

11. Circle the letters of the traits controlled by dominant alleles in Mendel's pea plants.

   a. tall   b. short   c. yellow   d. green

Segregation (pages 265–266)

12. How did Mendel find out whether the recessive alleles were still present in the

F$_1$ plants? _____

_____

_____

13. About one fourth of the F$_2$ plants from Mendel's F$_1$ crosses showed the trait controlled

by the _____ allele.

14. Circle the letter of each sentence that is true about Mendel's explanation of the results
from his F$_1$ cross.

    a. Mendel assumed that a dominant allele had masked the corresponding recessive
allele in the F$_1$ generation.

    b. The trait controlled by the recessive allele never showed up in any F$_2$ plants.

    c. The allele for shortness was always inherited with the allele for tallness.

    d. At some point, the allele for shortness was segregated, or separated, from the allele
for tallness.

15. What are gametes? _____

_____

16. Complete the following diagram to show how alleles segregate during the formation of
gametes.

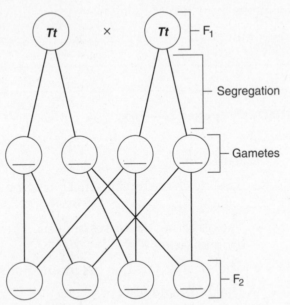

17. In the diagram above, the dominant allele is represented by _____ and the

recessive allele is represented by _____.

Section 11–2 Probability and Punnett Squares
(pages 267–269)

👓 Key Concepts
- How do geneticists use the principles of probability?
- How do geneticists use Punnett squares?

Genetics and Probability (page 267)

1. The likelihood that a particular event will occur is called _____.

2. Circle the letter of the probability that a single coin flip will come up heads.

   a. 100 percent   **b.** 75 percent   **c.** 50 percent   **d.** 25 percent

3. Is the following sentence true or false? The past outcomes of coin flips greatly affect the outcomes of future coin flips. _____

4. Why can the principles of probability be used to predict the outcomes of genetic crosses? _____

_____

Punnett Squares (page 268)

5. How do geneticists use Punnett squares? _____

_____

_____

6. Complete the Punnett square to show the possible gene combinations for the F$_2$ offspring.

PUNNETT SQUARE FOR *Tt* × *Tt*

	T	*t*
T		
t		

Match the terms with the definitions.

Terms	Definitions
_____ 7. genotype	**a.** Organisms that have two identical alleles for a particular trait (*TT* or *tt*)
_____ 8. homozygous	
_____ 9. phenotype	**b.** Organisms that have two different alleles for the same trait (*Tt*)
_____ 10. heterozygous	**c.** Physical characteristic of an organism (tall)
	d. Genetic makeup of an organism (*Tt*)

11. Is the following sentence true or false? Homozygous organisms are true-breeding for a particular trait. _____

12. Is the following sentence true or false? Plants with the same phenotype always have the same genotype. _____

Probability and Segregation (page 269)

13. Circle the letter of each sentence that is true about probability and segregation.

   a. In an F_1 cross between two hybrid tall pea plants (Tt), ½ of the F_2 plants will have two alleles for tallness (TT).

   b. The F_2 ratio of tall plants to short plants produced in a cross between two hybrid tall pea plants (Tt) is 3 tall plants for every 1 short plant.

   c. Mendel observed that about ¾ of the F_2 offspring showed the dominant trait.

   d. Segregation occurs according to Mendel's model.

14. In Mendel's model of segregation, what was the ratio of tall plants to short plants in the F_2 generation? _____

Probabilities Predict Averages (page 269)

15. Is the following sentence true or false? Probabilities predict the precise outcome of an individual event. _____

16. How can you be sure of getting the expected 50 : 50 ratio from flipping a coin?

_____

17. The _____ the number of offspring from a genetic cross, the closer the resulting numbers will get to expected values.

18. Is the following sentence true or false? The ratios of an F_1 generation are more likely to match Mendelian predicted ratios if the F_1 generation contains hundreds or thousands of individuals. _____

Reading Skill Practice

Taking notes helps the reader focus on the main ideas and the vocabulary of the reading. Take notes while rereading Section 11–2. Note the main ideas and the highlighted, boldface terms in the order in which they are presented. You may copy the ideas word for word or summarize them using your own words. Do your work on a separate sheet of paper.

Section 11–3 Exploring Mendelian Genetics
(pages 270–274)

🔑 **Key Concepts**
- What is the principle of independent assortment?
- What inheritance patterns exist aside from simple dominance?

Independent Assortment (pages 270–271)

1. In a two-factor cross, Mendel followed _____ different genes as they passed from one generation to the next.

2. Write the genotypes of the true-breeding plants that Mendel used in his two-factor cross.

   Phenotype   **Genotype**

   a. round yellow peas   _____

   b. wrinkled green peas   _____

3. Circle the letter that best describes the F_1 offspring of Mendel's two-factor cross.

   a. Homozygous dominant with round yellow peas

   b. Homozygous recessive with wrinkled green peas

   c. Heterozygous dominant with round yellow peas

   d. Heterozygous recessive with wrinkled green peas

4. Is the following sentence true or false? The genotypes of the F_1 offspring indicated to Mendel that genes assort independently.

   _____

5. How did Mendel produce the F_2 offspring? _____

6. Circle the letter of the phenotypes that Mendel would expect to see if genes segregated independently.

   a. round and yellow

   b. wrinkled and green

   c. round and green

   d. wrinkled and yellow

7. What did Mendel observe in the F_2 offspring that showed him that the alleles for seed shape segregate independently of those for seed color? _____

   _____

   _____

8. What were the phenotypes of the F_2 generation that Mendel observed? _____

   _____

© Pearson Education, Inc., publishing as Pearson Prentice Hall.

9. What was the ratio of Mendel's F$_2$ generation for the two-factor cross? _____

_____

10. Complete the Punnett square below to show the predicted results of Mendel's two-factor cross.

MENDEL'S TWO-FACTOR CROSS
RrYy × RrYy

	RY	*Ry*	*rY*	*ry*
RY				
Ry				
rY				
ry				

11. State Mendel's principle of independent assortment. _____

_____

_____

A Summary of Mendel's Principles (page 272)

12. Circle the letter of each sentence that is true about Mendel's principles.

   a. The inheritance of biological characteristics is determined by genes that are passed from parents to their offspring.

   b. Two or more forms of the gene for a single trait can never exist.

   c. The copies of genes are segregated from each other when gametes are formed.

   d. The alleles for different genes usually segregate independently of one another.

13. When two or more forms of the gene for a single trait exist, some forms of the gene

   may be _____ and others may be _____ .

Beyond Dominant and Recessive Alleles (pages 272–273)

14. Is the following sentence true or false? All genes show simple patterns of dominant

   and recessive alleles. _____

15. Complete the table of the different patterns of inheritance.

PATTERNS OF INHERITANCE

Type	Description	Examples
	One allele is not completely dominant over another. The heterozygous phenotype is somewhere in between the two homozygous phenotypes.	
	Both alleles contribute to the phenotype of the organism.	
	Genes have more than two alleles.	
	Two or more genes control a trait.	

Applying Mendel's Principles (page 274)

16. List three criteria Thomas Hunt Morgan was looking for in a model organism for genetic studies.

a. _____

b. _____

c. _____

17. Is the following sentence true or false? Mendel's principles apply not just to pea plants but to other organisms as well. _____

Genetics and the Environment (page 274)

18. Characteristics are determined by interaction between genes and the

_____.

Section 11–4 Meiosis (pages 275–278)

 Key Concepts
- What happens during the process of meiosis?
- How is meiosis different from mitosis?

Introduction (page 275)

1. List the two things that Mendel's principles of genetics required in order to be true.

    a. _____

    _____

    b. _____

    _____

    _____

Chromosome Number (page 275)

2. What does it mean when two sets of chromosomes are homologous? _____

_____

_____

_____

3. Circle the letter of each way to describe a diploid cell.

    a. 2N

    b. Contains two sets of homologous chromosomes

    c. Contains a single set of homologous chromosomes

    d. A gamete

4. Circle the letter of the number of chromosomes in a haploid *Drosophila* cell.

    a. 8   b. 4   c. 2   d. 0

Phases of Meiosis (pages 275–277)

5. Draw the chromosomes in the diagrams below to show the correct phase of meiosis.

Prophase I

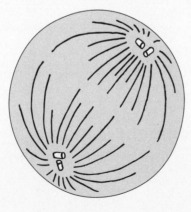

Metaphase I

Anaphase II

6. Identify which phase of meiosis is shown in the diagrams below.

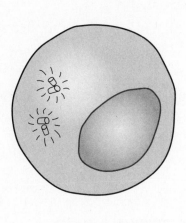
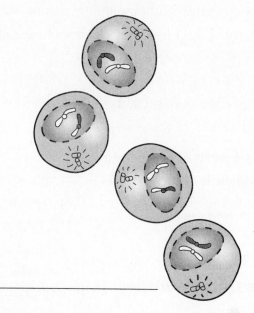

_____   _____

7. Why is meiosis described as a process of reduction division? _____

_____

_____

_____

8. What are the two distinct divisions of meiosis?

a. _____   **b.** _____

9. Is the following sentence true or false? The diploid cell that enters meiosis becomes 4 haploid cells at the end of meiosis. _____

10. How does a tetrad form in prophase I of meiosis? _____

_____

_____

11. Circle the number of chromatids in a tetrad.

a. 8   **b.** 6   **c.** 4   **d.** 2

12. What results from the process of crossing-over during prophase I? _____

_____

_____

_____

13. Circle the letter of each sentence that is true about meiosis.

   a. During meiosis I, homologous chromosomes separate.

   b. The two daughter cells produced by meiosis I still have the two complete sets of chromosomes, as does a diploid cell.

   c. During anaphase II, the paired chromatids separate.

   d. After meiosis II, the four daughter cells contain the diploid number of chromosomes.

Gamete Formation (page 278)

Match the products of meiosis with the descriptions.

Product of Meiosis	Description
_____ 14. eggs	a. Haploid gametes produced in males
_____ 15. sperm	b. Haploid gametes produced in females
_____ 16. polar bodies	c. Cells produced in females that do not participate in reproduction

Comparing Mitosis and Meiosis (page 278)

17. Circle the letter of each sentence that is true about mitosis and meiosis.

   a. Mitosis produces four genetically different haploid cells.

   b. Meiosis produces two genetically identical diploid cells.

   c. Mitosis begins with a diploid cell.

   d. Meiosis begins with a diploid cell.

Reading Skill Practice

You can often increase your understanding of what you've read by making comparisons. A compare-and-contrast table helps you to do this. On a separate sheet of paper, make a table to compare the processes of mitosis and meiosis. For more information about compare-and-contrast tables, see Organizing Information in Appendix A.

Section 11–5 Linkage and Gene Maps
(pages 279–280)

🔑 Key Concept

- What structures actually assort independently?

Gene Linkage (page 279)

1. Is the following sentence true or false? Thomas Hunt Morgan discovered that some genes violated the principle of independent assortment. _____

2. Morgan grouped the *Drosophila* genes that were inherited together into four _____ groups.

3. List the two conclusions that Morgan made about genes and chromosomes.

   a. _____

   _____

   b. _____

   _____

4. Why didn't Mendel observe gene linkage? _____

   _____

   _____

   _____

   _____

Gene Maps (pages 279–280)

5. Explain why two genes found on the same chromosome are not always linked forever.

   _____

   _____

   _____

   _____

6. The new combinations of alleles produced by crossover events help to generate genetic _____.

7. Is the following sentence true or false? Genes that are closer together are more likely to be separated by a crossover event in meiosis. _____

8. What is a gene map? _____

   _____

9. How is a gene map constructed? _____

   _____

   _____

   _____

Vocabulary Review

Labeling Diagrams *Use the words listed below to label the Punnett square. Some words may be used twice.*

heterozygous parent
dominant allele
recessive allele

homozygous offspring
heterozygous offspring

1. _____

6. _____

5. _____

4. _____

	H	h
H	HH	Hh
h	Hh	hh

2. _____

3. _____

Matching *In the space provided, write the letter of the definition that best matches each term.*

_____ 7. phenotype

_____ 8. gamete

_____ 9. genetics

_____ 10. probability

_____ 11. haploid

_____ 12. gene map

_____ 13. gene

_____ 14. multiple alleles

_____ 15. trait

a. likelihood that something will happen
b. shows the relative locations of genes on a chromosome
c. physical characteristics of an organism
d. containing one set of chromosomes
e. sex cell
f. chemical factor that determines traits
g. specific characteristic
h. scientific study of heredity
i. gene with more than two alleles

Completion *Fill in the blanks with terms from Chapter 11.*

16. The process in which two genes segregate independently is called

_____.

17. Plants that, if left to self-pollinate, produce offspring identical to themselves are called

_____.

18. The offspring of crosses between parents with different traits are called

_____.

19. The process during sexual reproduction in which male and female sex cells join is called

_____.

20. The process of reduction division in which the number of chromosomes per cell is cut

in half is called _____.

© Pearson Education, Inc., publishing as Pearson Prentice Hall.

Chapter 12   DNA and RNA

Summary

12–1 DNA

To understand genetics, biologists had to learn the chemical structure of the gene. Frederick Griffith first learned that some factor from dead, disease-causing bacteria turned harmless bacteria into disease-causing ones. Griffith called this process transformation. Griffith thought that the transforming factor might be a gene. Oswald Avery and his research group later found that DNA was the transforming factor. Alfred Hershey and Martha Chase also showed that genes are made of DNA.

Scientists began studying the structure of DNA to learn how it can carry information, determine an organism's traits, and replicate itself. DNA is a long molecule made up of units called nucleotides. Each nucleotide is made up of a 5-carbon sugar, a phosphate group, and a nitrogen-containing base. There are four kinds of bases: adenine, guanine, cytosine, and thymine.

James Watson and Francis Crick discovered that DNA is shaped like a double helix, or a twisted ladder, in which two strands are wound around each other. The two strands are held together by hydrogen bonds between adenine and thymine and between guanine and cytosine. The sugar phosphate backbone makes up the sides of the ladder.

12–2 Chromosomes and DNA Replication

Single-celled organisms without a nucleus have DNA in the cytoplasm. Most have one circular DNA molecule. In organisms with a nucleus, DNA is in the nucleus. The DNA is organized into different numbers of chromosomes, depending on the organism.

DNA molecules are very long. To fit inside cells, they must be tightly folded. The DNA in a chromosome is wound around proteins, called histones. The DNA and histones wind together to form nucleosomes.

Before a cell divides, it copies its DNA in a process called replication. The DNA molecule separates into two strands. Then, two new strands form, following the rules of base pairing. Each strand of the DNA molecule serves as a template, or model, for the new strand.

Many enzymes carry out DNA replication. One enzyme, called DNA polymerase, joins individual nucleotides to produce the DNA molecule. It also checks that the correct nucleotide is added.

12–3 RNA and Protein Synthesis

In order for a gene to work, the genetic instructions in the DNA molecule must be decoded. The first step is to copy the DNA sequence into RNA. RNA makes it possible for a single gene in a DNA molecule to make hundreds of copies.

RNA has a structure like DNA, except for three differences: (1) The sugar in RNA is ribose instead of deoxyribose; (2) RNA is single-stranded; and (3) RNA has uracil in place of thymine.

Three kinds of RNA molecules work together to make proteins. Messenger RNA has the instructions to put together amino acids to make a protein. Proteins are put together on ribosomes. Ribosomes are made up of proteins and ribosomal RNA. Transfer RNA carries each amino acid to the ribosome according to the coded message in messenger RNA.

RNA is copied from DNA in a process called transcription. The enzyme RNA polymerase binds to DNA and separates the two strands. Then, RNA polymerase builds a strand of RNA using one strand of DNA as the template. The sequence of DNA that signals RNA polymerase where to bind and start making RNA is called the promoter.

The instructions for making proteins are found in the order of the four nitrogenous bases. This code is read three letters, or nucleotides, at a time. Each codon, or group of three nucleotides, specifies a certain amino acid that makes up a protein. In the genetic code, some amino acids are specified by more than one codon. One codon is a start signal for translation. Three codons signal the end of translation.

Translation is the process in which the genetic code in RNA is used to make proteins. Translation takes place on ribosomes. Before translation can begin, messenger RNA is transcribed from DNA. Then, the messenger RNA moves into the cytoplasm and attaches to a ribosome. As each codon of the messenger RNA moves through the ribosome, the proper amino acid is brought into the ribosome by transfer RNA. The ribosome joins together each amino acid. In this way, the protein chain grows. When the ribosome reaches a stop codon, it falls away from the protein chain and the messenger RNA molecule. Transcription has ended.

12–4 Mutations

Mutations are changes in the sequence of DNA. Gene mutations are changes in a single gene. Chromosomal mutations cause changes in whole chromosomes. Gene mutations that occur at a single point in the DNA sequence are called point mutations. When a point mutation causes one base to replace another, only one amino acid is affected. If a nucleotide is added or taken away, it causes a frameshift mutation. All the groupings of three nucleotides, or codons, are changed. This can cause the gene to produce a completely different protein.

In a chromosomal mutation, there is a change in the number or the structure of chromosomes. There are four kinds of chromosomal mutations: deletions, duplications, inversions, and translocations.

12–5 Gene Regulation

Genes can be turned on and off when proteins are needed. In prokaryotes, some genes are turned on and off by a section of a chromosome called an operon. An operon is a group of genes that work together. Two sequences of DNA in the operon that control when genes are turned on and off are the operator and the promoter. When the cell needs a certain protein, RNA polymerase attaches to the promoter and produces a messenger RNA that is translated into the needed protein.

When the cell no longer needs the protein, it makes another special protein called the repressor. The repressor attaches to the operator, blocking the promoter so that RNA polymerase cannot attach to it. This turns the genes of the operon off.

In eukaryotes, there are several ways of turning genes on and off. One system uses a protein that binds directly to DNA. This either starts or increases the transcription of certain genes.

Chapter 12   DNA and RNA

Section 12–1 DNA (pages 287–294)

Key Concepts
- What did scientists discover about the relationship between genes and DNA?
- What is the overall structure of the DNA molecule?

Griffith and Transformation (pages 287–289)

1. What did Frederick Griffith want to learn about bacteria? _____
_____
_____

2. The strain of bacteria that caused pneumonia grew into _____ colonies
on culture plates; harmless bacteria produced colonies with _____ edges.

3. Circle the letter of each sentence that is true about Griffith's experiment.

   a. Mice injected with bacteria from smooth colonies died.

   b. Mice injected with bacteria from rough colonies died.

   c. Mice injected with heat-killed bacteria from smooth colonies died.

   d. Mice injected with a mixture of bacteria from heat-killed smooth colonies and live rough colonies died.

4. What result from Griffith's experiment suggested that the cause of pneumonia was not a chemical poison released by the disease-causing bacteria? _____
_____
_____

5. What is transformation? _____
_____

6. What hypothesis did Griffith form from the results of his experiments? _____
_____
_____

Avery and DNA (page 289)

7. Is the following sentence true or false? Avery and his colleagues thought that the molecule required in transformation might also be the molecule of the gene.
_____

8. Briefly describe how Avery and his group determined which molecule was most important for transformation. _____
_____
_____

9. Transformation did not occur when _____ was destroyed.

10. What was the conclusion from Avery's experiments? _____

_____

The Hershey-Chase Experiment (pages 289–290)

11. What is a bacteriophage? _____

_____

12. Circle the letter of each part that makes up a bacteriophage.

   a. lipid coat   c. carbohydrate core

   b. protein coat   d. DNA core

13. What happens when a bacteriophage infects a bacterial cell? _____

_____

_____

14. How would Hershey and Chase learn whether genes were made of protein or DNA?

_____

_____

_____

15. What results did Hershey and Chase observe? _____

_____

_____

16. Hershey and Chase concluded that the genetic material of the bacteriophage was

_____.

The Components and Structure of DNA (pages 291–294)

17. List the three critical things that genes were known to do.

   a. _____

   b. _____

   _____

   c. _____

18. What is the makeup of a nucleotide? _____

_____

19. Adenine, guanine, cytosine, and thymine are four kinds of _____ bases in DNA.

20. Identify the components of a nucleotide in the diagram below. Label the bases as purines or pyrimidines.

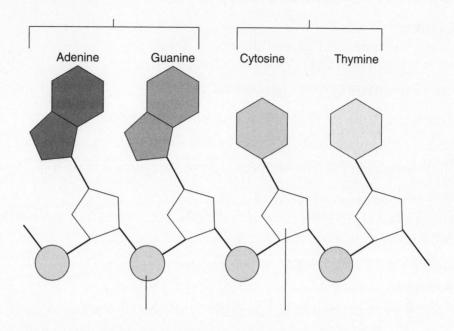

| Adenine | Guanine | Cytosine | Thymine |

21. Is the following sentence true or false? Adenine and guanine are larger molecules than cytosine and thymine because they have two rings in their structure. _____

22. What forms the backbone of a DNA chain? _____

_____

23. Is the following sentence true or false? The nucleotides must be joined together in a specific order. _____

24. According to Chargaff's rules, the percentages of _____ are equal to those of thymine and the percentages of _____ are equal to those of guanine in the DNA molecule.

25. Rosalind Franklin's work with X-ray diffraction showed that the DNA molecule is shaped like a(an) _____ and contains _____ strands.

26. How did Francis Crick and James Watson try to understand the structure of DNA?

_____

_____

27. How did Watson and Crick describe the structure of DNA? _____

_____

_____

28. Is the following sentence true or false? According to the principle of base pairing, hydrogen bonds could form only between adenine and cytosine. _____

Section 12–2 Chromosomes and DNA Replication (pages 295–299)

Key Concept
- What happens during DNA replication?

DNA and Chromosomes (pages 295–297)

1. Circle the letter of the location of DNA in prokaryotic cells.

   a. nucleus   **b.** mitochondria   **c.** cytoplasm   **d.** vacuole

2. Is the following sentence true or false? Most prokaryotes contain a single, circular DNA molecule. _____

3. Eukaryotic DNA is generally located in the cell _____ in the form of a number of chromosomes.

4. Is the following sentence true or false? All organisms have the same number of chromosomes. _____

5. Is the following sentence true or false? The *E. coli* chromosome is longer than the diameter of an individual *E. coli* bacterium. _____

6. Circle the letter of each sentence that is true about chromosome structure.

   a. The DNA in eukaryotic cells is very loosely packed.

   b. Prokaryotic cells contain more DNA than eukaryotic cells.

   c. A human cell contains more than 1 meter of DNA.

   d. The DNA of the smallest human chromosome is nearly 10 times as long as many bacterial chromosomes.

7. Eukaryotic chromosomes contain both DNA and protein, packed together to form

   _____.

8. What are histones? _____

   _____

9. Why are individual chromosomes visible only during mitosis? _____

   _____

   _____

10. Is the following sentence true or false? Changes in chromatin structure and histone-DNA binding are associated with changes in gene activity. _____

11. What do nucleosomes do? _____

   _____

   _____

© Pearson Education, Inc., publishing as Pearson Prentice Hall.

DNA Replication (pages 297–299)

12. What occurs during the process of replication? _____

_____

13. Complete the flowchart to describe the process of DNA replication.

The DNA molecule _____, or unzips, into two strands.

↓

Each strand serves as a(an) _____, or model, to produce the new strands.

↓

Two new _____ strands are produced, following the rules of _____.

14. Is the following sentence true or false? In eukaryotic chromosomes, DNA replication begins at a single point in the chromosome and proceeds in two directions. _____

15. The sites where DNA replication and separation occur are called _____.

16. What occurs when a molecule of DNA is "unzipped"? _____

_____

_____

17. What is the complementary strand of bases for a strand with the bases TACGTT?

_____

18. Is the following sentence true or false? Each DNA molecule resulting from replication has one original strand and one new strand. _____

19. List two major roles of DNA polymerase in the process of DNA replication.

a. _____

b. _____

Reading Skill Practice

The illustrations in textbooks can help you better understand a difficult concept. Look at Figure 12–10 on page 297. List in order, beginning with DNA, the levels of organization of eukaryotic DNA to form chromosomes. Do your work on a separate sheet of paper.

Section 12–3 RNA and Protein Synthesis
(pages 300–306)

Key Concepts
- What are the three main types of RNA?
- What is transcription?
- What is translation?

The Structure of RNA (page 300)

1. List the three main differences between RNA and DNA.

   a. _____

   b. _____

   c. _____

2. What is the importance of the cell's ability to copy a single DNA sequence into RNA?

   _____

   _____

Types of RNA (pages 300–301)

3. What is the one job in which most RNA molecules are involved? _____

   _____

4. Complete the table about the types of RNA.

TYPES OF RNA

Type	Function
	Carries copies of the instructions for assembling amino acids from DNA to the rest of the cell
Ribosomal RNA	
	Transfers each amino acid to the ribosome to help assemble proteins

Transcription (page 301)

5. Circle the letter of each sentence that is true about transcription.

   a. During transcription, DNA polymerase binds to RNA and separates the DNA strands.

   b. RNA polymerase uses one strand of DNA as a template to assemble nucleotides into a strand of RNA.

   c. RNA polymerase binds only to DNA promoters, which have specific base sequences.

   d. Promoters are signals in RNA that indicate to RNA polymerase when to begin transcription.

© Pearson Education, Inc., publishing as Pearson Prentice Hall.

RNA Editing (page 302)

6. Many RNA molecules from eukaryotic genes have sections, called _____, edited out of them before they become functional. The remaining pieces, called _____, are spliced together.

7. Is the following sentence true or false? RNA editing occurs in the cytoplasm of the cell. _____

8. What are two explanations for why some RNA molecules are cut and spliced?

   a. _____

   _____

   _____

   b. _____

   _____

   _____

The Genetic Code (pages 302–303)

9. Proteins are made by joining _____ into long chains called polypeptides.

10. How can only four bases in RNA carry instructions for 20 different amino acids?

    _____

    _____

    _____

11. What is a codon? _____

    _____

    _____

12. Circle the letter of the number of possible three-base codons.

    a. 4   b. 12   c. 64   d. 128

13. Is the following sentence true or false? All amino acids are specified by only one codon. _____

14. Circle the letter of the codon that serves as the "start" codon for protein synthesis.

    a. UGA   b. UAA   c. UAG   d. AUG

Translation (pages 303–305)

15. What occurs during the process of translation? _____

    _____

16. Where does translation take place? _____

    _____

17. Circle the letter of each sentence that is true about translation.

a. Before translation occurs, messenger RNA is transcribed from DNA in the nucleus.

b. Translation occurs in the nucleus.

c. It is the job of transfer RNA to bring the proper amino acid into the ribosome to be attached to the growing peptide chain.

d. When the ribosome reaches a stop codon, it releases the newly formed polypeptide and the mRNA molecule.

18. What is an anticodon? _____

_____

_____

The Roles of RNA and DNA (page 306)

Match the roles with the molecules. Molecules may be used more than once.

Roles	Molecules
_____ 19. Master plan	a. DNA
_____ 20. Goes to the ribosomes in the cytoplasm	b. RNA
_____ 21. Blueprint	
_____ 22. Remains in the nucleus	

Genes and Proteins (page 306)

23. Many proteins are _____, which catalyze and regulate chemical reactions.

24. Is the following sentence true or false? Genes are the keys to almost everything that living cells do. _____

Reading Skill Practice

A flowchart is useful for organizing the steps in a process. Make a flowchart that shows the steps in the process of translation. Look at Figure 12–18 on pages 304–305 for help. For more information about flowcharts, see Appendix A. Do your work on a separate sheet of paper.

Section 12–4 Mutations (pages 307–308)

⬭ **Key Concept**
- What are mutations?

Introduction (page 307)

1. What are mutations? _____

_____

_____

2. Is the following sentence true or false? Chromosomal mutations result from changes in a single gene. _____

Kinds of Mutations (pages 307–308)

3. Mutations that occur at a single point in the DNA sequence are _____ mutations.

4. A mutation involving the insertion or deletion of a nucleotide is a(an)

_____ mutation.

5. Complete the table of types of chromosomal mutations.

CHROMOSOMAL MUTATIONS

Type	Description	Examples
		ABC•DEF → AC•DEF
Duplication		
	Part of a chromosome becomes oriented in the reverse of its usual direction	
Translocation		

6. Circle the letter of each sentence that is true about gene mutations.

a. Point mutations affect just one nucleotide.

b. The substitution of one nucleotide for another in the gene never affects the function of the protein.

c. Point mutations that involve the insertion or deletion of a nucleotide change the reading frame of the genetic message.

d. Frameshift mutations affect every amino acid that follows the point of the mutation.

Significance of Mutations (page 308)

7. Mutations that cause dramatic changes in protein structure are often _____.

8. Mutations are a source of _____ in a species.

9. What is polyploidy? _____

_____

_____

Section 12–5 Gene Regulation (pages 309–312)

⚷ Key Concepts
- How are *lac* genes turned off and on?
- How are most eukaryotic genes controlled?

Introduction (page 309)

1. Label the parts of a typical gene in the diagram below.

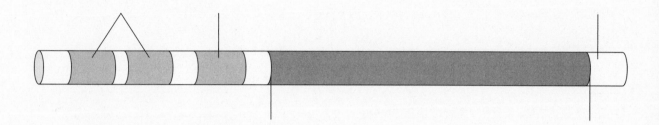

2. Where does RNA polymerase bind? _____
_____

3. Is the following sentence true or false? The actions of DNA-binding proteins help to determine whether a gene is turned on or turned off. _____

Gene Regulation: An Example (pages 309–310)

4. What is an operon? _____
_____
_____

5. What is the function of the genes in the *lac* operon? _____
_____
_____

6. Circle the letter of each sentence that is true about lactose.

   a. Lactose is a simple sugar.

   b. To use lactose for food, *E. coli* must take lactose across its cell membrane.

   c. The bond between glucose and galactose must be broken in order for *E. coli* to use lactose for food.

   d. Proteins encoded by the genes of the *lac* operon are needed only when *E. coli* is grown on a medium containing glucose.

7. What turns the *lac* operon off and on? _____
_____
_____

8. Complete the concept map to show how the *lac* operon is regulated.

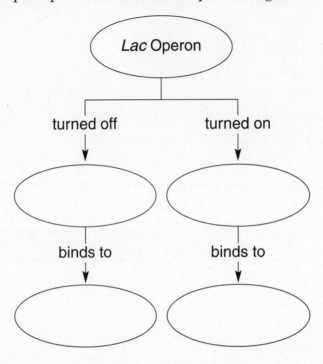

9. How does the repressor protein prevent transcription? _____

_____

_____

10. How does lactose cause the *lac* operon to turn on? _____

_____

_____

_____

11. Circle the letter of each sentence that is true about gene regulation in prokaryotic genes.

   a. The *lac* operon is the only example of genes regulated by repressor proteins.

   b. Many other genes are regulated by repressor proteins.

   c. Some genes are regulated by proteins that enhance the rate of transcription.

   d. Cells cannot turn their genes on and off as needed.

Eukaryotic Gene Regulation (page 311)

12. Is the following sentence true or false? Operons are frequently found in eukaryotes.

_____

13. How are eukaryotic genes usually controlled? _____

_____

_____

© Pearson Education, Inc., publishing as Pearson Prentice Hall.

14. What is the function of the TATA box? _____

_____

15. Eukaryotic promoters are usually found just _____ the TATA box, and they consist of a series of short _____ sequences.

16. List three ways in which proteins that bind to enhancer sequences of a gene can work to regulate gene expression.

a. _____

b. _____

c. _____

17. Why is gene regulation in eukaryotes more complex than in prokaryotes? _____

_____

_____

_____

_____

Development and Differentiation (page 312)

18. What role do the hox genes play in the development of an organism? _____

_____

_____

_____

19. Circle the letter of each sentence that is true about hox genes.

a. A mutation in a hox gene has no effect on the organs that develop in specific parts of the body.

b. In fruit flies, a mutation affecting the hox genes can replace a fly's antennae with a pair of legs.

c. The function of the hox genes in humans seems to be almost the same as it is in fruit flies.

d. A copy of the gene that controls eye growth in mice does not function in fruit flies.

20. Why do common patterns of genetic control for development exist among animals?

_____

_____

_____

Vocabulary Review

Matching   *In the space provided, write the letter of the definition that best matches each term.*

_____ **1.** base pairing

_____ **2.** nucleotide

_____ **3.** histone

_____ **4.** transcription

_____ **5.** intron

_____ **6.** translation

_____ **7.** transfer RNA

_____ **8.** promoter

_____ **9.** mutation

_____ **10.** polyploidy

_____ **11.** operon

_____ **12.** differentiation

a. making a protein using messenger RNA

b. having extra sets of chromosomes

c. hydrogen bonding between adenine and thymine

d. sequence in messenger RNA that is cut out

e. cells specializing in structure and function

f. carries amino acids to the ribosome during protein synthesis

g. unit of DNA

h. copying part of DNA into RNA

i. change in the genetic material

j. group of genes that work together

k. DNA sequence that binds RNA polymerase

l. protein that binds DNA into tight coils

Completion   *Fill in the blanks with terms from Chapter 12.*

13. A _____ is a type of virus that infects bacteria.

14. Eukaryotic chromosomes contain both DNA and protein, tightly packed together to form a substance called _____.

15. The duplication of DNA is called _____.

16. The principal enzyme involved in DNA replication is _____ because it joins individual nucleotides to produce a DNA molecule.

17. DNA sequences that code for proteins are called _____.

18. A _____ consists of three consecutive nucleotides that specify a single amino acid.

19. Gene mutations, known as _____, occur at a single point in the DNA sequence.

20. Differentiation of cells and tissues in the embryo is controlled by _____.

© Pearson Education, Inc., publishing as Pearson Prentice Hall.

Summary

13–1 Changing the Living World

For thousands of years, people have chosen to breed only the animals and plants with the desired traits. This technique is called selective breeding. Selective breeding takes advantage of naturally occurring genetic variation in a group of living things.

One tool used by selective breeders is hybridization. In hybridization, individuals with different traits are crossed. Hopefully, the offspring will have the best traits of both parents. The offspring of these crosses, called hybrids, are often hardier than the parents.

Once breeders have a group of plants or animals with the desired traits, they want to keep the traits. To do so, breeders use another tool called inbreeding. In inbreeding, individuals with similar characteristics are crossed. Inbreeding helps to ensure that the characteristics that make each breed unique will be preserved. Inbreeding does have the risk of bringing together two recessive alleles for a genetic defect.

Selective breeding would be nearly impossible without large amounts of variation in traits. Breeders can increase the variation in a group of organisms by causing mutations. Mutations are inheritable changes in DNA. Mutations do occur naturally. However, breeders can increase the rate of mutation by using radiation and chemicals. Many mutations are harmful. However with luck, breeders can produce useful mutations.

The use of mutations is particularly helpful with bacteria. Their small size enables millions of organisms to be treated with radiation or chemicals at the same time. Using this technique, scientists have been able to develop hundreds of beneficial bacteria strains, including bacteria that can digest the oil from oil spills.

New varieties of plants have also been developed using mutants. If chromosomes fail to separate, extra sets of chromosomes result. This is called polyploidy. In animals, polyploidy is usually fatal. In plants, however, the new species that result are larger and stronger than their diploid relatives.

13–2 Manipulating DNA

To increase variation, scientists can also make changes directly to the DNA molecule. In this group of techniques, called genetic engineering, scientists can change an organism's DNA.

Scientists can easily remove DNA from a cell and separate it from the other cell parts. Scientists can also cut DNA into smaller pieces using enzymes called restriction enzymes. Each restriction enzyme cuts DNA at a specific sequence of nucleotides. These DNA fragments can be separated and analyzed in a process called gel electrophoresis.

Scientists can also read the order of nucleotide bases in a DNA fragment. They use a technique in which a single strand of DNA is copied. However, the copy is made with colored nucleotides inserted at random places. Reading the order of colored bands in a gel gives the nucleotide sequence of the DNA fragment.

Scientists can change DNA sequences in many different ways. Short sequences of DNA made in the laboratory can be joined to the DNA molecule of an organism. DNA from one organism can be attached to the DNA of another organism. These DNA molecules are called recombinant DNA because they are made by combining DNA from different sources.

Scientists often need many copies of a certain gene to study it. A technique called polymerase chain reaction (PCR) allows scientists to do that. PCR is a chain reaction in which DNA copies become templates to make more DNA copies.

13–3 Cell Transformation

DNA fragments cannot work by themselves. They must be part of the DNA molecule in an organism. DNA fragments become part of a cell's DNA during the process of transformation. This is the same process that Griffith observed in his experiments.

To add DNA fragments to bacteria, a fragment is joined to a small, circular piece of DNA called a plasmid. Plasmids are found naturally in some bacteria. Scientists join the fragment to the plasmid by cutting both with the same restriction enzymes. The cut pieces join together because their ends match up.

When scientists transform bacteria, not all bacteria take in the plasmid. Scientists can identify those bacteria that carry the plasmid because the plasmid also carries a genetic marker. Usually, the genetic marker is a gene that gives the bacteria resistance to a certain antibiotic.

Plant cells can also be transformed. Scientists insert the DNA fragment into a plasmid. This plasmid is transformed into a bacterium that naturally infects plants. Plant cells in a culture that have had their cell walls removed will also take up DNA on their own. Scientists can also inject DNA directly into some plant cells.

Animal cells can be transformed in ways similar to those used for plant cells. Many egg cells are large enough that DNA can be directly injected into the nucleus. Once inside, the repair enzymes may help insert the DNA fragment into the chromosomes of the injected cell.

13–4 Applications of Genetic Engineering

Scientists wondered whether genes from one organism would work in a different organism. Some scientists isolated the gene from fireflies that allows them to glow. Then, they inserted this gene into the DNA of a plant. These plants glowed in the dark. This showed that plants and animals use the same process to translate DNA into proteins. The glowing plant is transgenic because it has a gene from another species.

Human genes have been added to bacteria. These transgenic bacteria are used to produce human proteins such as insulin, human growth hormone, and clotting factor.

Scientists have produced transgenic animals to study the function of genes and to improve the food supply. Transgenic animals might also be used to supply us with human proteins that can be collected in the animal's milk.

Transgenic plants have been produced that can make their own insecticide. Others are resistant to weed killers. Some have even been engineered to contain vitamins needed for human health.

A clone is a member of a population of genetically identical cells that were produced from a single cell. Clones are useful because it is one way to make copies of transgenic organisms. It is easy to produce cloned bacteria and plants.

Animals are very difficult to clone. However, scientists in Scotland successfully cloned a sheep, named Dolly. Animal cloning has risks. Studies suggest that cloned animals may have genetic defects and other health problems.

Name_____ Class_____ Date_____

Section 13–1 Changing the Living World
(pages 319–321)

🔑 **Key Concepts**
- What is the purpose of selective breeding?
- Why might breeders try to induce mutations?

Selective Breeding (pages 319–320)

1. What is meant by selective breeding? _____
_____
_____

2. Circle the letter of each organism that has been produced by selective breeding.

   a. horses   b. dogs   c. cats   d. potatoes

3. Who was Luther Burbank? _____
_____

4. Complete the table describing the types of selective breeding.

SELECTIVE BREEDING

Type	Description	Examples
	Crossing dissimilar individuals to bring together the best of both organisms	
	The continued breeding of individuals with similar characteristics	

5. Is the following sentence true or false? Hybrids are often hardier than either of the parents. _____.

6. What two plant traits did Luther Burbank try to combine in his crosses?

   a. _____
   b. _____

7. Is the following sentence true or false? To maintain the desired characteristics of a line of organisms, breeders often use hybridization. _____

8. Most members of a breed are genetically _____.

9. What are the risks of inbreeding? _____
_____
_____

Increasing Variation (pages 320–321)

10. Why are biologists interested in preserving the diversity of plants and animals in the wild? _____

_____

_____

11. Is the following sentence true or false? The genetic variation that exists in nature is enough to satisfy the needs of breeders. _____

12. Breeders can increase the genetic variation by inducing _____, which are the ultimate source of genetic variability.

13. Circle the letter of an inheritable change in DNA.

    a. variation   **b.** trait   **c.** mutation   **d.** genotype

14. Is the following sentence true or false? Mutations cannot occur spontaneously.

    _____

15. Name two methods used by breeders to increase the rate of mutation.

    a. _____   **b.** _____

16. Is it easy for breeders to produce mutants with desirable mutations? Explain.

    _____

    _____

    _____

17. Why are radiation and chemicals useful techniques for producing mutant bacteria?

    _____

    _____

    _____

18. Is the following sentence true or false? Scientists have produced bacteria that can digest oil. _____

19. What technique do scientists use to produce mutant plants? _____

    _____

    _____

20. Circle the letter of each sentence that is true about polyploidy.

    a. Polyploid plants have many sets of chromosomes.

    b. Polyploidy is usually fatal in animals.

    c. Polyploidy produces new species of plants that are weaker and smaller than their diploid relatives.

    d. Bananas and some citrus fruits are polyploid.

Section 13–2 Manipulating DNA (pages 322–326)

Key Concept
- How do scientists make changes to DNA?

The Tools of Molecular Biology (pages 322–323)

1. What is genetic engineering? _____

_____

2. Is the following sentence true or false? Making changes to the DNA code is similar to changing the code of a computer program. _____

3. Scientists use their knowledge of the _____ of DNA and its

_____ properties to study and change DNA molecules.

4. List four steps that molecular biologists use to study and change DNA molecules.

    a. _____

    b. _____

    c. _____

    d. _____

5. Explain how biologists get DNA out of a cell. _____

_____

_____

6. Biologists use _____ to cut DNA molecules at a specific sequence of nucleotides to make smaller fragments.

7. Circle the letter of the process by which DNA fragments are separated and analyzed.

    a. gel electrophoresis   c. transformation

    b. extraction   d. restriction

8. In the diagram below, label the positive and negative ends of the gel and identify the location of longer and shorter fragments.

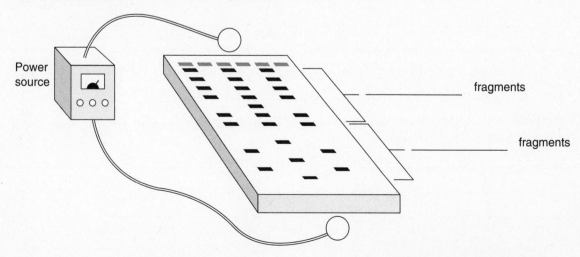

Power source

fragments

fragments

9. Circle the letter of each sentence that is true about gel electrophoresis.

   a. An electric voltage applied to the gel separates the DNA fragments.

   b. DNA molecules are positively charged.

   c. Gel electrophoresis is used to compare the genomes of different organisms.

   d. Gel electrophoresis can be used to locate and identify one particular gene in an individual's genome.

Using the DNA Sequence (pages 323–326)

10. Complete the concept map to show how researchers use the DNA sequence of an organism.

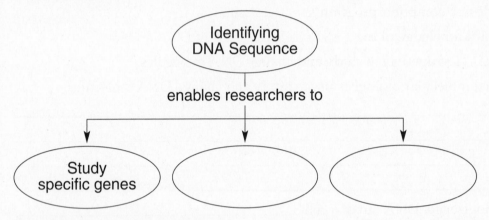

11. List four "ingredients" added to a test tube to produce tagged DNA fragments that can be used to read a sequence of DNA.

   a. _____

   b. _____

   c. _____

   d. _____

12. What does the reaction in the test tube generate when complementary DNA is made for

   reading DNA? _____

   _____

   _____

13. Is the following sentence true or false? The pattern of colored bands on a gel tells the

   exact sequence of bases in DNA. _____

14. Enzymes that splice DNA together can also be used to join _____ DNA sequences to natural DNA sequences.

15. How is recombinant DNA produced? _____

   _____

   _____

16. What is polymerase chain reaction (PCR)? _____

_____

_____

17. What is the role of the primers in PCR? _____

_____

_____

_____

18. Circle the letter of the first step in the polymerase chain reaction.

　　a. The copies become templates to make more copies.

　　b. The DNA is cooled to allow the primers to bind to the single-stranded DNA.

　　c. The DNA is heated to separate its two strands.

　　d. DNA polymerase makes copies of the region between the primers.

Reading Skill Practice

A flowchart is useful for organizing the steps in a process. Make a flowchart that shows the steps molecular biologists use to determine the order of bases in a segment of a DNA molecule.

Section 13–3 Cell Transformation (pages 327–329)

🔑 Key Concepts
- What happens during cell transformation?
- How can you tell if a transformation experiment has been successful?

Introduction (page 327)

1. What occurs during transformation? _____

_____

2. Is the following sentence true or false? Griffith's extract of heat-killed bacteria contained

DNA fragments. _____

Transforming Bacteria (pages 327–328)

3. Complete the flowchart to show the steps in transforming bacteria.

Foreign DNA is joined to a(an) _____, which is a small, circular DNA molecule found naturally in some bacteria.

↓

Recombinant plasmids are mixed with bacterial cells. Some bacterial cells take

in the recombinant DNA by the process of _____.

↓

The culture is treated with a(an) _____, a compound that kills bacteria.

↓

Only cells that have been transformed survive, because only they carry a(an) _____ for antibiotic resistance.

4. Give two reasons why a plasmid is useful for DNA transfer.

a. _____

_____

b. _____

_____

Transforming Plant Cells (pages 328–329)

5. When researchers transform plant cells using a bacterium that causes plant tumors, how do researchers prevent plant tumors from forming in the transformed cells?

_____

_____

6. Circle the letter of each sentence that is true about transforming plant cells.

   a. Many plant cells can be transformed by using a bacterium that will, in nature, insert a tumor-producing plasmid into plant cells.

   b. Sometimes plant cells in culture will take up DNA on their own when their cell walls are removed.

   c. It is impossible to inject DNA directly into plant cells.

   d. Plant cells that are transformed cannot develop into adult plants.

7. Describe what occurs in a successful transformation of cells. _____

   _____

   _____

   _____

Transforming Animal Cells (page 329)

8. Describe how animal cells can be transformed by directly injecting DNA.

   _____

   _____

   _____

   _____

9. Is the following sentence true or false? The DNA molecules used for transformation of animal cells do not require marker genes. _____

10. How is a DNA molecule constructed so that it will eliminate a particular gene?

   _____

   _____

   _____

   _____

11. Is the following sentence true or false? Gene replacement has made it possible to identify the specific functions of genes in many organisms. _____

Reading Skill Practice

When you read about related concepts, a compare-and-contrast table can help you focus on their similarities and differences. Construct a table to compare and contrast transformation in bacteria, plants, and animals. Look in Appendix A for more information about compare-and-contrast tables. Do your work on a separate sheet of paper.

Section 13–4 Applications of Genetic Engineering (pages 331–333)

💬 **Key Concept**
- How are transgenic organisms useful to human beings?

Introduction (page 331)

1. How do scientists know that plants and animals share the same basic mechanisms of

   gene expression? _____

   _____

Transgenic Organisms (pages 331–333)

2. What is a transgenic organism? _____

   _____

   _____

3. Describe how to make a transgenic organism. _____

   _____

   _____

   _____

   _____

4. Genetic engineering has spurred the growth of _____, a new
   industry that is changing the way we interact with the living world.

5. Circle the letter of each sentence that is true about transgenic microorganisms.

   a. Transgenic bacteria will never produce useful substances for health and industry.

   b. Transgenic bacteria produce human proteins cheaply and in great abundance.

   c. People with insulin-dependent diabetes are now treated with pure human insulin.

   d. In the future, transgenic organisms may produce the raw materials for plastics.

6. List four ways in which transgenic animals have been used.

   a. _____

   b. _____

   c. _____

   d. _____

7. Many transgenic plants contain genes that produce a natural _____, so
   the crops do not have to be sprayed with pesticides.

8. Circle the letter of each item that might soon be produced by transgenic plants.

    a. human antibodies   **c.** rot-resistant foods

    b. plastics   **d.** vitamin A-enriched rice

Cloning (page 333)

9. What is a clone? _____

_____

10. Is the following sentence true or false? For years, many scientists thought that it was

impossible to clone bacteria. _____

11. Complete the sentences in the diagram below to show the steps in cloning a sheep.

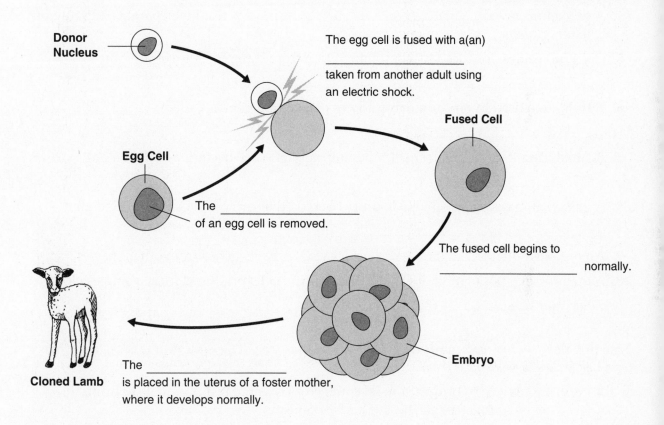

Donor Nucleus

The egg cell is fused with a(an) _____ taken from another adult using an electric shock.

Egg Cell

Fused Cell

The _____ of an egg cell is removed.

The fused cell begins to _____ normally.

Embryo

Cloned Lamb

The _____ is placed in the uterus of a foster mother, where it develops normally.

12. Is the following sentence true or false? All cloned animals are also transgenic.

_____

13. What kinds of mammals have been cloned in recent years? _____

_____

_____

Vocabulary Review

Completion   *Fill in the blanks with terms from Chapter 13.*

1. In the process of _____, only those animals with desired characteristics are allowed to produce the next generation.

2. The continued breeding of individuals with similar characteristics is

   _____.

3. Through the use of techniques in _____, which is the process of making changes in the DNA code of a living organism, scientists have produced bacteria that can make human proteins.

4. A procedure called _____ is used to separate a mixture of DNA fragments.

5. DNA molecules produced by combining DNA from different sources are called

   _____.

6. A technique used to produce many copies of a certain gene is called

   _____.

7. A small, circular DNA molecule found naturally in some bacteria is called a(an)

   _____.

8. A gene that makes it possible to identify bacteria that carry a plasmid is called a(an)

   _____.

9. An organism that is _____ contains genes from other species.

10. A member of a population of genetically identical cells produced from a single cell is

    called a(an) _____.

True or False   *In the space, write* true *if the statement is true. If the statement is false, write the term that makes the statement true.*

_____ 11. In <u>hybridization</u>, breeders cross dissimilar individuals to bring together the best of both organisms.

_____ 12. Breeders use <u>hybridization</u> to maintain a dog breed.

_____ 13. Scientists use <u>gel electrophoresis</u> to cut DNA at a specific nucleotide sequence.

_____ 14. A plant that glows in the dark is an example of a <u>transgenic</u> organism.

_____ 15. Dolly the sheep is an example of a <u>plasmid</u>.

© Pearson Education, Inc., publishing as Pearson Prentice Hall.

Chapter 14   The Human Genome

Summary

14–1 Human Heredity

Biologists can analyze human chromosomes by looking at a karyotype. A karyotype is a picture of the chromosomes from a cell arranged in homologous pairs.

Humans have 46 chromosomes. Two of these chromosomes, X and Y, are the sex chromosomes. Females have two X chromosomes (XX). Males have one X and one Y chromosome (XY). The other 44 chromosomes are called autosomes.

Human genes are inherited according to the same principles of genetics described by Mendel. To study the inheritance of human traits, biologists use a pedigree chart. A pedigree shows the relationships within a family. The inheritance of a certain trait in a family can be traced using a pedigree. From this, biologists can infer the genotypes of family members.

It is difficult to associate an observed human trait with a specific gene. Many human traits are polygenic, meaning that they are controlled by many genes. The environment also influences many traits.

Some of the first human genes to be identified were those that control blood type. Red blood cells can carry two different antigens, called A and B. Antigens are molecules that can be recognized by the immune system. The presence or absence of the A and B antigens produces four possible blood types: A, B, AB, and O. The ABO blood types are determined by a single gene with three alleles.

In addition to the ABO antigens, there is another antigen on red blood cells called the Rh antigen. People who have the Rh antigen are Rh positive. People without it are Rh negative. A single gene with two alleles determines the Rh blood group.

There are several human genetic disorders, including phenylketonuria (PKU), Huntington's disease, and sickle cell disease. PKU is caused by a recessive allele. It is expressed only in individuals who have inherited a recessive allele from each parent. Huntington's disease is caused by a dominant allele. It is expressed in any person who has that allele. Sickle cell disease is caused by a codominant allele.

Scientists are beginning to understand which changes in the DNA sequence cause certain genetic disorders. Cystic fibrosis is caused by the deletion of three bases in the middle of the sequence for a protein. This deletion inactivates the protein, which causes the symptoms of this disorder. Only one DNA base is changed in the allele that causes sickle cell disease. This base change produces a blood protein that is less soluble than normal.

14–2 Human Chromosomes

The two smallest human chromosomes, chromosomes 21 and 22, were the first chromosomes to have their DNA sequences identified. Both have many genes important for health. Both have regions of DNA that do not code for proteins.

Genes located on the X and Y chromosomes, the sex chromosomes, are said to be sex-linked. They are inherited in a different pattern than genes located on autosomes. For example, all alleles linked to the X chromosome, including those responsible for colorblindness, hemophilia, and Duchenne muscular dystrophy, are expressed in males even if they are recessive alleles. However, in order for these recessive alleles to be expressed in females, there must be two copies of them.

Females have two X chromosomes. Males have only one. To account for this difference, one X chromosome in females is randomly turned off. The turned-off chromosome forms a dense region in the nucleus known as a Barr body. Barr bodies are not found in males because their single X chromosome must be active.

The most common error during meiosis is nondisjunction. Nondisjunction is the failure of chromosomes to separate properly during meiosis. It causes abnormal numbers of chromosomes to find their way into gametes. This may result in a disorder of chromosome number. An example of autosomal nondisjunction is Down syndrome, in which there is an extra copy of chromosome 21. Nondisjunction can also occur in sex chromosomes. In Turner's syndrome, a female has only one X chromosome. In Klinefelter's syndrome, there are extra X chromosomes.

14–3 Human Molecular Genetics

Biologists can use techniques in molecular biology to read, analyze, and even change the DNA code of human genes. Genetic tests are available to test parents for the presence of recessive alleles for genetic disorders.

In a process called DNA fingerprinting, individuals can be identified by analyzing sections of DNA that have little or no known function. These sections of DNA vary widely from one person to the next.

In 1990, scientists around the world began the Human Genome Project. The goal was to identify the DNA sequence for the entire DNA in a human cell. In 2000, the human genome was sequenced. Now the project goal is to analyze these sequences. One way scientists are analyzing the DNA is by looking for genes. To do this, they look for promoter sequences. These are sequences that bind RNA polymerase.

Information about the human genome can be used to cure genetic disorders by gene therapy. In one method of gene therapy, a virus is used to deliver the normal gene into cells to correct the genetic defects. The virus is changed so that it cannot cause disease. The normal gene is attached to the DNA of the virus. The inserted gene can make proteins that correct the genetic defect.

There are risks and problems with gene therapy. Having the power to manipulate human DNA doesn't necessarily make it right. People in a society are responsible for making sure that the tools made available by science are used wisely.

Chapter 14   The Human Genome

Section 14–1 Human Heredity (pages 341–348)

⚷ Key Concepts
- How is sex determined?
- How do small changes in DNA cause genetic disorders?

Human Chromosomes (pages 341–342)

1. How do biologists make a karyotype? _____
_____
_____

2. Circle the letter of each sentence that is true about human chromosomes.

    a. The X and Y chromosomes are known as sex chromosomes because they determine an individual's sex.

    b. Males have two X chromosomes.

    c. All the chromosomes except the sex chromosomes are autosomes.

    d. Biologists would write 46,XY to indicate a human female.

3. Complete the Punnett square below to show how the sex chromosomes segregate during meiosis.

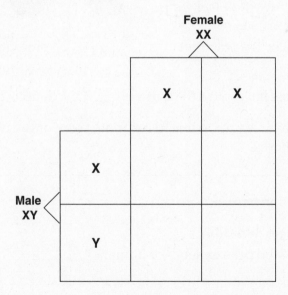

4. Why is there the chance that half of the zygotes will be female and half will be male?
_____
_____
_____

Human Traits (pages 342–343)

5. What does a pedigree chart show? _____

Match the labels to the parts of the pedigree chart shown below. Some of the parts of the pedigree chart may be used more than once.

Pedigree Chart

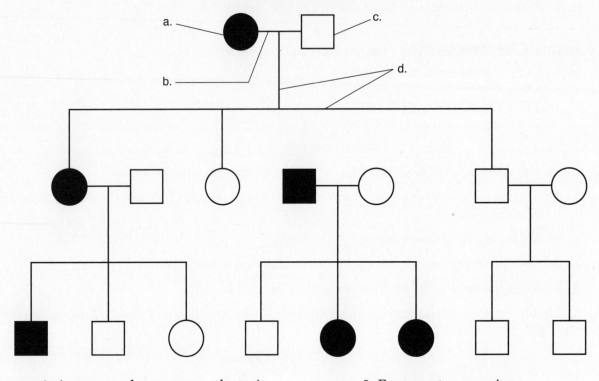

_____ **6.** A person who expresses the trait

_____ **7.** A male

_____ **8.** A person who does not express the trait

_____ **9.** Represents a marriage

_____ **10.** A female

_____ **11.** Connects parents to their children

12. Give two reasons why it is impossible to associate some of the most obvious human traits with single genes.

   a. _____

   b. _____

Human Genes (pages 344–346)

13. Why is it difficult to study the genetics of humans? _____

_____

14. Circle the letter of each sentence that is true about human blood group genes.

   a. The Rh blood group is determined by a single gene.

   b. The negative allele (Rh⁻) is the dominant allele.

   c. All of the alleles for the ABO blood group gene are codominant.

   d. Individuals with type O blood are homozygous for the *i* allele (*ii*) and produce no antigen on the surface of red blood cells.

15. Is the following sentence true or false? Many human genes have become known through the study of genetic disorders. _____

Match the genetic disorder with its description.

Genetic Disorder	Description
_____ **16.** Phenylketonuria (PKU)	**a.** Nervous system breakdown caused by an autosomal recessive allele
_____ **17.** Tay-Sachs disease	**b.** A form of dwarfism caused by an autosomal dominant allele
_____ **18.** Achondroplasia	**c.** A buildup of phenylalanine caused by an autosomal recessive allele
_____ **19.** Huntington's disease	**d.** A progressive loss of muscle control and mental function caused by an autosomal dominant allele

From Gene to Molecule (pages 346–348)

20. What is the normal function of the protein that is affected in cystic fibrosis?

_____

_____

21. A change in just one DNA base for the gene that codes for the protein _____ causes sickle-shaped red blood cells.

22. What is the advantage of being heterozygous for the sickle cell allele?

_____

_____

23. What makes an allele dominant, recessive, or codominant? _____

_____

_____

Section 14–2 **Human Chromosomes** (pages 349–353)

⬭ Key Concepts
- Why are sex-linked disorders more common in males than in females?
- What is nondisjunction, and what problems does it cause?

Human Genes and Chromosomes (page 349)

1. Circle the letter of each sentence that is true about human genes and chromosomes.

   a. Chromosomes 21 and 22 are the largest human chromosomes.

   b. Chromosome 22 contains long stretches of repetitive DNA that do not code for proteins.

   c. Biologists know everything about how the arrangements of genes on chromosomes affect gene expression.

   d. Human genes located close together on the same chromosome tend to be inherited together.

Sex-Linked Genes (pages 350–351)

2. What are sex-linked genes? _____

_____

3. Is the following sentence true or false? The Y chromosome does not contain any genes at all. _____

4. Complete the table describing sex-linked disorders.

SEX-LINKED DISORDERS IN HUMANS

Disorder	Description	Cause
Colorblindness		
		A recessive allele in either of two genes resulting in a missing protein required for normal blood clotting
		A defective version of the gene that codes for a muscle protein

5. Is the following sentence true or false? All X-linked alleles are expressed in males, even if they are recessive. _____

6. Complete the Punnett square to show how colorblindness is inherited.

$$X^cY$$

	X^c	Y
X^c		
X^c		

X^cX^c

X-Chromosome Inactivation (page 352)

7. How does the cell "adjust" to the extra X chromosome in female cells? _____

_____

_____

8. What is a Barr body? _____

_____

_____

9. Is the following sentence true or false? Barr bodies are found only in males.

_____

10. If you see a white cat with orange and black spots, is it most likely a male or a female? Explain. _____

_____

_____

_____

Chromosomal Disorders (pages 352–353)

11. What occurs during nondisjunction? _____

_____

_____

12. Is the following sentence true or false? If nondisjunction occurs, gametes may have abnormal numbers of chromosomes. _____

13. The condition in which an individual has three copies of a chromosome is known as _____, which means "three bodies."

14. Is the following sentence true or false? Down syndrome occurs when an individual has two copies of chromosome 21. _____

15. Circle the letter of the characteristic of Down syndrome.

    a. dwarfism

    c. colorblindness

    b. mental retardation

    d. muscle loss

16. Why does an extra copy of one chromosome cause so much trouble? _____

_____

_____

17. Circle the letter of each sentence that is true about sex chromosome disorders.

    a. A female with the karyotype 45,X has inherited only one X chromosome and is sterile.

    b. Females with the karyotype 47,XXY have Klinefelter's syndrome.

    c. Babies have been born without an X chromosome.

    d. The Y chromosome contains a sex-determining region that is necessary for male sexual development.

Reading Skill Practice

Writing an outline is a useful way to organize the important facts in a section. Write an outline of Section 14–2. Use the section headings as the headings in your outline. Include only the important facts and main ideas in your outline. Be sure to include the vocabulary terms. Do your work on a separate sheet of paper.

Section 14–3 Human Molecular Genetics
(pages 355–360)

⚬ **Key Concepts**
- What is the goal of the Human Genome Project?
- What is gene therapy?

Human DNA Analysis (pages 355–357)

1. Biologists search the volumes of the human genome using _____.

2. Why might prospective parents decide to have genetic testing? _____
_____
_____

3. Circle the letter of each sentence that is true about genetic testing.

    a. It is impossible to test parents to find out if they are carriers for cystic fibrosis or Tay-Sachs disease.

    b. Labeled DNA probes can be used to detect specific sequences found in disease-causing alleles.

    c. Some genetic tests use changes in restriction enzyme cutting sites to identify disease-causing alleles.

    d. DNA testing makes it possible to develop more effective therapy and treatment for individuals affected by genetic disease.

4. What is DNA fingerprinting? _____
_____
_____

5. Complete the flowchart to show the steps in DNA fingerprinting.

```
┌─────────────────────────────────────────────────────────────┐
│ Small sample of DNA is cut with a(an) _____ enzyme.│
└─────────────────────────────────────────────────────────────┘
                             │
                             ▼
┌─────────────────────────────────────────────────────────────┐
│ The fragments are separated by size using _____ .  │
└─────────────────────────────────────────────────────────────┘
                             │
                             ▼
┌─────────────────────────────────────────────────────────────┐
│ Fragments with highly variable regions are detected with a(an)│
│                                                               │
│ _____, revealing a series of DNA bands of various sizes.│
└─────────────────────────────────────────────────────────────┘
                             │
                             ▼
┌─────────────────────────────────────────────────────────────┐
│ The pattern of bands produced is the _____, which can be│
│ distinguished statistically from the pattern of any other individual in the world.│
└─────────────────────────────────────────────────────────────┘
```

6. Circle the letter of each source for a DNA sample from an individual.

    a. blood   **c.** clothing

    b. sperm   **d.** hair with tissue at the base

7. Is the following sentence true or false? DNA evidence is not reliable enough to be used to convict criminals. _____

The Human Genome Project (pages 357–358)

8. What is the Human Genome Project? _____

_____

_____

9. Circle the letter of each sentence that is true about the Human Genome Project.

    a. The human genome is the first genome entirely sequenced.

    b. The human genome is about the same size as the genome of *E. coli.*

    c. Researchers completed the genomes of yeast and fruit flies during the same time they sequenced the human genome.

    d. A working copy of the human genome was completed in June 2000.

10. What were the three major steps in the process of sequencing the human genome?

    a. _____

_____

    b. _____

_____

    c. _____

_____

11. What is an open reading frame, and what is it used for? _____

_____

_____

12. The mRNA coding regions of most genes are interrupted by _____.

13. List three other parts of the gene that researchers look for.

    a. _____

    b. _____

    c. _____

14. Why are biotechnology companies interested in genetic information? _____

_____

_____

15. Is the following sentence true or false? Human genome data are top secret and can be accessed only by certain people. _____

Gene Therapy (pages 359–360)

16. What is gene therapy? _____

_____

17. Circle the letter of each sentence that is true about gene therapy.

   a. When the normal copy of the gene is inserted, the body can make the correct protein, which eliminates the disorder.

   b. So far, no one has been successfully cured of a genetic disorder using gene therapy.

   c. Viruses are often used to carry the normal genes into cells.

   d. Viruses used in gene therapy often cause disease in the patients.

18. Is the following sentence true or false? All gene therapy experiments have been successful. _____

Ethical Issues in Human Genetics (page 360)

19. What other changes could be made to the human genome by manipulating human cells? _____

_____

_____

20. What is the responsibility of society in biology? _____

_____

_____

_____

21. Is the following true or false? Scientists should be expected to make all ethical decisions regarding advances in human genetics. _____

Chapter 14   The Human Genome

Vocabulary Review

Labeling Diagrams   *Use the words listed below to label the diagram.*

autosome   sex chromosome   karyotype

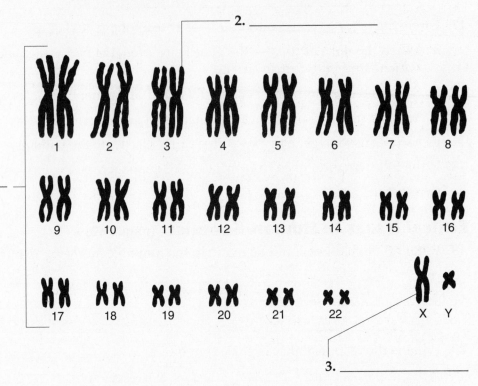

2. _____

1. _____

3. _____

Matching   *In the space provided, write the letter of the definition that best matches each term.*

_____ **4.** karyotype

_____ **5.** sex chromosomes

_____ **6.** autosomes

_____ **7.** pedigree

_____ **8.** sex-linked gene

_____ **9.** nondisjunction

_____ **10.** DNA fingerprinting

a. chart that shows the relationships within a family

b. failure of homologous chromosomes to separate in meiosis

c. picture of chromosomes arranged in pairs

d. test used to identify individuals by analyzing sections of DNA

e. chromosomes that determine an individual's sex

f. gene located on the X or Y chromosome

g. chromosomes that do not determine sex

Chapter 15   Darwin's Theory of Evolution

Summary

15–1 The Puzzle of Life's Diversity

The theory of evolution can explain the diversity of life on Earth. Evolution, or change over time, is the process by which modern organisms have descended from ancient organisms. A scientific theory is an explanation of natural events that is supported by evidence and can be tested with new evidence.

Charles Darwin contributed more than any other scientist to our understanding of evolution. During his trip on the *Beagle*, Darwin made many observations and collected a great deal of evidence. He observed tremendous diversity of organisms. He also noticed that many plants and animals were very well suited to their environment. Darwin collected fossils, or the preserved remains of ancient organisms. Some of the fossils were unlike any creatures he had ever seen. He wondered why the species represented by the fossils had disappeared.

Darwin's observations on the Galápagos Islands influenced him the most. The islands are close together but have different climates. Darwin noticed that the traits of many organisms—such as the shell shapes of tortoises—varied from island to island. Darwin wondered if animals living on different islands had once been members of the same species.

15–2 Ideas That Shaped Darwin's Thinking

In Darwin's day, most Europeans believed that Earth and all its life forms had been created just a few thousand years earlier. They also believed that species did not change through time. Several scientists who lived around the same time as Darwin began to challenge these ideas. These scientists had an important influence on the development of Darwin's theory of evolution.

Geologists James Hutton and Charles Lyell argued that Earth is many millions of years old. They also argued that the processes that changed Earth in the past were the same as the processes that are still changing Earth in the present. Knowing that Earth could change over time helped Darwin realize that life might change as well. Knowing that Earth was very old convinced Darwin that there had been enough time for life to evolve.

Jean-Baptiste Lamarck was one of the first scientists to recognize that evolution has occurred and that organisms are adapted to their environment. To explain evolution, Lamarck hypothesized that an organism could gain or lose traits during its lifetime by using or not using organs. He also hypothesized that these changes could be passed on to the organism's offspring and eventually change the species. Scientists now know that some of Lamarck's hypotheses about evolution are incorrect. However, his general ideas about evolution and adaptation are correct, and they influenced Darwin.

Another important influence on Darwin was the economist Thomas Malthus. Malthus thought that if the human population continued to grow unchecked, it would run out of living space and food. Darwin realized that this was true of all organisms and not just humans.

15-3 Darwin Presents His Case

Darwin was reluctant to publish his ideas because they were so radical. When he realized that another scientist, Alfred Russel Wallace, had the same ideas, Darwin finally published *On the Origin of Species* in 1859. In the book, Darwin provided evidence that evolution has occurred. He also explained his theory for how evolution comes about.

Darwin's theory was based on artificial selection. In artificial selection, animal breeders select for breeding only animals with the desired traits. For example, they select only the largest hogs or only the cows that produce the most milk. These traits are then passed on to the next generation.

Darwin thought that a process similar to artificial selection occurs in nature. He called this process natural selection. Darwin's theory of evolution by natural selection can be summed up as follows: Individuals differ, and some of the differences can be passed on to their offspring. More offspring are produced than can survive and reproduce. There is competition for limited resources, or a struggle for existence. Individuals best suited to their environment survive and reproduce most successfully. In other words, there is survival of the fittest. Fitness is the ability to survive and reproduce in a specific environment. It results from adaptations, or inherited characteristics that increase an organism's chance of survival. Only the fittest organisms pass on their traits. Because of this, species change over time.

Darwin argued that species alive today are descended, with modification, from ancestral species that lived in the past. Darwin also introduced the principle of common descent. According to this principle, all species come from common ancestors. The principle of common descent links all organisms on Earth into a single tree of life.

Darwin presented four types of evidence in support of evolution: the fossil record, the geographical distribution of living species, homologous structures of living organisms, and similarities in early development, or embryology. Comparing fossils from older and younger rock layers documents the fact that evolution has occurred. The presence of similar but unrelated organisms in similar environments suggests the operation of natural selection. Homologous structures have different mature forms but develop from the same embryonic tissues. They provide strong evidence that organisms have descended, with modifications, from common ancestors. Some homologous structures no longer serve important functions in descendants. If the structures are greatly reduced in size, they are called vestigial organs. The early stages, or embryos, of many animals are very similar. These similarities also provide evidence that the animals share common ancestors.

Scientific advances have supported most of Darwin's hypotheses. Today, evolutionary theory is called the "grand unifying theory of the life sciences." It gives insights to all biological and biomedical sciences.

Section 15–1 The Puzzle of Life's Diversity
(pages 369–372)

🔑 Key Concepts
- What was Charles Darwin's contribution to science?
- What pattern did Darwin observe among organisms of the Galápagos Islands?

Introduction (page 369)

1. The process by which modern organisms have descended from ancient organisms is called _____ .

2. A well-supported explanation of phenomena that have occurred in the natural world is a(an) _____ .

Voyage of the *Beagle* (pages 369–370)

3. Circle the letter of each sentence that is true about Charles Darwin.

   a. He was born in 1809.

   b. He was an English naturalist.

   c. He was 42 when he began the voyage on the *Beagle*.

   d. The voyage lasted five years and took him around the world.

4. Label the Galápagos Islands on the map below.

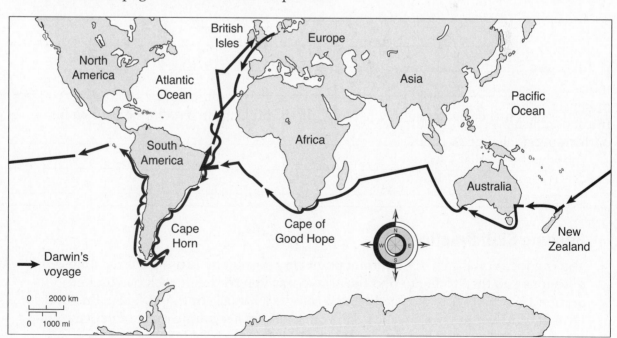

5. Is the following sentence true or false? Darwin was looking for a scientific explanation for the diversity of life on Earth. _____

Darwin's Observations (pages 370–372)

6. Circle the letter of each observation that Darwin made.

   a. An enormous number of species inhabit Earth.

   b. Many organisms seem to be poorly suited to their environment.

   c. The same sorts of animals are always found in the same ecosystems in different parts of the world.

   d. Some species that lived in the past no longer live on Earth.

7. The preserved remains of ancient organisms are called _____.

8. As Darwin studied fossils, what new questions arose? _____

   _____

   _____

9. How did Darwin explain differences in shell shape of tortoises from Hood Island and

   Isabela Island? _____

   _____

   _____

   _____

10. Darwin observed that small brown birds on the Galápagos Islands differed in the

    shape of their _____.

The Journey Home (page 372)

11. What did Darwin think about on his journey home to England? _____

    _____

    _____

    _____

12. After he returned to England, what hypothesis did Darwin develop to explain his

    findings? _____

    _____

    _____

Reading Skill Practice

You can focus on the most important points in a section by turning the headings into questions and then trying to find the answers as you read. For each heading in Section 15–1, first write the heading as a *how, what,* or *why* question. Then, find and write the answer to your question. Do your work on a separate sheet of paper.

Section 15–2 Ideas That Shaped Darwin's Thinking (pages 373–377)

Key Concepts

- How did Hutton and Lyell describe geological change?
- According to Lamarck, how did species evolve?
- What was Malthus's theory of population growth?

An Ancient, Changing Earth (pages 374–375)

1. Two scientists who helped Darwin and others recognize how old Earth is were _____ and _____.

2. Circle the letter of each idea that was proposed by James Hutton.

   a. Earth is a few thousand years old.

   b. Layers of rock are moved by forces beneath Earth's surface.

   c. Most geological processes operate extremely slowly.

   d. The processes that changed Earth in the past are different from the processes that operate in the present.

3. Circle the letter of each sentence that is true about Lyell's work.

   a. His book, *Principles of Geology*, was published after Darwin returned from his voyage.

   b. His work explained how awesome geological features could be built up or torn down over long periods of time.

   c. His publications helped Darwin appreciate the significance of the geological phenomena that he had observed.

   d. He stressed that scientists must explain past events in terms of processes that they can actually observe.

4. In what two ways did an understanding of geology influence Darwin? _____

   _____

   _____

   _____

Lamarck's Evolution Hyphotheses (page 376)

5. Is the following sentence true or false? Lamarck was among the first scientists to recognize that living things have changed over time. _____

6. Is the following sentence true or false? Lamarck proposed that all organisms have an innate tendency toward complexity and perfection. _____

7. How did Lamarck propose that species change over time? _____

_____

_____

_____

_____

8. How did Lamarck pave the way for the work of later biologists? _____

_____

_____

_____

9. Which step in the diagram below shows the inheritance of acquired traits as proposed by Lamarck? _____

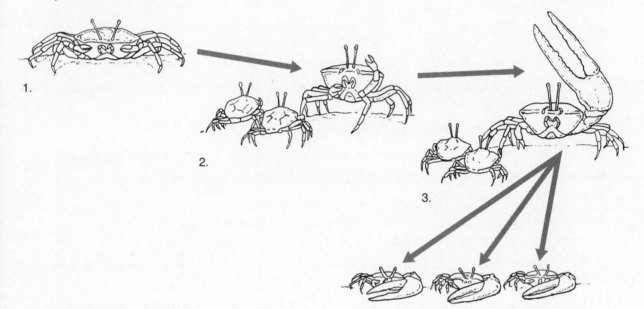

Population Growth (page 377)

10. Circle the letter of each sentence that is true about Thomas Malthus.

    a. He was an important influence on Darwin.

    b. He was an English naturalist.

    c. He believed that war, famine, and disease limit the growth of populations.

    d. His views were influenced by conditions in twentieth-century England.

11. Is the following sentence true or false? The overwhelming majority of a species' offspring survive. _____

Section 15–3 Darwin Presents His Case
(pages 378–386)

🔑 **Key Concepts**
- How is natural variation used in artificial selection?
- How is natural selection related to a species' fitness?
- What evidence of evolution did Darwin present?

Publication of *On the Origin of Species* (pages 378–379)

1. Is the following sentence true or false? When Darwin returned to England, he rushed to publish his thoughts about evolution. _____

2. The naturalist whose essay gave Darwin an incentive to publish his own work was

   _____.

3. Circle the letter of each sentence that is true about Darwin's book *On the Origin of Species*.

   a. It was published in 1869.

   b. It was ignored when it was first published.

   c. It contained evidence for evolution.

   d. It described natural selection.

Inherited Variation and Artificial Selection (page 379)

4. Differences among individuals of a species are referred to as _____.

5. Is the following sentence true or false? Genetic variation is found only in wild organisms in nature. _____

6. Circle the letter of each sentence that is true about artificial selection.

   a. It is also called selective breeding.

   b. It occurs when humans select natural variations they find useful.

   c. It produces organisms that look very different from their ancestors.

   d. It is no longer used today.

Evolution by Natural Selection (pages 380–382)

7. What was Darwin's greatest contribution? _____

   _____

Match each term with its definition.

Terms	Definitions
_____ 8. fitness	**a.** Any inherited characteristic that increases an organism's chance of survival
_____ 9. adaptation	**b.** Survival of the fittest
_____ 10. natural selection	**c.** The ability of an individual to survive and reproduce in its specific environment

11. What does the phrase *struggle for existence* mean? _____

    _____

12. Is the following sentence true or false? Adaptations can be physical characteristics but
    not more complex features such as behavior. _____

13. Explain what Darwin meant by the phrase *survival of the fittest*. _____

    _____

    _____

14. Circle the letter of each sentence that is true about natural selection.

    a. It selects traits that increase fitness.

    b. It takes place without human control.

    c. It can be observed directly in nature.

    d. It leads to an increase in a species' fitness.

15. The principle that living species descend, with changes, from other species over time is
    referred to as _____.

16. The principle that all species were derived from common ancestors is known as

    _____.

Evidence of Evolution (pages 382–385)

17. Is the following sentence true or false? Darwin argued that living things have been
    evolving on Earth for thousands of years. _____

18. Complete the concept map.

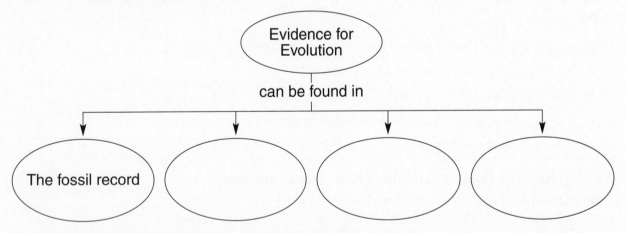

19. How do fossils that formed in different rock layers provide evidence of evolution?

    _____

    _____

20. Circle the letter of the way Darwin explained the distribution of finch species on the Galápagos Islands.

   a. They had descended with modification from a common mainland ancestor.

   b. They had descended with modification from several different mainland ancestors.

   c. They had remained unchanged since arriving on the Galápagos from the mainland.

   d. They had become more similar to one another after arriving on the Galápagos.

21. How did Darwin explain the existence of similar but unrelated species?

   _____

   _____

   _____

22. Structures that have different mature forms but develop from the same embryonic tissues are called _____.

23. Is the following sentence true or false? Homologous structures provide strong evidence that all four-limbed vertebrates have descended, with modifications, from common ancestors. _____

24. Organs that are so reduced in size that they are just vestiges, or traces, of homologous organs in other species are called _____.

Summary of Darwin's Theory (page 386)

25. Circle the letter of each idea that is part of Darwin's theory of evolution.

   a. There is variation in nature.

   b. Fewer organisms are produced than can survive.

   c. There is a struggle for existence.

   d. Species change over time.

26. According to Darwin's theory, what happens to individuals whose characteristics are not well suited to their environment? _____

   _____

27. Darwin believed that all organisms on Earth are united into a single tree of life by

   _____.

Strengths and Weaknesses of Evolutionary Theory (page 386)

28. What is the status of Darwin's hypotheses today? _____

   _____

   _____

Chapter 15   Darwin's Theory of Evolution

Vocabulary Review

Crossword Puzzle   *Complete the puzzle by entering the term that matches each numbered description.*

Across

1. scientist whose ideas about evolution and adaptation influenced Darwin
3. ship on which Darwin traveled
7. change over time
10. explanation of natural events that is supported by evidence and can be tested with new evidence
12. economist whose ideas about human population influenced Darwin
14. remains of ancient life
15. homologous structure that is greatly reduced in size

Down

1. geologist who influenced Darwin
2. inherited characteristic that increases an organism's chance of survival
4. type of selection in which humans select the variations
5. islands where Darwin observed variation in tortoises
6. ability of an individual to survive and reproduce in its specific environment
8. type of selection Darwin referred to as survival of the fittest
9. structures that have different mature forms but develop from the same embryonic tissues
11. scientist whose ideas about evolution were the same as Darwin's
13. geologist who influenced Darwin

Summary

16–1 Genes and Variation

Darwin's original ideas can now be understood in genetic terms. Beginning with variation, we now know that traits are controlled by genes and that many genes have at least two forms, or alleles. We also know that individuals of all species are heterozygous for many genes.

To understand evolution, genetic variation is studied in populations. A population is defined as a group of individuals of the same species that interbreed. Members of a population share a common group of genes, called a gene pool. A gene pool consists of all the genes, including all the different alleles, that are present in the population. In genetic terms, evolution is any change in the relative frequency of alleles in a population. The relative frequency of an allele is the number of times the allele occurs in a gene pool, compared with the number of times other alleles for the same gene occur.

The two main sources of genetic variation are mutations and gene shuffling. A mutation is any change in a sequence of DNA. Gene shuffling occurs during the production of gametes in sexual reproduction. It can result in millions of different combinations of genes. Mutation and gene shuffling do not change relative allele frequencies. However, they increase genetic variation by increasing the number of different genotypes.

The number of different phenotypes for a given trait depends on how many genes control the trait. A single-gene trait is controlled by one gene. If there are two alleles for the gene, two or three different genotypes are possible. An example in humans is the presence or absence of widow's peak. A polygenic trait is controlled by two or more genes, and each gene may have more than one allele. An example of a human polygenic trait is height.

Polygenic traits such as height produce many different phenotypes. Variation in a polygenic trait in a population often produces a bell-shaped curve, with most people falling near the middle of the curve.

16–2 Evolution as Genetic Change

Natural selection acts on individuals. Evolution acts on populations. Natural selection acting on individuals leads to the evolution of populations.

Natural selection on a trait controlled by a single gene with two alleles can cause one allele to increase and the other allele to decrease. Natural selection on polygenic traits is more complicated. Natural selection on polygenic traits can occur as directional selection, stabilizing selection, or disruptive selection. Directional selection takes place when individuals at one end of the bell-shaped curve have higher fitness than individuals near the middle or at the other end of the curve. The result of directional selection is a shift in the curve toward the higher fitness end. Stabilizing selection takes place when individuals near the middle of the curve have higher fitness than individuals at either end. The result of stabilizing selection is a narrowing of the curve around the middle. Disruptive selection takes place when individuals at the upper and lower ends of the curve have higher fitness than individuals near the middle. As a result of disruptive selection, the curve develops a peak at each end and a low point in the middle.

Natural selection is not the only source of evolutionary change. In small populations, alleles can become more or less common simply by chance. This kind of change in allele frequency is called genetic drift. It occurs when individuals with a particular allele leave more descendants than other individuals, just by chance. Over time, this can cause an allele to become more or less common in a population.

Genetic drift also may occur when a small group of individuals colonizes a new habitat. By chance, the small group may have different relative allele frequencies than the original population. When this happens, it is called the founder effect.

To understand how evolution occurs, scientists first had to answer the question: Under what conditions does evolution not occur? The answer to this question is called the Hardy-Weinberg principle. The principle states that allele frequencies in a population will remain constant unless one or more factors cause those frequencies to change. The situation in which allele frequencies remain constant is called genetic equilibrium. For a population to be in genetic equilibrium, five conditions are required: random mating, very large population size, no migrations, no mutations, and no natural selection. Random mating assures that each individual has an equal chance of reproducing. Very large population size prevents genetic drift from occurring. If all five conditions are met, relative allele frequencies will not change and evolution will not occur.

16–3 The Process of Speciation

Speciation means the formation of new species. For one species to evolve into two new species, the gene pools of two populations must become separated, or reproductively isolated. Reproductive isolation has occurred when the members of two populations cannot interbreed and produce fertile offspring. Reproductive isolation can involve behavioral, geographic, or temporal isolation.

Behavioral isolation occurs when populations have different courtship rituals or other behaviors involved in reproduction. Geographic isolation occurs when populations are separated by geographic barriers, such as mountains or rivers. Temporal isolation occurs when populations reproduce at different times.

Recently, Peter and Rosemary Grant proved that natural selection is still causing evolution of finches on the Galápagos Islands. The Grants showed that there was enough heritable variation in finch beaks to provide raw material for natural selection. They also showed that differences in beaks produced differences in fitness. These differences in fitness caused directional selection to occur.

Darwin thought that different finch species evolved on the Galápagos Islands from a single species of founding birds. We now know how this could have happened. A few finches may have traveled from mainland South America to one of the islands to found a new population. There, they survived and reproduced. Some birds crossed to a second island, and the two populations became geographically isolated. They no longer shared a gene pool. Seed sizes on the second island favored birds with larger beaks. The population on the second island evolved into a population with larger beaks. Eventually, the large-beaked birds on the second island became reproductively isolated and evolved into a new species.

Evolution continues today. For example, bacteria are evolving to have resistance to drugs. Evolutionary theory can help us understand these changes.

© Pearson Education, Inc., publishing as Pearson Prentice Hall.

Chapter 16   Evolution of Populations

Section 16–1 Genes and Variation (pages 393–396)

🔑 Key Concepts
- What are the main sources of heritable variation in a population?
- How is evolution defined in genetic terms?
- What determines the numbers of phenotypes for a given trait?

Introduction (page 393)

1. Is the following sentence true or false? Mendel's work on inheritance was published after Darwin's lifetime. _____

2. Which two important factors was Darwin unable to explain without an understanding of heredity? _____

_____

_____

How Common Is Genetic Variation? (page 393)

3. All organisms have additional _____ that is "invisible" because it involves small differences in biochemical processes.

Variation and Gene Pools (page 394)

4. A group of individuals of the same species that interbreed is a(an) _____.

5. All of the genes in a population are called a(an) _____.

6. Is the following sentence true or false? A gene pool typically contains just one allele for each inheritable trait. _____

7. The number of times that an allele occurs in a gene pool compared with the number of times other alleles for the same gene occur is called the _____ of the allele.

Sources of Genetic Variation (pages 394–395)

8. What is a mutation? _____

_____

9. Why do mutations occur? _____

_____

_____

Name_____ Class_____ Date _____

10. Complete the concept map.

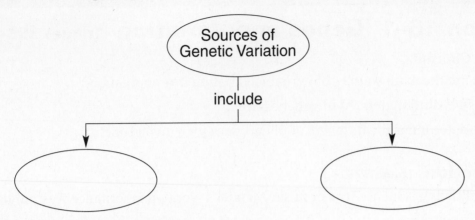

11. Circle the letter of each choice that is true about mutations.

  a. They do not always change an amino acid.

  b. They always affect lengthy segments of a chromosome.

  c. They always affect an organism's phenotype.

  d. They always affect an organism's fitness.

12. Is the following sentence true or false? Most heritable differences are due to gene shuffling that occurs during the production of gametes. _____

13. Circle the letter of each choice that is true about sexual reproduction.

  a. It is a major source of variation in many populations.

  b. It can produce many different phenotypes.

  c. It can produce many different genetic combinations.

  d. It can change the relative frequency of alleles in a population.

Single-Gene and Polygenic Traits (pages 395–396)

14. Is the following sentence true or false? The number of phenotypes produced for a given trait depends on how many genes control the trait. _____

15. Is the following sentence true or false? Most traits are controlled by a single gene.

_____

© Pearson Education, Inc., publishing as Pearson Prentice Hall.

16. Label the two graphs to show which one represents a single-gene trait and which one represents a polygenic trait.

_____   _____

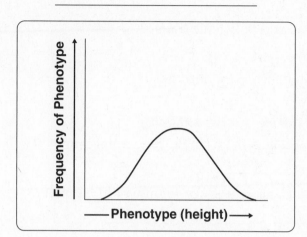

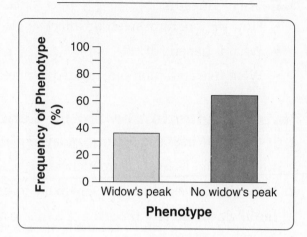

Reading Skill Practice

When you read about related concepts, making a graphic organizer such as a Venn diagram can help you focus on their similarities and differences. Make a Venn diagram comparing and contrasting single-gene and polygenic traits. For more information on Venn diagrams, see Appendix A of your textbook. Do your work on a separate sheet of paper.

Section 16–2 Evolution as Genetic Change
(pages 397–402)

👄 **Key Concepts**

- How does natural selection affect single-gene and polygenic traits?
- What is genetic drift?
- What five conditions are needed to maintain genetic equilibrium?

Natural Selection on Single-Gene Traits (pages 397–398)

1. Is the following sentence true or false? Natural selection on single-gene traits cannot lead to changes in allele frequencies. _____

2. If a trait made an organism less likely to survive and reproduce, what would happen to the allele for that trait? _____

_____

_____

3. If a trait had no effect on an organism's fitness, what would happen to the allele for that trait? _____

_____

_____

Natural Selection on Polygenic Traits (pages 398–399)

4. List the three ways that natural selection can affect the distributions of phenotypes.

   a. _____

   b. _____

   c. _____

Match the type of selection with the situation in which it occurs.

Type of Selection	**Situation**
_____ 5. Directional	a. Individuals at the upper and lower ends of the curve have higher fitness than individuals near the middle.
_____ 6. Stabilizing	b. Individuals at one end of the curve have higher fitness than individuals in the middle or at the other end.
_____ 7. Disruptive	c. Individuals near the center of the curve have higher fitness than individuals at either end.

8. An increase in the average size of beaks in Galápagos finches is an example of _____ selection.

9. Is the following sentence true or false? The weight of human infants at birth is under the influence of disruptive selection. _____

© Pearson Education, Inc., publishing as Pearson Prentice Hall.

10. Draw the missing graph to show how disruptive selection affects beak size.

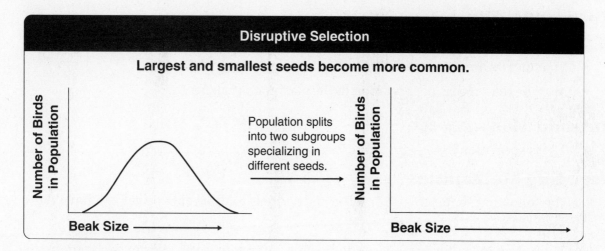

Genetic Drift (page 400)

11. Is the following sentence true or false? Natural selection is the only source of evolutionary change. _____

12. Random change in allele frequencies in small populations is called _____.

13. A situation in which allele frequencies change as a result of the migration of a small subgroup of a population is known as the _____.

14. What is an example of the founder effect? _____
_____
_____

Evolution Versus Genetic Equilibrium (pages 401–402)

15. What does the Hardy-Weinberg principle state? _____
_____
_____

16. The situation in which allele frequencies remain constant is called _____.

17. List the five conditions required to maintain genetic equilibrium.

a. _____   d. _____

b. _____   e. _____

c. _____

18. Why is large population size important in maintaining genetic equilibrium?
_____
_____

Section 16–3 The Process of Speciation
(pages 404–410)

🔑 **Key Concepts**
- What factors are involved in the formation of new species?
- Describe the process of speciation in the Galápagos finches.

Introduction (page 404)

1. What is speciation? _____

Isolating Mechanisms (pages 404–405)

2. Is the following sentence true or false? Individuals in different species can have the same gene pool. _____

3. What does it mean for two species to be reproductively isolated from each other?

   _____

   _____

4. What must happen in order for new species to evolve? _____

   _____

5. List three ways that reproductive isolation occurs.

   a. _____   c. _____

   b. _____

6. When does behavioral isolation occur? _____

   _____

   _____

7. Is the following sentence true or false? Eastern and Western meadowlarks are an example of behavioral isolation. _____

8. When does geographic isolation occur? _____

   _____

   _____

9. Abert and Kaibab squirrels in the Southwest are an example of _____ isolation.

10. Is the following sentence true or false? Geographic barriers guarantee the formation of new species. _____

11. What is an example of temporal isolation? _____

   _____

Testing Natural Selection in Nature (pages 406–407)

12. Is the following sentence true or false? The basic mechanisms of evolutionary change cannot be observed in nature. _____

13. Circle the letter of each hypothesis about the evolution of Galápagos finches that was tested by the Grants.

   a. The finches' beak size and shape has enough inheritable variation to provide raw material for natural selection.

   b. The different finch species are the descendants of a common mainland ancestor.

   c. Differences in the finches' beak size and shape produce differences in fitness that cause natural selection to occur.

   d. The evolution of the finches is proceeding slowly and gradually.

Speciation in Darwin's Finches (pages 408–409)

14. Complete the flowchart to show how speciation probably occurred in the Galápagos finches.

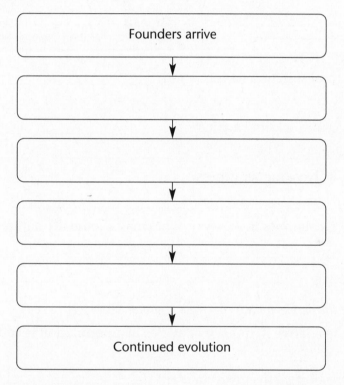

Founders arrive

Continued evolution

15. How could differences in beak size lead to reproductive isolation? _____

_____

_____

Studying Evolution Since Darwin (page 410)

16. Why is the study of evolution important? _____

_____

_____

Chapter 16   Evolution of Populations

Vocabulary Review

Interpreting Diagrams   *The diagrams show the distribution curves for time of mating in a popula-tion of insects. The diagram on the left represents the starting population. The diagram on the right represents the population several generations later. Study the diagrams and answer the questions below.*

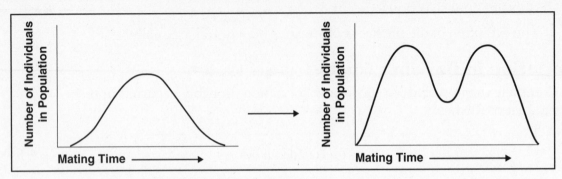

1. What type of natural selection has occurred? _____

_____

2. Which phenotypes are selected against? _____

_____

3. Which phenotypes have higher fitness? _____

_____

4. If natural selection continues in this way, what may eventually happen to the population?

_____

_____

Completion   *Fill in the blanks with terms from Chapter 16.*

5. Any change in the relative frequency of alleles in a population is called

_____.

6. A gene pool consists of all the genes in a(an) _____.

7. The two main sources of genetic variation are gene shuffling and

_____.

8. A random change in allele frequency is called _____.

9. When birds cannot interbreed because they have different mating songs, they are

characterized by _____ isolation.

10. A situation in which allele frequencies change as a result of the migration of a small

subgroup of a population is known as the _____.

11. Research on Galápagos finches by Peter and Rosemary Grant showed that a type of

natural selection called _____ selection was occurring.

12. Two related species that live in the same area but mate during different seasons are

separated by _____ isolation.

Chapter 17   The History of Life

Summary

17–1 The Fossil Record

Fossils are preserved traces and remains of ancient life. Scientists who study fossils are called paleontologists. They use fossils to infer what past life forms were like. All the information about past life provided by fossils is called the fossil record. The fossil record shows how life has changed over time. It shows that more than 99 percent of all species that ever lived on Earth have become extinct, or died out.

Few organisms are actually preserved as fossils. Most fossils that do form are found in sedimentary rock. As sediments build up in layers over time, they sometimes bury the remains of dead organisms. These dead organisms eventually turn into fossils.

Relative dating and radioactive dating are used to determine the age of fossils. Relative dating determines whether a fossil is older or younger than other fossils. It is based on where fossils are found in rock layers. Fossils from deeper rock layers are assumed to be older than fossils from rock layers closer to the surface. Index fossils represent species that lived for a short period of time but over a wide geographic range. Index fossils can help determine the relative age of fossils from different places. Radioactive dating determines a fossil's age in years. Radioactive elements in fossils decay, or break down, at a steady rate, called a half-life. A half-life is the length of time needed for half of the radioactive atoms in a sample to decay. A fossil's age is calculated from the half-life and the amount of remaining radioactive atoms the fossil contains.

The geologic time scale is used for evolutionary time. The scale begins with Precambrian Time. Following Precambrian Time, the scale is divided into three eras: the Paleozoic, Mesozoic, and Cenozoic eras. Each era is further divided into smaller lengths of time, called periods.

17–2 Earth's Early History

Earth is about 4.6 billion years old. At first, Earth was very hot and the atmosphere contained toxic gases. The atmosphere also contained water vapor but no oxygen. About 3.8 billion years ago, Earth's surface cooled and water vapor condensed. Thunderstorms soaked the surface, and oceans formed.

In the 1950s, Stanley Miller and Harold Urey simulated conditions on early Earth. They filled a container with water and gases found in Earth's early atmosphere. They passed electric sparks through the mixture to simulate lightning. Soon, organic compounds formed. The experiment showed that molecules needed for life could have evolved under conditions on early Earth. Sometimes large organic molecules form tiny bubbles called proteinoid microspheres. Structures similar to proteinoid microspheres might have become the first living cells. RNA and DNA also could have evolved from simple organic molecules.

The first known life forms evolved about 3.5 billion years ago. They were single celled and looked like modern bacteria. Some were preserved as microscopic fossils, or microfossils. Eventually, photosynthetic bacteria became common. During photosynthesis, the bacteria produced oxygen. The oxygen accumulated in the atmosphere. The rise of oxygen drove some life forms to extinction. At the same time, other life forms evolved that depended on oxygen.

The first eukaryotes, or organisms with nuclei, evolved about 2 billion years ago. One explanation for how eukaryotes evolved is the endosymbiotic theory. This theory proposes that smaller prokaryotes began living inside larger cells and evolved a symbiotic relationship with the larger cells.

Later, sexual reproduction evolved. Sexual reproduction increased genetic variation, so evolution could occur more quickly.

17–3 Evolution of Multicellular Life

During Precambrian Time, life arose and evolved into multicellular forms. However, life still existed only in the oceans. Few fossils exist from the Precambrian, because the animals did not yet have any hard parts.

There is much more fossil evidence from the Paleozoic Era. Animals with hard parts, such as trilobites, evolved then. Other important evolutionary events of the Paleozoic include the evolution of land plants, insects, amphibians, and reptiles. At the end of the Paleozoic, there was a mass extinction, in which many types of organisms became extinct at once.

Important evolutionary events in the Mesozoic Era include the appearance of flowering plants and the dominance of dinosaurs. Reptiles, in general, were so successful during the era that the Mesozoic is called the Age of Reptiles. At the close of the Mesozoic, another mass extinction occurred.

The Cenozoic Era is called the Age of Mammals. During the Cenozoic, mammals evolved adaptations that allowed them to live on land, in water, and in air. The first human fossils may have appeared about 200,000 years ago in Africa.

17–4 Patterns of Evolution

Macroevolution means large-scale evolution, or evolution above the level of the species. Six patterns of macroevolution are extinction, adaptive radiation, convergent evolution, coevolution, punctuated equilibrium, and changes in developmental genes.

Most of the time, extinctions have occurred because species could not compete for resources or adapt to gradually changing environments. Several times, however, mass extinctions have occurred. During these mass extinctions, huge numbers of species became extinct at once. This may have occurred because of a combination of events, such as volcanoes erupting and asteroids striking Earth.

Adaptive radiation is the process in which a single species evolves into diverse species that live in different ways. Convergent evolution is the process in which unrelated species come to look alike because they have evolved similar adaptations to similar environments. Coevolution is the process by which two species evolve in response to changes in each other over time. For example, plants evolved poisons that protected them from insects. In response, insects evolved ways of protecting themselves from the poisons.

Darwin thought evolution occurred slowly and gradually. The fossil record sometimes shows a different pattern of evolution, called punctuated equilibrium. In this pattern, long periods of little or no change are interrupted by short periods of rapid change.

Some genes, called hox genes, control the actions of many other genes. Small changes in hox genes can produce major differences in adult organisms. Some scientists think that changes in hox genes may contribute to major evolutionary changes.

Section 17–1 The Fossil Record (pages 417–422)

🔑 Key Concepts

- What is the fossil record?
- What information do relative dating and radioactive dating provide about fossils?
- What are the main divisions of the geologic time scale?

Fossils and Ancient Life (page 417)

1. Scientists who study fossils are called _____.

2. What is the fossil record? _____

_____

3. What evidence does the fossil record provide? _____

_____

_____

4. Species that died out are said to be _____.

5. Is the following sentence true or false? About half of all species that have ever lived on Earth have become extinct. _____

How Fossils Form (page 418)

6. Circle the letter of each sentence that is true about fossils.

    a. Most organisms that die are preserved as fossils.

    b. Fossils can include footprints, eggs, or other traces of organisms.

    c. Most fossils form in metamorphic rock.

    d. The quality of fossil preservation varies.

7. How do fossils form in sedimentary rock? _____

_____

_____

_____

Interpreting Fossil Evidence (pages 418–420)

8. List the two techniques paleontologists use to determine the age of fossils.

    a. _____

    b. _____

9. Circle the letter of each sentence that is true about relative dating.

    a. It determines the age of a fossil by comparing its placement with that of fossils in other layers of rock.

    b. It uses index fossils.

    c. It allows paleontologists to estimate a fossil's age in years.

    d. It provides no information about absolute age.

10. Is the following sentence true or false? Older rock layers are usually closer to Earth's surface than more recent rock layers. _____

11. Is the following sentence true or false? Scientists use radioactive decay to assign absolute ages to rocks. _____

12. The length of time required for half of the radioactive atoms in a sample to decay is called a(an) _____.

13. The use of half-lives to determine the age of a sample is called

_____.

14. How do scientists calculate the age of a sample using radioactive dating?

_____

_____

15. Is the following sentence true or false? All radioactive elements have the same half-life.

_____

Geologic Time Scale (pages 421–422)

16. Fill in the missing eras and periods in the geologic time scale below.

GEOLOGIC TIME SCALE

Era					Paleozoic						
Period	Quaternary		Cretaceous	Triassic	Permian		Devonian		Ordovician		Vendian
Time (millions of years ago)	1.8 – present	65 – 1.8	145 – 65	208 – 145	245 – 208	290 – 245	360 – 290	410 – 360	440 – 410	505 – 440	544 – 505	650 – 544

17. Circle the letter of the choice that lists the eras of the geologic time scale in order from the most recent to the oldest.

    a. Mesozioc, Paleozoic, Cenozoic

    b. Cenozoic, Paleozoic, Mesozoic

    c. Cenozoic, Mesozoic, Paleozoic

    d. Paleozoic, Mesozoic, Cenozoic

18. Circle the letter of each sentence that is true about the geologic time scale.

    a. The scale is used to represent evolutionary time.

    b. Major changes in fossil organisms separate segments of geologic time.

    c. Divisions of the scale cover standard lengths of 100 million years.

    d. Geologic time begins with the Cambrian Period.

19. After Precambrian time, what are the two basic divisions of the geologic time scale?

_____

20. During which era did dinosaurs roam the Earth? _____

21. During which era did mammals become common? _____

Reading Skill Practice

Writing a summary can help you remember the information you have read. When you write a summary, write only the important points. Write a summary of the information in Section 17–1. Your summary should be shorter than the text on which it is based.

Section 17–2 Earth's Early History (pages 423–428)

⬛ **Key Concepts**
- What substances made up Earth's early atmosphere?
- What did Miller and Urey's experiments show?
- What occurred when oxygen was added to Earth's atmosphere?
- What hypothesis explains the origin of eukaryotic cells?

Formation of Earth (pages 423–424)

1. List six components of Earth's early atmosphere.

   a. _____   c. _____   e. _____

   b. _____   d. _____   f. _____

2. Is the following sentence true or false? Liquid water first occurred on Earth more than 4 billion years ago. _____

The First Organic Molecules (page 424)

3. Label the diagram to show which part of Miller and Urey's apparatus simulated lightning storms on early Earth.

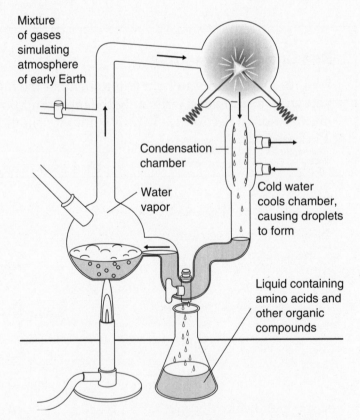

Mixture of gases simulating atmosphere of early Earth

Condensation chamber

Water vapor

Cold water cools chamber, causing droplets to form

Liquid containing amino acids and other organic compounds

4. Circle the letter of each sentence that is true about Miller and Urey's experiments.

   a. Their purpose was to determine how the first organic molecules evolved.

   b. They led to the formation of several amino acids.

   c. They accurately simulated conditions in Earth's early atmosphere.

   d. The results were never duplicated in experiments by other scientists.

The Puzzle of Life's Origins (page 425)

5. What are proteinoid microspheres? _____

_____

_____

6. Is the following sentence true or false? Scientists know how DNA and RNA evolved.

   _____

7. Why do scientists think that RNA may have evolved before DNA? _____

_____

_____

_____

8. Once DNA evolved, why would it have become the primary means of transmitting genetic information? _____

_____

_____

Free Oxygen (page 426)

9. Microscopic fossils are called _____.

10. Circle the letter of each sentence that is true about the earliest life forms on Earth.

    a. They resembled modern bacteria.

    b. They were eukaryotes.

    c. They relied on oxygen.

    d. They were not preserved as fossils.

11. How did early photosynthetic bacteria change Earth? _____

_____

_____

12. Is the following sentence true or false? The rise of oxygen in the atmosphere drove some life forms to extinction. _____

Origin of Eukaryotic Cells (pages 427–428)

13. Is the following sentence true or false? The ancestor of all eukaryotic cells evolved about 2 billion years ago. _____

14. What was the first step in the evolution of eukaryotic cells? _____

_____

_____

15. What does the endosymbiotic theory propose? _____

_____

_____

16. Circle the letter of each choice that provides support for the endosymbiotic theory.

   a. The membranes of mitochondria and chloroplasts resemble the plasma membranes of free-living prokaryotes.

   b. Mitochondria and chloroplasts do not have DNA.

   c. Mitochondria and chloroplasts have ribosomes that are similar in size and structure to those of bacteria.

   d. Mitochondria and chloroplasts reproduce by binary fission, as bacteria do.

Sexual Reproduction and Multicellularity (page 428)

17. How did sexual reproduction speed up the evolutionary process? _____

_____

_____

18. Is the following sentence true or false? Sexual reproduction evolved after the first

multicellular organisms appeared. _____

Reading Skill Practice

When you read a section that contains new or difficult material, identifying the sentence that best expresses the main topic under each heading can help you focus on the most important points. For each heading in Section 17–2, identify and copy the sentence that best expresses the main topic under that heading. Do your work on a separate sheet of paper.

Section 17–3 Evolution of Multicellular Life
(pages 429–434)

⬛ **Key Concept**

• What were the characteristic forms of life in the Paleozoic, Mesozoic, and Cenozoic eras?

Precambrian Time (page 429)

1. Is the following sentence true or false? Almost 90 percent of Earth's history occurred during the Precambrian. _____

2. Circle the letter of each sentence that is true about life in the Precambrian.

   a. Anaerobic and photosynthetic forms of life appeared.

   b. Aerobic forms of life evolved, and eukaryotes appeared.

   c. Multicellular life forms evolved.

   d. Life existed on the land and in the sea.

3. Why do few fossils exist from the Precambrian? _____

_____

Paleozoic Era (pages 429–431)

4. The first part of the Paleozoic Era is the _____ Period.

5. Is the following sentence true or false? Life was not very diverse during the Cambrian Period. _____

6. Circle the letter of each sentence that is true about the Cambrian Period.

   a. Organisms with hard parts first appeared.

   b. Most animal phyla first evolved.

   c. Many animals lived on the land.

   d. Brachiopods and trilobites were common.

Match the periods of the Paleozoic Era with the evolutionary events that occurred during them.

Periods	Events
_____ 7. Ordovician and Silurian	a. Reptiles evolved from amphibians, and winged insects evolved into many forms.
_____ 8. Devonian	b. The first vertebrates evolved, and insects first appeared.
_____ 9. Carboniferous and Permian	c. Many groups of fishes were present in the oceans, and the first amphibians evolved.

10. Animals first begin to invade the land during the _____ Period.

11. Where does the Carboniferous Period get its name? _____

_____

_____

12. When many types of living things become extinct at the same time, it is called a(an)

_____.

13. Is the following sentence true or false? The mass extinction at the end of the Paleozoic
affected only land animals. _____

Mesozoic Era (pages 431–432)

14. Complete the following table.

PERIODS OF THE MESOZOIC ERA

Period	Evolutionary Event
	First mammals
	First birds
	First flowering plants

15. The Mesozoic Era is called the Age of _____.

16. The first dinosaurs appeared in the _____ Period.

17. Is the following sentence true or false? The mammals of the Triassic Period were very
small. _____

18. Is the following sentence true or false? Many paleontologists think that birds are close
relatives of dinosaurs. _____

19. The dominant vertebrates throughout the Cretaceous Period were _____.

20. What advantage do flowering plants have over conifers? _____

_____

_____

21. Describe the mass extinction that occurred at the end of the Cretaceous Period.

_____

_____

_____

Cenozoic Era (pages 433–434)

22. Is the following sentence true or false? During the Cenozoic Era, mammals evolved adaptations that allowed them to live on land, in water, and in the air.

_____

23. The Cenozoic Era is called the Age of _____.

24. What were Earth's climates like during the Tertiary Period? _____

_____

_____

25. How did Earth's climate change during the Quaternary Period? _____

_____

_____

26. Is the following sentence true or false? The very earliest ancestors of our species appeared about 100,000 years ago. _____

Reading Skill Practice

When you read a section with many details, writing an outline may help you organize and remember the material. Outline Section 17–3 by first writing the section headings as major topics in the order in which they appear in the book. Then, beneath each major topic, list important details about it.

Section 17–4 Patterns of Evolution (pages 435–440)

⊂⊐ **Key Concept**
- What are six important patterns of macroevolution?

Introduction (page 435)

1. The large-scale evolutionary changes that take place over long periods of time are referred to as _____.

2. What are six patterns of macroevolution?

   a. _____   d. _____

   b. _____   e. _____

   c. _____   f. _____

Extinction (page 435)

3. What are possible causes of mass extinctions? _____

_____

_____

4. What effects have mass extinctions had on the history of life? _____

_____

_____

Adaptive Radiation (page 436)

5. The process of a single species or a small group of species evolving into diverse forms that live in different ways is called _____.

6. What led to the adaptive radiation of mammals? _____

_____

Convergent Evolution (pages 436–437)

7. The process by which unrelated organisms come to resemble one another is called

_____.

8. Circle the letter of each choice that is an example of convergent evolution.

   a. Bird's wing and fish's fin

   b. Shark's fin and dolphin's limb

   c. Human's arm and bird's wing

   d. Human's leg and dolphin's limb

Coevolution (pages 437–438)

9. The process by which two species evolve in response to changes in each other over time is called _____.

10. How have plants and plant-eating insects coevolved? _____

_____

_____

_____

Punctuated Equilibrium (page 439)

11. The idea that evolution occurs at a slow, steady rate is called _____.

12. What are some reasons rapid evolution may occur after long periods of equilibrium?

_____

_____

_____

13. The pattern of long, stable periods interrupted by brief periods of more rapid change is called _____.

14. Is the following sentence true or false? Evolution has often proceeded at different rates for different organisms. _____

Developmental Genes and Body Plans (page 440)

15. How can hox genes help reveal how evolution occurred? _____

_____

_____

_____

16. Is the following sentence true or false? Changes in the timing of genetic control during embryonic development can contribute to the variation involved in natural selection.

_____

Vocabulary Review

Multiple Choice   *In the space provided, write the letter of the answer that best completes each sentence.*

_____ 1. Index fossils are used in the type of dating called
  a. radioactive dating.   **c.** relative dating.
  b. periodic dating.   **d.** absolute dating.

_____ 2. Oxygen was added to Earth's atmosphere by the process of
  a. macroevolution.   **c.** coevolution.
  b. endosymbiosis.   **d.** photosynthesis.

_____ 3. Sexual reproduction evolved before the evolution of
  a. multicellular organisms.   **c.** eukaryotes.
  b. photosynthetic bacteria.   **d.** the earliest life forms.

_____ 4. The Age of Mammals occurred during the
  a. Mesozoic Era.   **c.** Cenozoic Era.
  b. Paleozoic Era.   **d.** Precambrian.

_____ 5. Dinosaurs were dominant during the
  a. Precambrian.   **c.** Paleozoic Era.
  b. Mesozoic Era.   **d.** Cenozoic Era.

Writing Descriptions   *Describe each pattern of macroevolution.*

6. coevolution _____

   _____

   _____

7. convergent evolution _____

   _____

   _____

8. mass extinction _____

   _____

   _____

9. punctuated equilibrium _____

   _____

   _____

10. adaptive radiation _____

   _____

   _____

Chapter 18   Classification

Summary

18–1 Finding Order in Diversity

There are millions of different species on Earth. To study this great diversity of organisms, biologists must give each organism a name. Biologists also must organize living things into groups in a logical way. Therefore, biologists need a classification system. Taxonomy is the discipline of naming and classifying organisms. To be useful, the names that are assigned should be universally accepted. A good classification system should also group together organisms that are more similar to each other than they are to organisms in other groups.

Common names for organisms vary by language and region. This creates confusion. By the 1700s, scientists had tried to solve this problem by agreeing to use a single name for each species. At first, the names they used were very long. Then, Carolus Linnaeus developed a two-word naming system, called binomial nomenclature. This system is still used today. In binomial nomenclature, each species is assigned a two-part scientific name. The first part of the name refers to the genus (plural: genera). A genus is a group of closely related species. For example, the genus *Ursus* contains six bear species. The second part of the name, along with the genus name, refers to a single species (plural: species). Recall that species consist of individuals who can interbreed. The name *Ursus maritimus*, for example, refers to the species polar bear.

Linnaeus's system of classification has seven different levels. From smallest to largest, the levels are species, genus, family, order, class, phylum, and kingdom. Each of the levels is called a taxon (plural: taxa). Just as a genus is a group of similar species, a family is a group of similar genera, an order a group of similar families, a class a group of similar orders, a phylum (plural: phyla) a group of similar classes, and a kingdom a group of similar phyla. Linnaeus named two kingdoms of living things, the Animalia (animal) and Plantae (plant) kingdoms.

18–2 Modern Evolutionary Classification

Linnaeus and other taxonomists have always tried to group organisms according to biologically important characteristics. However, they have not always agreed upon which characteristics are most important.

Early classifications were based on visible similarities. Biologists now group organisms according to evolutionary relationships. The study of evolutionary relationships among organisms is called phylogeny. Classification based on evolutionary relationships is called evolutionary classification. Species within one genus are more closely related to each other than to species in another genus. This is because all members of a genus share a recent common ancestor. All genera in a family also share a common ancestor. However, this common ancestor is farther in the past than the common ancestor of species within a genus. The higher the level of the taxon, the farther back in time is the common ancestor of all the organisms in that taxon.

Many biologists now use a method called cladistic analysis to determine evolutionary relationships. Cladistic analysis is based on derived characters. Derived characters are new traits that arise as a group evolves over time. Derived traits are therefore found in closely related organisms but not in their distant ancestors. Derived characters can be used to construct a cladogram. A cladogram is a diagram that shows the evolutionary relationships among a group of organisms. A cladogram is basically an evolutionary tree, much like a family tree.

All organisms have DNA and RNA. Because DNA and RNA are so similar across all forms of life, these molecules can be compared in different species. The more similar the molecules are in different species, the more recently the species shared a common ancestor. Therefore, the more closely related they are.

Comparisons of DNA can also be used to estimate the length of time that two species have been evolving independently. A model called a molecular clock can be used for this purpose. The model assumes that neutral mutations, which do not affect phenotype, accumulate in gene pools. Two species evolving independently from each other will accumulate different neutral mutations through time. The more there are of these different neutral mutations, the longer the two species have been evolving independently.

18–3 Kingdoms and Domains

As biologists learned more about the natural world, they realized that Linnaeus's two kingdoms, Animalia and Plantae, did not represent all life forms. First, microorganisms, such as bacteria, were discovered. Microorganisms did not seem to fit into either kingdom, so they were placed in their own kingdom, called Protista. Then, mushrooms, yeast, and molds were separated from plants and placed in their own kingdom, called Fungi. Later, bacteria were separated from other Protista and placed in another new kingdom, called Monera. Finally, the Monera were divided into two kingdoms: Eubacteria and Archaebacteria. By the 1990s, a six-kingdom system of classification was proposed. It includes the kingdoms Eubacteria, Archaebacteria, Protista, Fungi, Plantae, and Animalia.

A new taxon, called the domain, is now used by many biologists. The domain is one level higher than the kingdom. Three domains are recognized: Bacteria, Archaea, and Eukarya.

The domain Bacteria includes unicellular organisms without a nucleus. They have cell walls containing a substance called peptidoglycan. The domain Bacteria corresponds to the kingdom Eubacteria.

The domain Archaea also includes unicellular organisms without a nucleus. These organisms have cell walls that do not contain peptidoglycan. The domain Archaea corresponds to the kingdom Archaebacteria.

The domain Eukarya includes the four remaining kingdoms: Protista, Fungi, Plantae, and Animalia. All members of the domain Eukarya have cells with a nucleus. Most members of the kingdom Protista are unicellular organisms. Some Protista are autotrophs; others, heterotrophs. Most members of the kingdom Fungi are multicellular, and all are heterotrophs. All members of the kingdom Plantae are multicellular autotrophs. Most plants cannot move about, and their cells have cell walls. All members of the kingdom Animalia are multicellular heterotrophs. Most animals can move about, and their cells lack cell walls.

Section 18–1 Finding Order in Diversity
(pages 447–450)

🔑 Key Concepts
- How are living things organized for study?
- What is binomial nomenclature?
- What is Linnaeus's system of classification?

Why Classify? (page 447)

1. Why do biologists use a classification system to study the diversity of life?

   _____

   _____

2. The science of classifying organisms and assigning them universally accepted names is known as _____.

3. Is the following sentence true or false? In a good system of classification, organisms placed into a particular group are less similar to each other than they are to organisms in other groups. _____

Assigning Scientific Names (page 448)

4. Why is it confusing to refer to organisms by common names? _____

   _____

   _____

   _____

5. Circle the letter of each sentence that is true about early efforts at naming organisms.
   a. Names were usually in English.
   b. Names often described detailed physical characteristics of a species.
   c. Names could be very long.
   d. It was difficult to standardize the names.

6. The two-word naming system developed by Linnaeus is called _____

   _____.

7. Circle the letter of each sentence that is true about binomial nomenclature.
   a. The system is no longer in use today.
   b. Each species is assigned a two-part scientific name.
   c. The scientific name is always written in italics.
   d. The second part of the scientific name is capitalized.

8. What is the genus of the grizzly bear, *Ursus arctos*? _____

   _____

Linnaeus's System of Classification (pages 449–450)

9. A group or level of organization in taxonomy is called a taxonomic category, or

_____.

10. The largest taxonomic category in Linnaeus's system of classification is the

_____, and the smallest is the _____.

11. What two kingdoms did Linnaeus name? _____

_____

12. Fill in the name of each missing taxonomic category in the chart below.

Grizzly bear	Black bear	Giant panda	Red fox	Abert squirrel	Coral snake	Sea star	
							KINGDOM Animalia
							Chordata
							Mammalia
							Carnivora
							Ursidae
							Ursus
							SPECIES *Ursus arctos*

Reading Skill Practice

Taking notes can help you identify and remember the most important information when you read. Take notes on Section 18–1 by writing the main headings and under each heading listing the most important points. Include in your notes the boldface terms and sentences. Do your work on a separate sheet of paper.

Section 18–2 Modern Evolutionary Classification (pages 451–455)

⊂⊃ **Key Concepts**
- How are evolutionary relationships important in classification?
- How can DNA and RNA help scientists determine evolutionary relationships?

Introduction (page 451)

1. What traits did Linnaeus consider when classifying organisms? _____
_____
_____
_____

Which Similarities Are Most Important? (page 451)

2. What problems are faced by taxonomists who rely on body-structure comparisons?
_____
_____
_____
_____

Evolutionary Classification (page 452)

3. Is the following sentence true or false? Darwin's theory of evolution changed the way biologists thought about classification. _____

4. How do biologists now group organisms into categories? _____
_____
_____
_____

5. Is the following sentence true or false? Genera placed within a family should be less closely related to one another than to members of any other family. _____

6. The strategy of grouping organisms together based on their evolutionary history is called _____.

Classification Using Cladograms (page 453)

7. Circle the letter of each sentence that is true about cladistic analysis.

   a. It considers only traits that are evolutionary innovations.

   b. It considers all traits that can be measured.

   c. It considers only similarities in body structure.

   d. It is a method of evolutionary classification.

8. Characteristics that appear in recent parts of a lineage, but not in its older members, are called _____.

9. A diagram that shows the evolutionary relationships among a group of organisms is called a(an) _____.

10. Is the following sentence true or false? Derived characters are used to construct a cladogram. _____

Similarities in DNA and RNA (page 454)

11. Is the following sentence true or false? Some organisms do not have DNA or RNA.

_____

12. How do similarities in genes show that humans and yeasts share a common ancestry?

_____

_____

_____

_____

Molecular Clocks (page 455)

13. A model that uses DNA comparisons to estimate the length of time that two species have been evolving independently is known as a(an) _____.

14. A molecular clock relies on the repeating process of _____.

15. Why are only neutral mutations useful for molecular clocks? _____

_____

_____

_____

_____

16. Is the following sentence true or false? The degree of dissimilarity in DNA sequences is an indication of how long ago two species shared a common ancestor.

_____

17. Why are there many molecular clocks in a genome instead of just one?

_____

_____

Section 18–3 Kingdoms and Domains (pages 457–461)

🔑 Key Concepts
- What are the six kingdoms of life as they are now identified?
- What is the three-domain system of classification?

The Tree of Life Evolves (pages 457–458)

1. Is the following sentence true or false? The scientific view of life was more complex in Linnaeus's time. _____

2. What fundamental traits did Linnaeus use to separate plants from animals?

   _____

   _____

   _____

3. What type of organisms were later placed in the kingdom Protista?

   _____

   _____

4. Mushrooms, yeast, and molds have been placed in their own kingdom, which is called_____ .

5. Why did scientists place bacteria in their own kingdom, the Monera? _____

   _____

   _____

6. List the two groups into which the Monera have been separated.

   a. _____

   b. _____

7. Complete the concept map.

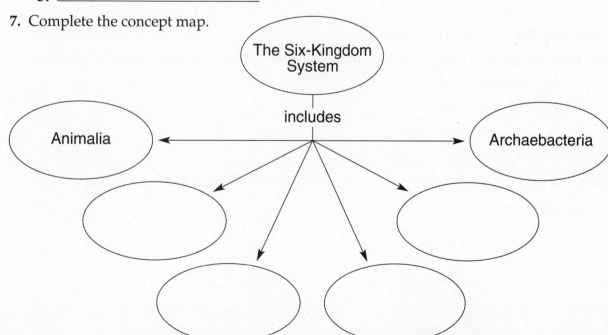

The Three-Domain System (page 458)

8. A more inclusive category than any other, including the kingdom, is the

   _____.

9. What type of analyses have scientists used to group modern organisms into

   domains? _____

10. List the three domains.

    a. _____

    b. _____

    c. _____

11. Complete the chart below.

CLASSIFICATION OF LIVING THINGS

Domain	Kingdom	Examples
	Eubacteria	*Streptococcus, Escherichia coli*
Archaea		
	Protist	
		Mushrooms, yeasts
	Plantae	
		Sponges, worms, insects, fishes, mammals

Domain Bacteria (page 459)

12. Circle the letter of each sentence that is true about members of the domain Bacteria.

    a. They are multicellular.

    b. They are prokaryotes.

    c. They have rigid cell walls.

    d. The cell walls contain peptidoglycans.

13. Is the following sentence true or false? All members of the domain Bacteria are

    parasites. _____

Domain Archaea (page 459)

14. Circle the letter of each sentence that is true about members of the domain Archaea.

    a. They are unicellular.   **c.** They lack cell walls.

    b. They are eukaryotes.   **d.** They lack cell membranes.

15. Is the following sentence true or false? Many members of the domain Archaea can survive only in the absence of oxygen. _____

Domain Eukarya (pages 460–461)

16. Circle the letter of each sentence that is true about all the members of the domain Eukarya.

    a. They have a nucleus.

    b. They are multicellular.

    c. They are heterotrophs.

    d. They have cell walls and chloroplasts.

Match each kingdom with the description that applies to members of that kingdom.

	Kingdom	Description
_____	**17.** Protista	**a.** They have cell walls of chitin.
_____	**18.** Fungi	**b.** They have no cell walls or chloroplasts.
_____	**19.** Plantae	**c.** They include slime molds and giant kelp.
_____	**20.** Animalia	**d.** They include mosses and ferns.

Name_____ Class _____ Date _____

Vocabulary Review

Crossword Puzzle   *Complete the puzzle by entering the term that matches each numbered description.*

Across

7. type of classification that is based on evolutionary history
8. discipline of classifying and naming organisms
10. taxon composed of similar orders
11. taxon composed of similar classes
12. type of clock that estimates how long species have been evolving independently

Down

1. kingdom in the Eukarya domain that includes single-celled autotrophs
2. study of evolutionary relationships among organisms
3. new taxon that is higher than the kingdom
4. taxon composed of similar genera
5. taxon composed of closely related species
6. diagram based on derived characters
8. general term for any level, or category, in a taxonomic system
9. taxon composed of similar families

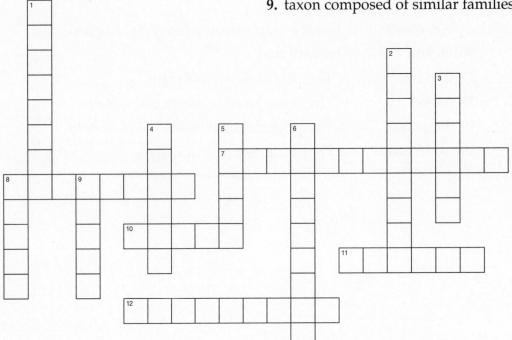

Answering Questions   *Write one or more sentences to answer each question.*

13. In what ways are members of the domain Bacteria and the domain Archaea similar?

_____

_____

14. Which domain includes only organisms with a nucleus in their cells? _____

_____

15. What are two ways that most members of the kingdom Plantae and the kingdom Animalia differ? _____

_____

Summary

19–1 Bacteria

The smallest and most common microorganisms are prokaryotes, which are unicellular organisms that lack a nucleus. Prokaryotes are divided into two kingdoms: Eubacteria and Archaebacteria. Eubacteria live almost everywhere. Eubacteria are usually surrounded by a cell wall, which contains a carbohydrate called peptidoglycan. Inside the cell wall is a cell membrane that surrounds the cytoplasm. Archaebacteria look very similar to eubacteria. Archaebacteria lack the peptidoglycan of eubacteria and have different membrane lipids. Also, the DNA sequences of key archaebacterial genes are more like those of eukaryotes than those of eubacteria. Archaebacteria may be the ancestors of eukaryotes.

Prokaryotes are identified by characteristics such as shape, the chemical nature of their cell walls, the way they move, and the way they obtain energy. Three differently shaped prokaryotes are bacilli, cocci, and spirilla. Bacilli (singular: bacillus) are rod-shaped; cocci (singular: coccus) are sphere-shaped; and spirilla (singular: spirillum) are spiral or corkscrew-shaped. Two different types of cell walls are found in prokaryotes. A method called Gram staining is used to tell them apart. Gram-positive bacteria appear violet when stained, while Gram-negative bacteria appear pink. Prokaryotes move in a variety of ways.

Most prokaryotes are heterotrophs—organisms that obtain energy by consuming other organisms. Other prokaryotes are autotrophs, organisms that can make their own food. Heterotrophic prokaryotes include chemoheterotrophs and photoheterotrophs. Autotrophic prokaryotes include photoautotrophs and chemoautotrophs.

Prokaryotes release energy by both cellular respiration and fermentation. Organisms that require a constant supply of oxygen to live are called obligate aerobes. Organisms that do not require oxygen are called obligate anaerobes. Organisms that can survive with or without oxygen are called facultative anaerobes.

When a bacterium has grown so that it has nearly doubled, it replicates its DNA and divides in half, producing two identical "daughter" cells. This asexual reproduction is called binary fission. Bacteria are also able to exchange genetic information by a process called conjugation. Many bacteria can form an endospore when conditions are bad.

Bacteria are vital to maintaining the living world. Some are producers that carry out photosynthesis. Others are decomposers that break down dead matter. Some soil bacteria convert natural nitrogen gas into a form plants can use through a process called nitrogen fixation. Humans use bacteria in industry, food production, and other ways.

19–2 Viruses

Viruses are particles of nucleic acid, protein, and, in some cases, lipids. All viruses have one thing in common: They enter living cells and, once inside, use the machinery of the infected cell to produce more viruses. A typical virus is composed of a core of DNA or RNA surrounded by a protein coat. A virus's protein coat is called its capsid. Viruses that infect bacteria are called bacteriophages.

Once the virus is inside a host cell, two different processes may occur. In a lytic infection, a virus enters a cell, makes copies of itself, and causes the cell to burst, releasing new virus particles that can attack other cells. The virus uses the materials of the host cell to make copies of its own DNA molecule. In a lysogenic infection, a virus integrates its DNA into the DNA of the host cell, and the viral genetic information replicates along with the host cell's DNA. The viral DNA that is embedded in the host's DNA is called a prophage. The prophage may remain part of the DNA of the host cell for many generations. Eventually, the prophage will remove itself from the host cell DNA and make new virus particles.

Some viruses, called retroviruses, contain RNA as their genetic information. In a retrovirus, the genetic information is copied backward—from RNA to DNA instead of from DNA to RNA. The virus that causes the disease AIDS is a retrovirus.

Viruses must infect a living cell in order to reproduce. Viruses are parasites. Because viruses are not made up of cells and cannot live independently, viruses are not considered to be living things.

19–3 Diseases Caused by Bacteria and Viruses

Disease-causing agents are known as pathogens. Bacteria and viruses can cause disease. Not all bacteria are pathogens. Some live in and on the human body and help the body perform essential functions. Other bacteria can produce human diseases such as tuberculosis, strep throat, and tooth decay.

Bacteria produce disease in one of two general ways. Some bacteria damage the cells and tissues of the infected organism directly by breaking down the cells for food. Other bacteria release toxins (poisons) that travel throughout the body interfering with the normal activity of the host.

Many bacterial diseases can be prevented by using a vaccine. A vaccine is a preparation of weakened or killed pathogens. A vaccine can prompt the body to produce immunity to the disease. Immunity is the body's natural way of killing pathogens. When a bacterial infection does occur, antibiotics can be used to fight the disease. Antibiotics are compounds that block the growth and reproduction of bacteria. Animals also suffer from bacterial diseases.

There are various methods to control bacterial growth, including sterilization, disinfectants, and food storage and food processing. Disinfectants include soaps and cleaning solutions. Food storage includes using a refrigerator.

Viruses produce disease by disrupting the body's normal equilibrium. In many viral infections, viruses attack and destroy certain body cells, causing the symptoms of the disease. Viral diseases in humans include the common cold, influenza, AIDS, chickenpox, and measles. Viruses produce other serious diseases in both animals and plants.

Two other viruslike particles can cause disease. Viroids are single-stranded RNA molecules that have no surrounding capsids. Viroids cause disease in plants. Prions are particles that contain only protein—there is no DNA or RNA. Prions cause disease in animals, including humans.

Section 19–1 Bacteria (pages 471–477)

🔑 Key Concepts
- How do the two groups of prokaryotes differ?
- What factors are used to identify prokaryotes?
- What is the importance of bacteria?

Introduction (page 471)

1. What are prokaryotes? _____

_____

2. Is the following sentence true or false? Prokaryotes are much smaller than most

   eukaryotic cells. _____

Classifying Prokaryotes (pages 471–472)

3. What are the two different groups of prokaryotes?

   a. _____   b. _____

4. Which is the larger of the two kingdoms of prokaryotes? _____

5. Where do eubacteria live? _____

_____

6. What protects a prokaryotic cell from injury? _____

_____

7. Circle the letter of what is within the cell wall of a prokaryote.

   a. another cell wall   c. archaebacteria

   b. cell membrane   d. pili

8. What is peptidoglycan? _____

_____

9. Some eubacteria have a second _____ outside the cell membrane.

10. Circle the letter of each sentence that is true about archaebacteria.

    a. Their membrane lipids are different from those of eubacteria.

    b. They lack a cell wall.

    c. They lack peptidoglycan.

    d. They look very similar to eubacteria.

11. What is significant about the DNA sequences of key archaebacterial genes?

_____

_____

12. How are archaebacteria related to eukaryotes? _____

_____

13. What are methanogens, and where do they live? _____

_____

_____

Identifying Prokaryotes (page 473)

14. Complete the illustration of a typical prokaryote by labeling the parts.

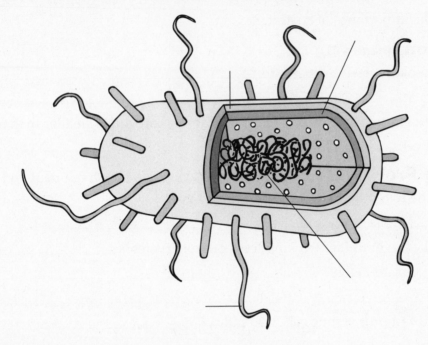

15. What are four characteristics used to identify prokaryotes?

a. _____

b. _____

c. _____

d. _____

16. What are each of the differently shaped prokaryotes called?

a. The rod-shaped are called _____.

b. The spherical-shaped are called _____.

c. The corkscrew-shaped are called _____.

17. A method of telling two different types of eubacteria apart by using dyes is called

_____.

18. What colors are Gram-positive and Gram-negative bacteria under the microscope

when treated with Gram stain? _____

_____

19. What are flagella? _____

20. Is the following sentence true or false? Some prokaryotes do not move at all.

_____

Metabolic Diversity (pages 473–474)

21. Complete the table about prokaryotes classified by the way they obtain energy.

GROUPS OF PROKARYOTES

Group	Description
	Organism that carries out photosynthesis in a manner similar to that of plants
Chemoautotroph	
	Organism that takes in organic molecules and then breaks them down
Photoheterotroph	

22. Members of which group of photoautotrophs contain a bluish pigment and chlorophyll *a*? _____

23. How do the chemoautotrophs that live near hydrothermal vents on the ocean floor obtain energy? _____

_____

24. Complete the table about prokaryotes classified by the way they release energy.

GROUPS OF PROKARYOTES

Group	Description
	Organisms that require a constant supply of oxygen
Obligate anaerobes	
Facultative anaerobes	

25. Facultative anaerobes can switch between cellular respiration and _____.

Growth and Reproduction (page 475)

26. What occurs in the process of binary fission? _____

_____

_____

27. What occurs during conjugation? _____

_____

28. Is the following sentence true or false? Most prokaryotes reproduce by conjugation.

_____

© Pearson Education, Inc., publishing as Pearson Prentice Hall.

29. What is an endospore? _____

_____

_____

Importance of Bacteria (pages 476–477)

30. How do decomposers help the ecosystem recycle nutrients when a tree dies?

_____

_____

_____

31. What would happen to plants and animals if decomposers did not recycle nutrients?

_____

_____

32. Why do plants and animals need nitrogen? _____

_____

_____

33. How does nitrogen fixation help plants? _____

34. What kind of relationship do many plants have with nitrogen-fixing bacteria?

_____

35. How can bacteria be used to clean up an oil spill? _____

_____

36. What have biotechnology companies begun to realize about bacteria adapted

to extreme environments? _____

_____

_____

Reading Skill Practice

Writing a summary can help you remember the information you have read. When you write a summary, write only the most important points. Write a summary of the information under the green heading Decomposers. Your summary should be shorter than the text on which it is based. Do your work on a separate sheet of paper.

Section 19–2 Viruses (pages 478–483)

🔑 **Key Concepts**
- What is the structure of a virus?
- How do viruses cause infection?

What Is a Virus? (pages 478–479)

1. What are viruses? _____

_____

2. What do all viruses have in common? _____

_____

_____

3. Is the following sentence true or false? Most viruses are so small that they can be seen only with the aid of a powerful electron microscope. _____

4. What is the structure of a typical virus? _____

_____

5. Complete the illustration of a T4 bacteriophage by labeling the parts.

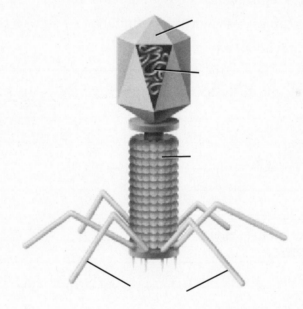

6. A virus's protein coat is called a(an) _____.

7. How does a typical virus get inside a cell? _____

_____

_____

Name_____ Class_____ Date _____

8. What occurs when viruses get inside cells? _____

_____

_____

_____

9. Why are most viruses highly specific to the cells they infect? _____

_____

_____

10. What are bacteriophages? _____

Viral Infection (pages 480–481)

11. Why is a lytic infection given that name? _____

_____

12. Circle the letter of each sentence that is true about a lysogenic infection.

    a. The virus lyses the host cell immediately.

    b. The virus embeds its DNA into the host's DNA.

    c. The virus's DNA is replicated along with the host cell's DNA.

    d. A host cell makes copies of the virus indefinitely.

13. Complete the flowchart about a lytic infection.

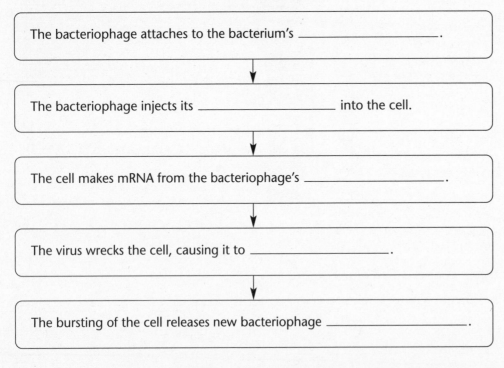

The bacteriophage attaches to the bacterium's _____.

↓

The bacteriophage injects its _____ into the cell.

↓

The cell makes mRNA from the bacteriophage's _____.

↓

The virus wrecks the cell, causing it to _____.

↓

The bursting of the cell releases new bacteriophage _____.

14. What is a prophage? _____

_____

Retroviruses (page 482)

15. What are retroviruses? _____

_____

16. What happens when retroviruses infect a cell? _____

_____

_____

Viruses and Living Cells (pages 482–483)

17. Circle the letter of each reason why some biologists do not consider viruses to be alive.

   a. They can't infect living cells.

   b. They can't evolve.

   c. They can't regulate gene expression.

   d. They can't reproduce independently.

18. Complete the table comparing viruses and cells.

Virus and Cells

Characteristic	Virus	Cell
Structure	DNA or RNA core, capsid	Cell membrane, cytoplasm; eukaryotes also contain nucleus and organelles
Reproduction		Independent cell division either asexually or sexually
Genetic Code		DNA
Growth and Development	No	
Obtain and Use Energy		Yes
Response to the Environment	No	
Change Over Time		

Section 19–3 Diseases Caused by Bacteria and Viruses (pages 485–490)

⬤ Key Concepts
- How do bacteria cause disease?
- How can bacterial growth be controlled?
- How do viruses cause disease?

Bacterial Disease in Humans (pages 485–486)

1. What are pathogens? _____

2. What are the two general ways that bacteria cause disease?

   a. _____

   _____

   b. _____

   _____

3. What kind of tissue do the bacteria that cause tuberculosis break down?

   _____

4. What are antibiotics? _____

   _____

5. What do you think is one of the major reasons for the dramatic increase in life expectancy during the past two centuries? _____

   _____

   _____

Bacterial Disease in Animals (page 486)

6. What is one example of a bacterial disease in animals? _____

   _____

Controlling Bacteria (pages 487–488)

7. What is sterilization? _____

8. A chemical solution that kills pathogenic bacteria is called a(an) _____.

9. Why will food stored at low temperatures keep longer? _____

   _____

   _____

Viral Disease in Humans (page 488)

10. What are some human diseases that viruses cause? _____

    _____

    _____

© Pearson Education, Inc., publishing as Pearson Prentice Hall.

Viral Disease in Animals (page 489)

11. What is one example of a viral disease in animals? _____

_____

12. Cancer-causing viruses are known as _____.

Viral Disease in Plants (page 489)

13. Why do plant viruses have a difficult time entering the cells they infect? _____

_____

_____

14. How are most plant viruses spread? _____

Viroids and Prions (page 490)

15. What are viroids? _____

_____

16. A disease-causing particle that contains only protein and not DNA or RNA is called

a(an) _____.

Chapter 19   Bacteria and Viruses

Vocabulary Review

Matching   *In the space provided, write the letter of the definition that best matches each term.*

_____   **1.** lysogenic infection

_____   **2.** eubacteria

_____   **3.** chemoautotroph

_____   **4.** toxin

_____   **5.** prion

_____   **6.** bacteriophage

_____   **7.** coccus

_____   **8.** chemoheterotroph

_____   **9.** antibiotic

_____   **10.** virus

_____   **11.** prokaryote

_____   **12.** spirillum

_____   **13.** prophage

_____   **14.** pathogen

_____   **15.** lytic infection

_____   **16.** endospore

_____   **17.** bacillus

_____   **18.** binary fission

_____   **19.** obligate anaerobe

_____   **20.** vaccine

a. spiral-shaped bacterium

b. pathogen that causes disease in animals by forming a protein clump

c. rod-shaped bacterium

d. organism that must take in organic molecules for both energy and a supply of carbon

e. a particle of nucleic acid, protein, and in some cases, lipids

f. process in which viral DNA becomes part of a host cell's DNA

g. disease-causing agent

h. spherical bacterium

i. process in which a host cell bursts after being invaded by a virus

j. organism consisting of one cell that lacks a nucleus

k. process in which a bacterium replicates its DNA and divides in half

l. organism that obtains energy from inorganic molecules

m. spore formed by bacteria when growth conditions become unfavorable

n. virus that infects bacteria

o. viral DNA that is embedded in the host's DNA

p. substance produced by some bacteria that poisons host cells

q. preparation of weakened or killed pathogens

r. compound that can destroy bacteria

s. organism that can live only in an oxygen-free environment

t. the larger of the two kingdoms of prokaryotes

Summary

20–1 The Kingdom Protista

The kingdom Protista is a diverse group. Protists are eukaryotes that are not members of the kingdoms Plantae, Animalia, or Fungi. Most protists are unicellular. The first eukaryotic organisms on Earth were protists.

Protists, which first appeared about 1.5 billion years ago, were the first group of eukaryotes to evolve. One explanation for the way the first eukaryotes developed from prokaryotes has been credited to Lynn Margulis. Margulis's hypothesis states that the first eukaryote—and the first protist—was formed by a symbiosis among several prokaryotes. Evidence to support this hypothesis includes structural similarities between certain eukaryotic organelles and bacteria.

Because protists are such a diverse group, scientists don't always agree on how to classify them. One way to classify protists is according to the way they obtain nutrition. There are animallike protists, plantlike protists, and funguslike protists.

20–2 Animallike Protists: Protozoans

Animallike protists—also called protozoans—are heterotrophs. The four phyla of animallike protists are classified according to they way they move.

Animallike protists that swim using flagella are classified in the phylum Zoomastigina. They are called zooflagellates. Members of the phylum Sarcodina move by means of temporary projections of cytoplasm known as pseudopods. Sarcodines use pseudopods for feeding and movement. Sarcodines called amoebas have thick pseudopods. The phylum Ciliophora is named for cilia, which are short hairlike projections similar to flagella. Ciliates use cilia for feeding and movement. Some of the best-known ciliates belong to the genus *Paramecium*. Members of the phylum Sporozoa are parasites and do not move on their own. Sporozoans reproduce by means of sporozoites.

Some animallike protists cause serious diseases. The sporozoan *Plasmodium* causes malaria. The zooflagellate *Trypanosoma* causes African sleeping sickness. Some animallike protists are beneficial to organisms. *Trichonympha* lives within the digestive system of termites and helps termites digest wood.

20–3 Plantlike Protists: Unicellular Algae

Plantlike protists are commonly called algae. Plantlike protists include four phyla that contain unicellular organisms. One of the key traits used to classify algae is the photosynthetic pigments they contain. Chlorophyll includes three forms. Each form absorbs a different wavelength of light. Many algae also have compounds called accessory pigments that absorb light at different wavelengths than chlorophyll.

Euglenophytes—members of the phylum Euglenophyta—are plantlike protists that have two flagella but no cell wall. Euglenophytes have chloroplasts, but in most other ways they are like the protozoans called zooflagellates.

Chrysophytes—members of the phylum Chrysophyta—are a diverse group of plantlike protists that have gold-colored chloroplasts. Diatoms—members of the phylum Bacillariophyta—produce thin, delicate cell walls rich in silicon. Silicon (Si) is the main component of glass. These walls are shaped like the two sides of a petri dish or a flat pillbox.

Dinoflagellates—members of the phylum Pyrrophyta—generally have two flagella. About half of the dinoflagellates are photosynthetic. The other half live as heterotrophs.

Plantlike protists play a major ecological role on Earth by being a considerable part of the phytoplankton. Phytoplankton are made up of the population of small photosynthetic organisms found near the surface of the ocean. Many protists grow rapidly in regions where sewage is dumped into water. When the amount of waste is excessive, algae grow into enormous masses called algal blooms.

20–4 Plantlike Protists: Red, Brown, and Green Algae

Three phyla of plantlike protists contain mostly multicellular organisms. The most important differences among these phyla are their photosynthetic pigments. Red algae—members of phylum Rhodophyta—are able to live at great depths due to their efficiency in harvesting light energy. Red algae contain chlorophyll *a* and reddish accessory pigments called phycobilins.

Brown algae—members of the phylum Phaeophyta—contain chlorophyll *a* and *c* as well as a brown accessory pigment called fucoxanthin. The largest alga is giant kelp, a brown alga that grows to be more than 60 meters in length.

Green algae—members of the phylum Chlorophyta—share many characteristics with plants. They share the same photosynthetic pigments, chlorophyll *a* and *b*. Both plants and green algae have cellulose in their cell walls. Also, green algae are like plants in that they store food in the form of starch. These shared characteristics lead scientists to hypothesize that the ancestors of modern land plants looked like green algae. Green algae include the unicellular *Chlamydomonas*. Several species of green algae live in multicellular colonies. *Ulva*, called "sea lettuce," is a true multicellular green alga.

The life cycles of many algae include both a diploid and a haploid generation. The process of switching back and forth between haploid stages and diploid stages in a life cycle is called alternation of generations.

Algae produce much of Earth's oxygen through photosynthesis. Algae are a major food source in the oceans. People also use algae for food. Industry uses algae in making plastics and other products.

20–5 Funguslike Protists

Funguslike protists are like fungi in that they are heterotrophs that absorb food from dead or decaying organic matter. Unlike most true fungi, though, funguslike protists have centrioles. They also lack the chitin cell walls of true fungi.

Slime molds are funguslike protists that play key roles in recycling organic material. At one stage of their life cycle, slime molds look just like amoebas. At other stages, they form moldlike clumps that produce spores, almost like fungi. In cellular slime molds, individual cells remain distinct during every phase of the life cycle. They spend most of their lives as free-living cells. In acellular slime molds, cells fuse to form large cells with many nuclei. These structures are known as plasmodia. Fruiting bodies, or sporangia, spring up from a plasmodium.

Water molds, or oomycetes, are members of the phylum Oomycota. Oomycetes thrive on dead or decaying organic matter in water. Some oomycetes are plant parasites on land.

Slime molds and water molds are important recyclers of organic material. Some funguslike protists can cause diseases in plants. An oomycete caused a disease in the Irish potato crop in 1845 and 1846, leading to mass starvation.

Chapter 20 Protists

Section 20–1 The Kingdom Protista (pages 497–498)

🔑 **Key Concept**
- What are protists?

What Is a Protist? (page 497)

1. What is a protist? _____

_____

2. Circle the letter of each sentence that is true about protists.

   a. All are unicellular.

   b. All cells have a nucleus.

   c. All cells have membrane-bound organelles.

   d. All are multicellular.

3. Why are some organisms that consist of thousands of cells considered to be protists?

_____

_____

Evolution of Protists (page 498)

4. The first eukaryotic organisms on Earth were _____.

5. What is biologist Lynn Margulis's hypothesis about where the first protists came from?

_____

_____

_____

_____

_____

Classification of Protists (page 498)

6. Complete the table about protist classification.

GROUPS OF PROTISTS

Group	Method of Obtaining Food
	Consume other organisms
Plantlike protists	
Funguslike protists	

7. What don't categories of protists based on the way they obtain food reflect about these organisms? _____

_____

Reading Skill Practice

By looking at illustrations in textbooks, you can help yourself remember better what you have read. Look carefully at Figure 20–1 on page 497. What important idea do these photographs communicate? Do your work on a separate sheet of paper.

Section 20–2 Animallike Protists: Protozoans
(pages 499–505)

Key Concepts
- What are the distinguishing features of the major phyla of animallike protists?
- How do animallike protists harm other living things?

Introduction (page 499)

1. At one time, what were all animallike protists called? _____

2. How are the four phyla of animallike protists distinguished from one another?

_____

_____

Zooflagellates (page 499)

3. What kind of protists are classified in the phylum Zoomastigina? _____

_____

4. How many flagella does a zooflagellate have? _____

_____

5. Zooflagellates reproduce asexually by means of _____.

6. Is the following sentence true or false? Some zooflagellates have a sexual life cycle.

_____

Sarcodines (page 500)

7. Sarcodines are members of the phylum _____.

8. What are pseudopods? _____

_____

9. What do sarcodines use pseudopods for? _____

10. The best known sarcodines are the _____.

11. What is amoeboid movement? _____

_____

12. What is a food vacuole? _____

_____

13. How do amoebas capture and digest food? _____

_____

_____

14. Amoebas reproduce by means of _____.

15. Circle the letter of each example of a sarcodine.

   a. foraminiferan   **b.** paramecium   **c.** amoeba   **d.** heliozoan

Ciliates (pages 501–502)

16. Ciliates are members of the phylum _____.

17. What are cilia? _____

18. What do ciliates use cilia for? _____

Match the ciliate structure with its description.

Structure	Description
_____ **19.** Trichocysts	**a.** Indentation on one side of a ciliate into which food is swept
_____ **20.** Macronucleus	**b.** Smaller nucleus containing a "reserve copy" of the cell's genes
_____ **21.** Micronucleus	**c.** Small, bottle-shaped structures used for defense
_____ **22.** Gullet	**d.** Region of cell membrane where waste-containing food vacuoles fuse
_____ **23.** Anal pore	**e.** Larger nucleus containing multiple copies of most of the cell's genes
_____ **24.** Contractile vacuole	**f.** Cavity in cytoplasm specialized to collect and pump out water

25. Label the illustration of a paramecium.

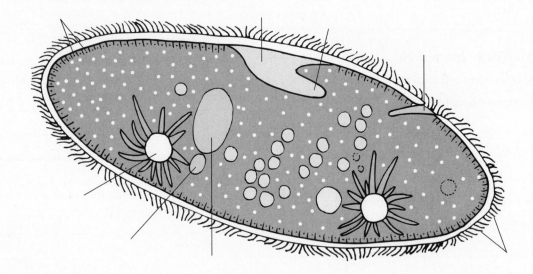

26. What is conjugation? _____

_____

27. Within a large population, how does conjugation benefit ciliates? _____

_____

Sporozoans (page 502)

28. Sporozoans are members of the phylum _____.

29. Circle the letter of each sentence that is true about sporozoans.

a. They are parasitic.   c. All have only one host.

b. They do not move on their own.   d. They reproduce by means of sporozoites.

Animallike Protists and Disease (pages 503–504)

30. What causes malaria? _____

_____

31. Complete the flowchart about the cycle of malarial infection.

An infected *Anopheles* mosquito bites a human and deposits *Plasmodium* spores into the

_____.

↓

The spores travel to the _____.

↓

Infected liver cells burst, releasing parasites that infect _____ cells.

↓

The human experiences the symptoms of _____.

↓

A mosquito bites the infected human and picks up the _____ cells.

Ecology of Animallike Protists (page 505)

32. Is the following sentence true or false? Some animallike protists recycle nutrients by breaking down dead organic matter. _____

33. How does the zooflagellate *Trichonympha* make it possible for termites to eat wood?

_____

_____

_____

_____

Section 20–3 Plantlike Protists: Unicellular Algae (pages 506–509)

Key Concepts

- What is the function of chlorophyll and accessory pigments in algae?
- What are the distinguishing features of the major phyla of unicellular algae?

Introduction (page 506)

1. Plantlike protists are commonly called _____.

2. Is the following sentence true or false? Algae include only multicellular organisms.

_____

Chlorophyll and Accessory Pigments (page 506)

3. In the process of photosynthesis, what substances trap the energy of sunlight?

_____

_____

4. How does water affect the sunlight that passes through it? _____

_____

5. Why does the dim blue light that penetrates deep into the sea contain little energy that chlorophyll *a* can use? _____

_____

6. How have various groups of algae adapted to conditions of limited light?

_____

_____

7. What are accessory pigments? _____

_____

8. Why are algae such a wide range of colors? _____

_____

_____

Euglenophytes (page 507)

9. Euglenophytes are members of the phylum _____.

10. Circle the letter of each sentence that is true about euglenophytes.

   a. They are remarkably similar to zooflagellates.

   b. They possess chloroplasts.

   c. They have a cell wall.

   d. They have two flagella.

© Pearson Education, Inc., publishing as Pearson Prentice Hall.

11. What is an eyespot, and what is its function? _____

_____

_____

12. Euglenas have a tough, intricate membrane called a(an) _____.

13. How do euglenas reproduce? _____

14. Label the illustration of a euglena.

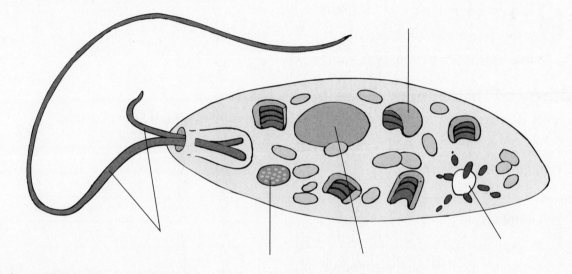

Chrysophytes (page 507)

15. The yellow-green algae and the golden-brown algae are members of the phylum

_____.

16. What color are the chloroplasts of chrysophytes? _____

17. Circle the letter of each sentence that is true about chrysophytes.

    a. The cell walls of some contain the carbohydrate pectin.

    b. They reproduce sexually but not asexually.

    c. They generally store food in the form of oil.

    d. Some form threadlike colonies.

Diatoms (page 507)

18. Diatoms are members of the phylum _____.

19. Circle the letter of each sentence that is true about diatoms.

    a. They are very rare in almost all environments.

    b. Their cell walls are rich in silicon.

    c. They are shaped like a petri dish or flat pillbox.

    d. They are among the most abundant organisms on Earth.

Dinoflagellates (page 508)

20. Dinoflagellates are members of the phylum _____.

21. How do dinoflagellates obtain nutrition? _____

_____

22. Circle the letter of each sentence that is true about dinoflagellates.

    a. They generally have one flagellum.

    b. Many species are luminescent.

    c. Most reproduce by binary fission.

Ecology of Unicellular Algae (pages 508–509)

23. How do plantlike protists make much of the diversity of aquatic life possible?

_____

24. What are phytoplankton? _____

_____

25. What are algal blooms? _____

_____

26. How can an algal bloom be harmful? _____

_____

_____

_____

Section 20–4 Plantlike Protists: Red, Brown, and Green Algae (pages 510–515)

🔑 Key Concepts
- What are the distinguishing features of the major phyla of multicellular algae?
- How do multicellular algae reproduce?

Introduction (page 510)

1. What are seaweeds? _____

2. What are the most important differences among the three phyla of multicellular algae?

_____

_____

Red Algae (page 510)

3. Red algae are members of the phylum _____.

4. Why are red algae able to live at great depths? _____

_____

5. What pigments do red algae contain? _____

_____

6. Which color of light are phycobilins especially good at absorbing?

   a. red   **b.** green   **c.** yellow   **d.** blue

7. Circle the letter of each sentence that is true about red algae.

   a. They can grow in the ocean at depths up to 260 meters.

   b. Most are unicellular.

   c. All are red or reddish-brown.

   d. Coralline algae play an important role in coral reef formation.

Brown Algae (page 511)

8. Brown algae are members of the phylum _____.

9. What pigments do brown algae contain? _____

_____

Match each structure with its description.

	Structure	Description
_____	**10.** Holdfast	**a.** Flattened stemlike structure
_____	**11.** Stipe	**b.** Gas-filled swelling
_____	**12.** Blade	**c.** Structure that attaches alga to the bottom
_____	**13.** Bladder	**d.** Leaflike structure

14. Where are brown algae commonly found growing? _____

_____

15. What is the largest known alga? _____

Green Algae (pages 511–512)

16. Green algae are members of the phylum _____.

17. What characteristics do green algae share with plants? _____

_____

18. What do scientists think is the connection between mosses and green algae?

_____

19. The freshwater alga *Spirogyra* forms long threadlike colonies called

_____.

20. How can the cells in a *Volvox* colony coordinate movement? _____

_____

21. "Sea lettuce" is the multicellular alga _____.

Reproduction in Green Algae (pages 512–514)

22. What occurs in the process known as alternation of generations? _____

_____

_____

23. The single-celled *Chlamydomonas* reproduces asexually by producing

_____.

24. Circle the letter of each sentence that is true about sexual reproduction in
Chlamydomonas.

    a. If conditions become unfavorable, cells release gametes.

    b. Paired gametes form a diploid zygote.

    c. A zygote quickly grows into an adult organism.

    d. The gametes are called male and female.

25. Complete the table about the generations in an organism's life cycle.

GENERATIONS IN A LIFE CYCLE

Generation	Definition	Diploid or Haploid?
	Gamete-producing phase	
	Spore-producing phase	

26. Complete the life cycle of *Ulva* by labeling the sporophyte, the male gametophyte, and the female gametophyte. Also, label the places where the processes of fertilization, mitosis, and meiosis occur.

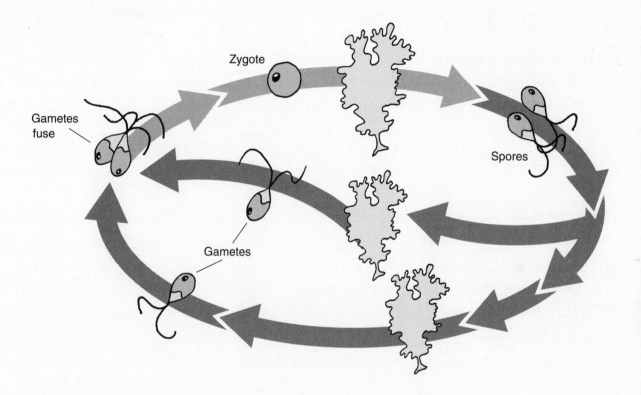

Human Uses of Algae (page 515)

27. Why have algae been called the "grasses" of the sea? _____

_____

28. Through photosynthesis, algae produce much of Earth's _____.

29. What is the compound agar derived from, and how is it used? _____

_____

_____

_____

Section 20–5 Funguslike Protists (pages 516–520)

Key Concepts
- What are the similarities and differences between funguslike protists and fungi?
- What are the defining characteristics of the slime molds and water molds?

Introduction (page 516)

1. How are funguslike protists like fungi? _____

_____

_____

2. How are funguslike protists unlike most true fungi? _____

_____

Slime Molds (pages 516–518)

3. What are slime molds? _____

_____

4. Cellular slime molds belong to the phylum _____.

5. Is the following sentence true or false? Cellular slime molds spend most of their lives as free-living cells. _____

6. What do cellular slime molds form when their food supply is exhausted? _____

_____

_____

7. What structure does a cellular slime mold colony produce, and what is that structure's function? _____

_____

_____

8. Acellular slime molds belong to the phylum _____.

9. What is a plasmodium? _____

_____

_____

10. The plasmodium eventually produces sporangia, which in turn produce haploid

_____.

Water Molds (pages 518–519)

11. Water molds, or oomycetes, are members of the phylum _____.

12. Water molds produce thin filaments known as _____.

13. What are zoosporangia? _____

_____

_____

14. Where are male and female nuclei produced in water mold sexual reproduction?

_____

_____

_____

15. Fertilization in water molds occurs in the _____.

Ecology of Funguslike Protists (page 519)

16. Why aren't there bodies of dead animals and plants littering the woods and fields you walk through? _____

_____

_____

17. What are examples of plant diseases that water molds cause? _____

_____

Water Molds and the Potato Famine (page 520)

18. What produced the Great Potato Famine of 1846? _____

_____

_____

19. What did the Great Potato Famine lead to? _____

_____

_____

Vocabulary Review

Matching   *In the space provided, write the letter of the description that best matches each organism.*

_____ **1.** sarcodines

_____ **2.** ciliates

_____ **3.** euglenophytes

_____ **4.** diatoms

_____ **5.** brown algae

_____ **6.** green algae

_____ **7.** slime molds

_____ **8.** water molds

a. unicellular algae that produce thin, delicate cell walls rich in silicon

b. funguslike protists that look just like amoebas at one stage of their life cycles

c. plantlike protists that share many characteristics with plants

d. protozoans that use pseudopods for feeding and movement

e. funguslike protists that thrive on dead or decaying organic matter in water

f. unicellular algae that have two flagella but no cell wall

g. protozoans that include those belonging to the genus *Paramecium*

h. multicellular algae that contain fucoxanthin

Completion   *Fill in the blanks with terms from Chapter 20.*

9. Any organism that is not a plant, an animal, a fungus, or a prokaryote is a(an)

_____.

10. A temporary cytoplasmic projection used in feeding and movement is called a(an)

_____.

11. The disease _____ is caused by the sporozoan *Plasmodium*.

12. Many algae have compounds called _____ pigments that absorb light at different wavelengths than chlorophyll.

13. _____ are the population of small, photosynthetic organisms found near the surface of the ocean.

14. The process of switching back and forth between haploid and diploid stages in a life cycle is known as _____ of generations.

15. The single structure with many nuclei produced by an acellular slime mold is called a(an) _____.

© Pearson Education, Inc., publishing as Pearson Prentice Hall.

Summary

21–1 The Kingdom Fungi

Fungi are eukaryotic heterotrophs that have cell walls. The cell walls of fungi are made up of chitin, a complex carbohydrate. Fungi do not ingest their food, as animals do. Instead, fungi digest food outside their bodies and then absorb it. Many fungi feed by absorbing nutrients from decaying matter. Some fungi are parasites.

All fungi except for yeasts are multicellular. Multicellular fungi are composed of thin filaments called hyphae. Each hypha is only one cell thick. The bodies of multicellular fungi are composed of many hyphae tangled together into a thick mass called a mycelium. The fruiting body of a fungus—such as the above-ground part of a mushroom—is a reproductive structure growing from the mycelium in the soil beneath it.

Most fungi reproduce both asexually and sexually. Asexual reproduction can occur when cells or hyphae break off and begin to grow on their own. Some fungi also produce spores. In some fungi, spores are produced in structures called sporangia. Sporangia are found at the tips of hyphae called sporangiophores. Sexual reproduction in fungi usually involves two different mating types.

Spores of fungi are found in almost every environment. Many fungi produce dry, almost weightless spores that are easily scattered in the wind.

21–2 Classification of Fungi

Fungi are classified according to their structure and method of reproduction. The four main groups of fungi are the common molds (phylum Zygomycota), the sac fungi (phylum Ascomycota), the club fungi (phylum Basidiomycota), and the imperfect fungi (Deuteromycota).

The common molds—zygomycetes—grow on meat, cheese, and bread. Zygomycetes have a life cycle that includes a zygospore. A zygospore is a resting spore that contains zygotes formed during the sexual phase of the mold's life cycle. The zygomycetes include the black bread mold, *Rhizopus stolonifer.* Black bread mold has two different kinds of hyphae. The rootlike hyphae that penetrate the bread's surface are rhizoids. The stemlike hyphae that run along the surface of bread are stolons. During the sexual phase in the bread mold, hyphae from different mating types fuse to produce gamete-forming structures called gametangia.

Sac fungi—ascomycetes—have a reproductive structure called an ascus, which contains spores. Sac fungi include the large cup fungi as well as the unicellular yeasts. The life cycle of an ascomycete includes both asexual and sexual reproduction. In asexual reproduction, tiny spores called conidia form at the tips of specialized hyphae called conidiophores. In sexual reproduction, haploid hyphae from two different mating types (+ and −) grow close together and produce a fruiting body. An ascus forms within the fruiting body. Two nuclei of different mating types fuse within the ascus to form a diploid zygote. Yeasts are unicellular ascomycetes. The process of asexual reproduction in yeasts is called budding.

The club fungi—basidiomycetes—have a specialized reproductive structure that resembles a club. The cap of the fruiting body of a basidiomycete—such as the familiar mushroom—is composed of tightly packed hyphae. The lower side of the cap is composed of gills, which are thin blades of tissue lined with basidia. A basidium is a spore-bearing structure. Two nuclei in each basidium fuse to form a diploid zygote cell. The zygote cell undergoes meiosis, forming clusters of spores called basidiospores. A single mushroom can produce billions of basidiospores. Club fungi include mushrooms, shelf fungi, and puffballs.

The imperfect fungi—deuteromycetes—include those fungi that are not placed in other phyla because researchers have never been able to observe a sexual phase in their life cycles. Most imperfect fungi look like ascomycetes, though others are similar to basidiomycetes or zygomycetes. An example of an imperfect fungus is *Penicillium notatum*, a mold that grows on fruit. It is the source of the antibiotic penicillin.

21–3 Ecology of Fungi

All fungi are heterotrophs. Many fungi are saprobes, which are organisms that obtain food from decaying organic matter. Others are parasites, and still others live in symbiosis with other species.

Fungi play an essential role in maintaining equilibrium in nearly every ecosystem. Fungi do this by recycling nutrients as they break down the bodies and wastes of other organisms. Many fungi feed by releasing digestive enzymes that break down organic material into simple molecules. Fungi food includes wastes and dead organisms. In breaking down this material, fungi promote the recycling of nutrients and essential chemicals. Without such decomposers, the energy-rich compounds that organisms accumulate would be lost forever.

Parasitic fungi cause serious plant and animal diseases. A few cause diseases in humans. Fungal diseases in plants include corn smut and wheat rust. Fungal diseases in humans include athlete's foot and ringworm, thrush, and yeast infections of the female reproductive tract.

Some fungi form symbiotic relationships in which both partners benefit, such as lichens and mycorrhizae. Lichens are not single organisms. Rather, lichens are symbiotic associations between a fungus and a photosynthetic organism. The photosynthetic organism in a lichen is either a green alga or a cyanobacterium, or both. The alga or cyanobacterium provides the fungus with a source of energy by carrying out photosynthesis. The fungus, in turn, provides the photosynthetic organism with water and minerals. The fungus also shades the alga or cyanobacterium from intense sunlight.

Mutualistic associations of plant roots and fungi are called mycorrhizae. The plant's roots are woven into a partnership with the web of fungal hyphae. The hyphae of fungi aid plants in absorbing water and minerals. In addition, the fungi release enzymes that free nutrients from the soil. The plants, in turn, provide the fungi with the products of photosynthesis. The presence of mycorrhizae is essential for the growth of many plants. Mycorrhizal associations were an adaptation that was critical in the evolution of plants.

Chapter 21   Fungi

Section 21–1 The Kingdom Fungi (pages 527–529)

⊂▬⊃ **Key Concepts**
- What are the defining characteristics of fungi?
- What is the internal structure of a fungus?
- How do fungi reproduce?

What Are Fungi? (page 527)

1. Circle the letter of each sentence that is true about fungi.

   a. They are heterotrophs.

   b. They have cell walls.

   c. They are photosynthetic.

   d. They are eukaryotic.

2. The cell walls of fungi are made of a complex carbohydrate called _____.

3. How do fungi digest their food? _____

   _____

4. Is the following sentence true or false? Some fungi are parasites. _____

Structure and Function of Fungi (pages 527–528)

5. Which group of fungi are not multicellular? _____

6. What are hyphae? _____

   _____

7. How thick is each hypha? _____

8. In some fungi, what divides the hyphae into cells containing one or two nuclei?

   _____

9. What is a mycelium? _____

   _____

   _____

10. Why is a mycelium well suited to absorb food? _____

   _____

   _____

11. What is a fruiting body of a fungus? _____

   _____

   _____

   _____

12. What is a fairy ring, and why does it form? _____

_____

_____

_____

13. Label the parts of the fungus.

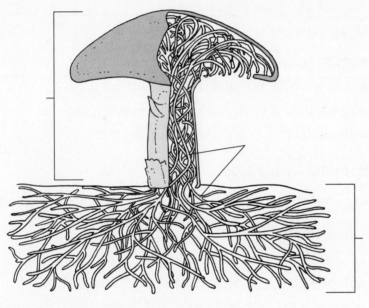

Reproduction in Fungi (pages 528–529)

14. Is the following sentence true or false? Most fungi can reproduce only asexually.

_____

15. How does asexual reproduction occur in fungi? _____

_____

_____

_____

16. In some fungi, spores are produced in structures called _____.

17. Where are sporangia found in a fungus? _____

_____

_____

18. Sexual reproduction in fungi usually involves two different _____.

19. What is a gametangium? _____

_____

_____

_____

20. How does a zygote form in fungal sexual reproduction? _____

_____

_____

_____

_____

_____

21. Circle the letter of each sentence that is true about sexual reproduction in fungi.

    a. The zygote is often the only diploid cell in the fungus's entire life cycle.

    b. Mating types are called male and female.

    c. Gametes of both mating types are about the same size.

    d. One mating type is a "+" (plus) and the other is a "−" (minus).

How Fungi Spread (page 529)

22. Is the following sentence true or false? The spores of many fungi scatter easily in the wind. _____

23. For a fungal spore to grow, where must it land? _____

_____

_____

_____

_____

Section 21–2 Classification of Fungi (pages 530–536)

Key Concept
- What are the characteristics of the four main phyla of fungi?

Introduction (page 530)

1. Complete the concept map about the four main groups of fungi.

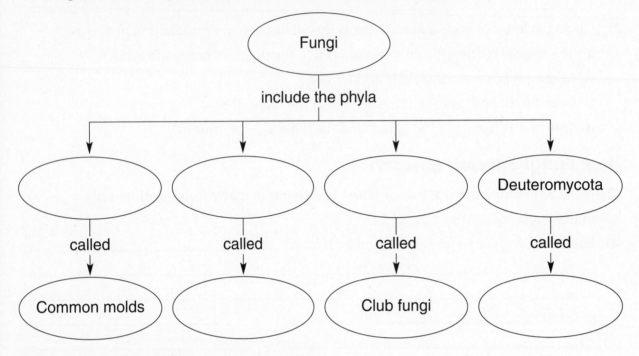

The Common Molds (pages 530–531)

2. What are zygomycetes? _____

_____

_____

3. The resting spore formed during the sexual phase of the mold's life cycle is called a(an)

_____.

4. Is the following sentence true or false? The hyphae of zygomycetes are generally

divided by cross walls. _____

5. What is the common name for *Rhizopus stolonifer*? _____

6. Complete the table about the kinds of hyphae of black bread mold.

KINDS OF HYPHAE

Kind	Description
Rhizoids	
Stolons	
	Hyphae that push up into the air and form sporangia at their tips

7. Complete the flowchart about sexual reproduction in zygomycetes.

> Two hyphae from different mating types come together, forming _____.

↓

> Haploid gametes from the mating types fuse to form diploid zygotes, which make up a single _____.

↓

> The zygospore eventually germinates, and a(an) _____ emerges.

↓

> The sporangium reproduces asexually by releasing _____.

The Sac Fungi (pages 532–533)

8. What is an ascus? _____

_____

9. Is the following sentence true or false? Ascomycetes make up the largest phylum in the kingdom Fungi. _____

10. What occurs among sac fungi during asexual reproduction? _____

_____

_____

11. Complete the flowchart about sexual reproduction in ascomycetes.

> Gametangia from two different mating types _____ together.

↓

> That fusion produces hyphae that contain haploid _____.

↓

> The N + N hyphae produce a fruiting body, inside of which the _____ forms.

↓

> Within the ascus, meiosis and mitosis occur to produce cells known as _____.

↓

> In a favorable environment, an ascospore germinates and grows into a haploid _____.

12. Is the following sentence true or false? Yeasts are multicellular ascomycetes.

_____

13. Why are yeasts classified as ascomycetes? _____

_____

14. What process do yeasts carry out to obtain energy when they are in a nutrient mixture such as bread dough? _____

The Club Fungi (pages 534–536)

15. From what does the phylum Basidiomycota get its name? _____

_____

16. Label the parts of a mushroom.

17. Where are basidia found on a basidiomycete? _____

_____

_____

18. The cap of a basidiomycete is composed of tightly packed _____ .

19. Is the following sentence true or false? The remarkable growth of mushrooms overnight is caused by cell enlargement. _____

20. Circle the letter of each example of basidiomycetes.

   a. puffballs   **b.** shelf fungi   **c.** rusts   **d.** yeasts

21. Why should you never pick or eat any mushrooms found in the wild?

_____

_____

22. Complete the flowchart about reproduction in basidiomycetes.

> A basidiospore germinates to produce a haploid primary _____ .

↓

> The mycelia of different mating types fuse to produce a(an) _____ .

↓

> A fruiting body pushes above ground, forming a(an) _____ at the soil's surface.

↓

> Two nuclei in each basidium fuse to form a diploid _____ .

↓

> Each zygote undergoes meiosis, forming clusters of diploid _____ .

The Imperfect Fungi (page 536)

23. The phylum Deuteromycota is composed of what fungi? _____

_____

_____

_____

24. What is *Penicillium notatum*, and where does it grow naturally? _____

_____

25. What is produced from *Penicillium notatum*? _____

_____

Reading Skill Practice

You can often increase your understanding of what you've read by making comparisons. A compare-and-contrast table helps you to do this. On a separate sheet of paper, make a table to compare the four main groups of fungi you read about in Section 21–2. For more information about compare-and-contrast tables, see Organizing Information in Appendix A of your textbook.

Section 21–3 Ecology of Fungi (pages 537–542)

Key Concepts
- What is the main role of fungi in natural ecosystems?
- What problems do parasitic fungi cause?
- What kinds of symbiotic relationships do fungi form with other organisms?

All Fungi Are Heterotrophs (page 537)

1. Fungi cannot manufacture their own food because they are _____.

2. What are saprobes? _____

_____

_____

Fungi as Decomposers (page 538)

3. Fungi recycle nutrients breaking down the bodies and wastes of other _____.

4. How do fungi break down leaves, fruit, and other organic material into simple

molecules? _____

_____

_____

Fungi as Parasites (pages 538–539)

5. Parasitic fungi cause serious plant and animal _____.

6. Circle the letter of each example of a fungal plant disease.

   a. wheat rust   **b.** corn smut   **c.** thrush   **d.** mildews

7. Rusts are members of the phylum _____.

8. What two kinds of plants do wheat rusts need to complete their life cycle?

_____

_____

_____

9. One deuteromycete can infect the areas between the human toes, causing an infection

known as _____.

10. What happens when the fungus that causes athlete's foot infects other areas of the

body? _____

_____

Symbiotic Relationships (pages 540–542)

11. Lichens and mycorrhizae are both examples of what kind of symbiotic relationship?

_____

12. What are lichens? _____

_____

13. What is the photosynthetic organism in a lichen? _____

_____

14. Where do lichens grow? _____

_____

15. What benefits do the fungus and the photosynthetic organism derive from the association in a lichen? _____

_____

_____

16. What are mycorrhizae? _____

17. Why is the presence of mycorrhizae essential for the growth of many plants?

_____

_____

Chapter 21   Fungi

Vocabulary Review

Labeling Diagrams   *Use terms from Chapter 21 to label the diagram.*

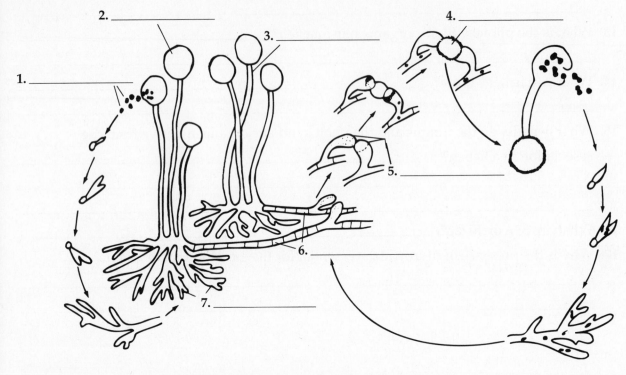

Completion   *Fill in the blanks with terms from Chapter 21.*

8. Multicellular fungi are composed of thin filaments called _____.

9. The bodies of multicellular fungi are composed of many hyphae tangled together into a thick mass called a(an) _____.

10. A(An) _____ body is a fungal reproductive structure growing from the mycelium.

11. The process of asexual reproduction in yeasts is called _____.

12. The spore-bearing structure of a club fungus is called the _____.

13. The phylum composed of fungi that have never been observed to have a sexual phase in their life cycles is the _____ fungi.

14. Organisms that obtain food from decaying organic matter are called

_____.

15. A(An) _____ is a symbiotic association between a fungus and a photosynthetic organism.

Chapter 22   Plant Diversity

Summary

22–1 Introduction to Plants

Plants provide the base for food chains on land. They also provide shade, shelter, and oxygen for animals. Plants are multicellular organisms with cells walls made of cellulose. They make their own food in the process of photosynthesis using green pigments called chlorophyll *a* and *b*.

Plant life cycles have two phases that alternate. This is known as alternation of generations. A diploid (2N) phase, called the sporophyte, alternates with a haploid (N) phase, called the gametophyte. The sporophyte produces haploid spores. The spores grow into haploid gametophytes. The gametophyte produces male and female reproductive cells, called gametes. Male and female gametes fuse during fertilization to produce a new sporophyte.

In order to survive, all plants need sunlight, water, minerals, oxygen, carbon dioxide, and a way to move water and nutrients to their cells. Plants have many adaptations to get these things.

Early land plants evolved from an organism that was like the multicellular green algae living today. As early land plants adapted to a dry habitat, several major groups of plants evolved. Botanists divide modern plants into four groups based on water-conducting tissues, seeds, and flowers. These four plant groups are mosses and their relatives, ferns and their relatives, cone-bearing plants, and flowering plants.

22–2 Bryophytes

Mosses, liverworts, and hornworts belong to the group called bryophytes. Bryophytes do not have tubes to move water and nutrients through the plant. Water simply moves from cell to cell. It moves from areas where there is plenty of water to areas where

water is needed. Examples of bryophytes include mosses, liverworts, and hornworts.

Bryophytes do not have true leaves, stems, and roots. Instead of roots, they have structures called rhizoids. Rhizoids anchor the plant to the ground.

Bryophytes reproduce sexually and asexually. They have several structures that produce reproductive cells. Structures called antheridia make sperm. Structures called archegonia produce egg cells.

Sperm cells must swim through water to fertilize eggs. This is why bryophytes must live in moist habitats. After fertilization, the diploid zygote grows to become a sporophyte. The sporophyte is made up of a capsule and a long stalk that remains attached to the gametophyte. It relies on the gametophyte for food and water. Spores are made inside the capsule. When the capsule ripens, it opens and the spores are carried off by wind and water. When a spore lands in a moist place, it grows into the plant we think of as moss. This green plant is the haploid gametophyte.

22–3 Seedless Vascular Plants

Ferns and their relatives were the first plants to have special tissues that carry water and food throughout a plant. These tissues are called vascular tissues. There are two types of vascular tissue. Xylem moves water from the roots to all parts of the plant. Special cells called tracheids make up xylem. They have thick, strong cell walls. The other type of vascular tissue is phloem. Phloem carries nutrients and food from place to place within the plant. Both xylem and phloem can move fluids through the plant body against the force of gravity. Many plants contain lignin, a substance that makes cell walls rigid.

Seedless vascular plants include club mosses, horsetails, and ferns. These plants have true roots, leaves, and stems. Roots absorb water and minerals. Leaves make food by photosynthesis. Stems support the plant and connect leaves and roots.

In the life cycle of ferns, the diploid sporophyte is the dominant stage. Fern sporophytes produce spores on the underside of the fronds in structures called sporangia. These spores are haploid. When spores are ripe, they burst from sporangia and are carried by wind and water. In the right conditions, they will grow to form haploid gametophytes.

The haploid gametophyte is a thin, heart-shaped structure. The antheridia and archegonia are found on the underside of the gametophyte. When mature, sperm from the antheridia swim to the archegonia to fertilize the eggs.

22–4 Seed Plants

Seed plants are divided into two groups: gymnosperms and angiosperms. Gymnosperms, or cone-bearing plants, produce seeds directly on the surface of cones. Angiosperms, which are flowering plants, produce seeds inside a tissue that protects them. Seed plants can live just about anywhere, because they do not need water for reproduction.

Like other plants, seed plants have alternation of generations. All of the seed plants that we see are sporophytes. The gametophytes of seed plants are made up of only a few cells. They grow and mature within flowers and cones. The entire male gametophyte fits in a tiny structure called a pollen grain. Pollen is carried to the female gametophyte by wind, birds, mammals, or insects. This process is called pollination.

Seeds protect the zygote of seed plants. After fertilization, the zygote grows into a tiny plant. This plant is called an embryo. When conditions are right, the embryo grows. It uses a supply of stored food inside the seed when it starts growing. A seed coat surrounds the embryo, protecting it from drying out.

Gymnosperms are the oldest surviving seed plants. Gymnosperms include gnetophytes, cycads, ginkgoes, and conifers. These plants produce seeds that are protected by a seed coat. However, the cone does not cover the seeds. This is why they are called naked seed plants.

22–5 Angiosperms—Flowering Plants

Angiosperms have reproductive organs called flowers. Flowers attract animals, which carry pollen from flower to flower. This is a more efficient way of pollination than the wind pollination of most gymnosperms. Unlike gymnosperms, the seeds of angiosperms are protected. The structure that protects the seeds develops into a fruit.

There are two groups of angiosperms: monocots and dicots. Monocot embryos have one seed leaf, or cotyledon. Dicot embryos have two cotyledons. Other differences between monocots and dicots include the arrangement of veins in leaves, the number of flower petals, the structure of roots, and the arrangement of vascular tissue in the stem.

Flowering plants can also be subdivided according to the characteristics of their stems. Woody plants—such as trees, shrubs, and vines—have cells with thick cell walls that support the plant body. Plant stems that are smooth and nonwoody are characteristic of herbaceous plants. Herbaceous plants include zinnias, petunias, and sunflowers.

Flowering plants have three different life spans. Annuals complete their life cycle within one growing season. Biennials complete their life cycle in two years. They produce seeds and die in the second growing season. Perennials live through many years. Some die each winter and regrow in spring.

Chapter 22   Plant Diversity

Section 22–1 Introduction to Plants (pages 551–555)

🔑 **Key Concepts**
- What is a plant?
- What do plants need to survive?
- How did the first plants evolve?

What Is a Plant? (page 551)

1. Circle the letter of each sentence that is true about plants.

    a. Plants are multicellular prokaryotes.

    b. Plants carry out photosynthesis.

    c. Plants have cell walls made of cellulose.

    d. Plants develop from multicellular embryos.

2. What pigments do plants use to carry out photosynthesis? _____

    _____

3. Is the following sentence true or false? All plants are autotrophs. _____

The Plant Life Cycle (page 552)

4. All plants have a life cycle that is characterized by _____

    _____.

5. Complete the diagram of the plant life cycle by writing the name of the plant generation
in the correct place. For each generation, indicate whether it is haploid or diploid by
writing either *N* or *2N*.

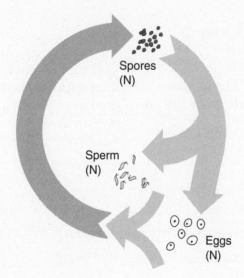

Spores
(N)

Sperm
(N)

Eggs
(N)

6. Complete the table about plant generations.

PLANT GENERATIONS

Generation	Description	Haploid or Diploid?
	Gamete-producing plant	
	Spore-producing plant	

7. Seed plants have evolved reproductive cycles that can be carried out without

_____ .

What Plants Need to Survive (page 552)

8. What are the four basic needs of plants?

a. _____

b. _____

c. _____

d. _____

9. Why are plant leaves typically broad and flat? _____

_____

10. Circle the letter of each sentence that is true about the basic needs of plants.

a. Plants require oxygen to support cellular respiration.

b. Plants must get rid of water as quickly as possible.

c. Water is one of the raw materials of photosynthesis.

d. Plants have specialized tissues to carry nutrients upward.

Early Plants (pages 553–554)

11. The history of plants can be understood in terms of the evolution of what kind

of structures? _____

_____

12. What did the first plants evolve from? _____

_____

13. Circle the letter of each sentence that is true about multicellular green algae.

a. They have the same photosynthetic pigments as plants.

b. They have the size, color, and appearance of plants.

c. They are classified as early plants.

d. They have reproductive cycles that are similar to those of early plants.

14. How were early plants similar to today's mosses? _____

_____

15. From the first plants, at least two major groups of plants evolved. What did those groups develop into? _____

_____

_____

Overview of the Plant Kingdom (page 555)

16. Circle the letter of each of the important features that botanists use to divide the plant kingdom into four groups.

    a. seeds

    b. water-conducting tissue

    c. stems

    d. flowers

17. What are the four main groups of living plants?

    a. _____

    b. _____

    c. _____

    d. _____

18. The great majority of plants alive today are _____.

Reading Skill Practice

Finding the main ideas of a section can help you organize the important points you need to remember. Skim Section 22–1 to find the main ideas. Write them on the left-hand side of a separate sheet of paper. Then, make a list of supporting details for each main idea on the right-hand side of the sheet.

Section 22–2 Bryophytes (pages 556–559)

⬡ **Key Concepts**
- What adaptations of bryophytes enable them to live on land?
- What are the three groups of bryophytes?
- How do bryophytes reproduce?

Introduction (page 556)

1. Mosses and their relatives are generally called _____.

2. Bryophyte life cycles are highly dependent on _____.

3. How does the lack of vascular tissue keep bryophytes small? _____

_____

_____

4. Why must bryophytes live in places where there is standing water for at least part of

the year? _____

_____

_____

Groups of Bryophytes (pages 556–557)

5. What are the three groups of plants that bryophytes include?

   a. _____

   b. _____

   c. _____

6. Where would you expect to find mosses growing? _____

_____

_____

7. Why are mosses the most abundant plants in polar regions? _____

_____

_____

8. Why is the thin, upright shoot of a moss plant not considered to be a true stem?

_____

_____

9. Complete the illustration by identifying which part of a typical moss plant is the gametophyte and which part is the sporophyte.

10. What do the mature gametophytes of liverworts look like? _____

_____

_____

11. What are gemmae? _____

_____

_____

12. How do liverworts reproduce asexually? _____

_____

_____

13. What does the hornwort sporophyte look like? _____

_____

_____

14. In what sort of soil would liverworts and hornworts be expected to be found?

_____

_____

_____

Life Cycle of Bryophytes (pages 558–559)

15. In bryophytes, which stage of the life cycle is dominant and carries out most of the plant's photosynthesis? _____

16. What fact of reproduction limits the distribution of bryophytes to habitats near water?

_____

_____

_____

17. When a moss spore germinates, what does it grow into? _____

_____

_____

18. Complete the table about bryophyte reproductive structures.

BRYOPHYTE REPRODUCTIVE STRUCTURES

Structure	Description	Structure Produces
Antheridia		Sperm
	Female reproductive structure	

19. What does the zygote depend on for water and nutrients? _____

_____

Human Use of Mosses (page 559)

20. In certain environments, the dead remains of sphagnum accumulate to form thick deposits of _____.

21. Why do gardeners add peat moss to soil? _____

_____

_____

Name_____ Class_____ Date _____

Section 22–3 Seedless Vascular Plants
(pages 560–563)

⚷ Key Concepts
- How is vascular tissue important to ferns and their relatives?
- What are the characteristics of the three phyla of seedless vascular plants?
- What are the stages in the life cycles of ferns?

Evolution of Vascular Tissue: A Transport System (page 560)

1. What is vascular tissue? _____

_____

2. What kind of cells did the first vascular plants have that were specialized to conduct water? _____

3. Circle the letter of each sentence that is true about tracheids.

   a. They are hollow cells.

   b. They are connected end to end.

   c. Their thick cell walls resist pressure.

   d. They are the key cells of phloem.

4. What is the function of xylem? _____

_____

5. What is the function of phloem? _____

_____

6. Is the following sentence true or false? Phloem and xylem cannot move water and nutrients against the force of gravity. _____

7. What is lignin? _____

Ferns and Their Relatives (pages 561–562)

8. Complete the table about plant structures.

PLANT STRUCTURES

Structure	Description
Roots	
Leaves	
Stems	

9. Spore-bearing vascular plants include what three types of plants?

   a. _____

   b. _____

   c. _____

10. Is the following sentence true or false? Vascular plants have true roots and stems.

    _____

11. The fossilized remains of ancient forests of club mosses exist today as huge beds of

    _____.

12. Circle the letter of each structure a horsetail has.

    a. stems   **b.** cones   **c.** leaves   **d.** roots

13. Ferns are members of phylum _____.

14. What are rhizomes? _____

    _____

15. The large leaves of ferns are called _____.

16. Fronds grow from what fern structures? _____

17. In what kind of habitats are ferns most abundant? _____

    _____

    _____

Life Cycle of Ferns (pages 562–563)

18. What is the dominant stage in the life cycle of ferns and other spore-bearing vascular

    plants? _____

    _____

19. Fern sporophytes produce haploid spores on the underside of their fronds in tiny

    containers called _____.

20. What are sori? _____

    _____

21. Are the spores of ferns haploid or diploid? _____

22. Label each drawing of a fern as either the sporophyte or the gametophyte.

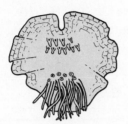 

_____   _____

23. Where are the antheridia and archegonia found in ferns? _____
_____

24. Why does fertilization in ferns require at least a thin film of water? _____
_____

25. Circle the letter of each sentence that is true about the life cycle of ferns.

    a. The zygote grows into a new gametophyte.

    b. The sporophyte is a heart-shaped, green structure.

    c. Fern sporophytes often live several years.

    d. When spores germinate, they grow into haploid gametophytes.

Section 22–4 Seed Plants (pages 564–568)

Key Concepts

- What adaptations allow seed plants to reproduce without standing water?
- What are the four groups of gymnosperms?

Introduction (page 564)

1. Complete the table about the two groups of seed plants.

SEED PLANTS

Group	Description	Examples
	Seed plants that bear seeds directly on the surfaces of cones	
	Seed plants that bear their seeds within a layer of protective tissue	

Reproduction Free From Water (pages 564–565)

2. What are three features that allow seed plants to reproduce without water?

   a. _____

   b. _____

   c. _____

3. What are cones and flowers? _____

_____

_____

_____

4. Why don't the gametophytes or the gametes of seed plants need standing water to

   function? _____

_____

_____

_____

5. What is pollination? _____

_____

_____

_____

© Pearson Education, Inc., publishing as Pearson Prentice Hall.

Match the structure with its description.

Structure	Description
_____ **6.** pollen grain	**a.** An embryo encased in a protective covering
_____ **7.** seed	**b.** Structure that surrounds and protects the plant embryo
_____ **8.** endosperm	**c.** Early developmental stage of an organism
_____ **9.** embryo	**d.** Male gametophyte of seed plants
_____ **10.** seed coat	**e.** Seed's food supply

11. What tissues or structures do seeds have that aid in their dispersal to other habitats?

_____

_____

12. What is the strategy that allows seeds to survive long periods of bitter cold, extreme heat, or drought? _____

_____

_____

_____

Evolution of Seed Plants (page 566)

13. How did conditions on Earth change during the Carboniferous and Devonian periods, and how did those changes affect plants? _____

_____

_____

_____

_____

_____

14. What link do seed ferns represent in the fossil record? _____

_____

_____

_____

15. What adaptations did seed plants have that allowed them to replace spore-bearing plants as continents became drier? _____

_____

_____

_____

_____

Gymnosperms—Cone Bearers (pages 566–568)

16. Complete the concept map about gymnosperms.

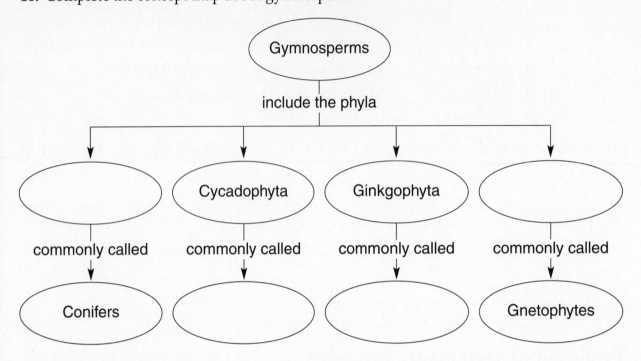

17. Where are the reproductive scales of gnetophytes found? _____

_____

18. What do cycads look like? _____

_____

19. In what kinds of habitats can cycads be found growing naturally today?

_____

_____

20. Why is the ginkgo tree sometimes called a living fossil? _____

_____

_____

21. What kinds of plants do conifers include? _____

_____

_____

22. Why are the leaves of most conifers long and thin, such as pine needles?

_____

_____

© Pearson Education, Inc., publishing as Pearson Prentice Hall.

23. In addition to the shape of the leaves, what are two other adaptations that help conifers conserve water?

    a. _____

    b. _____

    _____

24. Circle the letter of the reason conifers never become bare.

    a. They never lose their needles.

    b. The gametophyte supplies needles to the sporophyte.

    c. Older needles are gradually replaced by newer needles.

    d. The needles conserve water throughout the year.

25. How are larches and baldcypresses different from most other conifers?

    _____

    _____

Section 22–5 Angiosperms—Flowering Plants
(pages 569–572)

⊂⊃ **Key Concepts**
- What are the characteristics of angiosperms?
- What are monocots and dicots?
- What are the three categories of plant life spans?

Flowers and Fruits (page 569)

1. Angiosperms are members of the phylum _____.

2. Angiosperms have unique reproductive organs known as _____.

3. During which geologic period did flowering plants first appear? _____

   _____

   _____

4. In flowering plants, the seed is encased in a(an) _____.

5. What is a fruit? _____

6. Why is using fruit to attract animals one of the reasons for the success of flowering

   plants? _____

   _____

   _____

Diversity of Angiosperms (pages 570–572)

7. The seed leaves of plant embryos are called _____.

8. Complete the table about classes of angiosperms.

CLASSES OF ANGIOSPERMS

Class	Common Name	Number of Seed Leaves	Examples
Monocotyledonae			
Dicotyledonae			

9. Circle the letter of each plant feature that is characteristic of dicots.

   a. Parallel leaf veins

   b. Floral parts in multiples of 4 or 5

   c. Roots include a taproot

   d. Vascular bundles scattered throughout stem

10. Classify each of the following plants as either woody or herbaceous by writing the correct term on the line.

   a. Rose shrubs _____

   b. Oaks _____

   c. Tomato plants _____

   d. Sunflowers _____

   e. Grape vines _____

   f. Dandelions _____

11. Woody plants are made primarily of what kind of cells? _____

   _____

   _____

12. What characteristics do the stems of herbaceous plants have? _____

   _____

   _____

13. Complete the table about plant life spans.

PLANT LIFE SPANS

Category	Definition	Examples
Annuals		
Biennials		
Perennials		

Chapter 22   Plant Diversity

Vocabulary Review

Labeling Diagrams   *Use the following words to label the diagrams of the stages in a fern's life cycle:* antheridia, archegonia, frond, rhizoid, rhizome, root, sori.

Sporophyte   **Gametophyte**

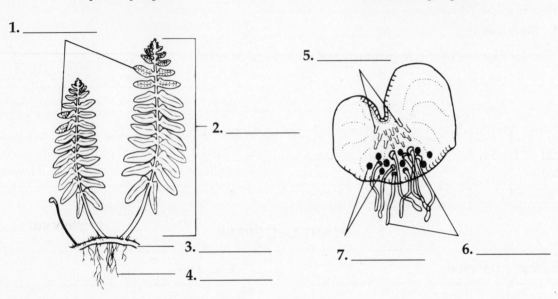

1. _____

2. _____

3. _____

4. _____

5. _____

6. _____

7. _____

Completion   *Fill in the blanks with terms from Chapter 22.*

8. A(An) _____ is the diploid phase of the plant life cycle.

9. A(An) _____ produces seeds directly on the surface of cones.

10. The seed-bearing structures of angiosperms are _____.

11. The transfer of pollen from the male to the female reproductive structures is called

_____.

12. A(An) _____ is a plant embryo with its food supply that is
protected by a seed coat.

13. The _____ is a wall of tissue surrounding the seed.

14. An angiosperm that has one cotyledon, or seed leaf, is called a(an)

_____.

15. Flowering plants that complete an entire life cycle within one growing season are called

_____.

Summary

23–1 Specialized Tissues in Plants

The cells of seed plants are organized into different tissues and organs. The three main plant organs are roots, stems, and leaves. These organs are made up of three main kinds of tissues: dermal tissue, vascular tissue, and ground tissue.

Dermal tissue is like the "skin" of a plant. It protects the plant and prevents water loss. Dermal tissue is made up of epidermal cells that have different shapes and functions.

Vascular tissue moves water and nutrients throughout the plant. It consists of xylem tissue and phloem tissue. Xylem tissue moves water. It is made up of two kinds of specialized cells called tracheids and vessel elements. Phloem tissue moves sugars. It consists of sieve tube elements and companion cells.

Ground tissue is made up of all the cells that lie between dermal and vascular tissues. Ground tissue is made up mostly of parenchyma cells. Parenchyma cells have thin cell walls and function in photosynthesis and storage. Collenchyma and sclerenchyma cells are also part of ground tissue. These cells have thick cell walls that help support the plant.

A fourth kind of tissue is responsible for plant growth. Meristematic tissue produces new cells by mitosis. These new cells have not yet become specialized for specific functions. As the new cells mature, they develop specialized structures and functions, a process called differentiation. Meristematic tissue is found at the tips of stems and roots.

23–2 Roots

As soon as a seedling begins to grow, it sends out a primary root. Other roots branch out from the primary root. They are called secondary roots.

In some plants, the primary root grows long and thick. The secondary roots stay small. This kind of primary root is called a taproot. In other plants, secondary roots grow and branch. The roots of these plants are called fibrous roots.

Roots are made up of cells from the four tissue systems—dermal, vascular, ground, and meristematic. A mature root has an outside layer of dermal tissue called the epidermis. It also has a central cylinder of vascular tissue called the vascular cylinder. Between these two tissues lies ground tissue, which is called the cortex. A thin layer of cells called the endodermis completely surrounds the vascular cylinder, separating it from the cortex. An apical meristem in the root causes it to grow in length.

Roots have two functions. One function is to anchor a plant in the ground. The other function is to absorb water and dissolved nutrients from the soil.

Once absorbed by the root hairs, water and nutrients move inward through the cortex. After passing through the endodermis into the vascular cylinder, the water cannot leave. This causes pressure to build up. This pressure is called root pressure. Root pressure forces water upward through the xylem toward the stem.

23–3 Stems

Stems have three important jobs. They produce leaves, branches, and flowers. They hold leaves up to the sunlight. They also carry water and nutrients between roots and leaves.

Like the rest of the plant, the stem is composed of dermal, vascular, and ground tissue. Stems are surrounded by a layer of epidermal cells that have thick cell walls and a waxy protective coating.

© Pearson Education, Inc., publishing as Pearson Prentice Hall.

In most plants, stems contain nodes (where leaves are attached) and internodes (regions between the nodes). Small buds are found where leaves attach to the nodes. Buds contain tissue that can produce new stems and leaves.

The arrangement of tissues in a stem differs among seed plants. In monocots, vascular bundles are scattered throughout the stem. In dicots and most gymnosperms, vascular bundles are arranged in a ring. These vascular bundles contain xylem and phloem tissue.

Plant stems can grow in two different ways. They have primary growth and secondary growth. In primary growth, stems grow longer as meristematic tissue at the ends of the stems produces new cells. In secondary growth, a stem grows wider as meristematic tissue on its sides produces new cells. This growth produces wood and bark. Only plants with woody stems have secondary growth.

23–4 Leaves

The leaves of a plant are its main organs of photosynthesis. In photosynthesis, plants make food. Sugars, starches, and oils made by plants provide food for all land animals.

Leaves have a structure that enables them to absorb light and make food. Most leaves have thin, flattened sections called blades to collect sunlight. The blade is attached to the stem at the petiole. Most leaves are also made up of a specialized ground tissue called mesophyll. Mesophyll cells have many chloroplasts. It is in these cells that photosynthesis occurs.

Xylem and phloem tissues in leaves are gathered in bundles called veins. These veins are connected to the xylem and phloem in the stem.

Plants must exchange gases with the air around them. They can lose a lot of water during this process. Leaves have an adaptation to prevent water loss. They allow air in and out of their waterproof covering only through small openings called stomata. Guard cells on the undersides of the leaves control the stomata and thus regulate the movement of gases into and out of leaf tissues. In general, the stomata are open during the day, when photosynthesis is active, and closed at night.

23–5 Transport in Plants

Xylem tissue forms tubes that stretch from roots through stems and out into leaves. Root pressure forces water and nutrients into the xylem. Other forces pull water and nutrients through the plant.

Water can be pulled up through xylem because its molecules are pulled together by a force called cohesion. Water molecules are also attracted to other molecules. This force is called adhesion. Together, cohesion and adhesion cause water to move upward. This movement is called capillary action.

Capillary action is too weak to pull water up the xylem tubes in a large plant. Another force pulls water up to the leaves. It is called transpiration pull. Transpiration pull happens because water moves from areas where there is plenty of water to areas where there is little water. When water evaporates from leaves, water is drawn upward from the roots to replace it.

Phloem transports the sugars made in photosynthesis. It carries sugars from the leaves into the stems and roots. The food is then either used or stored.

Scientists have only formed hypotheses to explain how phloem transport happens. One hypothesis is called the pressure-flow hypothesis. This hypothesis explains that sugars move from areas of high concentration to areas of low concentration. When sugars are pumped into or removed from phloem, the change in concentration causes a movement of sugars in that same direction.

Chapter 23   Roots, Stems, and Leaves

Section 23–1 Specialized Tissues in Plants
(pages 579–583)

🔑 **Key Concepts**
- What are the three principal organs and tissues of seed plants?
- What are the three main tissue systems of plants?
- What specialized cells make up vascular tissue?
- How does meristematic tissue differ from other plant tissue?

Seed Plant Structure (page 579)

1. What are the three principal organs of seed plants?

   a. _____ b. _____ c. _____

2. Circle the letter of each sentence that is true about a function that roots perform.

   a. They anchor plants in the ground.

   b. They compete with other plants for sunlight.

   c. They absorb water and nutrients from soil.

   d. They hold plants upright.

3. What does the transport system of stems do? _____

   _____

4. The principal organs in which plants carry out photosynthesis are the _____.

5. What do the adjustable pores of leaves help conserve, and what do they allow

   to enter and leave a plant? _____

   _____

Plant Tissue Systems (page 580)

6. What are the three tissue systems of plants?

   a. _____ c. _____

   b. _____

Dermal Tissue (page 580)

7. Dermal tissue typically consists of a single layer of _____.

8. What is the cuticle, and what is its function? _____

   _____

   _____

9. What is the function of the tiny projections known as trichomes? _____

   _____

10. What does dermal tissue consist of in roots, and what is its function? _____

    _____

Vascular Tissue (pages 580–581)

11. Complete the table about the types of vascular tissue.

TYPES OF VASCULAR TISSUE

Type	Function	Cell Types Within Tissue
	Transports water	
	Transports food	

Match the vascular-tissue cells with their descriptions.

Vascular-Tissue Cells	Description
_____ **12.** Tracheids	**a.** The main phloem cells
_____ **13.** Vessel elements	**b.** Long, narrow xylem cells with walls that are impermeable to water
_____ **14.** Sieve tube elements	**c.** Phloem cells that surround sieve tube elements
_____ **15.** Companion cells	**d.** Xylem cells arranged end to end on top of one another

16. How can water move from one tracheid into a neighboring cell? _____

_____

_____

17. How can materials move from one sieve tube element into the next? _____

_____

_____

18. What cells support the phloem cells? _____

Ground Tissue (page 582)

19. The cells that lie between dermal and vascular tissue make up what kind of tissue?

_____

20. Complete the table about ground-tissue cells.

GROUND-TISSUE CELLS

Type of Cell	Structure	Function
	Cells with thin cell walls and large central vacuoles	
	Cells with strong, flexible cell walls	
	Cells with extremely thick, rigid cell walls	

Plant Growth and Meristematic Tissue (pages 582–583)

21. What does indeterminate growth mean in a plant? _____

_____

_____

_____

22. Where are these cells produced? _____

_____

23. The only plant tissue that produces new cells by mitosis is called _____.

24. What occurs as meristematic cells mature? _____

_____

_____

25. What is an apical meristem? _____

_____

_____

26. Where else on many plants is there meristematic tissue other than at apical meristems?

_____

_____

_____

Section 23–2 Roots (pages 584–588)

Key Concepts

- What are the two main types of roots?
- What are the main tissues in a mature root?
- What are the different functions of roots?

Types of Roots (page 584)

1. How are primary roots and secondary roots different in some plants? _____

_____

2. Complete the table about types of roots.

TYPES OF ROOTS

Type of Root	Description	Mainly in Dicots or Monocots?	Examples
	Long and thick primary roots that grow deep into the soil		
	Roots that are usually shallow and consist of many thin roots		

Root Structure and Growth (page 585)

3. Label the parts of a root on the illustration.

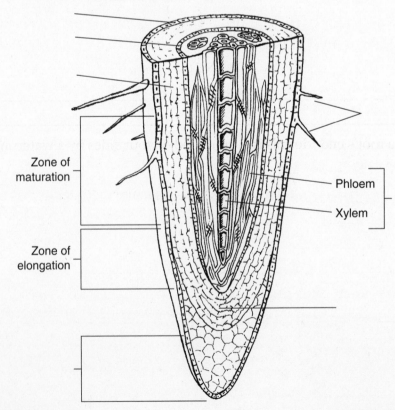

Zone of maturation

Zone of elongation

Phloem

Xylem

4. What is the structure of a mature root? _____

_____

_____

5. Water enters the plant through the large surface area provided by

the _____.

6. What does the cortex of a root consist of? _____

_____

7. The vascular tissue in the central region of a root is called the _____.

8. What protects the apical meristem of a root? _____

9. Where does most of the increase in root length occur? _____

_____

Root Functions (pages 586–588)

10. What are two functions of a plant's roots?

a. _____

b. _____

11. Is the following sentence true or false? The ingredients of a soil can determine what

kinds of plants grow in it. _____

12. Circle the letter of each sentence that is true about active transport of minerals in roots.

a. Water molecules move into the plant by active transport.

b. ATP is the source of energy used to pump mineral ions from the soil into the plant.

c. The cell membranes of root hairs contain active transport proteins.

d. Using active transport, a root actually pumps water into the plant.

13. What happens to the water and dissolved minerals after they move into the cortex?

_____

_____

14. Each of the cells of a root's endodermis is surrounded on four sides by a waterproof

strip called a(an) _____.

15. Why is there a one-way passage of materials into the vascular cylinder in plant roots?

_____

_____

_____

16. What is root pressure? _____

_____

Section 23–3 Stems (pages 589–594)

Key Concepts
- What are the three main functions of stems?
- How do monocot and dicot systems differ?
- How do primary growth and secondary growth occur in stems?

Stem Structure and Function (page 589)

1. What are the two important functions of stems?

   a. _____

   b. _____

2. What three tissue systems compose a stem? _____

   _____

Match the stem structure with its description.

	Structure	Description
_____	3. Node	a. A region between nodes
_____	4. Internode	b. Contains undeveloped tissue that can produce new stems and leaves
_____	5. Bud	c. Where leaves are attached

Monocot and Dicot Stems (page 590)

6. How does the arrangement of tissues in a stem differ among seed plants?

   _____

   _____

   _____

7. In a monocot stem, what does each vascular bundle contain? _____

   _____

8. The parenchyma cells inside the ring of vascular tissue in a dicot stem are known

   as _____.

9. What do the parenchyma cells outside the ring of vascular tissue form in a dicot stem?

   _____

Primary Growth of Stems (page 590)

10. What is primary growth in a plant? _____

    _____

    _____

11. Primary growth of stems is produced by cell division in the _____.

12. Is the following sentence true or false? Only dicot plants undergo primary growth. _____

Secondary Growth of Stems (pages 591–594)

13. The pattern of growth in which stems increase in width is called _____.

14. In conifers and dicots, where does secondary growth take place? _____
_____
_____

15. What type of lateral meristematic tissue produces vascular tissues and increases the thickness of stems over time? _____

16. What does cork cambium produce? _____

17. Circle the letter of each sentence that is true about the formation of vascular cambium.

   a. Vascular cambium forms between the xylem and phloem of individual vascular bundles.

   b. Divisions of vascular cambium give rise to new layers of xylem and phloem.

   c. Once secondary growth begins, vascular cambium appears as a thin layer.

   d. The production of new layers of xylem and phloem causes the stem to shrink when secondary growth begins.

18. Is the following sentence true or false? Most of what we call "wood" is actually layers of phloem. _____

19. What is heartwood? _____
_____
_____

20. The wood that is active in fluid transport and therefore lighter in color is called _____.

21. The alternation of dark and light wood produces what we commonly call _____.

22. How can you estimate the age of a tree? _____
_____

23. On most trees, what does bark include? _____
_____
_____
_____

24. Circle the letter of each sentence that is true about cork.

    a. Cork cells usually contain fats, oils, or waxes.

    b. Cork cells cause the loss of water from a stem.

    c. The outermost cork cells are usually dead.

    d. Cork cambium produces a thick, protective layer of cork.

25. Label the parts of the illustration of the cross section of a tree. Use the following terms : wood, bark, heartwood, cork, sapwood, cork cambium, vascular cambium, phloem.

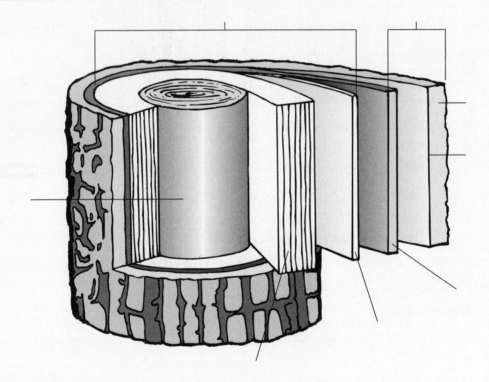

26. What are four kinds of modified stems that store food?

    a. _____

    b. _____

    c. _____

    d. _____

Section 23–4 Leaves (pages 595–598)

🔑 **Key Concepts**
- How does the structure of a leaf enable it to carry out photosynthesis?
- How does gas exchange take place in a leaf?

Leaf Structure (page 595)

1. The structure of a leaf is optimized for what purposes? _____
_____

2. What is a leaf blade? _____

3. The blade is attached to the stem by a thin stalk called a(an) _____.

4. Circle the letter of the type of tissue that covers a leaf.
   a. vascular   **b.** dermal   **c.** ground   **d.** petiole

5. The vascular tissues of leaves are connected directly to the vascular tissues of
_____.

Leaf Functions (pages 596–598)

6. The bulk of most leaves is composed of a specialized ground tissue known
as _____.

7. How do the carbohydrates produced in photosynthesis get to the rest of the
plant? _____
_____

Match the leaf structure with its description.

Structure	Description
_____ 8. Palisade mesophyll	**a.** A bundle of xylem and phloem tissues
_____ 9. Spongy mesophyll	**b.** Specialized cells that control the opening and closing of stomata
_____ 10. Vein	**c.** A layer of mesophyll cells that absorb much of the light that enters the leaf
_____ 11. Stomata	**d.** Openings in the underside of the leaf
_____ 12. Guard cells	**e.** A loose tissue with many air spaces between its cells

13. How do the air spaces in the spongy mesophyll connect with the exterior of the leaf?
_____
_____

14. What is transpiration? _____
_____

15. Why must a plant have its stomata open at least part of the time? _____
_____

16. What would probably happen to a plant that kept its stomata open all the time?

_____

_____

17. What is the balance plants maintain that prevents them from losing too much water?

_____

_____

_____

18. Complete the flowchart about guard cells.

Guard cells are forced into a curved shape when water pressure becomes _____.

↓

The guard cells pull away from one another, opening the _____.

↓

Guard cells straighten out when water pressure _____.

↓

The guard cells pull together, closing the _____.

19. Is the following sentence true or false? In general, stomata are closed at night. _____

20. How is the structure of the leaves of a pine tree an adaptation to dry conditions?

_____

_____

21. What are cactus leaves adapted for? _____

_____

22. Why must carnivorous plants rely on insects for their source of nitrogen?

_____

Reading Skill Practice

Writing a summary can help you remember the information that you have read. When you write a summary, write only the most important points. Write a summary of the information under the blue heading Leaf Functions. Your summary should be shorter than the text on which it is based. Do your work on a separate sheet of paper.

Section 23–5 Transport in Plants (pages 599–602)

🔖 **Key Concepts**
- How is water transported throughout a plant?
- How are the products of photosynthesis transported throughout a plant?

Water Transport (pages 599–601)

1. What combination of factors provides enough force to move water through the xylem tissue of even the tallest plant? _____

_____

_____

2. Complete the table about attraction between molecules.

ATTRACTION BETWEEN MOLECULES

Type of Attraction	Definition
Cohesion	
Adhesion	

3. The tendency of water to rise in a thin tube is called _____.

4. How does the thinness of a tube affect how high water will rise because of capillary action? Show your answer by drawing how high water would rise in each of the tubes on the illustration.

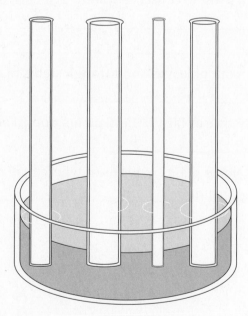

5. The tubelike structures of what two kinds of cells use capillary action to raise water above the level of ground?

a. _____ b. _____

Name_____ Class_____ Date_____

6. How do vessel elements form continuous tubes through which water can move freely?
_____

7. What causes the process known as transpiration pull? _____
_____
_____
_____

8. What normally keeps a plant's leaves and stems rigid? _____
_____
_____

9. High transpiration rates can lead to water loss that is severe enough to
cause _____.

10. How does the loss of osmotic pressure in leaves slow down the rate of transpiration?
_____
_____
_____

Nutrient Transport (pages 601–602)

11. How is the water content of a leaf kept constant? _____
_____
_____

12. How does wilting help a plant to conserve water? _____
_____
_____

13. The movement of sugars out of leaves and through stems to fruits takes place in what
kind of vascular tissue? _____

14. Is the following sentence true or false? Many plants pump food down into their roots
for winter storage. _____

15. The hypothesis that considers plants in terms of where they produce and use materials
from photosynthesis is called the _____.

© Pearson Education, Inc., publishing as Pearson Prentice Hall.

16. Complete the flowchart about the pressure-flow hypothesis.

Photosynthesis produces a high concentration of sugars in a cell, called the

_____ cell.

↓

Sugars move from the cell to phloem, and water also moves into the phloem by

the process of _____.

↓

Water moving into the phloem causes an increase in _____.

↓

The pressure causes fluid to move through the phloem toward a cell where

sugars are lower in concentration, called the _____ cell.

Reading Skill Practice

When you read a section, taking notes can help you organize and remember the information. As you read or review Section 23–5, take notes by writing each heading and listing the main points under each heading. Do your work on a separate sheet of paper.

Vocabulary Review

Multiple Choice   *In the space provided, write the letter of the answer that best completes each sentence or answers the question.*

_____ **1.** The main phloem cells are
  a. epidermal cells.
  b. sieve tube elements.
  c. vessel elements.
  d. meristems.

_____ **2.** Which of the following cells are found in ground tissue and have thin cell walls and large vacuoles?
  a. parenchyma
  b. sclerenchyma
  c. collenchyma
  d. companion cells

_____ **3.** The spongy layer of ground tissue just inside the epidermis of a root is called the
  a. root cap.
  b. endodermis.
  c. cortex.
  d. vascular cylinder.

_____ **4.** The meristematic tissue that produces the outer covering of stems is called
  a. pith.
  b. cork cambium.
  c. vascular cambium.
  d. bark.

_____ **5.** Which of the following is made up of tall, columnar cells that absorb light?
  a. petioles
  b. spongy mesophyll
  c. palisade mesophyll
  d. stomata

Matching   *In the space provided, write the letter that best matches each term.*

_____ **6.** apical meristem

_____ **7.** differentiation

_____ **8.** root hairs

_____ **9.** Casparian strip

_____ **10.** bud

_____ **11.** heartwood

_____ **12.** mesophyll

_____ **13.** transpiration

_____ **14.** adhesion

_____ **15.** capillary action

a. structure that makes cells of the endodermis waterproof

b. force of attraction between unlike molecules

c. cells that divide to increase root and stem length

d. older xylem that no longer conducts water

e. tendency of water to rise in a thin tube

f. tiny projections on the root epidermis that absorb water

g. specialized ground tissue in leaves where photosynthesis occurs

h. process in which cells develop special structures and functions

i. loss of water through leaves

j. part of a stem that contains undeveloped tissue

Summary

24–1 Reproduction With Cones and Flowers

Seed plants are completely adapted to life on land. Because they do not need water for reproduction, seed plants can reproduce nearly everywhere.

In the seed plant life cycle, the spore-producing generation (sporophyte) alternates with the gamete-producing generation (gametophyte). In seed plants, the familiar form of the plant is the sporophyte. The gametophyte of seed plants is hidden within the cones and flowers. Cones and flowers are two different methods of reproduction.

Pine trees and other gymnosperms use cones for reproduction. Pollen cones produce the male gametophyte, which are called pollen grains. Seed cones produce the female gametophyte in ovules. A few large egg cells form within the ovules. When a pollen grain lands near an ovule, it grows a pollen tube into the ovule. A sperm from the pollen tube fertilizes the egg in the ovule. A zygote forms and grows into an embryo. The embryo becomes enclosed in a seed.

Angiosperms, or flowering plants, reproduce with flowers. Flowers are organs that are made up of four kinds of leaves: sepals, petals, stamens, and carpels. Sepals make up the outermost circle of floral parts and are often green. They protect the flower bud. Colorful petals form the next circle. Petals attract insects and other pollinators to the flower.

The inner circles of a flower are fertile leaves. Stamens form the first inner circle. Each stamen has a long filament that supports an anther. The anther produces male gametophytes. One or more carpels form the innermost circle. Carpels, also called pistils, produce female gametophytes. Each

carpel has a broad base called the ovary. The carpel's stalk is called the style. At the top of the style is the stigma. The stigma has a sticky surface where pollen grains land. Angiosperms may have stamens and carpels within the same flower or in separate flowers on the same plant.

Reproduction in flowering plants takes place inside the flower. Inside the anthers, each cell undergoes meiosis to produce four haploid spore cells. Each of these cells becomes a pollen grain. Inside the ovaries are the ovules, where the female gametophyte develops. A single cell goes through meiosis to produce four haploid cells. One of these cells goes through mitosis, producing the embryo sac. This is the female gametophyte. Within the embryo sac is the egg cell.

During pollination, pollen is transferred from the anther to the stigma. Most gymnosperms are wind pollinated. Animals pollinate most angiosperms. Animal-pollinated flowers have many adaptations to attract the animals. Animals have evolved body shapes that let them reach nectar deep within the flowers. Animal pollination is more efficient than wind pollination.

When a pollen grain lands on a stigma, it grows a pollen tube to the ovary. Two sperm nuclei enter the embryo sac. Two distinct fertilizations take place in the embryo sac. First, one sperm nucleus fuses with the egg to form a diploid zygote. The zygote will grow into the plant embryo. Then, the other sperm nucleus fuses with two other nuclei in the embryo sac to form the endosperm. The endosperm provides food for the embryo. This is known as double fertilization.

24–2 Seed Development and Germination

Seeds helped to make angiosperms successful on land. Seeds nourish and protect embryos. As angiosperm seeds mature, the ovary walls thicken to form a fruit. The fruit encloses the seed. Some fruits are fleshy like grapes. Others are tough like pea pods.

Fleshy fruits often attract animals. When animals eat the fruit, they also eat the seeds. The animals disperse the seeds in their feces, often in areas far from the parent plant. Seeds that are spread by wind and water are usually lightweight. They easily float in the air or on water.

Many seeds enter a period of dormancy. They are alive but not growing. Dormancy gives time for seeds to spread to new areas or wait for better growing conditions. The right temperature and moisture can cause seeds to germinate, ending dormancy.

Germination is the stage of early growth of the plant embryo. When seeds germinate, they absorb water. This makes a seed swell and crack open. The young root emerges through the crack and begins to grow. In most monocots, a shoot emerges, protected by a sheath. The cotyledon stays underground. In some dicots, the cotyledons emerge above the ground. They protect the stem and the first leaves. In other dicots, the cotyledons stay underground to provide food for the seedling.

24–3 Plant Propagation and Agriculture

The production of seeds and fruits is sexual reproduction. Many plants also reproduce asexually by vegetative reproduction. This enables a single plant to produce many offspring that are genetically identical.

Plants reproduce asexually in many different ways. Some plants send out long, horizontal stems that produce roots or new shoots. Other plants produce tiny plants, called plantlets, on their leaves or stems. These plantlets detach and grow into new plants. Some plants can even produce new plants when a leaf drops to the ground and grows roots.

Plant growers often use vegetative reproduction to make exact copies of a useful or pretty plant. One method is to make a cutting of a stem that has meristematic tissue. The stem is partially buried in soil and treated with a special rooting mixture.

Grafting and budding are other methods used by plant growers. New plants are grown on plants that have a strong root system. A scion is a piece cut from the parent plant. It is attached to the plant with strong roots, called the stock. In grafting, stems are used as scions. In budding, buds are used as scions.

Agriculture, or the cultivation of plants, is the foundation of human society. Farmers in North America produce enough food to feed millions of people around the world. Most people of the world depend on a few crop plants—wheat, rice, and corn. Most food from crop plants is taken from the seeds.

Over time, farmers have increased the amount of crops they can harvest in an acre of land. Selective breeding of crop plants and improved farming techniques have made crop production more efficient.

Chapter 24   Reproduction of Seed Plants

Section 24–1 Reproduction With Cones and Flowers (pages 609–616)

🔑 **Key Concepts**

- What are the reproductive structures of gymnosperms and angiosperms?
- How does pollination differ between angiosperms and gymnosperms?

Alternation of Generations (page 609)

1. Circle the letter of each sentence that is true about alternation of generations in plants.

   a. In all plants, the sporophyte generation is diploid.

   b. The gametophyte in seed plants is hidden within the sporophyte plant.

   c. The recognizable part of a seed-bearing plant is the gametophyte.

   d. In all plants, the gametophyte generation is haploid.

2. An important trend in plant evolution is the reduction in the size of the _____.

3. Where are the gametophytes found in gymnosperms and angiosperms?

   _____

   _____

Life Cycle of Gymnosperms (pages 610–611)

4. Reproduction in gymnosperms takes place in _____.

5. Circle the letter of what produces cones in gymnosperms.

   a. mature sporophyte   **c.** pine trees

   b. mature gametophyte   **d.** pollen seeds

6. What kind of cone produces male gametophytes? _____

7. The male gametophytes of gymnosperms are called _____.

8. Circle the letter of each sentence that is true about seed cones.

   a. They produce pollen grains.

   b. They produce female gametophytes.

   c. They have two ovules at the base of each scale.

   d. They are generally much larger than pollen cones.

9. Is the following sentence true or false? Each mature female gametophyte contains hundreds of egg cells ready for fertilization. _____

10. How long does the gymnosperm life cycle typically take to complete?

    _____

11. In the gymnosperm life cycle, how do the pollen grains reach the female cones?

_____

_____

12. What ensures that pollen grains stay on the scales of a female cone? _____

_____

_____

13. A structure grown by a pollen grain that contains two sperm nuclei is called

a(an) _____.

14. What happens to the two sperm cells once the pollen tube reaches the female

gametophyte? _____

_____

_____

15. Circle the letter of what a gymnosperm embryo can be called.

a. mature gametophyte

b. new sporophyte

c. mature sporophyte

d. new gametophyte

16. What are the three generations of the gymnosperm life cycle that are contained in a

gymnosperm seed? _____

_____

_____

_____

Structure of Flowers (pages 612–613)

17. What are the four kinds of specialized leaves that compose a flower?

a. _____

b. _____

c. _____

d. _____

Match the floral part with its description.

	Floral Part	Description
_____	**18.** Sepals	**a.** Stalk with the stigma at the top
_____	**19.** Petals	**b.** Structures where male gametophytes are produced
_____	**20.** Stamen	**c.** Flower part that contains one or more ovules
_____	**21.** Filament	**d.** Outermost, green floral parts
_____	**22.** Anthers	**e.** Long, thin structure that supports an anther
_____	**23.** Carpels	**f.** Innermost floral parts that produce female gametophytes
_____	**24.** Ovary	**g.** Sticky, top portion of style
_____	**25.** Style	**h.** Male structure made up of an anther and a filament
_____	**26.** Stigma	**i.** Brightly colored parts just inside the sepals

27. Label the parts of the flower on the illustration.

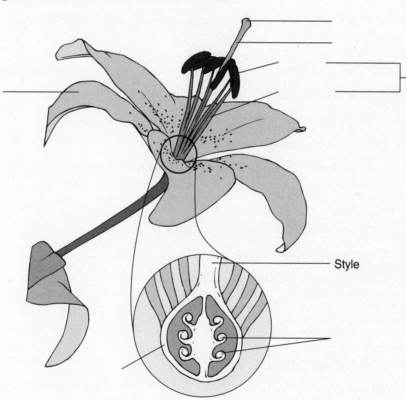

Style

28. What is a pistil? _____

_____

29. What are the separate male and female flowers on a corn plant? _____

_____

_____

_____

Life Cycle of Angiosperms (pages 614–615)

30. Where does reproduction in angiosperms take place? _____

_____

31. Inside the anthers, each cell undergoes meiosis and produces four haploid cells that each develop into a(an)_____.

32. In angiosperms, the pollen grain is the entire _____.

33. The female gametophyte of an angiosperm, contained within the ovary, is called the _____.

34. Circle the letter of each sentence that is true about the life cycle of angiosperms.

   a. The cycle begins when the mature sporophyte produces flowers.

   b. A pollen grain stops growing when it is released from the stigma.

   c. The female gametophyte develops in the ovule.

   d. The egg nucleus is one of the eight nuclei in the embryo sac.

Pollination (page 615)

35. How are most gymnosperms pollinated? _____

36. How are most angiosperms pollinated? _____

37. What are three kinds of animals that pollinate angiosperms? _____

_____

_____

Fertilization in Angiosperms (page 616)

38. What are the two distinct fertilizations that take place in angiosperms?

   a. _____

   _____

   b. _____

   _____

39. The food-rich tissue that nourishes a seedling as it grows is known as

_____.

40. Why is fertilization in angiosperms known as double fertilization? _____

_____

_____

41. Complete the flowchart about the life cycle of angiosperms.

> Inside the anthers, each cell undergoes _____ to produce megaspores.

↓

> Each megaspore becomes a(an) _____.

↓

> The nucleus of each pollen grain produces two haploid _____.

↓

> The pollen grain lands on a stigma and begins to grow a(an) _____
>
> that eventually reaches the ovary and enters the _____.

↓

> One of the sperm nuclei fuses with the egg nucleus to produce a(an) _____, and
>
> the other sperm nucleus fuses with two other nuclei to form a cell that grows into the _____.

Reading Skill Practice

Outlining is a way you can help yourself understand better and remember what you
have read. Write an outline for Section 24–1, Reproduction With Cones and Flowers.
In your outline, use the blue headings for the first level and the green subheadings
for the second level. Then, list the details that support, or back up, the main ideas.

Section 24–2 Seed Development and Germination (pages 618–621)

Key Concepts

- How do fruits form?
- How are seeds dispersed?
- What factors influence the dormancy and germination of seeds?

Seed and Fruit Development (page 618)

1. What is a fruit? _____

2. What happens as angiosperm seeds mature after fertilization is complete?

_____

_____

3. The outer layer of the seed that protects the embryo and its food supply is called a(an)

_____ .

4. Is the following sentence true or false? Both cucumbers and tomatoes are fruits.

_____

5. Circle the letter of each sentence that is true about fruits.

   a. As seeds mature, the ovary walls thicken to form a fruit.

   b. Fruits can carry one seed or several seeds.

   c. A fruit is a ripened ovary that encloses a seed or seeds.

   d. The inner wall of the ovary never touches the seed.

Seed Dispersal (page 619)

6. Why are seeds that are dispersed by animals typically contained in fleshy, nutritious

   fruits? _____

_____

7. Circle the letter of why seeds dispersed by animals are covered with tough coatings.

   a. The seeds need to be able to float on water.

   b. The coatings enable the seeds to pass through an animal unharmed.

   c. The seeds need to be digested by the animal that eats them.

   d. The coatings prevent the seeds from being eaten by animals.

8. Why are seeds dispersed by wind or water typically lightweight?

_____

_____

9. How are the seeds of ash and maple trees dispersed long distances from the parent

   plants? _____

_____

10. What adaptation does a coconut seed have that helps its dispersal? _____

_____

_____

_____

Seed Dormancy (page 620)

11. What is dormancy? _____

_____

12. What are two environmental factors that can cause a seed to end dormancy and germinate?

    a. _____   **b.** _____

13. What are two purposes served by seed dormancy?

    a. _____

    b. _____

14. Is the following sentence true or false? Some pine tree seeds remain dormant until the high temperatures generated by a forest fire cause cones to open and release the seeds.

_____

Seed Germination (page 621)

15. What is seed germination? _____

_____

16. Complete the flowchart about seed germination.

When a seed germinates, it absorbs _____.

↓

The water causes the endosperm to swell, which cracks open the _____.

↓

Through the cracked seed coat, the young _____ begins to grow.

17. Circle the letter of each sentence that is true about seed germination.

    a. In some dicots, the cotyledons protect the first foliage leaves.

    b. In most monocots, the cotyledon remains within the seed.

    c. In some dicots, the cotyledons remain below the soil and provide food for the seedling.

    d. In most monocots, the cotyledon emerges above ground to protect the leaves.

Section 24–3 Plant Propagation and Agriculture
(pages 622–626)

⬭ **Key Concepts**
- What forms of vegetative reproduction occur in plants?
- What is plant propagation?
- Which crops are the major food supply for humans?

Vegetative Reproduction (page 622)

1. The method of asexual reproduction used by many flowering plants is

   called _____.

2. What does vegetative reproduction enable a single plant that is well adapted to the

   environment to do? _____

   _____

   _____

3. Vegetative reproduction includes the production of new plants from what three kinds of
   plant structures?

   a. _____

   b. _____

   c. _____

4. Why does vegetative reproduction enable plants to reproduce very quickly?

   _____

   _____

5. What do spider plants produce that allows them to reproduce vegetatively?

   _____

6. Is the following sentence true or false? New plants can grow from the leaves of a parent
   plant if the leaves fall to the ground and the conditions are right.

   _____

7. How do strawberry plants reproduce vegetatively? _____

   _____

   _____

8. How do bamboo plants reproduce asexually? _____

   _____

Plant Propagation (page 623)

9. What do horticulturists use plant propagation for? _____

   _____

© Pearson Education, Inc., publishing as Pearson Prentice Hall.

10. Why might a horticulturist not want a plant to reproduce sexually by seeds?

_____

_____

11. Circle the letter of what a cutting must have to form roots when placed in a rooting mixture.

   a. Several stolons   c. Buds containing meristematic tissue

   b. A taproot   d. Buds without meristematic tissue

12. When a piece of stem or a lateral bud is cut from a parent plant and attached to another plant, what are the cut piece and the plant to which it is attached called?

_____

_____

13. When stems are used as scions, the process is called _____.

14. What is the process called when buds are used as scions? _____

15. In what kind of cases do growers use grafting and budding? _____

_____

Agriculture (pages 624–626)

16. Circle the letter showing when evidence suggests that agriculture developed in many parts of the world.

   a. about 1–2 million years ago   c. about 10,000–12,000 years ago

   b. about 1000–2000 years ago   d. about 100,000 years ago

17. What are three crop plants that most people of the world depend on for the bulk of their food supply?

   a. _____ b. _____ c. _____

18. The food taken from crops such as wheat, rice, and corn is stored in their

_____.

19. What are the four crops that 80 percent of all U.S. cropland is used to grow?

_____

20. What important crops were unknown in Europe before they were introduced there from the Americas? _____

_____

21. What are two ways in which the efficiency of agriculture has been improved?

   a. _____

   b. _____

22. How has the use of pesticides and fertilizers affected crop yields? _____

_____

_____

Name_____ Class_____ Date_____

Vocabulary Review

Labeling Diagrams   *Use the following words to label the parts of the flower:* anther, carpel, filament, ovary, ovule, petal, sepal, stamen, stigma, and style.

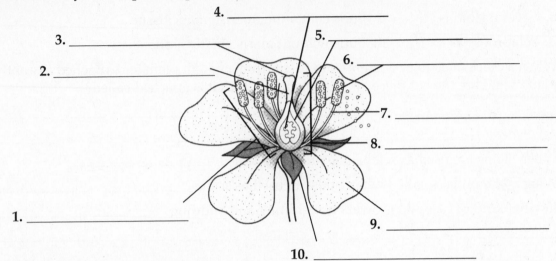

3. _____

2. _____

4. _____

5. _____

6. _____

7. _____

8. _____

1. _____

9. _____

10. _____

Completion   *Fill in the blanks with terms from Chapter 24.*

11. In gymnosperms, pollen grains form in _____.

12. The female gametophyte is produced by _____ in gymnosperms.

13. When a pollen grain lands on a stigma, it begins to grow a(an)

_____.

14. Brightly colored _____ attract pollinators to flowers.

15. In angiosperms, pollen grains are produced within the _____.

16. The sticky portion of the carpel where pollen grains often land is called the

_____.

17. The female gametophyte of the flowering plant consisting of eight nuclei and the

surrounding membrane is called the _____.

18. A food-rich tissue that nourishes the seedling as it grows is called the

_____.

19. The process of _____ in angiosperms produces a diploid
zygote and a triploid endosperm.

20. During _____, plant embryos are alive but not growing.

21. Seed _____ is the early growth stage of the plant embryo.

22. When flowering plants reproduce asexually, it is called _____.

23. Strawberry plants send out long trailing stems called _____ that
produce roots when they touch the ground.

24. In _____, stems are used as scions.

25. When buds are used as scions, the process is called _____.

© Pearson Education, Inc., publishing as Pearson Prentice Hall.

Chapter 25   Plant Responses and Adaptations

Summary

25–1 Hormones and Plant Growth

Plant growth is not precisely determined. However, plant growth still follows general growth patterns that differ among species. Plant growth never stops. New cells are always being made in meristems. Meristems are found at the tips of stems and roots. New cells later develop into specialized tissues.

Plants grow in response to environmental factors like light, moisture, gravity, and temperature. Certain plant chemicals also control plant growth. These chemicals are called hormones. A hormone is a substance that is produced in one part of an organism and affects another part of the same organism. The part of the organism affected by a hormone is the target cell or target tissue. Different kinds of target cells can respond to the same hormone. A single hormone may affect two different tissues in different ways.

One important group of plant hormones is auxins. Auxins have different effects on different tissues. Auxins make stems grow toward light and away from the pull of gravity. The tendency of a plant to grow toward light is called phototropism. Gravitropism is the response of a plant to the pull of gravity. Auxins make roots grow away from light and toward the pull of gravity. Auxins also control plant branching by keeping the buds on the sides of the stem from growing.

Growing roots and developing fruits and seeds make hormones called cytokinins. Cytokinins stimulate cell division and make dormant seeds sprout. Their effects are often opposite to the effects of auxins.

In the 1920s, Japanese scientists identified a substance produced by a fungus that stimulated plant growth. They named this substance gibberellin. Later, scientists learned that plants also produce gibberellins. Gibberellins cause dramatic increases in size and rapid growth.

Ethylene is another plant hormone. Plants release ethylene in response to auxins. Ethylene stimulates fruits to ripen.

25–2 Plant Responses

Plants respond to changes in their environment. They respond to gravity, light, and touch. These responses are called tropisms. Gravitropism is the response of a plant to gravity. Phototropism is the response of a plant to light. A plant's response to touch is called thigmotropism.

Some plants have a rapid response to touch that does not involve growth. This kind of response is caused by changes in the osmotic pressure of some cells. These pressure changes cause leaves to fold up or snap shut. This response enables a Venus' flytrap to trap an insect.

Many plants respond to periods of light and darkness. This is called photoperiodism. It is caused by changes in the length of periods of light and darkness. These changes affect plant pigments called phytochromes, causing plants to flower. Some plants, known as short-day plants, flower when days are short. Others, known as long-day plants, flower when the days are long.

Some plants lose their leaves and become dormant during the winter. Auxins and other hormones work together to control this. Changes in the length of light and dark periods cause a change in the chemistry of phytochrome. This change in phytochrome causes auxin production to drop. The production of ethylene increases. The leaves stop making chlorophyll. Other pigments in the leaves become visible as the green coloring disappears. The cells that join a leaf to the stem become weak, and an abscission layer forms. The abscission layer seals the leaf off from the rest of the plant. The leaves fall from the tree. Thick, waxy bud scales form. They cover the buds at the ends of the branches. The bud scales protect the buds from winter cold.

25–3 Plant Adaptations

Flowering plants live in many different environments. Through natural selection, plants have evolved different adaptations to live successfully in each environment.

Aquatic plants often live in mud that does not contain much oxygen. To get enough oxygen, many aquatic plants have air-filled spaces in their tissues. Oxygen diffuses through these spaces from the leaves to the roots.

Some plants can grow in salt water or in very salty air near the ocean. Many salt-tolerant plants have special cells that pump salt out of the plant tissues and onto the leaf surface. There, the rain washes off the salt.

Plants that live in the desert are called xerophytes. These plants must tolerate high daytime heat, sandy soil, strong winds, and little rain. These plants often have extensive roots, reduced leaves, and thick stems that can store water. Seeds of many desert plants can remain dormant for years. These seeds will germinate only when enough moisture guarantees them a chance to survive.

Some plants grow in soil with few nutrients. Carnivorous plants and parasites have adapted to living in environments with poor soil. Carnivorous plants trap and digest insects to get nitrogen. Parasites get water and nutrients directly from a host plant. Like all parasites, these plants harm their host plants.

Epiphytes are plants that are not rooted in soil. They grow directly on the bodies of other plants. Epiphytes are not parasites. They gather their own moisture, generally from rainfall. They also make their own food. Most epiphytes live in rain forests.

Many plants produce chemicals that are poisonous to the animals that eat them. These chemical defenses protect plants from potential predators.

Chapter 25   Plant Responses and Adaptations

Section 25–1 Hormones and Plant Growth
(pages 633–638)

🔑 **Key Concepts**

- What are plant hormones?
- How do auxins, cytokinins, gibberellins, and ethylene affect plant growth?

Patterns of Plant Growth (page 633)

1. Is the following sentence true or false? Plant growth follows patterns that are the same

   for all species. _____

2. Circle the letter of each sentence that is true about plant growth.

   a. Chemicals direct, control, and regulate plant growth.

   b. Meristems are found at places where plants grow rapidly.

   c. Plants stop growing when they reach maturity.

   d. Even very old plants continue to grow.

Plant Hormones (page 634)

3. What is a hormone? _____

   _____

   _____

4. What are two ways in which plant hormones control plant growth?

   a. _____

   _____

   b. _____

   _____

5. What is a target cell? _____

   _____

6. Circle the letter of each sentence that is true about hormones and plant growth.

   a. Plant hormones are produced in growing flowers and fruits.

   b. A single hormone may affect two different tissues in different ways.

   c. Hormones can activate the transcription of certain genes.

   d. All plant cells are affected by all plant hormones.

Auxins (pages 634–636)

7. What is phototropism? _____

   _____

8. From their experiment with oak seedlings, what did the Darwins

   suspect about the seedlings? _____

   _____

9. How do auxins affect plant cells? _____

10. Where are auxins produced, and how are they distributed in a plant? _____

_____

_____

11. Complete the flowchart about phototropism.

```
┌─────────────────────────────────────────────────┐
│  When light hits one side of a stem, a higher     │
│  concentration of                                 │
│                                                   │
│  auxins develops on the _____ side.     │
└─────────────────────────────────────────────────┘
                         │
                         ▼
┌─────────────────────────────────────────────────┐
│  The concentration of auxins stimulates cells on  │
│  the shaded side                                  │
│                                                   │
│  to _____.                              │
└─────────────────────────────────────────────────┘
                         │
                         ▼
┌─────────────────────────────────────────────────┐
│  As a result, the stem bends toward the _____.│
└─────────────────────────────────────────────────┘
```

12. What is gravitropism? _____

_____

13. Circle the letter of each sentence that is true about auxins.

   a. Auxins cause roots to grow downward.

   b. Auxins regulate cell division in meristems.

   c. Snipping off the tip of a plant removes the source of auxins.

   d. In roots, auxins stimulate cell elongation.

14. What is a lateral bud? _____

_____

15. The closer a bud is to the stem's tip, the more it is inhibited. What is this phenomenon

   called? _____

16. What are herbicides? _____

_____

Cytokinins (page 636)

17. What are cytokinins? _____

_____

_____

18. Circle the letter of each sentence that is true about cytokinins.

    a. They delay the aging of leaves.

    b. They stop cell division and the growth of lateral buds.

    c. They often produce effects opposite to those of auxins.

    d. They cause dormant seeds to sprout.

19. What are two examples of how cytokinins produce effects opposite to those of auxins?

    a. _____

    _____

    b. _____

    _____

Gibberellins (page 637)

20. What are gibberellins? _____

_____

21. Particularly in stems and fruits, gibberellins produce dramatic increases in

    _____.

Ethylene (page 638)

22. What do fruit tissues do in response to auxins? _____

_____

_____

23. Ethylene is a plant hormone that causes fruits to _____.

Section 25–2 Plant Responses (pages 639–642)

⬭ **Key Concepts**
- What are plant tropisms?
- What is photoperiodism?
- How do deciduous plants prepare for winter?

Tropisms (page 639)

1. What are tropisms? _____

_____

2. What do tropisms demonstrate about plants? _____

_____

_____

3. Complete the table about plant tropisms.

PLANT TROPISMS

Tropism	Definition
Gravitropism	
Phototropism	
	The response of a plant to touch

4. Circle the letter of each sentence that is true about the effects of thigmotropism.
   a. The tendrils of a grapevine wrap tightly around any object they encounter.
   b. A plant that is touched regularly may be stunted in growth.
   c. The stems of climbing plants don't grow straight up.
   d. When the tip of a vine encounters an object, it breaks off.

Rapid Responses (page 640)

5. The folding together of mimosa leaflets when touched is the result of what

   changes in cells at the base of each leaflet? _____

_____

6. What does a fly trigger in a Venus' flytrap that causes the leaf to snap shut?

_____

Photoperiodism (page 641)

7. Why are plants such as chrysanthemums and poinsettias called short-day plants?

_____

8. What are long-day plants? _____

9. What is photoperiodism? _____

_____

10. What is photoperiodism in plants responsible for? _____

_____

_____

11. What plant pigment is responsible for photoperiodism? _____

12. How does phytochrome control photoperiodism? _____

_____

_____

_____

Winter Dormancy (pages 641–642)

13. What is dormancy? _____

_____

14. How do shorter days and lower temperatures affect photosynthesis? _____

_____

15. As cold weather approaches, what happens to deciduous plants? _____

_____

_____

16. When days shorten at summer's end, what changes start a series of events that gradually shuts down the leaves of a flowering plant? _____

_____

_____

17. The layer of cells at the petiole that seals off a leaf from the vascular system is called the _____.

18. Why doesn't a tree's sap freeze during a cold winter? _____

_____

_____

_____

Reading Skill Practice

A flowchart can help you remember the order in which events occur. On a separate sheet of paper, create a flowchart that describes the steps that take place when flowering plants lose their leaves as winter approaches. This process is explained in the subsection Winter Dormancy. For more information about flowcharts, see Organizing Information in Appendix A at the back of your textbook.

Section 25–3 Plant Adaptations (pages 643–646)

⊂⊃ **Key Concepts**
- How are plants adapted to different environments?
- How do plants obtain nutrients from sources other than photosynthesis?
- How do plants defend themselves from insects?

Aquatic Plants (page 643)

1. What adaptation do aquatic plants have that allows them to grow in mud that is saturated with water and nearly devoid of oxygen? _____

_____

2. How do waterlilies get oxygen to their roots? _____

_____

_____

3. Circle the letter of each sentence that is true about the adaptations of aquatic plants.

   a. All aquatic plants grow very slowly after germination.

   b. In waterlilies, oxygen diffuses from open spaces in petioles into the roots.

   c. The knees of mangrove trees bring oxygen-rich air down to the roots.

   d. The seeds of some aquatic plants can float in water.

Salt-Tolerant Plants (page 644)

4. What adaptation do the leaves of salt-tolerant plants have that protects them against high salt concentration? _____

_____

_____

Desert Plants (pages 644–645)

5. What are three plant adaptations to a desert climate?

   a. _____

   b. _____

   c. _____

6. What are xerophytes? _____

7. Why do the roots of xerophytes have many hairs? _____

_____

8. Where is most of a desert plant's photosynthesis carried out? _____

_____

9. Why do cactuses have small leaves or no leaves at all? _____

_____

© Pearson Education, Inc., publishing as Pearson Prentice Hall.

10. What is the advantage for many desert plants that have seeds that can remain dormant for years? _____

_____

Nutritional Specialists (page 645)

11. The Venus' flytrap is an example of what kind of nutritional specialist?

_____

12. What nutrient do carnivorous plants need to obtain from insects that they can't otherwise get from the environment? _____

13. How does a Venus' flytrap obtain the nutrient it needs from an insect it catches?

_____

_____

_____

14. What common plant grows as a parasite on conifers in the western United States?

_____

Epiphytes (page 645)

15. What are epiphytes? _____

_____

16. Why aren't epiphytes considered to be plant parasites? _____

_____

_____

Chemical Defenses (page 646)

17. How do many plants defend themselves against insect attack? _____

_____

_____

18. How does nicotine protect a tobacco plant from potential predators? _____

_____

_____

Vocabulary Review

True or False   *In the space, write* true *if the statement is true. If the statement is false, write the term that makes the statement true.*

_____ 1. <u>Auxins</u> are plant hormones that stimulate cell elongation.

_____ 2. A(An) <u>abscission layer</u> is a meristematic area on the side of a stem that gives rise to side branches.

_____ 3. <u>Cytokinins</u> are plant hormones that increase the overall size of plants.

_____ 4. <u>Tropisms</u> are the responses of plants to external stimuli.

_____ 5. <u>Long-day</u> plants flower when days are short.

_____ 6. In <u>dormancy</u>, plant growth and activity decrease or stop.

_____ 7. <u>Xerophytes</u> are plants that are not rooted in soil and grow directly on other plants.

Matching   *In the space provided, write the letter that best matches each term.*

_____ 8. hormone

_____ 9. phototropism

_____ 10. gravitropism

_____ 11. apical dominance

_____ 12. herbicide

_____ 13. thigmotropism

_____ 14. photoperiodism

_____ 15. phytochrome

a. inhibition of lateral bud growth near stem tips

b. response of a plant to touch

c. response of a plant to the force of gravity

d. substance produced in one part of an organism that affects another part of the organism

e. plant pigment that responds to periods of light and darkness

f. compound that is toxic to plants

g. response of a plant to periods of light and darkness

h. response of a plant to light

Chapter 26   Sponges and Cnidarians

Summary

26–1 Introduction to the Animal Kingdom

All members of the kingdom Animalia share certain characteristics. Animals are multicellular, eukaryotic heterotrophs whose cells lack cell walls. The bodies of most animals contain tissues. Over 95 percent of all animal species are often grouped in a single, informal category: invertebrates. Invertebrates are animals that do not have a backbone, or vertebral column. The other 5 percent of animals are called vertebrates, because they have a backbone.

Animals carry out the following essential functions: feeding, respiration, circulation, excretion, response, movement, and reproduction. The study of the functions of organisms is called physiology. The structure, or anatomy, of an animal's body enables it to carry out physiological functions.

Many body functions help animals maintain homeostasis. Homeostasis is often maintained by internal feedback mechanisms. Most of these mechanisms involve feedback inhibition, in which the product or result of a process stops or limits the process.

Complex animals tend to have high levels of cell specialization and internal body organization, bilateral symmetry, a front end or head with sense organs, and a body cavity.

Animals that reproduce sexually begin life as zygotes. The zygote undergoes a series of divisions to form a blastula, a hollow ball of cells. The blastula folds in on itself, forming a single opening called a blastopore. The blastopore leads to a central tube that becomes the digestive tract. A protostome is an animal whose mouth is formed from the blastopore. A deuterstome is an animal whose anus is formed from the blastopore. The anus is the opening through which wastes leave the digestive tract.

During early development, the cells of most animal embryos differentiate into three layers, called germ layers. The endoderm is the innermost germ layer; the mesoderm is the middle germ layer; and the ectoderm is the outermost germ layer.

With the exception of sponges, every kind of animal exhibits some type of body symmetry. Some animals exhibit radial symmetry, in which any number of imaginary planes can be drawn through the center, each dividing the body into equal halves. More complex animals have bilateral symmetry, in which only a single imaginary plane can divide the body into two equal halves. Animals with bilateral symmetry usually exhibit cephalization, which is the concentration of sense organs and nerve cells at the front of the body. Most animals have a body cavity, which is a fluid-filled space that lies between the digestive tract and the body wall.

26–2 Sponges

Sponges make up the phylum Porifera. Sponges are sessile, meaning that they live their entire adult lives attached to a single spot. Sponges are classified as animals because they are multicellular, are heterotrophic, have no cell walls, and contain a few specialized cells.

Sponges are asymmetrical—they have no front or back ends. Sponges have specialized cells, called choanocytes, that move a steady current of water through the body. This water enters through pores in the body wall and leaves through the osculum, a large hole at the top of the central cavity. The movement of water through the sponge provides a simple mechanism for feeding, respiration, circulation, and excretion.

Sponges are filter feeders that sift microscopic food particles from the water. Digestion is intracellular, meaning that it takes place inside cells. Sponges can reproduce either sexually or asexually. In sexual reproduction, eggs are fertilized inside the sponge's body, a process called internal fertilization. After fertilization occurs, the resulting zygote develops into a larva. A larva is an immature stage of an organism that looks different from the adult form.

Sponges provide habitats for marine animals such as snails and sea stars. Sponges also form partnerships with photosynthetic organisms.

26–3 Cnidarians

Cnidarians are soft-bodied, carnivorous animals. They have stinging tentacles arranged around their mouths. Cnidarians are the simplest animals to have body symmetry and specialized tissues. Cnidarians get their name from cnidocytes, which are stinging cells on their tentacles.

Cnidarians exhibit radial symmetry. They have a central mouth surrounded by numerous tentacles. Cnidarians typically have a life cycle that includes two different-looking stages: a polyp and a medusa. A polyp has a cylindrical body with armlike tentacles. In a polyp, the mouth points upward. A medusa has a bell-shaped body with the mouth at the bottom. Polyps are usually sessile, while medusas are motile.

A cnidarian has a gastrovascular cavity, which is a digestive chamber with one opening. Food enters and wastes leave the same opening. Digestion is extracellular, meaning that it takes place outside of cells. For gathering information from the environment, cnidarians have a nerve net. A nerve net is a loosely organized network of nerve cells that together allow cnidarians to detect stimuli. Some cnidarians have a hydrostatic skeleton. In most cnidarians, sexual reproduction takes place with external fertilization in the water. External fertilization takes place outside the female's body.

Cnidarians include jellyfishes, hydras and their relatives, and sea anemones and corals. The class Scyphozoa contains the jellyfishes. Scyphozoans live their lives primarily as medusas. The class Hydrozoa contains hydras and related animals. The polyps of most hydrozoans grow in branching colonies. The Portuguese man-of-war is a colonial hydrozoan composed of many specialized polyps. The class Anthozoa contains sea anemones and corals. Anthozoans have only the polyp stage in their life cycles. Most corals are colonial, and their polyps grow together in large numbers. As the colonies grow, they secrete an underlying skeleton of calcium carbonate (limestone). Coral colonies produce the structures called coral reefs. Many coral reefs are now suffering from the effects of human activity.

Section 26–1 Introduction to the Animal Kingdom (pages 657–663)

Key Concepts
- What characteristics do all animals share?
- What essential functions do animals carry out?
- What are the important trends in animal evolution?

What Is an Animal? (page 657)

1. Is the following sentence true or false? The cells that make up animal bodies are eukaryotic. _____

2. What characteristics do all animals share? _____

_____

3. Complete the table about animals.

CATEGORIES OF ANIMALS

Category	Percentage of Species	Description	Examples
		Animals without backbones	
		Animals with backbones	

What Animals Do to Survive (pages 658–659)

4. What are seven essential functions that animals carry out?

   a. _____   e. _____

   b. _____   f. _____

   c. _____   g. _____

   d. _____

5. Complete the table about types of feeders.

TYPES OF FEEDERS

Type of Feeder	Description
	Feeds on plants
Carnivore	
Filter feeder	
	Feeds on decaying plant and animal material

6. Explain the difference between a parasite and a host. _____
_____
_____

7. What does an animal do when it respires? _____
_____

8. What does the excretory system of most animals do? _____
_____
_____

9. Animals respond to events in their environment using specialized cells called
_____.

10. What are receptors, and what is their function? _____
_____
_____

11. What does it mean that an animal is motile? _____
_____

12. What enables motile animals to move around? _____
_____
_____

13. Circle the letter of the process that helps a species maintain genetic diversity.

    a. asexual reproduction   **c.** response

    b. movement   **d.** sexual reproduction

14. What does asexual reproduction allow animals to do? _____
_____
_____

Trends in Animal Evolution (pages 660–663)

15. What are four characteristics that complex animals tend to have?

    a. _____

    b. _____

    c. _____

    d. _____

16. How have the cells of animals changed as animals have evolved? _____
_____
_____

17. Groups of specialized cells form _____, which form organs, which form _____.

18. After a zygote undergoes a series of divisions, it becomes a(an) _____

19. What is a protostome? _____

_____

20. What is a deuterostome? _____

_____

21. Is the following sentence true or false? Most invertebrates are deuterostomes.

_____

22. In the development of a deuterostome, when is the mouth formed? _____

_____

23. Complete the table about germ layers.

GERM LAYERS

Germ Layer	Location	Develops Into These Body Structures
	Innermost layer	
	Middle layer	
	Outermost layer	

24. Complete the table about body symmetry.

BODY SYMMETRY

Type of Symmetry	Description	Examples
	Body parts that repeat around the center	
	A single plane divides the body into two equal halves	

25. In an animal with radial symmetry, how many imaginary planes can be drawn through the center of the animal that would divide the animal in half? _____

_____

_____

Match the term with its meaning.

	Term		Meaning
_____	**26.** anterior	**a.**	Upper side
_____	**27.** posterior	**b.**	Back end
_____	**28.** dorsal	**c.**	Front end
_____	**29.** ventral	**d.**	Lower side

30. A body that is constructed of many repeated and similar parts, or segments, exhibits

_____ .

31. What is cephalization? _____

_____

32. How do animals with cephalization respond differently to the environment than

animals without cephalization? _____

_____

_____

33. What is a body cavity? _____

_____

34. Why is having a body cavity important? _____

_____

_____

Reading Skill Practice

An outline can help you remember the main points of a section. Write an outline of
Section 26–1. Use the section's blue headings for the first level of your outline and
the section's green headings for the second level. Support your headings with
details from the section. Do your work on a separate sheet of paper.

Section 26–2 Sponges (pages 664–667)

Key Concepts

- Why are sponges classified as animals?
- How do sponges carry out essential functions?

What Is a Sponge? (page 664)

1. Sponges are placed in the phylum _____.

2. What are pores, and where are pores on a sponge's body? _____
_____
_____

3. What does it mean that sponges are sessile? _____
_____
_____

4. Why are sponges classified as animals? _____
_____
_____

Form and Function in Sponges (pages 664–667)

5. Is the following sentence true or false? Sponges have no tissues. _____

6. What does the movement of water through a sponge provide? _____
_____
_____

Match the body part with its description.

Body Part	Description
_____ 7. Choanocyte	a. Cell that makes spicules
_____ 8. Spicule	b. Cell that uses flagella to move water through the sponge
_____ 9. Osculum	c. A large hole at the top of the sponge
_____ 10. Archaeocyte	d. A spike-shaped structure

11. Where does digestion take place in sponges? _____
_____

12. Circle the letter of each sentence that is true about sponges.

    a. Sponges are filter feeders.

    b. Sponges reproduce only asexually.

    c. Sponges rely on water movement to carry out body functions.

    d. Sponges do not have a nervous system.

13. How do many sponges protect themselves from predators? _____
_____

14. An immature stage of an organism that looks different from the adult form is
called a(an) _____.

15. How is a sponge larva different from the adult form? _____
_____

16. What are gemmules, and what is their role in sponge reproduction? _____
_____
_____
_____

Ecology of Sponges (page 667)

17. Why do you think many sponges are colored green? _____
_____

18. What adaptation may allow sponges to survive in a wide range of habitats?
_____
_____

Section 26–3 Cnidarians (pages 669–675)

Key Concepts
- What is a cnidarian?
- What two body plans exist in the cnidarian life cycle?
- What are the three groups of cnidarians?

Introduction (page 669)

1. Cnidarians are members of the phylum _____.

What Is a Cnidarian? (page 669)

2. What important features unite the cnidarians as a group? _____
_____
_____

3. What are cnidocytes? _____
_____

4. A poison-filled, stinging structure within a cnidocyte that contains a tightly coiled
dart is called a(an) _____.

Form and Function in Cnidarians (pages 670–672)

5. Is the following sentence true or false? Cnidarians have bilateral symmetry.
_____

6. What are the two stages in the cnidarian life cycle?
   a. _____   b. _____

7. Write labels on each illustration below to identify the life-cycle stage and to name the
different body parts.

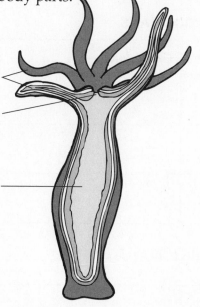
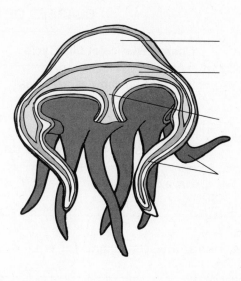

_____   _____

Match the cnidarian structure with its description.

Structure	Description
_____ 8. Gastroderm	a. Digestive chamber with single opening
_____ 9. Mesoglea	b. Sensory cells that help determine direction of gravity
_____ 10. Gastrovascular cavity	c. Inner lining of the gastrovascular cavity
_____ 11. Nerve net	d. Loosely organized network of nerve cells
_____ 12. Statocysts	e. Layer that lies between gastroderm and epidermis
_____ 13. Ocelli	f. Eyespots that detect light

14. Circle the letter of each sentence that is true about form and function in cnidarians.

    a. In a polyp, the mouth points downward.

    b. Materials that cannot be digested are passed out of the body through the mouth.

    c. Cnidarians respire by diffusion through their body walls.

    d. Most cnidarians reproduce sexually and asexually.

15. What does a cnidarian's hydrostatic skeleton consist of? _____

_____

16. Cnidarian polyps can reproduce asexually by _____ .

17. In the *Aurelia* life cycle, how are young medusas released? _____

_____

Groups of Cnidarians (pages 672–674)

18. Complete the table about classes of cnidarians.

CLASSES OF CNIDARIANS

Class	Characteristics of Life Cycle	Examples
	Live lives primarily as medusas	
	Polyps of most grow in branching colonies; some lack a medusa stage	
	Have only the polyp stage	

19. What is bioluminescence, and for what do jellyfishes use it? _____

_____

20. How do hydras differ from other cnidarians in the class Hydrozoa?

_____

_____

21. Circle the letter of each sentence that is true about corals.

    a. Corals secrete an underlying skeleton of calcium carbonate.

    b. Corals are solitary polyps that live at all depths of the ocean.

    c. Coral colonies growing near one another produce coral reefs.

    d. Most corals are colonial.

22. Is the following sentence true or false? Sea anemones are solitary polyps.

_____

23. How are coral reefs produced? _____

_____

_____

Ecology of Corals (page 675)

24. What variables determine the worldwide distribution of corals?

    a. _____

    b. _____

    c. _____

25. What do corals depend on to capture solar energy, recycle nutrients, and help lay down their skeletons? _____

_____

26. Circle the letter of each way that coral reefs can be harmed.

    a. Sediments from logging can smother corals.

    b. Overfishing can upset the ecological balance of coral reefs.

    c. Algae can remove energy from corals.

    d. Industrial pollutants can poison corals.

27. What is coral bleaching? _____

_____

_____

Chapter 26   Sponges and Cnidarians

Vocabulary Review

Completion   *Fill in the blanks with terms from Chapter 26.*

1. An animal without a backbone is called a(an) _____.

2. In sexual reproduction, the zygote undergoes a series of divisions to form a(an) _____, a hollow ball of cells.

3. A(An) _____ is an animal whose mouth is formed from the blastopore.

4. In _____ symmetry, only a single imaginary plane can divide the body into two equal halves.

5. The concentration of sense organs and nerve cells at the front end of the body is called _____.

6. A(An) _____ is an immature stage of an organism that looks different from the adult form.

7. Sponges are placed in the phylum _____.

8. A(An) _____ is a stage in the cnidarian life cycle in which the mouth points upward.

9. A digestive chamber with one opening is called a(an) _____ cavity.

Answering Questions   *In the space provided, write an answer to each question.*

10. What are the names of an animal's three germ layers? _____

_____

11. What is a body cavity? _____

_____

_____

12. What does the movement of water through a sponge provide for the sponge?

_____

_____

13. What kind of fertilization do sponges use? _____

_____

14. Which way does the mouth point in a medusa? _____

_____

15. What structures do coral colonies produce? _____

_____

Summary

27–1 Flatworms

The phylum Platyhelminthes consists of the flatworms. Flatworms are soft, flattened worms that have tissues and internal organ systems. They are the simplest animals to have three embryonic germ layers, bilateral symmetry, and cephalization. Flatworms are known as acoelomates, which means that there is no coelom between the tissues of flatworms. A coelom is a fluid-filled body cavity that is lined with tissue derived from mesoderm.

All flatworms rely on diffusion for some essential body functions, such as respiration, excretion, and circulation. Flatworms have a digestive cavity with a single opening, or mouth. Near the mouth is a muscular tube called a pharynx that pumps food into the digestive cavity. In free-living flatworms, several ganglia, or groups of nerve cells, control the nervous system. Many free-living flatworms have eyespots that detect changes in light. Asexual reproduction in free-living flatworms takes place by fission, in which an organism splits in two.

Turbellarians are free-living flatworms. Most live in marine or fresh water. Flukes are parasitic flatworms. Most flukes infect the internal organs of their hosts. Flukes reproduce sexually in the primary host and reproduce asexually in the intermediate host. Tapeworms are long, flat, parasitic worms that are adapted to life inside the intestines of their hosts.

27–2 Roundworms

The phylum Nematoda consists of the roundworms. Roundworms are slender, unsegmented worms. Most species are free-living. Roundworms have a body cavity between the endoderm and mesoderm tissues. This body cavity is called a pseudo-coelom, because it is only partially lined with mesoderm tissue. Roundworms have a digestive tract with two openings—a mouth and an anus.

Roundworms depend on diffusion for respiration, circulation, and excretion. In roundworms, the muscles and fluid in the pseudocoelom function as a hydrostatic skeleton. Roundworms reproduce sexually by internal fertilization.

Parasitic roundworms include trichinosis-causing worms, filarial worms, ascarid worms, and hookworms. Trichinosis is a disease caused by the roundworm *Trichinella*. Adult worms live and mate in the intestines of their hosts, including humans and pigs. *Trichinella* larvae form cysts. The roundworm completes its life cycle only when another animal eats muscle tissue containing these cysts.

Filarial worms are transmitted from host to host through biting insects. Filarial worms cause elephantiasis. Ascarid worms are serious parasites of humans and other animals. Hookworms infect one quarter of the people in the world.

27–3 Annelids

The phylum Annelida consists of earthworms and other annelids. The body of an annelid is divided into segments that are separated by septa, which are internal walls. Most segments are similar to one another. Some segments may be modified to perform special functions, including segments with eyes or antennae. In many annelids, bristles called setae are attached to each segment. Annelids are worms with segmented bodies. They have a true coelom that is lined with tissue derived from mesoderm.

Annelids have complex organ systems. Many annelids get their food using a pharynx. In earthworms, food moves through the crop, where it can be stored. Then, food moves through the gizzard, where it is ground into smaller pieces. Annelids typically have a closed circulatory system, in which blood is contained in a network of blood vessels.

Aquatic annelids often breathe through gills. A gill is an organ specialized for the exchange of gases underwater. Most annelids reproduce sexually. Some annelids, including earthworms, are hermaphroditic. When eggs are ready to be fertilized, a clitellum—a band of thickened segments—secretes a mucus ring in which fertilization takes place.

There are three classes of annelids: oligochaetes, leeches, and polychaetes. The oligochaetes are annelids that typically have streamlined bodies and relatively few setae. Most oligochaetes, including earthworms, live in soil or fresh water. The class Hirudinea includes the leeches. Leeches are typically external parasites that suck the blood and body fluids of their hosts. The polychaetes are marine annelids that have paired, paddlelike appendages tipped with setae.

Earthworms mix and aerate soil. Their tunnels provide passageways for plants. Their feces enrich the soil.

27–4 Mollusks

Mollusks—phylum Mollusca—are soft-bodied animals that usually have an internal or external shell. Many mollusks share similar developmental stages. Many aquatic mollusks have a free-swimming larval stage called a trochophore.

The body plan of most mollusks has four parts. The muscular foot is used for crawling, burrowing, or catching prey. The mantle is a thin layer of tissue that covers most of the mollusk's body. The shell is made by glands in the mantle that secrete calcium carbonate (limestone). Just beneath the mantle is the visceral mass, which consists of the internal organs.

Mollusks can be herbivores, carnivores, filter feeders, detritivores, or parasites. Snails and slugs feed using a flexible, tongue-shaped structure called a radula. Mollusks have an open circulatory system, in which blood is pumped through vessels and through sinuses.

There are three major classes of mollusks. The gastropods include pond snails, land slugs, and nudibranchs. Gastropods are shell-less or single-shelled mollusks that move by using a muscular foot located on the ventral (lower) side. The bivalves include clams, oysters, mussels, and scallops. Bivalves have two shells that are held together by one of two powerful muscles. Cephalopods include octopi, squids, cuttlefishes, and nautiluses. Cephalopods are typically soft-bodied mollusks in which the head is attached to a single foot. The foot is divided into tentacles. Most cephalopods have only small internal shells or no shells at all. Cephalopods have numerous complex sense organs.

Section 27–1 Flatworms (pages 683–688)

Key Concepts
- What are the defining features of flatworms?
- What are the characteristics of the three groups of flatworms?

What Is a Flatworm? (page 683)

1. Flatworms make up the phylum _____.

2. What are the defining features of flatworms? _____

_____

_____

3. A fluid-filled body cavity that is lined with tissue derived from mesoderm is called a(an) _____.

4. Why are flatworms known as acoelomates? _____

_____

5. Is the following sentence true or false? Flatworms are the simplest animals to have three germ layers. _____

Form and Function in Flatworms (pages 684–686)

6. Circle the letter of each sentence that is true about flatworms.

   a. Parasitic species are typically simpler in structure than free-living species.

   b. Free-living flatworms have organ systems for digestion, excretion, response, and reproduction.

   c. Free-living species probably evolved from parasitic ancestors.

   d. All flatworms rely on diffusion for some essential functions.

7. What do free-living flatworms feed on? _____

_____

_____

8. A muscular tube near the mouth at the end of the gastrovascular cavity is called a(an) _____.

9. What is the function of the pharynx? _____

_____

_____

10. What are flame cells, and what is their function? _____

_____

_____

11. What are ganglia, and what do they do in flatworms? _____

_____

_____

12. A group of cells that can detect changes in the amount of light in a flatworm's environment is called a(an) _____.

13. How do cilia help flatworms move, and what do muscle cells allow them to do?

_____

_____

_____

14. What is a hermaphrodite? _____

_____

_____

15. What occurs during fission? _____

_____

_____

16. Is the following sentence true or false? Free-living flatworms often have complex life cycles that involve both sexual and asexual reproduction. _____

Groups of Flatworms (pages 686–688)

17. Complete the table about the main groups of flatworms.

GROUPS OF FLATWORMS

Common Name	Class	Description
	Turbellaria	
		Parasitic flatworms that infect hosts' internal organs or outside parts
	Cestoda	

18. Circle the letter of each sentence that is true of turbellarians.

a. Most live in marine or fresh water.

b. Most are the same color, form, and size.

c. Most are bottom dwellers.

d. The most familiar are the planarians.

19. How does the blood fluke *Schistosoma mansoni* infect humans? _____
_____

20. In which host do blood flukes reproduce sexually, and in which do they reproduce asexually? _____
_____

21. On the illustration of the blood fluke's life cycle, label the primary host and the intermediate host.

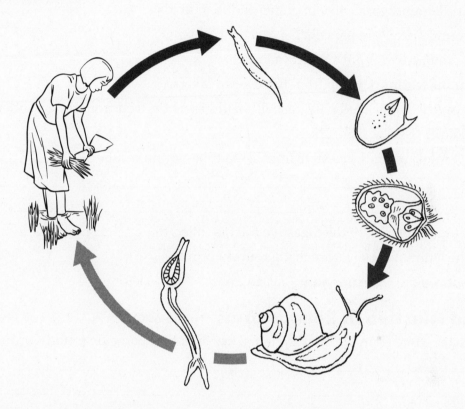

22. In what areas is schistosomiasis particularly widespread? _____
_____
_____

23. The head of an adult tapeworm is called a(an) _____.

24. What does a tapeworm use its scolex for? _____
_____

25. What are proglottids? _____

26. Sperm are produced by male reproductive organs, called _____.

27. Is the following sentence true or false? Sperm produced by a tapeworm's testes can fertilize the eggs of the same individual. _____

Section 27–2 Roundworms (pages 689–693)

Key Concepts
- What are the defining features of roundworms?
- What roundworms are important in human disease?

What Is a Roundworm? (page 689)

1. Circle the letter of each sentence that is true about roundworms.

   a. Parasitic roundworms live in plants and in animals.

   b. All roundworms are parasitic.

   c. Some roundworms are a meter in length.

   d. All roundworms develop from three germ layers.

2. A body cavity that is lined only partially with tissue derived from the mesoderm is called a(an) _____.

3. How is a roundworm's digestive tract like a tube-within-a-tube? _____

   _____

   _____

4. The posterior opening of the digestive tract is called the _____.

5. Circle the letter of each feature that a roundworm has.

   a. pseudocoelom   b. mouth   c. anus   d. coelom

Form and Function in Roundworms (page 690)

6. Which have more complex body systems, free-living or parasitic roundworms?

   _____

   _____

7. Is the following sentence true or false? Many free-living roundworms are predators.

   _____

8. Roundworms exchange gases and excrete metabolic wastes through their

   _____.

9. What can roundworms' sense organs detect? _____

   _____

10. Do roundworms reproduce sexually or asexually? _____

Roundworms and Human Disease (pages 690–692)

11. How do *Trichinella* roundworms cause pain in their hosts? _____

    _____

    _____

    _____

12. Complete the table about roundworms and human disease.

DISEASE-CAUSING ROUNDWORMS

Roundworm	Disease or Condition Caused	How Disease Is Spread
Trichinella		
	Elephantiasis	
Ascarid worms		
	Weakness and poor growth	

13. What is elephantiasis? _____

_____

_____

14. Circle the letter of each sentence that is true about the life cycle of *Ascaris*.

   a. Larvae in the lungs are coughed up and swallowed.

   b. The eggs develop into larvae in the lungs.

   c. Fertilized eggs leave the host's body in feces.

   d. The host ingests *Ascaris* eggs in contaminated food or water.

15. How are ascarid worms commonly spread? _____

_____

_____

16. Where do hookworm eggs hatch and develop? _____

_____

Research on *C. elegans* (page 693)

17. Circle the letter of each sentence that is true about *C. elegans*.

   a. It is a free-living roundworm.

   b. Its DNA was the first of any multicellular animal's to be sequenced completely.

   c. It feeds on rotting vegetation.

   d. Its DNA has 30 times the number of base pairs that human DNA has.

Name_____ Class_____ Date _____

Section 27–3 Annelids (pages 694–699)

Key Concepts
- What are the defining features of annelids?
- What are the characteristics of the three classes of annelids?

Introduction (page 694)

1. Of what phylum are earthworms a member? _____

2. What evidence is there that annelids are more closely related to clams and snails than to flatworms or roundworms? _____

_____

What Is an Annelid? (page 694)

3. What is a septum? _____

_____

4. Attached to each annelid segment are bristles called _____.

5. Annelids are among the simplest animals to have a true _____.

Form and Function in Annelids (pages 695–696)

6. How is the pharynx used differently in carnivorous species than in annelids that feed on decaying vegetation? _____

_____

_____

_____

7. What is a closed circulatory system? _____

_____

_____

8. What is a gill? _____

_____

9. How do aquatic annelids respire differently than land-dwelling annelids?

_____

_____

_____

10. How do annelids keep their skins moist? _____

11. What are the two major groups of body muscles in annelids called?

a. _____

b. _____

12. Marine annelids have paddlelike appendages called _____.

13. What is a clitellum, and what is its function? _____

_____

_____

14. Write labels on the illustration of the annelid for each of the features pointed to.

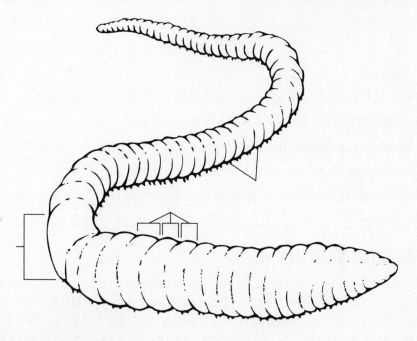

Groups of Annelids (pages 697–698)

15. Complete the table about common types of oligochaetes.

OLIGOCHAETES

Type of Oligochaete	Description	Habitat
	Long, pinkish-brown worms with few setae	
	Red, threadlike worms with few setae	

16. Circle the letter of each sentence that is true about leeches.

   a. They suck blood and body fluids from their hosts.

   b. Most live in moist, tropical habitats.

   c. They are typically external parasites.

   d. All are carnivores that feed on snails.

17. Circle the letter of each sentence that is true about polychaetes.

   a. They typically have only a few setae.

   b. They have paired, paddlelike appendages tipped with setae.

   c. They suck the blood of their host.

   d. They are marine annelids.

18. What annelids do polychaetes include? _____
_____

Ecology of Annelids (page 699)

19. How do the tunnels of earthworms affect other organisms? _____

_____

_____

_____

20. Circle the letter of each sentence that is true about annelids.

    a. Earthworms are important to the diet of birds.

    b. Annelids bring minerals from deep soil layers to the surface.

    c. Marine annelids spend their lives burrowing through soil.

    d. Annelid larvae form part of the animal plankton.

Reading Skill Practice

A flowchart can help you remember the order in which a process or series of events occurs. On a separate sheet of paper, make a flowchart for the process in earthworms of feeding and digestion, described on page 695. For more information about flowcharts, see Organizing Information in Appendix A of your textbook.

Section 27–4 Mollusks (pages 701–708)

🔑 Key Concepts
- What are the defining features of mollusks?
- What is the basic body plan of mollusks?
- What are the characteristics of the three main classes of mollusks?

What Is a Mollusk? (page 701)

1. Mollusks are members of the phylum _____.

2. Circle the letter of each sentence that is true about mollusks.

   a. They share similar developmental stages.

   b. They usually have an internal or external shell.

   c. They are the ancestors of annelids.

   d. They are soft-bodied animals.

3. What is a trochophore? _____

Form and Function in Mollusks (pages 702–704)

4. What are the four parts of the body plan of most mollusks?

   a. _____   c. _____

   b. _____   d. _____

5. What forms does the muscular mollusk foot take? _____

   _____

   _____

6. The thin layer of tissue that covers most of the mollusk's body is called the

   _____.

7. How is the mollusk shell made? _____

   _____

8. Snails and slugs feed using a tongue-shaped structure known as a(an) _____.

9. What is a siphon? _____

   _____

10. Why do land snails and slugs typically live only in moist places? _____

    _____

    _____

    _____

11. How does an open circulatory system carry blood to all parts of a mollusk's body?

    _____

    _____

    _____

12. A large saclike space in the body is called a(an) _____.

13. Ammonia is removed from the blood and released out of the body by tube-shaped

_____.

14. Circle the letter of each sentence that is true about mollusk response.

   a. Clams have a simple nervous system.

   b. Octopi and their relatives have the most highly developed
      nervous system of all invertebrates.

   c. Clams have well-developed brains.

   d. Vertebrates are more intelligent than octopi.

15. Where does fertilization take place in tentacled mollusks and certain snails?

_____

Groups of Mollusks (pages 705–707)

16. Complete the table about groups of mollusks.

GROUPS OF MOLLUSKS

Class	Common Name	Description of Shell	Examples
	Gastropods		
	Bivalves		
	Cephalopods		

17. Circle the letter of each sentence that is true about bivalves.

   a. Mussels use sticky threads to attach themselves to rocks.

   b. Some bivalves feed on material deposited in sand or mud.

   c. Clams move by flapping their shells rapidly when threatened.

   d. Scallops sting predators with recycled cnidarian nematocysts.

18. How do gastropods move? _____

_____

19. The cephalopod head is attached to a single _____.

20. What is a cephalopod's foot divided into? _____

21. What allows squids to locate a wide variety of prey? _____

_____

_____

22. The only present-day cephalopods with external shells are _____.

Ecology of Mollusks (page 708)

23. What allows mollusks to inhabit the extreme environment around deep-sea volcanic vents? _____

_____

_____

_____

24. Why can careful checks of bivalves warn public health officials of possible health problems to come? _____

_____

_____

_____

Vocabulary Review

Crossword Puzzle   *Use the clues below to fill in the spaces of the puzzle with the correct words.*

Across

3. process of asexual reproduction in free-living flatworms
6. annelid that sucks blood
7. structure in mollusks made of calcium carbonate
8. mollusk with tentacles
10. organism that has no coelom
12. type of annelid that includes the earthworm
14. thin layer of tissue that covers most of a mollusk's body
15. body cavity only partially lined with mesoderm

Down

1. soft-bodied invertebrate with an internal or external shell
2. structure in mollusks that contains the internal organs
4. marine annelid with appendages
5. fluid-filled body cavity lined with mesoderm tissue
9. structure used for respiration in mollusks
11. groups of nerve cells that control the nervous system in free-living flatworms
13. single-shelled mollusk that moves using its muscular foot

Summary

28–1 Introduction to the Arthropods

Phylum Arthropoda includes animals such as crabs, spiders, and insects. Arthropods have a segmented body, a tough exoskeleton, and jointed appendages. An exoskeleton is an external body covering. An arthropod exoskeleton is made from protein and a carbohydrate called chitin. All arthropods have jointed appendages. Appendages are structures such as legs and antennae that extend from the body wall.

The evolution of arthropods—by natural selection and other processes—has led to fewer body segments and highly specialized appendages for feeding, movement, and other functions. Most living arthropods have only two or three segments. Living arthropods have specialized appendages such as antennae, walking legs, wings, and mouthparts.

Arthropods include herbivores, carnivores, and omnivores. Most terrestrial arthropods breathe through a network of branching tracheal tubes that extend throughout the body. Air enters and leaves the tracheal tubes through small openings called spiracles. Other terrestrial arthropods, such as spiders, respire using book lungs. Most aquatic arthropods have gills. Arthropods have an open circulatory system. Most terrestrial arthropods dispose of nitrogen-containing wastes using saclike organs called Malpighian tubules. Terrestrial arthropods have internal fertilization. Aquatic arthropods have internal or external fertilization.

When arthropods outgrow their exoskeltons, they undergo periods of molting. During molting, an arthropod sheds its entire exoskeleton and manufactures a larger one to take its place.

28–2 Groups of Arthropods

Arthropods are classified based on the number and structure of their body segments and appendages—particularly their mouthparts.

Crustaceans—subphylum Crustacea—include crabs, shrimps, lobsters, crayfishes, and barnacles. Crustaceans typically have two pairs of antennae, two or three body sections, and chewing mouthparts called mandibles. Crustaceans with three body sections have a head, a thorax, and an abdomen. The thorax lies just behind the head and houses most of the internal organs. In crustaceans with two sections, the head and thorax are fused, forming a cephalothorax.

Chelicerates—subphylum Chelicerata—include horseshoe crabs, spiders, ticks, and scorpions. Chelicerates have mouthparts called chelicerae and two body sections. Nearly all chelicerates have four pairs of walking legs. Chelicerates are divided into two main classes—Merostomata and Arachnida. Class Merostomata includes horseshoe crabs. Horseshoe crabs are the oldest living arthropods. Class Arachnida includes spiders, mites, ticks, and scorpions. Spiders are the largest group of arachnids. Spiders spin strong webs by forcing liquid silk through spinnerets, organs that contain silk glands.

Uniramians—subphylum Uniramia—include centipedes, millipedes, and insects. Uniramians have jaws, one pair of antennae, and unbranched appendages. Centipedes have a few to more than 100 pairs of legs. Most body segments have one pair of legs each. Centipedes are carnivores. Millipedes have two, not one, pairs of legs per segment. Millipedes feed on dead or decaying plant material.

28–3 Insects

Insects have a body divided into three parts—head, thorax, and abdomen. Three pairs of legs are attached to the thorax. A typical insect has a pair of antennae, a pair of compound eyes, and two pairs of wings. Compound eyes are made of many lenses, and they detect minute changes in color and movement.

Insects have three pairs of appendages used as mouthparts, including a pair of mandibles. Insect mouthparts are a variety of shapes.

The growth and development of insects usually involve metamorphosis, which is a process of changing shape and form. In incomplete metamorphosis, the immature forms of insects look very much like adults. The immature forms are called nymphs. Nymphs gradually acquire adult structures, such as wings, and functional sex organs. Insects such as bees, moths, and beetles undergo complete metamorphosis. These insects hatch into larvae that look and act nothing like adults. A larva changes into a pupa, the stage in which an insect changes from larva to adult.

Insects are known for their destructive effects. Termites destroy wood, and mosquitoes bite humans. Yet, insects are also beneficial to humans. For example, insects pollinate many crops.

Insects communicate using sound, chemical, and other types of signals. Pheromones are specific chemical messengers that affect behavior or development in other individuals of the same species.

Ants, bees, termites, and some of their relatives form complex associations called societies. A society is a group of animals of the same species that work together for the benefit of the whole group.

28–4 Echinoderms

Phylum Echinodermata consists of animals such as sea stars, sea urchins, and sand dollars. Echinoderms are characterized by spiny skin, a water vascular system, and suction-cuplike structures called tube feet. Echinoderms have an endoskeleton, which is an internal skeleton. Most adult echinoderms exhibit five-part radial symmetry. Echinoderm larvae exhibit bilateral symmetry. Echinoderms are deuterostomes—an indication that echinoderms and vertebrates are closely related.

Echinoderms have a system of internal tubes called a water vascular system. The water vascular system is filled with fluid. It carries out many essential body functions in echinoderms, including respiration, circulation, and movement. It opens to the outside through a sievelike structure called a madreporite. In sea stars, the madreporite connects to a ring canal. From the ring canal, five radial canals extend along body segments. Attached to each radial canal are hundreds of tube feet. A tube foot is a structure that operates much like a suction cup. In most echinoderms, waste is released as feces through the anus. Most echinoderms move using their tube feet. Echinoderms reproduce by external fertilization.

Classes of echinoderms include sea urchins and sand dollars, brittle stars, sea cucumbers, sea stars, and sea lilies and feather stars. Echinoderms are common in a variety of marine habitats. Sea urchins help control the distribution of algae and other forms of marine life. Sea stars are important predators that help control the numbers of clams and corals.

Section 28–1 Introduction to the Arthropods
(pages 715–719)

Key Concepts
- What are the main features of arthropods?
- What are the important trends in arthropod evolution?
- What happens when an arthropod outgrows its exoskeleton?

What Is an Arthropod? (page 715)

1. What is the basic body plan of all arthropods? _____
_____
_____

2. A tough body wall that protects and supports the body of arthropods is called a(an)
_____ .

3. What is chitin? _____
_____
_____

4. Circle the letter of each sentence that is true about arthropod exoskeletons.
   a. The exoskeletons of many land-dwelling species have a waxy covering.
   b. All arthropod exoskeletons are the same shape.
   c. Lobster exoskeletons cannot be crushed by hand.
   d. An exoskeleton is an external covering.

5. What are appendages? _____
_____
_____

6. Is the following sentence true or false? The appendages of arthropods are jointed.
_____

Evolution of Arthropods (page 716)

7. Where did the first arthropods appear more than 600 million years ago?
_____

8. What are two ways in which arthropods have evolved since they first appeared?
   a. _____
   b. _____

9. Circle the letter of each sentence that is true about arthropod evolution.

  a. Most primitive arthropods had only one or two body segments.

  b. Arthropod appendages evolved into different forms.

  c. The early body plan was modified gradually.

  d. Appendages of living arthropods include wings, flippers, and mouthparts.

Form and Function in Arthropods (pages 716–719)

10. Is the following sentence true or false? Arthropods include herbivores, carnivores, and omnivores. _____

Match the arthropod structure with its description.

Structure	Description
_____ **11.** Tracheal tubes	**a.** Saclike organs that extract wastes from the blood and add them to feces
_____ **12.** Spiracles	**b.** Network of branching tubes through which arthropods breathe
_____ **13.** Book lungs	**c.** Organs through which horseshoe crabs respire
_____ **14.** Book gills	**d.** Layers of respiratory tissue stacked like the pages of a book through which spiders respire
_____ **15.** Malpighian tubules	**e.** Small openings on the side of the body through which air enters and leaves tracheal tubes

16. Complete the concept map about arthropod respiration.

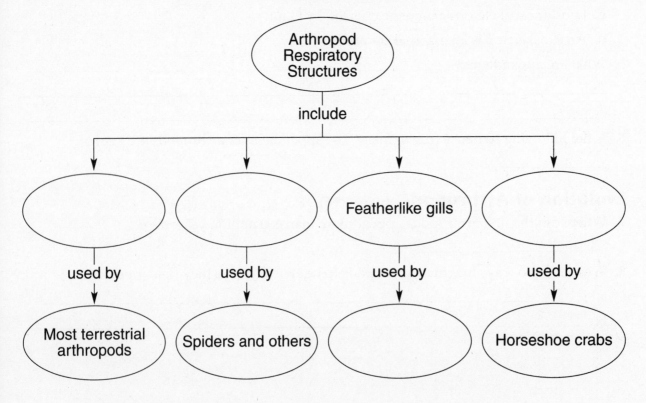

© Pearson Education, Inc., publishing as Pearson Prentice Hall.

17. Circle the letter of each sentence that is true about the response to the environment by arthropods.

   a. Most arthropods have sophisticated sense organs.

   b. All arthropods have a brain.

   c. Ganglia along a ventral nerve cord coordinate the movements of individual legs.

   d. Very few arthropods have a well-developed nervous system.

18. How do aquatic arthropods carry out excretion? _____

_____

_____

19. How do arthropods move? _____

_____

20. Circle the letter of each sentence that is true about arthropod reproduction.

   a. Aquatic arthropods have only internal fertilization.

   b. In some species, males have an organ that places sperm inside females.

   c. Terrestrial arthropods may have internal or external fertilization.

   d. In some aquatic species, males shed sperm around eggs released into the environment.

Growth and Development in Arthropods (page 719)

21. When do arthropods undergo periods of molting? _____

_____

22. What occurs in arthropods during molting? _____

_____

_____

Section 28–2 Groups of Arthropods
(pages 720–725)

⊂▭ **Key Concepts**
- How are arthropods classified?
- What are the distinguishing features of the three major groups of arthropods?

Introduction (page 720)

1. What characteristics do biologists use to classify arthropods? _____
_____
_____

2. What are the three major groups of arthropods?

   a. _____

   b. _____

   c. _____

Crustaceans (pages 720–721)

3. Circle the letter of each description of structures that crustaceans typically have.

   a. two pairs of branched antennae

   b. four or five body sections

   c. chewing mouthparts called mandibles

   d. two or three body sections

4. Label the two body sections of a typical crustacean.

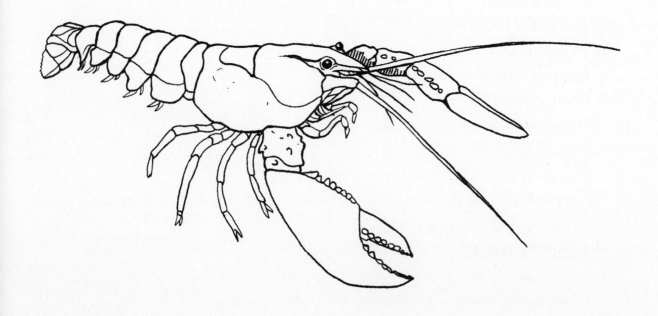

5. The largest group of crustaceans is the _____.

6. Complete the table about crustacean body parts.

CRUSTACEAN BODY PARTS

Body Part	Description
Thorax	
	Fusion of the head with the thorax
Abdomen	
	The part of the exoskeleton that covers the cephalothorax
Mandible	
	First pair of legs in decapods, which bear large claws
Swimmerets	

7. Circle the letter of each sentence that is true about barnacles.

a. They are sessile.

b. They have an outer, shell-like covering.

c. They move backward by snapping a tail.

d. They attach themselves to rocks and marine animals.

Spiders and Their Relatives (pages 722–724)

8. Horseshoe crabs, spiders, ticks, and scorpions are grouped as _____.

9. Circle the letter of each description of structures that chelicerates have.

a. four or five pairs of legs

b. three or four body sections

c. two pairs of branched antennae

d. mouthparts called chelicerae

10. What is the function of the chelicerae? _____

_____

_____

11. The appendages near the mouth that are usually modified to grab prey are called

_____.

12. How do spiders respire? _____

_____

_____

13. What arthropods do arachnids include? _____

_____

14. How are horseshoe crabs like and unlike crabs? _____

_____

_____

15. Why must spiders liquefy their food to swallow it? _____

_____

16. Circle the letter of each sentence that is true about spiders and silk.

   a. Spiders spin silk into cocoons for eggs.

   b. Spinning webs seems to be a programmed behavior.

   c. Spinnerets are organs that contain silk glands.

   d. Tarantulas cannot produce silk.

17. Is the following sentence true or false? Mites and ticks are often parasitic.

_____

18. Scorpions have pedipalps that are enlarged into _____.

19. What do ticks transmit that cause Rocky Mountain spotted fever and Lyme disease?

_____

_____

Insects and Their Relatives (page 725)

20. Centipedes, millipedes, and insects are all grouped as _____.

21. Circle the letter of each description of structures that uniramians have.

   a. one pair of antennae

   b. unbranched appendages

   c. mouthparts called chelicerae

   d. jaws

22. Why are centipedes restricted to moist or humid areas? _____

_____

_____

23. How many pairs of legs does each body segment of most centipedes have? _____

_____

_____

24. How many pairs per segment do millipedes have?

_____

_____

Section 28–3 Insects (pages 726–733)

☞ Key Concepts

- What are the distinguishing features of insects?
- What two types of development can insects undergo?
- What types of insects form societies?

Introduction (page 726)

1. What are three characteristics of insects that have contributed to their evolutionary success?

   a. _____

   b. _____

   c. _____

What Is an Insect? (pages 727–729)

2. Label the three body parts of an insect.

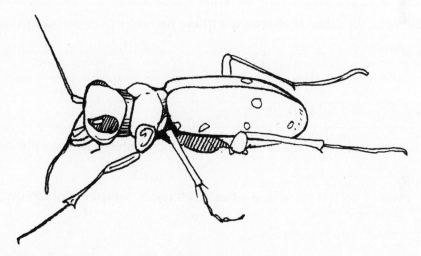

3. How many pairs of legs does an insect have, and where are they attached?

   _____

4. Circle the letter of each sentence that is true about a typical insect.

   a. It has tracheal tubes used for respiration.

   b. It has a pair of compound eyes on the head.

   c. It has two pairs of wings on the abdomen.

   d. It has a pair of antennae on the head.

5. What is the multiple-lens structure of the compound eye better at detecting than the human eye? _____

6. Where do insects have chemical receptors for taste and smell? _____

   _____

   _____

© Pearson Education, Inc., publishing as Pearson Prentice Hall.

7. Is the following sentence true or false? Many insects have well-developed ears.
   _____

8. Why do insect mouthparts take on a variety of shapes? _____
   _____
   _____

9. How many pairs of wings does a flying insect typically have, and what are they made of? _____
   _____
   _____

10. What has the evolution of flight allowed insects to do? _____
    _____
    _____
    _____

11. What is metamorphosis? _____
    _____

12. What is the main difference between complete metamorphosis and incomplete metamorphosis? _____
    _____
    _____
    _____

13. The immature forms of an insect that undergo incomplete metamorphosis are called _____.

14. Circle the letter of each type of insect that undergoes complete metamorphosis.
    a. moths
    b. bees
    c. chinch bugs
    d. beetles

15. What do the insects that undergo complete metamorphosis hatch into?
    _____

16. The stage in which an insect changes from larva to adult is called a(an)
    _____.

17. Circle the letter of each sentence that is true about complete metamorphosis.
    a. The nymphs gradually acquire adult structures.
    b. During the pupal stage, the body is completely remodeled inside and out.
    c. The larva molts a few times but changes little in appearance.
    d. The adult that emerges seems like a completely different animal from the larva.

Insects and Humans (page 730)

18. Is the following sentence true or false? Only male mosquitoes bite humans and other animals to get a blood meal. _____

19. How do insects contribute beneficially to agriculture? _____

_____

_____

_____

Insect Communication (page 731)

20. Circle the letter of each sentence that is true about insect communication.

   a. To attract females, male crickets chirp.

   b. Much of an insect's communication involves finding a mate.

   c. Insects communicate using visual signals.

   d. Fireflies use sound cues to communicate with potential mates.

21. What are pheromones? _____

_____

_____

Insect Societies (pages 732–733)

22. What is a society? _____

_____

_____

23. Circle the letter of each sentence that is true about castes.

   a. Each caste has a body form specialized for its role.

   b. Most insect societies have multiple queens.

   c. Groups of individuals in a society are specialized to perform particular tasks.

   d. The queen is typically the largest individual in the colony.

24. What does a honeybee's round dance tell the other bees? _____

_____

25. What does a honeybee's waggle dance tell the other bees? _____

_____

Reading Skill Practice

By looking carefully at illustrations in textbooks, you can help yourself understand better what you have read. Look carefully at Figure 28–16 on page 728. What important idea do these illustrations communicate? Do your work on a separate sheet of paper.

Section 28–4 Echinoderms (pages 734–738)

Key Concepts
- What are the distinguishing features of echinoderms?
- What functions are carried out by the water vascular system of echinoderms?
- What are the different classes of echinoderms?

Introduction (page 734)

1. An internal skeleton is called a(an) _____.

2. What forms an echinoderm's endoskeleton? _____
_____

3. In what environment do all echinoderms live? _____

What Is an Echinoderm? (page 734)

4. Is the following sentence true or false? The bodies of most echinoderms are
two-sided. _____

5. What are five features that characterize echinoderms?
   a. _____   d. _____
   b. _____   e. _____
   c. _____

6. What characteristic of echinoderms indicates that they are closely related to
vertebrates? _____

Form and Function in Echinoderms (pages 735–736)

7. What functions does the water vascular system carry out in echinoderms?
_____

8. The water vascular system opens to the outside through a sievelike structure called
a(an) _____.

9. What is a tube foot? _____

10. Is the following sentence true or false? Sea stars usually feed on mollusks.
_____

11. In most echinoderms, how are solid wastes released? _____
_____

12. What is the structure of the nervous system in most echinoderms? _____
_____
_____

13. What do most echinoderms use to move? _____

14. Is the following sentence true or false? Echinoderms reproduce by internal
fertilization. _____

© Pearson Education, Inc., publishing as Pearson Prentice Hall.

Groups of Echinoderms (pages 737–738)

15. Complete the table about groups of echinoderms.

GROUPS OF ECHINODERMS

Group	Description of Feeding	Description of Body
	Many are detritivores or grazers	Disk-shaped
Sea cucumbers		Look like warty, moving pickles
Sea stars	Carnivores	
		Long, feathery arms and attached to the ocean bottom by a stalk

16. How do sand dollars defend themselves? _____

_____

17. When a brittle star is attacked, it sheds one or more arms. How does this help the

echinoderm? _____

_____

18. Where are most sea cucumbers found? _____

19. What happens if a sea star is pulled into pieces? _____

_____

20. Where do many feather stars live? _____

Ecology of Echinoderms (page 738)

21. What is the effect of a sudden rise or fall in the number of echinoderms in a marine

habitat? _____

22. Circle the letter of each sentence that is true about the ecology of echinoderms.

a. The crown-of-thorns sea star is a major threat to coral reefs.

b. Sea urchins help control the distribution of algae.

c. Echinoderms feed almost exclusively on coral.

d. Sea stars help control the number of clams and corals.

Chapter 28 Arthropods and Echinoderms

Vocabulary Review

Labeling Diagrams   *Use terms from Chapter 28 to label the diagram below.*

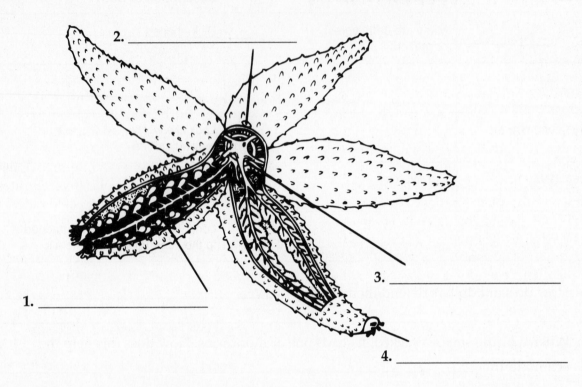

2. _____

3. _____

1. _____

4. _____

Completion   *Fill in the blanks with terms from Chapter 28.*

5. A(An) _____ is a tough external covering of the body.

6. A structure that extends from the body wall of an arthropod is called a(an)

_____.

7. The chewing mouthparts of crustaceans are called _____.

8. Chelicerates have _____ pairs of walking legs.

9. Arachnids include mites, ticks, scorpions, and _____.

10. Insects have a body divided into three parts—a head, a(an) _____,
and an abdomen.

11. In complete metamorphosis, the stage in which an insect changes from larva to adult is

called a(an) _____.

12. Specific chemical messengers that affect the behavior or development of individuals of

the same insect species are called _____.

13. A(An) _____ is an internal skeleton.

14. Most echinoderms exhibit five-part _____ symmetry.

Summary

29–1 Invertebrate Evolution

Paleontologists have identified microscopic fossils from between 610 and 570 million years ago. From the same time period, they have identified trace fossils, which are tracks and burrows made by soft-bodied animals. The fossils of some of the earliest and most primitive animals known were discovered in the Ediacara Hills of Australia. The Ediacaran animals, which lived between 575 and 543 million years ago, were flat and plate-shaped. They lived on the bottom of shallow seas and were made of soft tissues. They were segmented and had bilateral symmetry. However, the fossils show little evidence of cell specialization or a front and back end.

The Cambrian Period, which began 544 million years ago, is marked by the abundance of different fossils. One of the best-known sites of Cambrian fossils is the Burgess Shale of Canada. In just a few million years, animals had evolved complex body plans. Because of the extraordinary growth in animal diversity, events of the early Cambrian Period are called the Cambrian Explosion. The anatomies of Burgess Shale animals typically had body symmetry, segmentation, some type of skeleton, a front and a back end, and appendages adapted for many functions.

The appearance of each animal phylum in the fossil record represents the evolution of a successful and unique body plan. Modern sponges and cnidarians have little internal specialization. As larger and more complex animals have evolved, specialized cells join together to form tissues, organs, and organ systems.

All invertebrates except sponges exhibit some type of body symmetry. Cnidarians and echinoderms exhibit radial symmetry—body parts extend from the center of the body. Worms, mollusks, and arthropods exhibit bilateral symmetry—they have mirror-image right and left sides. The evolution of bilateral symmetry was accompanied by the trend toward cephalization, which is the concentration of sense organs and nerve cells in the front of the body. Invertebrates with cephalization can respond to the environment in more sophisticated ways than can simpler invertebrates.

Most complex animals are coelomates, with a true coelom that is lined with tissue derived from mesoderm. A coelom is a body cavity. Flatworms are acoelomates—they don't have a coelom. Roundworms are pseudocoelomates—their coelom is only partially lined with mesoderm. Annelids, mollusks, arthropods, and echinoderms have true coeloms.

In most invertebrates, the zygote divides to form a blastula. In protostomes, the blastopore develops into a mouth. In deuterostomes, the blastopore develops into an anus. Worms, arthropods, and mollusks are protostomes. Echinoderms (and chordates) are deuterostomes.

29–2 Form and Function in Invertebrates

In many ways, each animal phylum represents an "experiment" in the adaptation of body structures to carry out the essential functions of life. Biologists can learn a great deal about the nature of life by comparing body systems among the various living invertebrates.

The simplest animals—sponges—break down food primarily through intracellular digestion, which is the process of digesting food inside cells. More complex animals—mollusks, annelids, arthropods, and echinoderms—use extracellular digestion, which is the process of breaking down food outside the cells in a digestive cavity or tract. Complex animals digest food in a tube called the digestive tract. Food enters the body through the mouth and leaves the body through the anus.

All respiratory systems share two basic features: (1) Respiratory organs have large surface areas that are in contact with the air or water. (2) For diffusion to occur, the respiratory surfaces must be moist. Aquatic animals naturally have moist respiratory surfaces. Aquatic mollusks, arthropods, and many annelids exchange gases through gills. In terrestrial animals, surfaces are covered with water or mucus. Such covering prevents water loss from the body and also moistens air as it travels through the body to the respiratory surface.

All cells require a constant supply of oxygen and nutrients. Also, cells must remove wastes. The smallest and thinnest animals accomplish these tasks by diffusion between their bodies and the environment. Most complex animals move blood through their bodies using one or more hearts. Some animals use an open circulatory system, in which blood is only partially contained within blood vessels. The blood moves through vessels into a system of sinuses, where the blood directly contacts tissues. Other animals have a closed circulatory system. In a closed circulatory system, a heart or heartlike organ forces blood through vessels that extend throughout the body.

Multicellular animals must control the amount of water in their tissues. But they also have to get rid of ammonia, a poisonous nitrogen-containing waste produced as a result of metabolism. Most animals have an excretory system that rids the body of metabolic wastes while controlling the amount of water in the tissues. Many land animals convert ammonia into a compound called urea, which is eliminated from the body through urine.

Invertebrates show three trends in the evolution of the nervous system: centralization, cephalization, and specialization. The more complex an animal's nervous system is, the more developed its sense organs are.

Invertebrates have one of three main kinds of skeletal systems: hydrostatic skeletons, exoskeletons, or endoskeletons. Annelids and certain cnidarians have a hydrostatic skeleton, in which muscles surround a fluid-filled body cavity that supports the muscles. Arthropods have an exoskeleton, which is an external skeleton. Echinoderms have an endoskeleton, which is structural support located inside the body.

Most invertebrates reproduce sexually during at least part of their life cycle. Depending on environmental conditions, however, many invertebrates may also reproduce asexually. In external fertilization, eggs are fertilized outside the female's body. In internal fertilization, eggs are fertilized inside the female's body.

Section 29–1 Invertebrate Evolution
(pages 745–750)

Key Concept
- What are the major trends in invertebrate evolution?

Introduction (page 745)

1. What are three places where fossils have been found that shed light on the origins of invertebrates?

    a. _____

    b. _____

    c. _____

Origin of the Invertebrates (pages 745–747)

2. What are trace fossils? _____

    _____

    _____

    _____

3. Circle the letter of how old the fossils of the Ediacaran fauna are.

    a. 700–600 years old

    b. 6500–7500 years old

    c. 60–75 million years old

    d. 610–570 million years old

4. Is the following sentence true or false? Most fossils of Ediacaran fauna show little evidence of cell specialization. _____

5. What is the best known site of Cambrian fossils? _____

    _____

    _____

6. Circle the letter of each sentence that is true about animals of the Burgess Shale.

    a. They were ancestors of most modern animal phyla.

    b. They had features that are characteristic of most invertebrates living today.

    c. They had specialized cells, tissues, and organs.

    d. They were far less diverse than animals that lived earlier.

7. What features of the Burgess Shale animals made them so successful? _____

    _____

    _____

    _____

Invertebrate Phylogeny (page 747)

8. To which group of invertebrates are chordates most closely related?

_____

9. Number the features below according to the sequence in which they evolved. Number the feature that evolved first *1*.

_____ **a.** Deuterostome development

_____ **b.** Tissues

_____ **c.** Coelom

_____ **d.** Protostome development

Evolutionary Trends (pages 748–750)

10. What does the appearance of each phylum in the fossil record represent in terms of evolution? _____

_____

11. As larger and more complex animals evolved, in what ways did specialized cells join together? _____

_____

_____

12. Circle the letter of each animal group that has organ systems.

a. flatworms

b. cnidarians

c. mollusks

d. arthropods

13. What are the two kinds of symmetry that invertebrates exhibit? _____

_____

14. What is cephalization? _____

_____

_____

15. What body plan and lifestyle characterize invertebrates that have evolved cephalization? _____

_____

_____

16. What are the three germ layers that most invertebrates develop from?

a. _____

b. _____

c. _____

17. What is a coelom? _____

18. Label each of the cross sections of the acoelomate, pseudocoelomate, and coelomate.

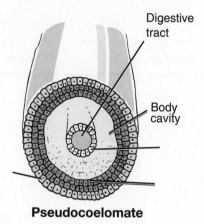

Digestive
tract

Body
cavity

Pseudocoelomate

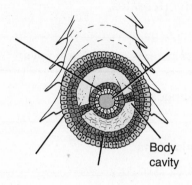

Body
cavity

Coelomate

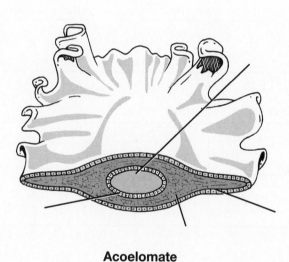

Acoelomate

19. What does segmentation allow an animal to do with a minimum of new genetic material?

_____

20. Most complex animal phyla have a true coelom that is lined completely with

_____.

21. In most invertebrates, the zygote divides repeatedly to form a(an)

_____.

22. What is the difference in early development between a protostome and a

deuterostome? _____

_____

_____

23. Which groups of invertebrates are protostomes? _____

_____

24. Complete the table that shows the general characteristics of the main groups of invertebrates.

Invertebrate	Germ Layer	Body Symmetry	Cephalization	Coelom
Sponges				
Cnidarians				
Flatworms				
Roundworms				
Annelids				
Mollusks				
Arthropods				
Echinoderms				

Reading Skill Practice

A good way to show similarities and differences between items is with a Venn diagram, which consists of two or more circles that overlap. Create Venn diagrams that compare these groups of invertebrates: (1) cnidarians and roundworms, (2) annelids and mollusks, and (3) arthropods and echinoderms. Use the table in Figure 29–5 for the information to be contained in your diagrams. For more information about Venn diagrams, see Organizing Information in Appendix A of your textbook.

Section 29–2 Form and Function in Invertebrates (pages 751–758)

🔑 **Key Concept**
- How do different invertebrate phyla carry out life functions?

Introduction (page 751)

1. What are seven essential tasks all animals perform to survive? _____
_____
_____

2. Why aren't more complicated systems in living animals necessarily better than simpler systems in other living animals? _____
_____
_____

Feeding and Digestion (pages 751–752)

3. How is the digestion of food different in simple animals compared to that in more complex animals? _____
_____
_____

4. Complete the table about types of digestion.

TYPES OF DIGESTION

Type	Definition
	Digestion of food inside cells
Extracellular digestion	

5. More-complex animals digest food in a tube called a(an) _____.

Respiration (pages 752–753)

6. Why do respiratory organs have large surface areas? _____
_____
_____

7. Why are respiratory surfaces kept moist? _____
_____

8. What are gills? _____
_____

9. What are book lungs made of? _____
_____

Circulation (page 754)

10. How do the smallest and thinnest animals meet the requirement of supplying oxygen and nutrients to cells and removing metabolic wastes? _____

_____

_____

11. Complex animals move fluid through their bodies using one or more

_____ .

12. Label each of the organisms below according to which has a closed circulatory system and which has an open circulatory system.

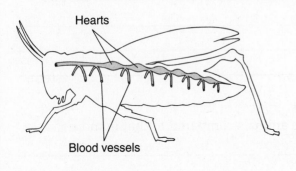

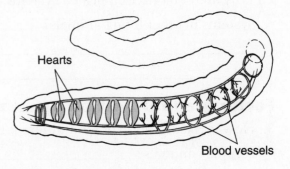

_____   _____

13. Closed circulatory systems are characteristic of what kinds of animals? _____

_____

_____

Excretion (pages 754–755)

14. What does the excretory system of most animals do? _____

_____

_____

15. How do aquatic invertebrates rid their bodies of ammonia? _____

_____

_____

16. Circle the letter of each way that terrestrial invertebrates eliminate nitrogenous wastes from their bodies.

a. Ammonia diffuses from body tissues into the surrounding water.

b. They convert ammonia into urea.

c. They convert ammonia into uric acid.

d. They form a thick paste that leaves the body through the rectum.

Name_____ Class_____ Date _____

Response (page 756)

17. What three trends do invertebrates show in the evolution of the nervous system?

    a. _____

    b. _____

    c. _____

18. Number the following groups of invertebrates according to how centralized their nervous system is. Number the group with the simplest nervous system *1*.

    _____ **a.** Flatworms

    _____ **b.** Cnidarians

    _____ **c.** Arthropods

19. What is cephalization? _____

    _____

20. Is the following sentence true or false? The more complex an animal's nervous system, the more developed its sense organs are. _____

Movement and Support (pages 756–757)

21. What are the three main kinds of skeletal systems among invertebrates?

    a. _____

    b. _____

    c. _____

22. What invertebrates have endoskeletons? _____

Sexual and Asexual Reproduction (pages 757–758)

23. What is the difference between external and internal fertilization? _____

    _____

    _____

24. Circle the letter of each sentence that is true about invertebrate reproduction.

    a. Most invertebrates reproduce sexually in one part of their life cycle.

    b. Asexual reproduction maintains genetic diversity in a population.

    c. Asexual reproduction includes budding and division in two.

    d. Most invertebrates have separate sexes.

Vocabulary Review

Answering Questions   *In the space provided, write an answer to each question.*

1. Why are events of the early Cambrian Period called the Cambrian Explosion? _____

_____

_____

2. What is the advantage of cephalization? _____

_____

_____

3. What are the two basic features that all respiratory systems share? _____

_____

_____

_____

Matching   *In the space provided, write the letter of the definition that best matches each term.*

_____   **4.** acoelomate

_____   **5.** hydrostatic skeleton

_____   **6.** intracellular digestion

_____   **7.** internal fertilization

_____   **8.** deuterostome

_____   **9.** extracellular digestion

_____   **10.** pseudocoelomate

_____   **11.** protostome

_____   **12.** external fertilization

_____   **13.** exoskeleton

_____   **14.** coelomate

_____   **15.** endoskeleton

a. fertilization inside the body of the female

b. animal whose blastopore develops into its mouth

c. fluid-filled body cavity surrounded and supported by muscles

d. fertilization outside the body of the female

e. animal whose blastopore develops into its anus

f. animal whose body cavity is fully lined with mesoderm

g. animal with no body cavity

h. food is broken down in a digestive cavity or tract

i. hard body covering

j. structural support inside the body

k. animal whose body cavity is partly lined with mesoderm

l. food is broken down within cells

Summary

30–1 The Chordates

A chordate is an animal that has, for at least some stage of its life, a hollow nerve cord, a notochord, pharyngeal pouches, and a tail.

The hollow nerve cord runs along the back of the body. Nerves branch from it and connect to organs and muscles.

The notochord is a long supporting rod that runs just below the nerve cord. Most chordates have a notochord only as embryos.

Pharyngeal pouches are paired structures in the throat. In some chordates, they develop into gills.

Most chordates are vertebrates. Vertebrates have a backbone made of segments called vertebrae. The backbone replaces the notochord. The backbone gives support and protects the spinal cord. It also gives the muscles a place to attach.

Two groups of chordates do not have backbones. Tunicates are filter feeders that live in the ocean. Adult tunicates have neither a notochord nor a tail. Larval tunicates have the chordate characteristics.

The other group of chordates without a backbone is the lancelet. Lancelets are small, fishlike animals. Adult lancelets have all four chordate characteristics. They also have a definite head region.

30–2 Fishes

Fishes are animals with backbones that live in water. They usually have paired fins, scales, and gills.

Fishes were the first vertebrates to evolve. The evolution of jaws and paired fins was the most important development in fish evolution. Jaws improved defense and expanded food choices. Paired fins gave more control of body movement.

Fishes have various modes of feeding. Fishes are herbivores, carnivores, parasites, filter feeders, and detritus feeders. One fish may even have several different modes of feeding, depending on the food available.

Most fishes breathe with gills. Gills have many tiny blood vessels. This provides a large surface area for oxygen and carbon to be exchanged. Most fishes breathe by pulling water through the mouth and pumping it over the gills and out through openings in the sides of the pharynx.

Fishes have a closed circulatory system that pumps blood in a single loop—from the heart to the gills, from the gills to the body, and back to the heart. The heart is made up of four parts: the sinus venosus, atrium, ventricle, and bulbus arteriosus. The ventricle is the actual pumping portion of the heart. The atrium is a one-way compartment for blood that is going to enter the ventricle.

Most fishes get rid of wastes as ammonia. Some wastes pass through the gills into the water. Other wastes are removed from the blood by the kidneys. Kidneys also help fishes control the amount of water in their bodies.

Fishes have well-developed nervous systems. The brain has several parts. The olfactory bulbs and cerebrum are involved with the sense of smell. The optic lobes process information from the eyes. The cerebellum coordinates body movements. Most fishes have a lateral line system that senses currents and vibrations in the water.

Most fishes move by contracting muscles on either side of the backbone. Fins propel the fish forward and help it steer. Many fishes have a gas-filled swim bladder that keeps them from sinking.

Fishes reproduce in a number of ways. Their eggs are fertilized either externally or internally, depending on the species. Some lay eggs. They are called oviparous. In ovo-viviparous fishes, the eggs develop inside the female. The embryos are fed by an attached yolk sac. In viviparous fishes, the embryos get their food from the mother's body, not from an egg.

All fishes can be classified into three groups: jawless fishes, cartilaginous fishes, and bony fishes. Lampreys and hagfishes are jawless fishes. Their bodies are supported by a notochord. They do not have true teeth or jaws. They are parasites and scavengers.

The cartilaginous fishes include sharks, rays, and skates. All members of this group of fishes have a skeleton made of cartilage. Most also have toothlike scales covering their skin.

Bony fishes have skeletons made of bone. Almost all bony fishes belong to the group known as the ray-finned fishes. Their fins have thin, bony spines that are joined together by a thin layer of skin.

30–3 Amphibians

Amphibians have some—but not all—of the adaptations necessary to live on land. As larvae, they live in water. As adults, they live on land. Adult amphibians breathe with lungs and have moist skin that has mucous glands. They do not have scales and claws.

Early amphibians had several adaptations that helped them live on land. Leg bones became stronger to hold weight and allow movement. Lungs and moist skin allowed them to get oxygen from air. The breastbone supported and protected internal organs.

Amphibian larvae are filter feeders or herbivores. They have long, coiled intestines. This helps them break down plant material. Adults have a much shorter intestine because they are carnivores.

In most larvae, gas exchange occurs through the skin as well as lungs. Lungs usually replace gills when an amphibian becomes an adult. However, some gas exchange occurs through the skin and the lining of the mouth.

In adult amphibians, the circulatory system forms a double loop. The first loop carries oxygen-poor blood from the heart to the lungs. It returns oxygen-rich blood to the heart from the lungs. The second loop carries oxygen-rich blood from the heart to the body and returns to the heart with oxygen-poor blood. The amphibian heart has three separate chambers: left atrium, right atrium, and ventricle.

Kidneys remove wastes from blood. Urine passes to the cloaca. From there, it either passes directly to the outside or is stored in a small bladder.

Amphibian eggs do not have shells. The female usually lays eggs in water. The male fertilizes them externally. The eggs hatch into larvae, which are often called tadpoles. Tadpoles gradually change into adults that live on land.

Amphibians have well-developed nervous systems and sense organs. Frogs have keen vision to spot and respond to moving insects. Tympanic membranes, or eardrums, receive sound vibrations.

The amphibian groups are salamanders, frogs and toads, and caecilians. Salamanders have long bodies, legs, and tails. Frogs and toads do not have tails and can jump. Caecilians do not have legs.

Section 30–1 The Chordates (pages 767–770)

Key Concepts
- What characteristics do all chordates share?
- What are the two groups of nonvertebrate chordates?

What Is a Chordate? (page 767)

1. List the four key characteristics of a chordate.

   a. _____

   b. _____

   c. _____

   d. _____

Use the diagram below to match the description of the chordate characteristic with its structure.

Structure

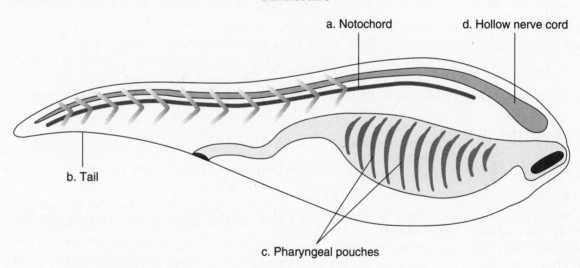

a. Notochord   d. Hollow nerve cord

b. Tail

c. Pharyngeal pouches

Description

_____ 2. Connects nerves to internal organs, muscles, and sense organs

_____ 3. Long supporting rod located just below the nerve cord

_____ 4. Paired structures in the throat region

_____ 5. Contains bone and muscle

Most Chordates Are Vertebrates (page 768)

6. What structure do most vertebrates have? _____

7. What chordate structure becomes the spinal cord in vertebrates? _____

8. The backbone is made of individual segments called _____ that enclose and protect the spinal cord.

9. Circle the letter of each sentence that is true about vertebrates.

   a. A vertebrate's backbone is part of an endoskeleton.

   b. The endoskeleton supports and protects the animal's body.

   c. The endoskeleton must be shed as the animal grows.

   d. The endoskeleton is made entirely of nonliving material.

Nonvertebrate Chordates (pages 769–770)

10. How are tunicates and lancelets similar to each other? _____

_____

11. What evidence indicates that vertebrates and nonvertebrate chordates evolved from a common ancestor? _____

_____

_____

12. Circle the letter of each characteristic found only in tunicate larvae and not in tunicate adults.

   a. tunic   c. hollow nerve cord

   b. tail   d. notochord

13. Is the following sentence true or false? Both larval and adult tunicates are filter feeders.

   _____

14. Circle the letter of each characteristic found in lancelets.

   a. definite head region   c. notochord

   b. jaws   d. fins

15. Is the following sentence true or false? Lancelets use the pharynx for feeding and gas exchange. _____

16. How is blood moved through the body of a lancelet? _____

_____

_____

Reading Skill Practice

A Venn diagram is a useful tool to compare and contrast two things. Construct a Venn diagram to compare and contrast the characteristics of tunicates and lancelets. See Appendix A for more information about Venn diagrams. Do your work on a separate sheet of paper.

Section 30–2 Fishes (pages 771–781)

Key Concepts
- What are the basic characteristics of fishes?
- What were the important developments during the evolution of fishes?
- How are fishes adapted for life in water?
- What are the three main groups of fishes?

What Is a Fish? (page 771)

1. Write the function of each characteristic of fishes.

   a. Paired fins _____

   b. Scales _____

   c. Gills _____

2. Is the following sentence true or false? The characteristics of living fishes are very uniform and almost no diversity exists among fishes. _____

Evolution of Fishes (pages 772–773)

3. Circle the letter of each sentence that is true about the evolution of fishes.

   a. Fishes were the first vertebrates to evolve.

   b. Fishes arose directly from tunicates and lancelets.

   c. Fishes changed little during the course of their evolution.

   d. Early fishes were jawless and covered with bony plates.

4. Which period is known as the Age of Fishes?

   a. Cambrian   c. Silurian

   b. Ordovician   d. Devonian

5. Jawless fishes with little armor of the Devonian Period were the ancestors of modern _____ and _____.

6. Why were jaws an extremely useful adaptation? _____

   _____

   _____

7. A strong tissue that supports the body and is more flexible than bone is

   _____.

8. Is the following sentence true or false? Paired fins gave fishes less control over their movement. _____

Form and Function in Fishes (pages 774–778)

9. What are the different modes of feeding found in fishes? _____

   _____

© Pearson Education, Inc., publishing as Pearson Prentice Hall.

10. Is the following sentence true or false? A single fish may exhibit only one mode of feeding. _____

Match the internal organ with its function.

Internal Organ	Function
_____ **11.** Pyloric ceca	**a.** Short tube connecting the fish's mouth to the stomach
_____ **12.** Intestine	**b.** Where food is first partially broken down
_____ **13.** Pancreas	**c.** Fingerlike pouches in which food is processed and nutrients absorbed
_____ **14.** Esophagus	**d.** Adds digestive enzymes and other substances to food as it moves through the gut
_____ **15.** Anus	**e.** Completes the process of digestion and nutrient absorption
_____ **16.** Stomach	**f.** Opening through which undigested material is eliminated

17. What does the capillary network in each gill filament provide? _____
_____
_____

18. Describe how fishes with gills exchange gases. _____
_____
_____
_____

19. The protective bony cover over the gill slit from which water is pumped out of a fish's body is called a(an) _____.

20. How do lungfishes survive in oxygen-poor water? _____
_____
_____

21. Is the following sentence true or false? Fishes have an open circulatory system.

_____

Match each chamber of the heart in fishes with its function.

Heart Chamber	Function
_____ **22.** Ventricle	**a.** Collects oxygen-poor blood from the veins
_____ **23.** Sinus venosus	**b.** Large muscular cavity that serves as a one-way compartment for blood entering the ventricle
_____ **24.** Bulbus arteriosus	**c.** Thick-walled, muscular chamber that is the actual pumping portion of the heart
_____ **25.** Atrium	**d.** Large, muscular tube that connects to the ventricle and moves blood through the aorta toward the gills

26. What form of nitrogenous waste do most fishes excrete?

_____

27. How does the function of kidneys in saltwater fishes differ from their function in

freshwater fishes? _____

_____

_____

Match the structures of the fish's brain with their functions.

Structure	Function
_____ **28.** Olfactory bulb	**a.** Controls the functioning of many internal organs
_____ **29.** Cerebrum	**b.** Primarily processes the sense of smell in fishes
_____ **30.** Optic lobe	**c.** Coordinates body movements
_____ **31.** Cerebellum	**d.** Involved with the sense of smell, or olfaction
_____ **32.** Medulla oblongata	**e.** Processes information from the eyes

33. Circle the letter of each sentence that is true about the sense organs of fishes.

a. Fishes have poorly developed sense organs.

b. Many fishes have chemoreceptors that sense tastes and smells.

c. Fishes have a lateral line system used for sensing sounds.

d. Some fishes can sense low levels of electric current.

34. What are two ways that fins help fish to move?

a. _____

b. _____

35. The streamlined body shapes of most fishes help reduce the amount of

_____ as they move through the water.

36. What is the function of the swim bladder? _____

_____

_____

37. In which mode of fish reproduction do the embryos develop inside the mother's body
using the egg yolk for nourishment?

a. oviparous

c. viviparous

b. ovoviviparous

d. herbivorous

Groups of Fishes (pages 778–780)

38. Fishes are divided into groups according to _____ structure.

39. Complete the table about the groups of fishes.

GROUPS OF FISHES

Type	Description	Examples
	No true teeth; skeletons made of fibers and cartilage; keep their notochord as adults	
Cartilaginous fishes		Sharks, rays, skates
		Ray-finned fishes, such as flounder, angelfish, and flying fish and lobe-finned fishes, such as lungfishes and the coelacanth

40. Is the following sentence true or false? Hagfishes are filter feeders as larvae and parasites as adults. _____

41. Circle the letter of each characteristic of a shark.

    a. torpedo-shaped body

    b. secretes slime

    c. many teeth

    d. winglike fins

42. Is the following sentence true or false? Lobe-finned fishes have fleshy fins supported by bones that are sometimes jointed. _____

Ecology of Fishes (page 781)

43. Fishes that spend most of their lives in the ocean but migrate to fresh water to breed are called _____.

44. Fishes that live in fresh water but migrate to the ocean to breed are called

_____.

Section 30–3 Amphibians (pages 782–789)

🔑 **Key Concepts**
- What is an amphibian?
- How are amphibians adapted for life on land?
- What are the main groups of living amphibians?

What Is an Amphibian? (page 782)

1. Is the following sentence true or false? Amphibian adults are fishlike aquatic animals that respire using gills. _____

2. Circle the letter of each characteristic of amphibians.

   a. scales   **b.** claws   **c.** moist skin   **d.** mucus glands

Evolution of Amphibians (pages 782–783)

3. List three challenges that had to be overcome by vertebrates colonizing land habitats.

   a. _____

   b. _____

   c. _____

4. List three adaptations that evolved in amphibians that helped them live at least part of their lives out of water.

   a. _____

   b. _____

   c. _____

5. Amphibians became the dominant form of animal life during the _____ Period, also known as the Age of Amphibians.

6. Why did most amphibian groups become extinct by the end of the Permian Period?

   _____

   _____

   _____

7. What three orders of amphibians survive today?

   a. _____

   b. _____

   c. _____

Form and Function in Amphibians (pages 784–787)

8. Circle the letter of each characteristic of a tadpole.

   a. carnivore

   b. herbivore

   c. long intestines

   d. short intestines

9. Circle the letter of each characteristic of an adult amphibian.

   a. carnivore

   b. herbivore

   c. sticky tongue

   d. long intestines

10. Briefly describe the path of food in a frog's digestive system.

    _____

    _____

    _____

11. Circle the letter of each sentence that is true about respiration.

    a. In tadpoles, gas exchange occurs only through the skin.

    b. Lungs replace gills when an amphibian becomes an adult.

    c. Gas exchange in adults can also occur through the skin.

    d. All adult amphibians have lungs.

12. Amphibians have _____ that filter wastes from the blood.

13. Complete the captions in the diagram about the stages in the life cycle of a frog.

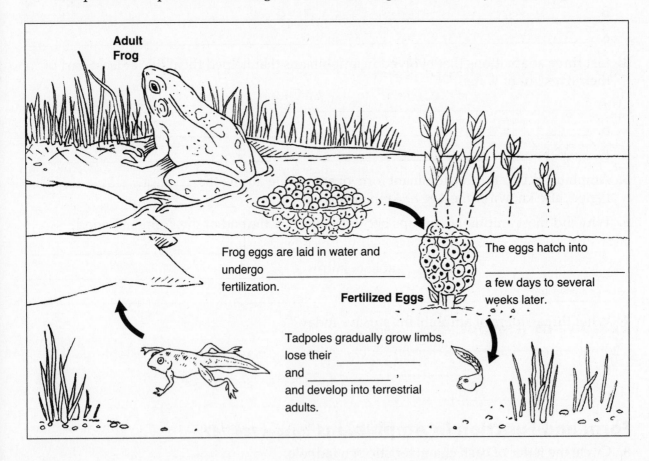

Adult Frog

Frog eggs are laid in water and undergo _____ fertilization.

Fertilized Eggs

The eggs hatch into _____ a few days to several weeks later.

Tadpoles gradually grow limbs, lose their _____ and _____, and develop into terrestrial adults.

14. How is the first loop in the circulatory system of an adult amphibian different from the second loop? _____

_____

_____

Match the type of amphibian with its method of movement.

Amphibian	Method of Movement
_____ **15.** Tadpoles	**a.** Flattened tail for propulsion
_____ **16.** Adult salamanders	**b.** Well-developed hind limbs for jumping
_____ **17.** Frogs and toads	**c.** Legs push backward against the ground

18. Circle the letter of each sentence that is true about response in amphibians.

a. An amphibian's brain is structured very differently from a fish's.

b. An amphibian's eye is protected from damage and kept moist by the nictitating membrane.

c. Frogs probably do not see color as well as fishes.

d. Amphibians hear through tympanic membranes, or eardrums.

Groups of Amphibians (page 788)

19. Circle the letter of each characteristic of salamanders.

a. tail   **c.** herbivore

b. carnivore   **d.** short body

20. Circle the letter of each characteristic of frogs and toads.

a. tail   **c.** able to jump

b. no tail   **d.** adults have gills

21. Circle the letter of each characteristic of caecilians.

a. legless   **c.** able to jump

b. long legs   **d.** some scales

Ecology of Amphibians (page 789)

22. What are two ways in which amphibians protect themselves from predators?

a. _____

b. _____

23. Is the following sentence true or false? For the past several decades, the number of living species of amphibians has been increasing. _____

Name_____ Class_____ Date_____

Vocabulary Review

Labeling Diagrams   *Use the following words to label the structures of the animal below:* nerve cord, notochord, pharyngeal pouches, *and* tail. *Then, complete the sentence.*

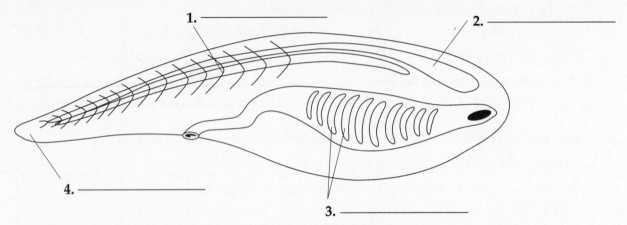

1. _____

2. _____

4. _____

3. _____

5. The animal diagrammed above is an example of a(an) _____.

Matching   *In the space provided, write the letter of the definition that best matches each term.*

_____ **6.** vertebrae

_____ **7.** cartilage

_____ **8.** atrium

_____ **9.** ventricle

_____ **10.** cerebrum

_____ **11.** cerebellum

_____ **12.** medulla oblongata

_____ **13.** lateral line system

_____ **14.** swim bladder

_____ **15.** oviparous

a. part of the brain responsible for voluntary activities

b. part of the brain that controls many internal organs

c. chamber of the heart into which blood enters from the body

d. method of development in which eggs hatch outside the mother's body

e. receptors in fishes that sense motion and vibrations in water

f. tissue that is softer and more flexible than bone

g. individual segments that make up the backbone

h. part of the brain that coordinates body movements

i. the actual pumping portion of the heart

j. gas-filled organ in fishes that adjusts buoyancy

Completion   *Fill in the blanks with terms from Chapter 30.*

16. In _____ animals, the eggs develop inside the mother's body, and the embryo uses the yolk for nourishment.

17. In _____ animals, the embryos develop inside the mother's body and obtain their nourishment from their mother, not the egg.

18. The muscular cavity at the end of the large intestine in amphibians is called the

_____.

19. Transparent eyelids, called _____ membranes, protect an amphibian's eyes underwater and keep them moist in air.

20. Amphibians hear through _____ membranes, or eardrums.

Summary

31–1 Reptiles

Reptiles are vertebrates that are adapted to live entirely on land. They have dry skin that is covered with protective scales. This helps hold water in their bodies. They have efficient lungs that get oxygen from air. Reptiles also have eggs with a shell and several membranes.

As the climate became drier at the end of the Carboniferous Period, amphibians began dying out. This opened up many new habitats for reptiles. The Mesozoic Era is often called the Age of Reptiles because of the diversity and large numbers of reptiles that lived. Dinosaurs were everywhere. The Age of Reptiles ended with a mass extinction at the end of the Cretaceous Period.

Reptiles are ectotherms. They control their body temperature by their behavior. To warm up, they bask in the sun. To cool down, they move into shade, go for a swim, or move to an underground burrow.

Reptiles eat a wide range of foods. They also have many different ways of eating.

Reptile lungs have more gas-exchange area than amphibian lungs. Reptiles also have muscles around their ribs. They are able to expand their chest to inhale and collapse it to exhale.

Reptiles have a double-loop circulatory system. One loop carries blood to and from the lungs. The other loop carries blood to and from the rest of the body. Most reptiles have a three-chambered heart with a partially separated ventricle. Crocodiles have two atria and two ventricles.

Reptiles get rid of liquid wastes as urine. The urine contains either ammonia or uric acid. Reptiles that live in water excrete ammonia. Reptiles that live on land convert ammonia to uric acid. Uric acid is less toxic and requires less water to dilute it.

The reptilian brain is similar to the amphibian brain. However, the cerebrum and cerebellum are larger. Reptiles have well-developed sense organs.

Reptiles have larger and stronger limbs than amphibians. Their legs are rotated further under the body than those of amphibians. In this position, the legs can carry more body weight.

Reptiles have internal fertilization. Most are oviparous, laying eggs that develop outside the mother's body. The embryos are covered with membranes and a protective shell. This amniotic egg keeps the embryo from drying out. Some snakes and lizards are ovoviviparous, and the young are born alive.

Four groups of reptiles survive today. Lizards and snakes (order Squamata) have legs, clawed toes, external ears, and movable eyelids. Snakes are lizards that have lost their legs during their evolution.

Crocodilians (order Crocodilia) have long, broad snouts and a squat appearance. They are fierce carnivores that live only in tropical climates. Crocodilians include alligators, crocodiles, caimans, and gavials.

Turtles and tortoises (order Testudines) have backbones fused to a shell, which provides protection. Turtles usually live in water. Tortoises usually live on land. Instead of teeth, these reptiles have horny ridges on their jaws.

The tuatara (order Sphenodonta) is found only on a few islands near New Zealand. They look somewhat like lizards, but do not have external ears and have primitive scales. They also have a "third eye," which is part of a sense organ on the top of the brain.

31–2 Birds

Birds are reptilelike animals that have a constant internal body temperature. They have two legs that are covered with scales. Their front legs are modified into wings. Birds are covered with feathers. Feathers help birds fly and keep them warm. Birds have different kinds of feathers.

Paleontologists agree that birds evolved from extinct reptiles. Some think that birds evolved directly from dinosaurs. Others think that birds and dinosaurs evolved from an earlier common ancestor.

Birds have many adaptations that enable them to fly. Birds are endotherms. They produce their own body heat. Their high metabolic rate produces heat. Feathers help conserve this heat.

Birds need to eat large amounts of food to maintain their high metabolic rate. Birds have bills adapted to the type of food they eat. Some birds have digestive organs called a crop and a gizzard. The crop is located at the end of the esophagus. Food is stored and moistened in the crop. The gizzard is part of the stomach. It grinds and crushes food so that it is easier to digest.

Birds have a very efficient respiratory system. A system of air sacs and breathing tubes ensures that air flows into the air sacs and out through the lungs in one direction.

The lungs are constantly exposed to oxygen-rich air. This helps birds maintain their high metabolic rate.

Birds have a four-chambered heart and two circulatory loops. A bird's heart has two separate ventricles. Oxygen-rich blood and oxygen-poor blood are completely separated.

Birds have an excretory system similar to that of reptiles. Nitrogenous wastes are converted to uric acid and sent to the cloaca. The cloaca reabsorbs most of the water from the wastes before they are expelled.

Birds have a well-developed brain and sense organs. The cerebrum and cerebellum are large in relation to body size. These adaptations enable birds to respond quickly to stimuli and coordinate the movements for flight. Birds have well-developed sight and hearing but do not sense smells or tastes very well.

The bodies, wings, legs, and feet of birds are adapted to many different habitats and lifestyles. Some of these adaptations, like air spaces in bones, help birds fly. All birds, however, do not fly.

Birds have internal fertilization. They lay amniotic eggs that have a hard shell. Most birds keep their eggs warm until they hatch. One or both parents may care for the offspring.

Section 31–1 Reptiles (pages 797–805)

🔑 Key Concepts
- What are the characteristics of reptiles?
- How are reptiles adapted to life on land?
- What are the four living orders of reptiles?

What Is a Reptile? (page 797)

1. List three characteristics shared by all reptiles.

   a. _____

   b. _____

   c. _____

2. What is the disadvantage of reptilian scaly skin? _____

   _____

   _____

Evolution of Reptiles (pages 798–799)

3. Circle the letter of each sentence that is true about the evolution of reptiles.

   a. Reptiles evolved rapidly in the warm, humid climate of the Carboniferous Period.

   b. Mammal-like reptiles dominated many land habitats until near the end of the Triassic Period.

   c. All dinosaurs were enormous.

   d. Some dinosaurs may have had feathers.

4. Is the following sentence true or false? The extinction of dinosaurs opened up new niches on land and in the sea, providing opportunities for other kinds of organisms to evolve.

   _____

Form and Function in Reptiles (pages 800–802)

5. How do ectotherms control their body temperature? _____

   _____

   _____

6. Is the following sentence true or false? All reptiles are herbivores. _____

7. Circle the letter of each adaptation reptiles have for respiration.

   a. lungs   c. strong rib muscles

   b. moist skin   d. gill slits

8. Circle the letter of each sentence that is true about circulation in reptiles.

   a. Reptiles have a double-loop circulatory system.

   b. All reptile hearts have only one atrium.

   c. Most reptiles have one ventricle with partial internal walls.

   d. Crocodiles have the least developed heart of living reptiles.

9. What is the advantage of uric acid to terrestrial reptiles? _____

_____

_____

10. Circle the letter of each sentence that is true about response in reptiles.

   a. The reptilian cerebrum is smaller than that of amphibians.

   b. Reptiles that are active during the day tend to have complex eyes.

   c. Reptiles do not have ears.

   d. Snakes sense vibrations in the ground through bones in their skulls.

11. Explain why reptiles are able to carry more body weight than amphibians.

_____

_____

12. All reptiles reproduce by _____ fertilization in which the male deposits sperm inside the body of the female.

13. In the diagram below, label the four membranes in the amniotic egg that surround the developing embryo.

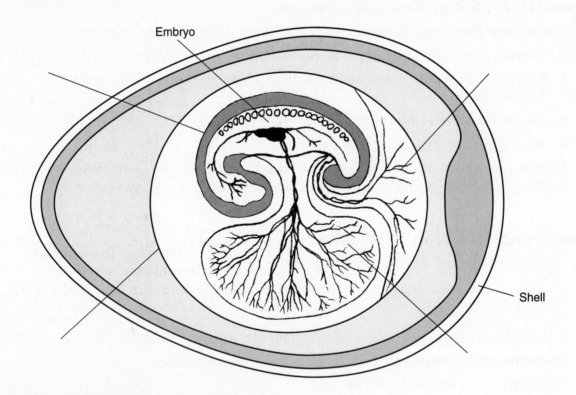

Embryo

Shell

Groups of Reptiles (pages 803–805)

14. List the four living orders of reptiles.

   a. _____

   b. _____

   c. _____

   d. _____

© Pearson Education, Inc., publishing as Pearson Prentice Hall.

15. Is the following sentence true or false? Both snakes and lizards have scaly skin and clawed toes. _____

16. Circle the letter of each characteristic of crocodilians.

    a. long snout   **c.** herbivore

    b. long legs   **d.** protective of young

17. Members of the order Testudines that live on land are referred to as

_____.

18. How do most turtles and tortoises protect themselves? _____

_____

19. Circle the letter of each characteristic of turtles and tortoises.

    a. teeth   **c.** strong limbs

    b. strong jaws   **d.** long, broad snout

20. Describe how tuataras differ from lizards. _____

_____

_____

Ecology of Reptiles (page 805)

21. Circle the letter of each sentence that is true about the ecology of reptiles.

    a. Reptiles are in no danger of disappearing.

    b. Reptilian habitats have been expanding.

    c. Humans hunt reptiles for food, to sell as pets, and for their skins.

    d. Conservation programs are in place to help reptiles survive.

Reading Skill Practice

Flowcharts can help you to order the steps in a process or the stages in a series of events. Construct a flowchart that shows the stages in the evolution of reptiles, beginning at the end of the Carboniferous Period and ending with the extinction of dinosaurs at the end of the Cretaceous Period. See Appendix A for more information about flowcharts. Do your work on a separate sheet of paper.

Section 31–2 Birds (pages 806–814)

⬤ **Key Concepts**
- What characteristics do birds have in common?
- How are birds adapted for flight?

What Is a Bird? (page 806)

1. Circle the letter of each characteristic of birds.

   a. feathers

   b. four legs

   c. wings

   d. scales

2. The single most important characteristic that separates birds from all other living animals is _____.

3. List two functions of feathers.

   a. _____

   b. _____

4. Identify each type of feather diagrammed below.

_____   _____

Evolution of Birds (page 807)

5. In what ways is the early bird *Archaeopteryx* different from modern birds?

   _____

   _____

6. Is the following sentence true or false? Scientists know for certain that birds evolved directly from dinosaurs. _____

Form, Function, and Flight (pages 808–812)

7. What adaptations do birds have that enable them to fly? _____

_____

_____

8. For what two things do birds require energy?

a. _____

b. _____

9. Is the following sentence true or false? Birds have a low metabolic rate compared to

reptiles. _____

Match the type of bird bill with the type of food it is adapted to eat.

	Bird Bill	Food
_____	**10.** Short and fine	**a.** Flower nectar
_____	**11.** Short and thick	**b.** Seeds
_____	**12.** Strong and hooked	**c.** Insects
_____	**13.** Long and thin	**d.** Animal prey

14. What is the main function of the crop? _____

_____

15. Why might a bird swallow gravel or small stones? _____

_____

_____

16. What is an advantage of the one-way airflow through a bird's lungs? _____

_____

_____

17. What type of circulatory system do birds have? _____

_____

18. Circle the letter of the form of nitrogenous waste excreted by birds.

a. ammonia

b. urea

c. uric acid

d. nitrate

19. Circle the letter of each sentence that is true about response in birds.

    a. Birds have brains that quickly interpret and respond to signals.

    b. The cerebrum controls behaviors, such as nest building.

    c. The cerebellum in birds is much like that in reptiles.

    d. Birds can sense tastes and smells quite well.

20. What are two ways in which the skeleton of a flying bird is strengthened for flight?

    a. _____

    b. _____

21. How are the amniotic eggs of birds different from the eggs of reptiles? _____

_____

_____

22. Is the following sentence true or false? Bird parents do not ever care for their offspring.

_____

Groups of Birds (pages 812–813)

Match the bird group with its characteristics. Use Figure 31–19 as a guide.

Bird Groups	Characteristics
_____ **23.** Birds of prey	**a.** Largest order of birds, which includes songbirds
_____ **24.** Ostriches and their relatives	**b.** Fierce predators with hooked bills, large wingspans, and sharp talons
_____ **25.** Parrots	**c.** Flightless birds that move by running
_____ **26.** Perching birds	**d.** Adapted to wading in aquatic habitats
_____ **27.** Herons and their relatives	**e.** Colorful, noisy birds that use their feet to hold up food
_____ **28.** Cavity-nesting birds	**f.** Birds found in all types of aquatic ecosystems; have four toes connected by a web
_____ **29.** Pelicans and their relatives	**g.** Multicolored birds that live in holes made in trees, mounds, or underground tunnels

Ecology of Birds (page 814)

30. Circle the letter of each way in which birds interact with natural ecosystems.

    a. pollinate flowers

    b. disperse seeds

    c. control insects

    d. produce toxic wastes

31. Is the following sentence true or false? Some species of migrating birds use stars and other celestial bodies as guides. _____

32. Is the following sentence true or false? Birds are not affected by changes in the environment. _____

Reading Skill Practice

By looking at illustrations in textbooks, you can help yourself remember better what you have read. Look carefully at Figure 31–14 on page 809. What important information does the illustration communicate? Do your work on a separate sheet of paper.

Chapter 31   Reptiles and Birds

Vocabulary Review

Matching   *In the space provided, write the letter of the definition that best matches each term.*

_____ **1.** ectotherms

_____ **2.** endotherms

_____ **3.** carapace

_____ **4.** plastron

_____ **5.** crop

_____ **6.** gizzard

a. digestive structure that grinds and crushes food

b. animals that can generate their own body heat

c. animals that rely on behavior to control body temperature

d. ventral part of a turtle shell

e. dorsal part of a turtle shell

f. digestive structure that stores and moistens food

Completion   *Fill in the blanks with terms from Chapter 31.*

7. One of the most important adaptations to life on land is the _____, which protects the growing embryo and keeps it from drying out.

8. An outer covering of _____ helps birds fly and keeps them warm.

9. In birds, _____ direct air through the lungs in an efficient, one-way flow.

Labeling Diagrams   *Use the following words to label the amniotic egg:* allantois, amnion, chorion, embryo, shell, *and* yolk sac.

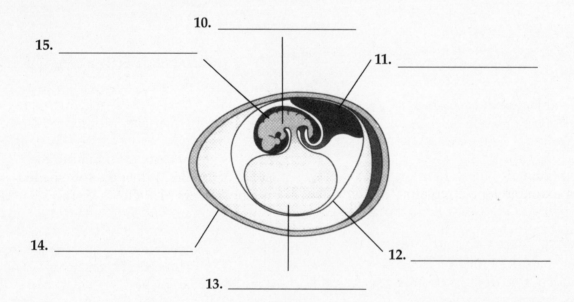

10. _____

15. _____

11. _____

14. _____

12. _____

13. _____

Summary

32–1 Introduction to the Mammals

All mammals have hair and mammary glands. In females, mammary glands produce milk to nourish the young. In addition to hair and mammary glands, all mammals breathe air, have four-chambered hearts, and can generate their body heat internally.

Mammals descended from ancient reptiles. Early mammals, which lived during the time of dinosaurs, were small and active only at night. When the dinosaurs became extinct, mammals evolved to fill many different niches.

Mammals have many different adaptations that allow them to live in diverse habitats. Like birds, mammals are endotherms. Their metabolism creates their body heat. They have body fat and fur or hair to prevent heat loss. Many have sweat glands to conserve body heat.

Mammals must eat a lot of food to maintain their high metabolic rate. Mammals have specialized teeth, jaws, and digestive systems for eating plants or animals or both.

All mammals use lungs to breathe. Well-developed muscles in the chest, including the diaphragm, help pull air into the lungs and push air out.

Mammals have a four-chambered heart and a double-loop circulatory system. One loop brings blood to and from the lungs, and the other loop brings blood to and from the rest of the body. Each side of the heart has an atrium and a ventricle. Oxygen-rich blood is completely separated from oxygen-poor blood.

Highly developed kidneys help control the amount of water in the body. This enables mammals to live in many different habitats. The kidneys filter nitrogenous wastes from the blood, forming urine.

Mammals have the most highly developed brains of any animals. Mammalian brains consist of a cerebrum, cerebellum, and medulla oblongata. The cerebrum contains a well-developed outer layer called the cerebral cortex. It is the center of thinking and other complex behaviors.

Mammals, like other vertebrates, have endocrine glands that are part of an endocrine system. Endocrine glands regulate body activities by releasing hormones that affect other organs and tissues.

Mammals have many different adaptations for movement. Variations in the structure of limb bones allow mammals to run, walk, climb, burrow, hop, fly, and swim.

Mammals reproduce by internal fertilization. All newborn mammals feed on the mother's milk. Most mammal parents care for their young for a certain amount of time after birth. The length of care varies among species.

32–2 Diversity of Mammals

The three groups of living mammals are the monotremes, marsupials, and placentals. They differ in their means of reproduction and development. Monotremes lay eggs. They also have a cloaca, similar to the cloaca of reptiles. When the soft-shelled monotreme eggs hatch, the young are nourished by the mother's milk.

Marsupials bear live young that complete their development in an external pouch. The young are born at a very early stage of development. They crawl across the mother's fur and attach to a nipple. They continue to drink milk until they are large enough to survive on their own.

Placental mammals are the most familiar. Placental mammals are named for the placenta—an internal structure that is formed when the embryo's tissues join with tissues from within the mother's body. Nutrients, oxygen, carbon dioxide, and wastes are passed between the embryo and mother through the placenta. After birth, most placental mammals care for their offspring.

32–3 Primates and Human Origins

All primates share several important adaptations. Many of these adaptations are useful for a life spent mainly in trees. These adaptations include binocular vision, a well-developed cerebrum, flexible fingers and toes, and arms that rotate in broad circles.

Very early in evolutionary history, primates split into several groups. Prosimians are small, nocturnal primates with large eyes adapted for seeing in the dark. Anthropoids include monkeys, apes, and humans.

Very early in their evolutionary history, anthropoids split into two major groups. One group evolved into the monkeys found today in Central and South America. This group is called the New World monkeys. All New World monkeys have a prehensile tale. A prehensile tail is a tail that can coil tightly around a branch to serve as a "fifth hand." The other group of anthropoids includes the Old World monkeys and the great apes. Old World monkeys do not have prehensile tails. Great apes, which are also called hominoids, include gorillas, chimpanzees, and humans.

The hominoid line gave rise to the branch that leads to modern humans. This group, called the hominids, evolved adaptations for upright walking, thumbs adapted for grasping, and larger brains.

Many recent fossil finds have changed the way paleontologists think about hominid evolution. Now researchers think that hominid evolution occurred in a series of complex adaptive radiations. This produced a large number of different species rather than one species that led directly to the next.

Researchers agree that our genus, *Homo*, first appeared in Africa. However, researchers do not agree when the first hominids began migrating from Africa. They are also not sure when and where *Homo sapiens* arose. The multiregional model suggests that modern humans evolved independently in several parts of the world. The out-of-Africa model proposes that modern humans arose in Africa and then migrated out.

About 500,000 years ago, two main groups of hominids are known to have existed. *Homo neanderthalensis* lived in Europe and western Asia. Fossil evidence suggests that they used stone tools and lived in organized groups. The other group is the first *Homo sapiens*. Researchers think that they lived side by side with Neanderthals.

According to one hypothesis, around 50,000–40,000 years ago, *H. sapiens* dramatically changed their way of life. They made more sophisticated tools. They produced cave paintings. They also began burying their dead with elaborate rituals. In other words, they began to behave more like modern humans. The Neanderthals disappeared about 30,000 years ago. It is not yet known why. Since then, *H. sapiens* has been the only hominid on Earth.

Section 32–1 Introduction to the Mammals
(pages 821–827)

Key Concepts

- What are the characteristics of mammals?
- When did mammals evolve?
- How do mammals maintain homeostasis?

Introduction (page 821)

1. List the two notable features of mammals.

   a. _____

   b. _____

2. Circle the letter of each characteristic of mammals.

   a. breathe air   c. ectotherm

   b. three-chambered heart   d. endotherm

Evolution of Mammals (page 821)

3. What three characteristics help scientists identify mammalian fossils?

   a. _____

   b. _____

   c. _____

4. The ancestors of mammals diverged from ancient _____ during the

   Permian Period.

5. Circle the letter of each sentence that is true about the evolution of mammals.

   a. The first true mammals were as large as dinosaurs.

   b. During the Cretaceous Period, mammals were probably nocturnal.

   c. After dinosaurs disappeared, mammals increased in size and filled many
      new niches.

   d. The Permian Period is usually called the Age of Mammals.

Form and Function in Mammals (pages 822–827)

6. List two ways in which mammals conserve body heat.

   a. _____

   b. _____

7. Is the following sentence true or false? Mammals have a low rate of metabolism.
_____

8. Circle the letter of each way mammals are able to rid themselves of excess heat.
  a. fat   **c.** sweat glands
  b. hair   **d.** panting

9. The ability of mammals to regulate their body heat from within is an example of _____ .

10. Is the following sentence true or false? Animals that are omnivores consume only meat. _____

11. As mammals evolved, the form and function of their _____ and _____ became adapted to eat foods other than insects.

12. Complete the table about the different kinds of teeth found in mammals.

TEETH ADAPTATIONS IN MAMMALS

Type	Description
Canines	
	Chisellike incisors used for cutting, gnawing, and grooming
Molars and premolars	

13. In which type of animal would you expect to find sharp canine teeth? _____

14. How are herbivores' molars adapted for their diet? _____
_____
_____

15. Is the following sentence true or false? Carnivores have a shorter intestine than herbivores. _____

16. Complete the flowchart to show how cows digest their food.

Newly swallowed food is stored and processed in the _____.

↓

Symbiotic bacteria in the rumen digest the _____ of most plant tissues.

↓

The cow _____ the food from the rumen into its mouth, and food is chewed and swallowed again.

↓

The food is swallowed again and moves through the rest of the _____ and _____.

17. How does the diaphragm work to help move air into and out of the lungs?

_____

_____

_____

_____

18. Is the following sentence true or false? Mammals have a four-chambered heart that pumps blood into two separate circuits around the body. _____

19. Where does the right side of the heart pump oxygen-poor blood? _____

20. After blood picks up oxygen in the lungs, where does it go? _____

_____

21. How do mammalian kidneys help to maintain homeostasis? _____

_____

_____

_____

Match each part of the mammalian brain with its function.

Part of the brain	Function
_____ **22.** medulla oblongata	**a.** Involved in thinking and learning
_____ **23.** cerebral cortex	**b.** Controls muscular coordination
_____ **24.** cerebrum	**c.** Regulates involuntary body functions
_____ **25.** cerebellum	**d.** Part of the cerebrum that is the center of thinking and other complex behaviors

26. What are endocrine glands? _____

_____

_____

27. What body system helps to protect mammals from disease? _____

28. Is the following sentence true or false? Mammals have a rigid backbone, as well as rigid shoulder and pelvic girdles for extra stability. _____

29. Mammals reproduce by _____ fertilization.

30. Is the following sentence true or false? All mammals are viviparous, or live-bearing.

_____

31. What do young mammals learn from their parents? _____

_____

_____

Section 32–2 Diversity of Mammals (pages 828–832)

🔑 **Key Concepts**
- How do the three groups of living mammals differ from one another?
- How did convergent evolution cause mammals on different continents to be similar in form and function?

Introduction (page 828)

1. List the three groups of living mammals.

   a. _____ b. _____ c. _____

2. The three groups of mammals differ greatly in their means of _____ and development.

Monotremes and Marsupials (pages 828–829)

3. The mammals that lay eggs are _____. Those that bear live young at a very early stage of development are _____.

4. What two characteristics do monotremes share with reptiles?

   a. _____

   _____

   b. _____

   _____

5. How do monotremes differ from reptiles? _____

   _____

   _____

6. Circle the letter of each mammal that is a marsupial.

   a. koala   c. platypus

   b. echidna   d. kangaroo

7. Describe how marsupial embryos develop. _____

   _____

   _____

   _____

   _____

   _____

Placental Mammals (pages 829–831)

8. What is the placenta? _____

   _____

   _____

9. What four substances are exchanged between the embryo and the mother through the placenta?

a. _____   c. _____

b. _____   d. _____

10. Is the following sentence true or false? After birth, most placental mammals care for their young and provide them with nourishment by nursing. _____

Match the main order of placental mammal with its description. Use Figure 32–12 on pages 830–831.

Order	Description
_____ **11.** Insectivores	**a.** Hoofed mammals with an even number of digits on each foot
_____ **12.** Sirenians	**b.** Herbivores with two pairs of incisors in the upper jaw and hind legs adapted for leaping
_____ **13.** Chiropterans	**c.** Herbivores that live in rivers, bays, and warm coastal waters
_____ **14.** Artiodactyls	**d.** The only mammals capable of true flight
_____ **15.** Proboscideans	**e.** Insect eaters with long, narrow snouts and sharp claws
_____ **16.** Lagomorphs	**f.** Mammals that have trunks

Biogeography of Mammals (page 832)

17. Is the following sentence true or false? During the Paleozoic Era, the continents were one large landmass. _____

18. What effect on the evolution of mammals was caused when the continents drifted apart? _____

_____

_____

_____

_____

Reading Skill Practice

A compare-and-contrast table is a useful tool for organizing similarities and differences. Make a table to compare the three groups of living mammals. Include information about the reproduction and development of each group. For more information about compare-and-contrast tables, look in Appendix A of your textbook. Do your work on a separate sheet of paper.

© Pearson Education, Inc., publishing as Pearson Prentice Hall.

Section 32–3 Primates and Human Origins
(pages 833–841)

⚙ Key Concepts
- What characteristics do all primates share?
- What are the major evolutionary groups of primates?
- What is the current scientific thinking about hominid evolution?

What Is a Primate? (pages 833–834)

1. What characteristic distinguished the first primates from other mammals? _____
_____
_____

2. List four adaptations that are shared by primates.

   a. _____

   b. _____

   c. _____

   d. _____

3. Circle the letter of each sentence that is true about primates.

   a. Primates are well adapted to a life of running on the ground.

   b. Many primates can hold objects firmly in their hands.

   c. A well-developed cerebrum enables primates to display elaborate social behaviors.

   d. Because primates have a flat face, both eyes point to the sides.

4. What is binocular vision? _____
_____
_____
_____

Evolution of Primates (pages 834–835)

5. Circle the letter of each characteristic of prosimians.

   a. nocturnal   b. diurnal   c. small in size   d. small eyes

Match the characteristics to the anthropoid group. Each anthropoid group may be used more than once.

	Characteristic	**Anthropoid Group**
_____	6. Found today in Central and South America	**a.** New World monkeys
_____	7. Found today in Africa and Asia	**b.** Old World monkeys
_____	8. Includes baboons and macaques	
_____	9. Includes squirrel monkeys and spider monkeys	
_____	10. Lack prehensile tails	
_____	11. Long, prehensile tails and long, flexible arms	

Name_____ Class_____ Date_____

12. Complete the concept map to show the evolution of primates.

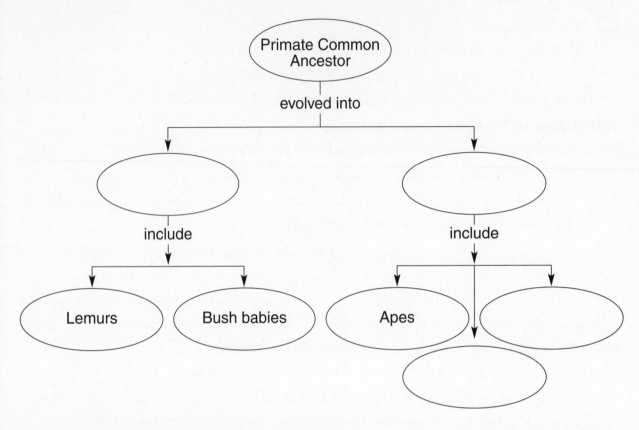

13. The anthropoid group that includes Old World monkeys also includes the great apes,

or _____.

Hominid Evolution (pages 835–838)

14. What was the importance of bipedal locomotion that evolved in the hominid family?

_____

_____

15. The hominid hand evolved a(an) _____ thumb that enabled grasping objects and using tools.

16. Is the following sentence true or false? Hominids have a much larger brain than the

other hominoids, such as chimpanzees. _____

17. Is the following sentence true or false? Only one fossil species exists that links humans

with their nonhuman primate ancestors. _____

18. Circle the letter of each characteristic of the hominid genus *Australopithecus*.

a. bipedal apes

b. never lived in trees

c. fruit eaters

d. very large brains

388 Chapter 32

© Pearson Education, Inc., publishing as Pearson Prentice Hall.

19. Is the following sentence true or false? Fossil evidence shows that hominids walked bipedally long before they had large brains. _____

20. Based on their teeth, what kind of diet did the known *Paranthropus* species probably eat?

_____

21. Is the following sentence true or false? Currently, researchers completely understand the evolution of the hominid species. _____

The Road to Modern Humans (pages 839–840)

22. *Homo habilis* was found with tools made of _____.

23. Describe the two hypotheses that explain how modern *Homo sapiens* might have evolved from earlier members of the genus *Homo*.

a. _____

_____

b. _____

_____

Modern *Homo sapiens* (page 841)

24. Circle the letter of each characteristic of Neanderthals.

a. stone tools

b. lived in social groups

c. gave rise to *H. sapiens*

d. made cave paintings

25. Is the following sentence true or false? Neanderthals and *Homo sapiens* lived side by side for around 50,000 years. _____

26. What fundamental changes did some populations of *H. sapiens* make to their way of life around 50,000–40,000 years ago? _____

_____

_____

Vocabulary Review

Multiple Choice   *In the space provided, write the letter of the answer that best completes each sentence.*

_____ 1. Mammals are characterized by hair and
   a. lungs.
   b. mammary glands.
   c. four-chambered hearts.
   d. prehensile tails.

_____ 2. The outer layer of the cerebrum that is the center of thinking is the
   a. cerebellum.
   b. medulla oblongata.
   c. cerebral cortex.
   d. subcutaneous fat.

_____ 3. Mammals that lay eggs are
   a. monotremes.
   b. placental mammals.
   c. marsupials.
   d. primates.

_____ 4. Small, nocturnal primates with large eyes adapted to seeing in the dark belong to the primate group called
   a. prosimians.
   b. hominoids.
   c. anthropoids.
   d. hominids.

_____ 5. Members of the primate group in which the only living members are humans are called
   a. prosimians.
   b. hominoids.
   c. anthropoids.
   d. hominids.

Completion   *Fill in the blanks with terms from Chapter 32.*

6. The layer of fat located beneath the skin is called _____.

7. The _____ is a stomach chamber in which newly swallowed plant food is stored and processed.

8. A powerful muscle called the _____ pulls the bottom of the chest cavity downward, pulling air into the lungs.

9. Mammals bearing live young that complete their development in a pouch are called _____.

10. A structure called a(an) _____ forms when an embryo's tissues join with tissues from the mother's body.

11. The ability to merge visual images from both eyes is called _____.

12. Members of the primate group that includes monkeys, apes, and humans are called _____.

13. A tail that can coil tightly around a branch is called a(an) _____ tail.

14. The evolution of _____, or two-foot, locomotion freed the hands to use tools.

15. The hominid hand evolved a(an) _____ that enabled grasping objects and using tools.

Summary

33–1 Chordate Evolution

Scientists have learned the most about chordates by studying the embryos of living organisms. Scientists have found evidence of early chordates in the fossilized remains of *Pikaia*. *Pikaia* had a notochord and paired muscles. On the basis of this early evidence, scientists classify *Pikaia* as an early chordate.

Chordates include both vertebrates and nonvertebrates. These two groups share a common invertebrate ancestor. Modern amphibians, reptiles, birds, and mammals share more recent common ancestors.

Scientists infer how vertebrates have evolved by studying fossils and the characteristics of living chordates. Scientists believe that the appearance of new adaptations, such as jaws and paired appendages, has led to adaptive radiations. Adaptive radiation results in many new species with different adaptations. Even though these species might look different, they are related.

Another trend in evolution, called convergent evolution, occurs when unrelated species adapt to similar environments. Convergent evolution produces species that look and behave alike even though they are not related.

33–2 Controlling Body Temperature

Controlling body temperature is important for maintaining homeostasis. The chemical reactions that carry out life functions can occur only within a certain temperature range. Vertebrates have different ways to control body temperature. These ways depend on a source of body heat, a way to conserve heat, and a way to get rid of excess heat.

In terms of how they generate and control their body heat, vertebrates are classified into two basic groups: ectotherms and endotherms. Ectotherms rely on the temperature of the environment for body heat. Ectotherms have low rates of metabolism. They do not have good insulation and easily lose heat to the environment.

Endotherms generate their own body heat. They have high metabolic rates. They conserve heat within their bodies with outer coverings, such as feathers, fat, and fur or hair. They get rid of excess heat by sweating or panting.

Endotherms can survive in cool temperatures. However, they require a lot of food. Ectotherms need much less food. However, they cannot survive in very cold environments.

The first land vertebrates were most likely ectotherms. Scientists do not know exactly when endothermy evolved. Some scientists think that dinosaurs were endotherms; others do not. Evidence suggests that endothermy might have evolved more than once.

33–3 Form and Function in Chordates

Organ systems of different vertebrates are specialized to perform specific functions. The complexity of these systems increases from fishes to mammals.

The skulls and teeth of vertebrates are adapted for feeding on a wide variety of foods. For example, the hummingbird's long bill and the narrow snout of the honey possum are adaptations for feeding on nectar. Invertebrates' digestive systems are also adapted for different feeding habits. Carnivores have shorter digestive tracts than herbivores. Herbivores often house bacteria to help break down plant fibers.

Chordates have two basic structures for respiration. Animals that live in water use gills for respiration. Animals that live on land use lungs. As you move from amphibians to mammals, the surface area of the lungs increases. Birds have the most efficient gas exchange. The combination of air sacs and tubes ensures that oxygen-rich air is always in the lungs.

Vertebrates with gills have a single-loop circulatory system. Blood travels from the heart to the gills, then to the rest of the body, and back to the heart. Vertebrates with lungs have a double-loop circulatory system. The first loop carries blood between the heart and the lungs. The second loop carries blood between the heart and the body.

As chordates evolved, the heart developed chambers to separate oxygen-rich blood from oxygen-poor blood. Fish have two chambers: an atrium to receive blood from the body and a ventricle to pump blood. Amphibians have three chambers: two atria and one ventricle. Most reptiles also have a three-chambered heart, but the ventricle has a partial partition. Birds, mammals, and crocodiles have a four-chambered heart. Oxygen-rich blood is completely separated from oxygen-poor blood.

The excretory system removes nitrogenous wastes from the body. It also controls the amount of water in the body. In nonvertebrate chordates and fishes, wastes leave the body through gills and gill slits. These wastes are in the form of ammonia. In most other vertebrates, the kidneys filter out wastes. Vertebrates that live on land excrete wastes in less toxic forms such as urea or uric acid. This enables land vertebrates to conserve water.

Nonvertebrate chordates have a relatively simple nervous system. They do not have specialized sense organs. Vertebrates have a much more complex brain. Each region of the brain is distinct and has a different function. The sense organs and nerve cells in vertebrates are concentrated at the front of the body. From fishes to mammals, the size and complexity of the cerebrum and cerebellum increase.

Vertebrates are much more mobile than nonvertebrate chordates. All vertebrates, except jawless fishes, have an internal skeleton of bone, or in some fishes, cartilage. The bones are held together with tough, flexible tissues that allow movement and keep the bones in place. Body muscles and limb placement help vertebrates move. Amphibians have limbs that stick out sideways. Reptiles, birds, and mammals have limbs directly under the body. This supports more body weight.

Almost all chordates reproduce sexually. Fishes and amphibians have external fertilization. The eggs of reptiles, birds, and mammals are fertilized internally.

Chordates may be oviparous, ovoviviparous, or viviparous. In oviparous species, the eggs develop outside the mother's body. Most fishes, amphibians, reptiles, and all birds are oviparous. In ovoviviparous species like sharks, the eggs develop inside the mother's body. The embryo gets nutrients from the egg yolk. The young are born alive. In viviparous species like most mammals, the embryos get nutrients directly from the mother. Like ovoviviparous species, the young of viviparous animals are born alive.

Section 33–1 Chordate Evolution (pages 849–852)

⚷ Key Concepts

- What are the roots of the chordate family tree?
- What is a main trend in the evolution of chordates?

Chordate Origins (page 849)

1. Studies of embryos of living organisms suggest that the most ancient chordates were closely related to _____.

2. Why do scientists consider *Pikaia* to be an early chordate and not a worm?

   _____

   _____

3. In the diagram below, label the notochord, head region, paired muscle blocks, tentacle, and tail fin of *Pikaia*.

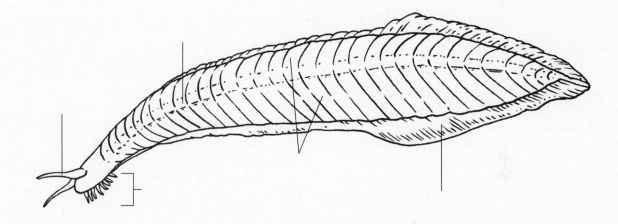

4. A flexible, supporting structure found only in chordates is a(an) _____.

5. Is the following question true or false? Scientists study tunicate larvae to better understand the early evolution of chordates. _____

The Chordate Family Tree (page 850)

6. Circle the letter of each sentence that is true about the chordate family tree. See Figure 33–2 on page 850.

   a. Vertebrates share a common invertebrate ancestor with tunicates and lancelets.

   b. Mammals and fishes share a more recent common ancestor than mammals and birds.

   c. Lungs evolved before paired appendages.

   d. Endothermy evolved after the amniotic egg.

Evolutionary Trends in Vertebrates (page 851)

7. What two things do scientists use to study the evolutionary trends in vertebrates?

   a. _____

   b. _____

8. What effect has the appearance of new adaptations had on the evolution of

   vertebrates? _____

   _____

   _____

   _____

9. What is convergent evolution? _____

   _____

   _____

10. When does convergent evolution occur? _____

    _____

    _____

11. What is one example of convergent evolution? _____

    _____

    _____

Chordate Diversity (pages 851–852)

12. Is the following sentence true or false? The chordate species alive today are a small fraction of the total number of chordate species that have existed over time.

    _____

13. List the six living chordate groups.

    a. _____

    b. _____

    c. _____

    d. _____

    e. _____

    f. _____

Reading Skill Practice

By looking carefully at photographs and illustrations in textbooks, you can help yourself better understand what you have read. Look carefully at Figure 33–3 on page 851. What idea does the photograph communicate?

Section 33–2 Controlling Body Temperature
(pages 854–856)

🔑 **Key Concepts**

- How is the control of body temperature an important aspect of vertebrate life?
- What is the difference between ectotherms and endotherms?

Body Temperature and Homeostasis (pages 854–855)

1. Circle the letter of each sentence that is true about body temperature.

   a. Essential life functions in animals can be carried out most efficiently at any temperature.

   b. If muscles are too cold, they may contract slowly.

   c. If an animal gets too hot, its muscles will work more efficiently.

   d. The control of body temperature is important for maintaining homeostasis.

2. List three features that vertebrates need in order to control their body temperature.

   a. _____

   b. _____

   c. _____

Match each description with the method of controlling body heat. Methods may be used more than once.

	Description	**Method**
_____	**3.** An animal whose body temperature is controlled from within	**a.** Ectotherm
_____	**4.** Examples include reptiles, fishes, and amphibians	**b.** Endotherm
_____	**5.** Warm up by basking in the sun	
_____	**6.** High metabolic rates that generate a significant amount of heat	
_____	**7.** An animal whose body temperature is mainly determined by the temperature of its environment	
_____	**8.** Have feathers, body fat, or hair for insulation	
_____	**9.** Easily lose heat to the environment	
_____	**10.** Low metabolic rate	
_____	**11.** Cools off by panting or sweating	

Comparing Ectotherms and Endotherms (page 856)

12. Name one advantage and one disadvantage of endothermy.

Advantage: _____

_____

Disadvantage: _____

_____

13. Is the following sentence true or false? Ectothermy is a more energy-efficient way to

live in cold environments. _____

Evolution of Temperature Control (page 856)

14. Circle the letter of each sentence that is true about the evolution of temperature control.

a. The first land vertebrates were ectotherms.

b. Scientists know when endothermy evolved.

c. Some biologists hypothesize that dinosaurs were endotherms.

d. Evidence suggests that endothermy evolved more than once.

Section 33–3 Form and Function in Chordates
(pages 857–864)

⊂━━ Key Concept
- How do the organ systems of the different groups of chordates carry out essential life functions?

Feeding (pages 857–858)

1. Most tunicates and all lancelets are _____. They remove plankton from the water that passes through their _____.

2. Circle the letter of the vertebrates that are filter feeders.
   a. tunicates   **b.** flamingoes   **c.** manta rays   **d.** crocodiles

3. What adaptations do vertebrates have to feed on nectar? _____
_____

4. Is the following sentence true or false? Mammals with sharp canine teeth and incisors are filter feeders. _____

5. Circle the letter of the vertebrates that typically have short digestive tracts that produce enzymes.
   a. herbivores   **b.** endotherms   **c.** carnivores   **d.** ectotherms

Respiration (pages 858–859)

6. Is the following sentence true or false? Generally, aquatic chordates use lungs for respiration. _____

7. List three examples of respiratory adaptations or structures used by chordates in addition to gills and lungs.

   a. _____
   _____

   b. _____
   _____

   c. _____

8. Describe the basic process of breathing among land vertebrates. _____
_____
_____
_____

9. Is the following sentence true or false? Mammals typically have more surface area in their lungs than amphibians. _____

10. Bubblelike structures in the lungs that provide an enormous surface area for gas exchange are called _____.

11. Complete the flowchart that describes the path of water as it moves through a fish. See Figure 33–9 on page 859.

Water flows in through the fish's _____, where muscles pump the water across

the _____.

As water passes over the gill filaments, _____ molecules diffuse into blood in the

capillaries. At the same time, _____ diffuses from blood into water.

Water and carbon dioxide are pumped out through the _____.

12. Why do mammals need large amounts of oxygen? _____

_____

_____

13. Why are the lungs of birds most efficient? _____

_____

_____

Circulation (pages 860–861)

14. Is the following sentence true or false? Chordates that use gills for respiration have a single-loop circulatory system. _____

15. Identify where the blood is carried in each loop of a double-loop circulatory system.
   First loop: _____
   Second loop: _____

16. Is the following sentence true or false? In a double-loop system, oxygen-poor blood from the heart is carried to the body. _____

17. In vertebrates with gills, the heart consists of _____ chambers.

18. What is the advantage of the reptilian heart over the amphibian heart? _____

_____

_____

19. Why is a four-chambered heart sometimes described as a double pump? _____

_____

Excretion (page 861)

20. In nonvertebrate chordates and fishes, _____ play an important role in excretion. However, most vertebrates rely on _____.

21. Circle the letter of each chordate that eliminates nitrogenous wastes as urea.

    a. tunicates   **c.** birds

    b. reptiles   **d.** mammals

22. How do vertebrate kidneys help maintain homeostasis? _____

_____

_____

Response (page 862)

23. Is the following sentence true or false? Nonvertebrate chordates have a complex brain with distinct regions. _____

24. Circle the letter of the part of the brain that controls the function of many internal organs.

    a. medulla oblongata   **c.** olfactory bulbs

    b. optic lobes   **d.** cerebrum

25. Is the following sentence true or false? The cerebrum and cerebellum are most developed in birds and mammals. _____

Movement (page 863)

26. Although nonvertebrate chordates lack bones, they do have _____.

27. What structures make it possible for vertebrates to control movement? _____

_____

_____

Reproduction (page 864)

28. Is the following sentence true or false? Vertebrate evolution shows a general trend from internal to external fertilization. _____

29. Circle the letter of development in which the eggs develop internally and the embryos receive nutrients from the yolk surrounding them.

    a. oviparous   **c.** viviparous

    b. ovoviviparous   **d.** asexual

Chapter 33   Comparing Chordates

Vocabulary Review

Labeling Diagrams   *Study the diagrams of the vertebrate brains below. Then, write the vertebrate group to which each brain belongs.*

   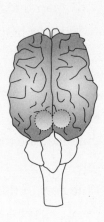 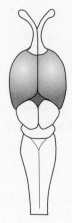

_____   _____   _____   _____   _____

Multiple Choice   *In the space provided, write the letter of the answer that best completes each sentence or answers the question.*

_____ **6.** Which of the following best describes a notochord?
  a. develops into gills in fishes   **c.** is dorsal and hollow
  b. is a flexible, supporting structure   **d.** extends posterior to the anus

_____ **7.** The rapid diversification of species as they adapt to new conditions is
  a. adaptive radiation.   **c.** convergent evolution.
  b. divergent evolution.   **d.** homeostasis.

_____ **8.** Which of the following is NOT true about ectotherms?
  a. The environment determines their body temperature.
  b. These animals have low metabolic rates.
  c. Examples include birds and mammals.
  d. Examples include reptiles, fishes, and amphibians.

_____ **9.** Endotherms get rid of excess heat by
  a. seeking shelter in underground burrows.
  b. basking in the sun.
  c. fluffing up feathers.
  d. panting or sweating.

_____ **10.** Alveoli are located in the
  a. digestive system.   **c.** circulatory system.
  b. brain.   **d.** lungs.

Summary

34–1 Elements of Behavior

Behavior is the way an organism reacts to changes within its body or in its environment. Behaviors usually occur when an animal reacts to a stimulus. The single, specific reaction to a stimulus is a response. Animals detect stimuli with their sense organs. When an animal responds, the nervous system and the muscles work together to produce the behavior.

Animal behavior is important to survival and reproduction. Some behaviors are controlled by genes. They are influenced by natural selection. Organisms with a certain behavior may survive and reproduce better than organisms without the behavior. Over time, most individuals in the population will have that behavior.

Some behaviors are innate. These behaviors are fully functional the first time they are performed, even though the animal may have had no previous experience with the stimuli to which it responds. Examples of innate behaviors are the suckling of a newborn mammal and the weaving of a spider web.

Learning is the way animals change their behavior as a result of experience. Acquired behavior is another name for learning, because these behaviors develop over time. Animals learn in different ways. These include habituation, classical conditioning, operant conditioning, and insight learning.

Habituation is the simplest way in which animals learn. In habituation, an animal's response to a stimulus decreases or stops when the animal is neither rewarded nor harmed for responding.

Classical conditioning occurs when an animal makes a mental connection between a stimulus and a good or bad event. One famous example was described by Ivan Pavlov. Pavlov discovered that if he rang a bell when he fed his dog, the dog would begin to salivate whenever he rang the bell.

In operant conditioning, an animal learns to behave in a certain way in order to receive a reward or to avoid punishment. Operant conditioning is also called trial-and-error learning because it begins with a random behavior that is rewarded.

Insight learning, or reasoning, is the most complicated form of learning. In insight learning, an animal applies something it has already learned to a new situation. Insight learning is found most often in humans.

Most behaviors are the result of innate behavior and learning combined. One example of this is imprinting. Newborn ducks and geese have an innate urge to follow the first moving object they see. They are not born knowing what that object will look like. The newborn must learn from experience what object to follow.

34–2 Patterns of Behavior

Many animal behaviors occur in patterns. These patterns often follow the natural cycles of day and night, seasonal changes, or moon phases. Examples of cycles of behavior include dormancy, migration, and circadian rhythms. Dormancy allows an animal to survive periods when food and other resources may not be available. Migration is the periodic movement from one place to another and then back again. Circadian rhythms occur in a daily pattern, like sleeping at night and going to school during the day.

Animal behaviors also help animals reproduce. Courtship behaviors help an animal find a healthy mate. Some courtship behaviors involve an elaborate series of rituals. Most rituals have specific signals and responses.

Animals have social behavior whenever they interact with members of their own species. Many animals form societies. A society is a group of related animals of the same species that interact closely and often cooperate with one another. Termites form societies. So do zebras, wild dogs, and primates. Animal societies use their strength in numbers to improve their ability to hunt, protect their territory, guard their young, and fight rivals.

Some animal behaviors help prevent others from using limited resources. These behaviors help protect territories. A territory is the area occupied and protected by an animal or group of animals. Territories contain resources, such as food, water, and shelter, that an animal needs to survive and reproduce.

Competition occurs when two or more animals claim the same territory. During competition, an animal may use threatening behavior, or aggression, to gain control over the other animal.

Communication is the passing of information from one animal to another. Animals use many different ways to communicate. Animals with good eyesight often use visual signals such as movement and color to communicate.

Animals with a well-developed sense of smell produce chemicals called pheromones. These chemicals affect the behavior of other members of the species, to mark a territory, for example.

Animals with strong vocal abilities communicate with sound. Birds, toads, crickets, and dolphins use sound to communicate.

Language is the most complicated form of communication. Language combines sounds, symbols, and gestures according to sets of rules about word order and meaning. Only humans are known to use language.

Chapter 34 Animal Behavior

Section 34–1 Elements of Behavior (pages 871–876)

Key Concepts
- What produces behavior in animals?
- What is an innate behavior?
- What are the major types of learning?

Stimulus and Response (pages 871–872)

1. How do biologists define behavior? _____

_____

_____

2. Behaviors are usually performed when an animal reacts to a(an) _____.

3. What is a response? _____

_____

4. Circle the letter of each response.
   a. alarm ringing
   c. answering the phone
   b. hunger pangs
   d. swimming toward moving prey

5. Circle the letter of each stimulus.
   a. light
   c. heat
   b. sound
   d. odors

6. Is the following sentence true or false? All animals can detect all types of stimuli.

_____

7. What body systems interact to produce a behavior in response to a stimulus?

_____

_____

_____

8. Is the following sentence true or false? Animals with more complex nervous systems can

respond to stimuli with more complicated and precise behaviors. _____

Behavior and Evolution (page 872)

9. Is the following sentence true or false? Animal behaviors are not influenced by genes.

_____

10. Explain how natural selection works in the evolution of behaviors in a population.

_____

_____

_____

_____

_____

Innate Behavior (page 873)

11. What is an innate behavior? _____

_____

_____

_____

12. What two things interact to cause innate behaviors?

a. _____

b. _____

Learned Behavior (pages 873–875)

13. What is learning? _____

_____

14. List the four major types of learning.

a. _____   c. _____

b. _____   d. _____

15. The process by which an animal decreases or stops its response to a repetitive stimulus that neither rewards nor harms the animal is called _____.

16. What is the advantage of habituation? _____

_____

_____

17. Identify the type of learning illustrated below. _____
What is the stimulus? _____ What is the reward or
punishment that is associated with the stimulus? _____

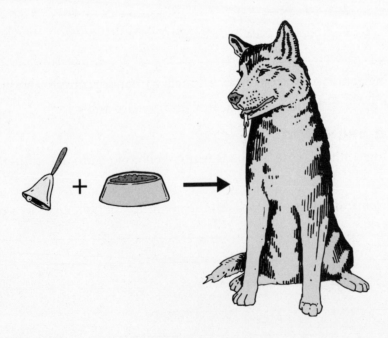

18. What is operant conditioning? _____
_____

19. How does a Skinner box work in operant conditioning? _____
_____
_____
_____

20. When does insight learning occur? _____
_____
_____

21. Is the following sentence true or false? Insight learning is common among reptiles and amphibians. _____

Instinct and Learning Combined (page 876)

22. What is the purpose of imprinting? _____
_____
_____

23. Is the following sentence true or false? Imprinting can be changed after it has occurred.
_____

Reading Skill Practice

When you read a section, taking notes can help you organize and remember the information. As you read or review Section 34–1, take notes by writing each heading and listing the main points under each heading. Do your work on a separate sheet of paper.

Section 34–2 Patterns of Behavior (pages 878–882)

⊂ミ Key Concepts
- How do environmental changes affect animal behavior?
- How do courtship and social behaviors increase an animal's evolutionary fitness?
- How do animals communicate?

Behavioral Cycles (page 878)

Match the behavioral cycle with its description.

Behavioral Cycle	Description
_____ 1. Dormancy	a. A sleeplike state that allows an animal to survive periods when food or other resources may not be available
_____ 2. Migration	b. Behavioral cycles that occur in daily patterns, such as sleeping at night and attending school during the day
_____ 3. Circadian rhythms	c. The periodic movement from one place to another and then back again to take advantage of favorable environmental conditions

Courtship (page 879)

4. Circle the letter of each sentence that is true about courtship.

   a. Courtship behavior helps animals identify healthy mates.

   b. In courtship, an individual sends out stimuli to attract a member of the opposite sex.

   c. Fireflies have an elaborate dance to indicate their readiness to mate.

   d. Courtship rituals always involve a single behavior.

Social Behavior (page 880)

5. Is the following sentence true or false? Courtship is an example of a social behavior.

_____

6. A group of related animals of the same species that interact closely and often cooperate with one another is called a(an) _____ .

7. What are the advantages of animal societies? _____

_____

_____

8. How does helping a relative survive improve an individual's evolutionary fitness?

_____

_____

_____

_____

_____

Competition and Aggression (page 881)

9. What is a territory? _____
_____
_____

10. Circle the letter of each resource that animals need to survive and reproduce.

   a. odors   **c.** nesting sites

   b. mates   **d.** water

11. When does competition occur? _____
_____
_____

12. A threatening behavior that one animal uses to gain control over another is

   _____.

Communication (pages 881–882)

13. What is communication? _____
_____

14. Is the following sentence true or false? Animals with poor eyesight often use visual signals involving movement and color. _____

15. Some animals communicate using _____, chemical messengers that affect the behavior of other individuals of the same species.

16. Is the following sentence true or false? Some animals that use sound to communicate, such as dolphins, might live in places where vision is not very useful. _____

Vocabulary Review

Completion   *Fill in the blanks with terms from Chapter 34.*

1. The way an animal reacts to changes within itself or its environment is called

   _____.

2. A single, specific reaction to a stimulus is a(an) _____.

3. Animals that change their behavior as a result of experience are

   _____.

4. In _____ conditioning, an animal learns to make a mental connection between a stimulus and a reward or punishment.

5. A behavioral cycle that occurs in a daily pattern is a(an) _____.

6. A specific area that is occupied and protected by an animal is its

   _____.

7. The passing of information from one organism to another is called

   _____.

8. The system of communication that only humans are known to use is

   _____.

True or False   *In the space, write* true *if the statement is true. If the statement is false, write the term that makes the statement true.*

_____ 9. A <u>stimulus</u> is any kind of signal that carries information and can be detected.

_____ 10. An <u>innate behavior</u> is an instinct.

_____ 11. <u>Insight learning</u> occurs when an animal stops its response to a repetitive stimulus that is harmless.

_____ 12. Ducklings exhibit <u>operant conditioning</u> when they follow the first moving object they see.

_____ 13. <u>Migration</u> is the periodic movement from one place to another and back again.

_____ 14. In <u>learning</u>, an individual sends out stimuli in order to attract a member of the opposite sex.

_____ 15. <u>Aggression</u> is a threatening behavior that one animal uses to gain control over another.

Chapter 35   Nervous System

Summary

35–1 Human Body Systems

The levels of organization in a multicellular organism include cells, tissues, organs, and organ systems. Cells are the basic units of structure and function in living things. In multicellular organisms, cells are specialized to perform certain functions. Tissues are groups of similar cells that perform a single function. There are four different types of tissues. Epithelial tissue covers body surfaces. Connective tissue supports the body and connects its parts. Nervous tissue carries messages throughout the body. Muscle tissue enables the body to move. An organ is a group of tissues that work together to perform a complex function. An organ system is a group of organs that perform related functions. Humans have 11 organ systems.

Organ systems work together to maintain stable conditions in the body. The process of maintaining stable internal conditions is called homeostasis. Homeostasis may involve feedback inhibition, or negative feedback. For example, the nervous system senses when the body cools and signals the cells to produce more heat.

35–2 The Nervous System

The nervous system controls and coordinates functions throughout the body and responds to internal and external stimuli. Messages carried by the nervous system are electrical signals called impulses. Cells that transmit impulses are called neurons. A neuron has a cell body containing the nucleus. Short branches, called dendrites, carry impulses toward the cell body. A long fiber, called the axon, carries impulses away from the cell body. A myelin sheath surrounds parts of the axon in some neurons. Impulses can jump over the myelin and travel faster.

A resting neuron is one that is not transmitting an impulse. Resting potential is the difference in electrical charge across the cell membrane of a resting neuron. An impulse begins when a resting neuron is stimulated by another neuron or by the environment. The impulse is a sudden reversal of charge across the cell membrane, called an action potential. The lowest level of stimulus needed to activate a neuron is known as the threshold.

At the end of the axon is a synapse. A synapse is the location at which a neuron can transfer an impulse to another cell. Chemicals called neurotransmitters transmit impulses across the synapse.

35–3 Divisions of the Nervous System

The nervous system has two major divisions: the central nervous system and the peripheral nervous system. The central nervous system is the control center of the body. It relays messages, processes information, and analyzes information. The peripheral nervous system carries messages back and forth between the environment and the central nervous system.

The central nervous system consists of the brain and spinal cord. Both are wrapped in layers of tissue called meninges. Between the meninges and nervous tissue is cerebrospinal fluid, which cushions and protects nervous tissue.

The brain is divided into several regions. The cerebrum controls voluntary actions. The cerebellum controls actions of the muscles. The brain stem controls basic body functions. The thalamus receives impulses from the senses and sends them to the cerebrum. The hypothalamus connects the nervous and endocrine systems.

The spinal cord connects the brain to the rest of the body. Certain kinds of information, including some reflexes, are processed directly in the spinal cord. A reflex is a quick, automatic response to a stimulus. A reflex allows your body to respond to danger immediately, without spending time thinking about a response. Animals rely heavily on reflex behaviors for survival.

The peripheral nervous system has two divisions. The sensory division transmits impulses from sensory neurons to the central nervous system. The motor division transmits impulses from the central nervous system to muscles and glands. The motor division is further divided into somatic and autonomic nervous systems. The somatic nervous system controls voluntary actions. The autonomic nervous system controls involuntary actions.

35–4 The Senses

Sensory receptors are neurons that react to stimuli in the environment and send impulses to the central nervous system. There are five types of sensory receptors. Pain receptors respond to pain. Thermoreceptors respond to temperature. Mechanoreceptors respond to pressure. Chemoreceptors respond to chemicals. Photoreceptors respond to light.

Light enters the eye through the pupil, which is a small opening at the front of the eye. Light then passes through the lens, which focuses the light on the retina. Photoreceptors called rods and cones are located in the retina. Rods are sensitive to dim light. Cones are sensitive to colors.

Sound vibrations enter the ear and create pressure waves in a fluid-filled structure called the cochlea. Sensory receptors in the cochlea send impulses to the brain. Three tiny canals in the ear, called semicircular canals, help the central nervous system maintain balance.

The sense organs that detect taste are the taste buds. Skin—the largest sense organ—contains sensory receptors that respond to temperature, touch, and pain.

35–5 Drugs and the Nervous System

A drug is any substance, other than food, that changes the structure or function of the body. Several types of drugs can affect the nervous system. Stimulants increase actions controlled by the nervous system, such as heart rate. Stimulants also increase the release of neurotransmitters in the brain. Depressants decrease actions, such as heart rate, that are controlled by the brain. Cocaine causes the sudden release in the brain of a neurotransmitter called dopamine. Opiates act like natural brain chemicals called endorphins, which normally help overcome pain. Marijuana can cause memory and concentration problems.

Alcohol is a depressant. It slows down the central nervous system. Drinking alcohol during pregnancy may cause fetal alcohol syndrome (FAS). Babies born with FAS have birth defects. People who are addicted to alcohol have a disease called alcoholism.

Addiction is an uncontrollable dependence on a drug. Drug abuse is the intentional misuse of any drug for nonmedical purposes. The best way to avoid the effects of drugs is to avoid drugs.

Section 35–1 Human Body Systems (pages 891–896)

⊂⊃ **Key Concepts**
- How is the human body organized?
- What is homeostasis?

Organization of the Body (pages 891–894)

1. List the levels of organization in a multicellular organism, from smallest to largest.

    a. _____

    b. _____

    c. _____

    d. _____

Match the organ system with its function.

Organ System

_____ 2. Nervous system

_____ 3. Skeletal system

_____ 4. Integumentary system

_____ 5. Endocrine system

_____ 6. Lymphatic/immune systems

_____ 7. Muscular system

_____ 8. Reproductive system

_____ 9. Respiratory system

_____ 10. Excretory system

_____ 11. Circulatory system

_____ 12. Digestive system

Function

a. Stores mineral reserves and provides a site for blood cell formation

b. Provides oxygen and removes carbon dioxide

c. Coordinates the body's response to changes in its internal and external environments

d. Helps produce voluntary movement, circulate blood, and move food

e. Controls growth, development, metabolism, and reproduction

f. Eliminates wastes and maintains homeostasis

g. Serves as a barrier against infection and injury

h. Converts food so it can be used by cells

i. Helps protect the body from disease

j. Produces reproductive cells

k. Brings materials to cells, fights infection, and helps to regulate body temperature

13. What are four types of tissues found in the human body? _____

_____

_____

14. The eye is an example of a(an) _____.

15. Circle the letter of the type of tissue that covers interior and exterior body surfaces.

    a. nervous

    b. connective

    c. epithelial

    d. muscle

16. Circle the letter of the type of tissue that connects body parts.

    a. nervous   **c.** epithelial

    b. connective   **d.** integumentary

Maintaining Homeostasis (pages 895–896)

17. The process of maintaining a controlled, stable internal environment is called

    _____.

18. The process in which a stimulus produces a response that opposes the original

    stimulus is referred to as _____.

19. Fill in the missing labels in the diagram to show how a thermostat uses feedback

    inhibition to maintain a stable temperature in a house.

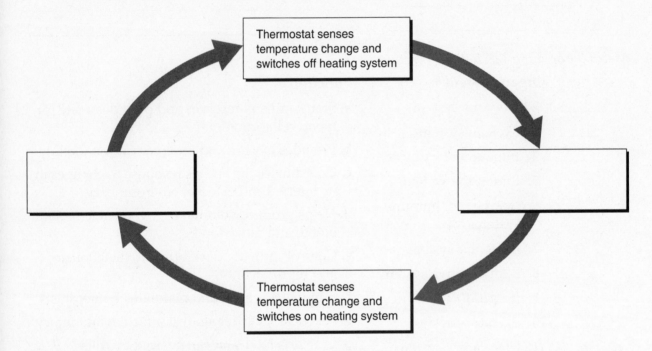

Thermostat senses temperature change and switches off heating system

Thermostat senses temperature change and switches on heating system

20. Is the following sentence true or false? The part of the brain that monitors and controls body temperature is the hypothalamus. _____

21. What happens if nerve cells sense that the core body temperature has dropped

    below 37°C? _____

    _____

    _____

22. What happens if the body temperature rises too far above 37°C? _____

    _____

    _____

Section 35–2 The Nervous System (pages 897–900)

🔑 Key Concepts
- What are the functions of the nervous system?
- How is the nerve impulse transmitted?

Introduction (page 897)

1. What is the function of the nervous system? _____

_____

_____

Neurons (pages 897–898)

2. How are neurons classified? _____

_____

3. What are three types of neurons?

  a. _____

  b. _____

  c. _____

4. Is the following sentence true or false? Sensory neurons carry impulses from the brain and the spinal cord to muscles and glands. _____

5. Label the following features in the drawing of a neuron: cell body, dendrites, and axon.

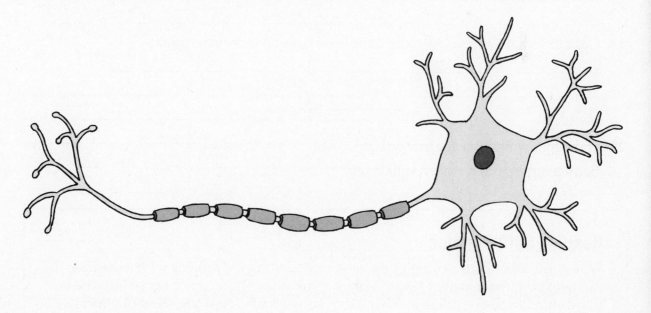

6. What is the function of the myelin sheath? _____

_____

The Nerve Impulse (pages 898–899)

7. The electrical charge across the cell membrane of a neuron in its resting state is called its

   _____.

8. How does a nerve impulse begin? _____

   _____

   _____

   _____

9. Circle the letter of the choice that describes an action potential.

   a. Reversal of charges due to the flow of positive ions into a neuron

   b. Increase in negative ions in a neuron due to the flow of potassium out of the cell

   c. Change to a negative charge due to the flow of sodium ions out of a neuron

   d. Reversal of charges due to the flow of negative ions into a neuron

10. The minimum level of a stimulus that is required to activate a neuron is called the

    _____.

11. How does a nerve impulse follow the all-or-nothing principle? _____

    _____

    _____

The Synapse (page 900)

12. What are neurotransmitters? _____

    _____

    _____

13. Describe what happens when an impulse arrives at an axon terminal.

    _____

    _____

    _____

    _____

    _____

Reading Skill Practice

When you read about a complex process, representing the process with a diagram
can help you understand it better. Make a diagram to show how a nerve impulse is
transmitted from one cell to another. Do your work on a separate sheet of paper.

© Pearson Education, Inc., publishing as Pearson Prentice Hall.

Section 35–3 Divisions of the Nervous System
(pages 901–905)

Key Concepts
- What are the functions of the central nervous system?
- What are the functions of the two divisions of the peripheral nervous system?

Introduction (page 901)

1. What is the function of the central nervous system? _____
_____
_____

The Central Nervous System (page 901)

2. The central nervous system consists of the _____ and the
_____.

3. Is the following sentence true or false? Three layers of connective tissue known as meninges protect the brain and spinal cord. _____

4. The brain and spinal cord are bathed and protected by _____.

The Brain (pages 902–903)

Match the part of the brain with its function.

	Part of Brain	Function
_____	5. Cerebrum	**a.** Coordinates and balances the actions of the muscles
_____	6. Cerebellum	**b.** Regulates the flow of information between the brain and the rest of the body
_____	7. Brain stem	**c.** Controls voluntary activities of the body
_____	8. Thalamus	**d.** Controls hunger, thirst, fatigue, anger, and body temperature
_____	9. Hypothalamus	**e.** Receives and relays messages from the sense organs

10. The two hemispheres of the brain are connected by a band of tissue called the
_____.

11. Identify the four lobes of the brain.

   a. _____   c. _____

   b. _____   d. _____

12. Is the following sentence true or false? The left hemisphere of the cerebrum controls the body's left side. _____

13. Is the following sentence true or false? The outer layer of the cerebrum is called the cerebral cortex. _____

14. What is gray matter, and where is it found? _____
_____

15. The two regions of the brain stem are the _____ and the

_____.

The Spinal Cord (page 903)

16. What is the advantage of a reflex? _____

_____

_____

The Peripheral Nervous System (pages 903–904)

17. Circle the letter of each choice that is part of the peripheral nervous system.

   a. cranial nerves   **c.** ganglia

   b. spinal nerves   **d.** spinal cord

18. Complete the concept map.

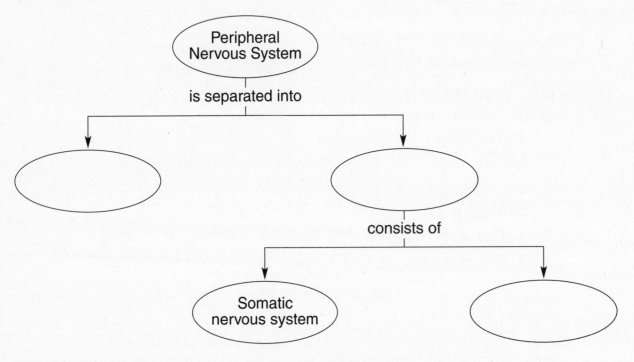

19. Circle the letter of each activity that is controlled by the somatic nervous system.

   a. Beating of the heart   **c.** Wiggling the toes

   b. Lifting a finger   **d.** Pulling foot away from tack

20. What does the autonomic nervous system regulate? _____

_____

_____

21. Why is it important to have two systems that control the same organs?

_____

_____

Section 35–4 The Senses (pages 906–909)

🗝 Key Concept
- What are the five types of sensory receptors?

Introduction (page 906)

1. What are sensory receptors? _____
_____
_____

2. List the five general categories of sensory receptors.

 a. _____

 b. _____

 c. _____

 d. _____

 e. _____

3. Which category of sensory receptors are sensitive to touch, sound, and motion?
_____
_____

Vision (pages 906–907)

4. Circle the letter of each sentence that is true about the structures of the eye.

 a. Light enters the eye through the cornea.

 b. The chamber behind the cornea is filled with vitreous humor.

 c. The pupil changes in size to let more or less light enter the eye.

 d. The lens focuses light on the retina.

5. Is the following sentence true or false? The function of the iris is to adjust the size of the pupil. _____

6. Where are the photoreceptors located in the eye? _____
_____

7. What do photoreceptors do? _____
_____

8. Is the following sentence true or false? Cones are extremely sensitive to light, but they do not distinguish different colors. _____

9. How do impulses travel from the eyes to the brain? _____
_____

10. What are the two types of photoreceptors? _____

Hearing and Balance (pages 908–909)

11. List the two sensory functions of the ear.

a. _____

b. _____

12. Label each of the following structures in the drawing of the ear: auditory canal, tympanum, semicircular canals, and cochlea.

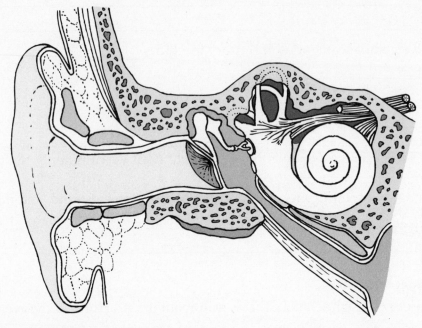

13. Is the following sentence true or false? The tympanum sends nerve impulses

to the brain. _____

14. Complete the flowchart.

Vibrations enter the ear through the _____.

↓

The vibrations cause the _____ to vibrate.

↓

These vibrations are picked up by three tiny bones, called the _____, _____, and _____.

↓

The last bone transmits the vibrations to the _____, creating pressure waves in the _____.

↓

Tiny hair cells inside the _____ produce nerve impulses that are sent to the brain through the _____ nerve.

15. What is the role of hair cells in the cochlea? _____

_____

_____

16. How do the semicircular canals help maintain balance? _____

_____

_____

Smell and Taste (page 909)

17. Is the following sentence true or false? Your sense of smell is actually an ability to

detect pressure. _____

18. How does the body detect smell? _____

_____

_____

19. Is the following sentence true or false? Much of what we commonly call the "taste" of

food and drink is actually smell. _____

20. The sense organs that detect taste are the _____.

21. List the four different categories of tastes.

   a. _____

   b. _____

   c. _____

   d. _____

Touch and Related Senses (page 909)

22. What is the largest sense organ? _____

_____

23. Is the following sentence true or false? The skin contains sensory receptors that

respond to temperature, touch, and pain. _____

24. Circle the letter of each choice that is true about the sense of touch.

   a. Unlike the other senses, the sense of touch is not found in one particular place.

   b. All parts of the body are equally sensitive to touch.

   c. The greatest density of touch receptors is found on the arms and legs.

   d. Touch is detected by mechanoreceptors.

25. Where is the greatest density of touch receptors found on the body? _____

_____

_____

Section 35–5 Drugs and the Nervous System
(pages 910–914)

Key Concepts
- What are the different classes of drugs that directly affect the central nervous system?
- What is the effect of alcohol on the body?

Introduction (page 910)

1. Is the following sentence true or false? A drug is any illegal substance that changes the structure or function of the body. _____

2. Is the following sentence true or false? Among the most powerful drugs are the ones that cause changes in the nervous system, especially to the brain and the synapses between neurons. _____

3. How can drugs disrupt the functioning of the nervous system? _____

_____

_____

Drugs That Affect the Synapse (pages 910–914)

Match the drug or type of drug with one way that it can affect the body.

Drug or Type of Drug	Effect on the Body
_____ 4. Stimulant	a. Acts on pleasure centers of brain
_____ 5. Depressant	b. Destroys liver cells
_____ 6. Cocaine	c. Reduces pain
_____ 7. Opiate	d. Decreases heart rate
_____ 8. Marijuana	e. Increases blood pressure
_____ 9. Alcohol	f. Causes lung damage

10. Circle the letter of each choice that is a stimulant drug.

   a. nicotine   c. amphetamine

   b. cocaine   d. codeine

11. Circle the letter of each choice that is a depressant drug.

   a. alcohol   c. tranquilizer

   b. morphine   d. barbiturate

12. Cocaine causes the sudden release in the brain of a neurotransmitter called

   _____.

13. Is the following sentence true or false? The most widely abused illegal drug is marijuana. _____

14. Circle the letter of each choice that is a result of long-term use of marijuana.

    a. Loss of memory   **c.** Increase in testosterone

    b. Inability to concentrate   **d.** Cirrhosis of the liver

15. Is the following sentence true or false? Alcohol is one of the most abused legal drugs.

_____

16. What is fetal alcohol syndrome, or FAS? _____

_____

_____

17. People who have become addicted to alcohol suffer from a disease called

_____ .

18. How does long-term alcohol use affect the body? _____

_____

_____

Drug Abuse (page 914)

19. The intentional misuse of any drug for nonmedical purposes is referred to as

_____ .

20. An uncontrollable dependence on a drug is known as _____ .

21. What is psychological dependence on a drug? _____

_____

22. When does physical dependence on a drug occur? _____

_____

_____

23. How can drug use increase the transmission of HIV, the virus that causes AIDS?

_____

_____

_____

Vocabulary Review

Completion   *Fill in the blanks in the table.*

Tissue Type	Function
Epithelial	1. _____
Connective	2. _____
Nervous	3. _____
Muscle	4. _____

True or False   *Determine whether each statement is true or false. If it is true, write* true *in the space provided. If the statement is false, change the underlined word or words to make the statement true.*

_____ **5.** The process by which organisms keep internal conditions relatively constant is called <u>homeostasis</u>.

_____ **6.** Cells that transmit nerve impulses are known as <u>meninges</u>.

_____ **7.** The long fiber that carries impulses away from the cell body of a nerve cell is the <u>dendrite</u>.

_____ **8.** The lowest level of stimulus needed to activate a neuron is called the <u>action potential</u>.

_____ **9.** The location at which a neuron can transfer an impulse to another cell is referred to as a(an) <u>synapse</u>.

_____ **10.** The part of the brain that controls voluntary actions is the <u>brain stem</u>.

_____ **11.** The part of the brain that receives impulses from the senses and sends them to the cerebrum is the <u>hypothalamus</u>.

_____ **12.** Light enters the eye through a small opening called the <u>pupil</u>.

_____ **13.** Photoreceptors in the eye that are sensitive to colors are known as <u>rods</u>.

_____ **14.** Drugs called <u>opiates</u> increase actions controlled by the nervous system.

_____ **15.** An uncontrollable dependence on a drug is known as drug <u>abuse</u>.

Answering Questions   *In the space provided, write an answer to each question.*

16. List the levels of organization in a multicellular organism, from smallest to largest.

_____

_____

17. What is resting potential? _____

_____

18. What is the function of the autonomic nervous system? _____

_____

19. How does alcohol affect the central nervous system? _____

_____

20. To which type of stimulus do thermoreceptors react? _____

Summary

36–1 The Skeletal System

The skeletal system supports the body, protects internal organs, provides for movement, stores mineral reserves, and provides a site for blood cell formation. The skeleton is divided into two parts: the axial skeleton and the appendicular skeleton. The axial skeleton includes the skull, ribs, and spine. The appendicular skeleton includes all the bones associated with the arms and legs, including bones of the shoulders, hips, hands, and feet.

The bones that make up the skeletal system are living tissue. Bones are a solid network of living cells and protein fibers that are surrounded by deposits of calcium salts. A typical bone is surrounded by a tough layer of connective tissue called the periosteum. Beneath the periosteum is a thick layer of compact bone. Running through compact bone is a network of tubes called Haversian canals. These canals contain blood vessels and nerves. Inside the layer of compact bone is spongy bone. Spongy bone is quite strong and adds strength to bones without adding mass. Within bones are cavities that contain a soft tissue called bone marrow. Bone marrow can be yellow or red. Yellow marrow is made up of fat. Red marrow produces blood cells.

The skeleton of an embryo is composed almost entirely of cartilage. Cartilage is a type of connective tissue that is tough but flexible. Cartilage is replaced by bone during the process of bone formation, or ossification. Ossification starts before birth and continues until adulthood.

A place where one bone attaches to another bone is called a joint. Joints permit bones to move without damaging each other. Depending on its type of movement, a joint is classified as immovable, slightly movable, or freely movable. Immovable joints, such as the joints in the skull, allow no movement. Slightly movable joints, such as the joints in the spine, allow a small amount of restricted movement. Freely movable joints permit movement in one or more directions. Freely movable joints are classified by the type of movement they permit.

Ball-and-socket joints, such as the shoulder, allow the widest range of movement of any joint. Hinge joints, such as the knee, permit only back-and-forth movement. Pivot joints, such as the elbow, allow one bone to rotate around another. Saddle joints, such as those in the hand, allow one bone to slide in two directions.

Strips of tough connective tissue, called ligaments, hold bones together in a joint. The bony surfaces of the joint are covered with cartilage. A substance called synovial fluid forms a thin film on the cartilage and makes the joint surfaces slippery.

Bones and joints can be damaged by excessive strain or disease. Arthritis is a disorder that involves inflammation of the joints. Osteoporosis is a condition in which bones weaken. Weak bones are likely to fracture, or break.

36–2 The Muscular System

Muscle tissue is found everywhere in the body. There are three different types of muscle tissue: skeletal, smooth, and cardiac. Skeletal muscles are usually attached to bones. They appear to be striped, so they are also called striated muscles. Skeletal muscles are responsible for voluntary movements such as dancing.

© Pearson Education, Inc., publishing as Pearson Prentice Hall.

Smooth muscles line blood vessels and the digestive tract. They are not striated or under conscious control. Smooth muscles move food through the digestive tract and control the flow of blood through the circulatory system. Cardiac muscle is found only in the heart. Like smooth muscle, it is not under conscious control.

Skeletal muscle cells are called muscle fibers. Muscle fibers are composed of smaller structures called myofibrils. Each myofibril is made up of even smaller structures called filaments. Filaments can be thick or thin. Thick filaments are made of a protein called myosin. Thin filaments are made of a protein called actin. A muscle contracts when the thin filaments in the muscle fiber slide over the thick filaments.

Impulses from motor neurons control the contraction of skeletal muscles. The point of contact between a motor neuron and a muscle fiber is called a neuromuscular junction. A neurotransmitter named acetylcholine is released by the motor neuron into the synapse. Acetylcholine transmits the impulse across the synapse to the skeletal muscle cell. The more muscle cells that are stimulated to contract, the stronger the contraction.

Skeletal muscles are joined to bones by tough connective tissues called tendons. Tendons pull on bones and make them work like levers. Muscles provide the force to move the bones. Most skeletal muscles work in opposing pairs. When one muscle contracts, the other relaxes.

Regular exercise is important in maintaining the strength and flexibility of muscles. Regular exercise also strengthens bones. Strong bones and muscles are less likely to become injured.

36–3 The Integumentary System

The skin is the single largest organ of the body. It is also the largest component of the integumentary system. The integumentary system serves as a barrier against infection and injury, helps to regulate body temperature, removes waste products from the body, and provides protection against ultraviolet radiation from the sun.

The skin is made up of two main layers: the epidermis and the dermis. The epidermis is the outer layer of the skin. Cells of the epidermis produce keratin. Keratin is a tough, fibrous protein that helps keep the epidermis flexible and waterproof. The epidermis also contains cells, called melanocytes, that produce melanin. Melanin is a dark drown pigment that helps protect the skin from ultraviolet rays.

The dermis is the inner layer of skin. It contains nerves, blood vessels, glands, and other structures not found in the epidermis. The dermis works with other organs to maintain homeostasis. It helps to regulate body temperature. Sweat glands in the dermis produce sweat when the body gets too hot. When the sweat evaporates from the skin, it cools the body.

Too much sunlight can produce skin cancer. You can protect against skin cancer by wearing a hat, sunglasses, and protective clothing. You also should use sunscreen with a sun protection factor (SPF) of at least 15.

In addition to the skin, the integumentary system includes the hair and nails. Both hair and nails are composed mainly of keratin. Hair on the head protects the scalp from sunlight and cold. Hair in the nostrils and around the eyes prevents dirt from entering the body. Hair is produced by structures called hair follicles. Hair follicles are located in the dermis. Nails grow from an area called the nail root. Nails protect the tips of the fingers and toes.

Chapter 36 Skeletal, Muscular, and Integumentary Systems

Section 36–1 The Skeletal System (pages 921–925)

⌬ Key Concepts
- What are the functions of the skeletal system?
- What is the structure of a typical bone?
- What are the three different kinds of joints?

Introduction (page 921)

1. What forms the skeletal system? _____
_____

The Skeleton (page 921)

2. List the functions of the skeletal system.

a. _____ d. _____

b. _____ e. _____

c. _____

3. Is the following sentence true or false? Most bones act like levers on which muscles act to produce movement. _____

4. Is the following sentence true or false? There are 106 bones in the adult human skeleton.

_____

5. Complete the concept map.

6. What is the general function of the axial skeleton? _____

_____

Structure of Bones (page 922)

7. The two minerals that make up most of the mass of bone are _____

and _____.

8. Is the following sentence true or false? Bones are living tissue. _____

Match each structure in a bone with its description.

Structure	Description
_____ **9.** Periosteum	**a.** Network of tubes running through bone
_____ **10.** Compact bone	**b.** Soft tissue contained in bone cavities
_____ **11.** Haversian canals	**c.** Tough layer of connective tissue surrounding bone
_____ **12.** Spongy bone	**d.** Thick layer of dense bone beneath the periosteum
_____ **13.** Bone marrow	**e.** Bone with a latticework structure

14. Cells that produce bone are called _____.

Development of Bones (pages 922–923)

15. The skeleton of an embryo is composed almost entirely of a type of connective tissue

called _____.

16. The network of fibers in cartilage is made from two proteins called _____

and _____.

17. Circle the letter of each sentence that is true about cartilage.

a. It contains blood vessels.   **c.** It cannot support weight.

b. It is dense and fibrous.   **d.** It is extremely flexible.

18. Cartilage is replaced by bone during the process of bone formation called

_____.

19. Is the following sentence true or false? By adulthood, all the cartilage in the body has been

replaced by bone. _____

Types of Joints (page 924)

20. What is a joint? _____

_____

21. List the three classifications of joints, based on their type of movement.

a. _____

b. _____

c. _____

22. What are examples of immovable joints? _____

_____

_____

23. Is the following sentence true or false? The joints between the two bones of the lower leg are slightly movable joints. _____

24. Identify the type of freely movable joint represented in each of the drawings below.

 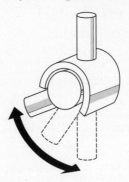 

_____ _____ _____

25. Is the following sentence true or false? Ball-and-socket joints permit the widest range of movement. _____

Structure of Joints (pages 924–925)

26. Circle the letter of each sentence that is true about the structure of joints.

    a. Cartilage protects the ends of bones as they move against each other at joints.

    b. Ligaments hold bones together at joints.

    c. Synovial fluid prevents the ends of bones from slipping past each other at joints.

    d. A bursa is a swelling caused by inflammation of a joint.

Skeletal System Disorders (page 925)

27. Inflammation of a bursa is called _____.

28. A serious disorder that involves inflammation of one or more joints is

_____.

Section 36–2 The Muscular System (pages 926–931)

⊂━ **Key Concepts**
- What are the three types of muscle tissue?
- How do muscles contract?
- Why is exercise important?

Types of Muscle Tissue (pages 926–927)

1. List the three different types of muscle tissue.

   a. _____   b. _____   c. _____

2. Is the following sentence true or false? Each type of muscle has the same function.

   _____

3. Is the following sentence true or false? Skeletal muscles are usually attached to bones.

   _____

4. Circle the letter of each sentence that is true about skeletal muscles.

   a. They have striations.

   b. Most of them are consciously controlled by the central nervous system.

   c. Their cells have just one nucleus.

   d. Their cells are long and slender.

5. Circle the letter of each sentence that is true about smooth muscle cells.

   a. They are spindle-shaped.

   b. They can function without nervous stimulation.

   c. They have two or more nuclei.

   d. They are connected by gap junctions.

6. What are three functions of smooth muscles? _____

   _____

   _____

   _____

7. Is the following sentence true or false? Cardiac muscle cells always have two nuclei.

   _____

8. Complete the table that compares and contrasts the three types of muscle tissue.

TYPES OF MUSCLE TISSUE

Muscle Tissue Type	Striated/Not Striated	What It Controls
Skeletal	Striated	
	Not striated	Involuntary movements
Cardiac		

Muscle Contraction (page 928)

9. Circle the letter of the choice that lists the muscle structures from largest to smallest.

   a. Myofibrils, filaments, muscle fibers

   b. Muscle fibers, myofibrils, filaments

   c. Muscle fibers, filaments, myofibrils

   d. Myofibrils, muscle fibers, filaments

Match each type of muscle filament with the protein it contains.

Type of Filament	Protein It Contains
_____ 10. thick	**a.** Actin
_____ 11. thin	**b.** Myosin

12. The filaments are arranged along the muscle fiber in units called _____.

13. Is the following sentence true or false? When a muscle is relaxed, there are only thin filaments in the center of a sarcomere. _____

14. How does a muscle contract according to the sliding-filament model of muscle contraction? _____

15. The energy for muscle contraction is supplied by _____.

Control of Muscle Contraction (page 929)

16. Complete the flowchart to show the missing steps in the stimulation of a muscle cell by a neuron.

```
┌─────────────────────────────────────────┐
│   Diffusion of acetylcholine across synapse │
└─────────────────────────────────────────┘
                    │
                 produces
                    ↓
┌─────────────────────────────────────────┐
│   Impulse in membrane of muscle cell      │
└─────────────────────────────────────────┘
                    │
                  causes
                    ↓
┌─────────────────────────────────────────┐
│                                           │
└─────────────────────────────────────────┘
                    │
                 affects
                    ↓
┌─────────────────────────────────────────┐
│          Regulatory proteins              │
└─────────────────────────────────────────┘
                    │
                  allow
                    ↓
┌─────────────────────────────────────────┐
│                                           │
└─────────────────────────────────────────┘
```

17. Is the following sentence true or false? Impulses from motor neurons control the contraction of skeletal muscles. _____

18. The point of contact between a motor neuron and a skeletal muscle cell is a(an)

_____ .

19. What terminates a muscle contraction? _____

_____

_____

20. Is the following sentence true or false? A single motor neuron can form synapses with many muscle cells. _____

21. What is the difference between a strong muscle contraction and a weak muscle contraction? _____

_____

_____

How Muscles and Bones Interact (page 930)

22. Is the following sentence true or false? Individual muscles can pull in only one direction. _____

23. Circle the letter of the term that refers to the tough connective tissue joining skeletal muscle to bone.

    a. cartilage   **b.** ligament   **c.** tendon   **d.** bursa

24. If bones are like levers, what functions as a fulcrum? _____

25. What does it mean for muscles to "work in opposing pairs"? _____

_____

Exercise and Health (page 931)

26. Why is regular exercise important? _____

_____

Reading Skill Practice

When you read a section with many details, writing an outline may help you organize and remember the material. Outline Section 36–2 by first writing the section headings as major topics in the order in which they appear in the book. Then, beneath each major topic, list important details about it. Title your outline *The Muscular System*. Do your work on a separate sheet of paper.

Section 36–3 The Integumentary System
(pages 933–936)

Key Concept
- What are the functions of the integumentary system?

Introduction (page 933)

1. Circle the letter of each choice that is part of the integumentary system.

   a. skin   c. cartilage

   b. bones   d. nails

The Skin (pages 933–936)

2. The most important function of the skin is _____.

3. List the four functions of the integumentary system.

   a. _____

   b. _____

   c. _____

   d. _____

4. The largest component of the integumentary system is the _____.

5. The outer layer of skin is called the _____.

6. Is the following sentence true or false? The inner layer of the epidermis is made up of dead cells. _____

7. Label the structures of the skin.

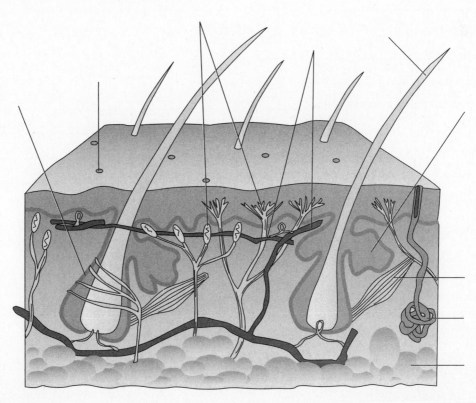

Match each term with its definition.

	Term	**Definition**
_____	**8.** keratin	**a.** Tough, fibrous protein
_____	**9.** melanin	**b.** Inner layer of the skin
_____	**10.** dermis	**c.** Dark brown pigment

11. Circle the letter of each sentence that is true about melanocytes.

   a. Melanocytes are cells that produce melanin.

   b. Most people have roughly the same number of melanocytes in their skin.

   c. All melanocytes produce about the same amount of melanin.

   d. Most people have the same distribution of melanocytes in their skin.

12. Is the following sentence true or false? The epidermis contains blood vessels.

   _____

13. Circle the letter of each type of structure that is found in the dermis.

   a. blood vessels   **c.** glands

   b. nerve endings   **d.** hair follicles

14. How does the dermis help regulate body temperature? _____

_____

_____

_____

_____

15. List the two types of glands contained in the dermis.

   a. _____

   b. _____

16. How does sweat help keep you cool? _____

_____

17. What is the function of sebum? _____

_____

Hair and Nails (page 936)

18. The basic structure of human hair and nails is _____.

19. List the two functions of head hair.

    a. _____

    b. _____

20. How does hair in the nose and ears and around the eyes help protect the body?

_____

_____

_____

21. Hair is produced by cells called _____.

22. Is the following sentence true or false? Hair is composed of cells that have died.

_____

23. What causes hair to grow? _____

_____

24. What is the nail root? _____

_____

_____

Vocabulary Review

Crossword Puzzle   *Complete the puzzle by entering the term that matches each numbered description.*

Across

3. type of canals in bone that contain blood vessels and nerves
5. tough layer of connective tissue that surrounds bone
7. tough connective tissue that holds bones together in a joint
10. layer of skin that contains glands and blood vessels
12. place where one bone attaches to another bone
13. protein found in thin muscle filaments

Down

1. type of connective tissue that is replaced by bone as a person grows
2. protein found in hair and nails
4. layer of skin where melanocytes are located
6. process in which cartilage is replaced by bone
8. protein found in thick muscle filaments
9. tough connective tissue that joins skeletal muscle to bone
11. dark brown pigment in skin

Completion   *Fill in the blanks with terms from Chapter 36.*

The three different types of muscle tissue are _____,

_____, and _____. Skeletal muscles are controlled

by motor neurons. A motor neuron and a skeletal muscle cell meet at a point called

a(an) _____. The motor neuron releases a neurotransmitter,

called _____, which transmits the impulse to the muscle cell.

Summary

37–1 The Circulatory System

The human circulatory system consists of the heart, blood vessels, and blood. Together with the respiratory system, the circulatory system supplies the body's cells with nutrients and oxygen and removes carbon dioxide and other wastes from the body.

The heart is located near the center of the chest. It is composed almost entirely of muscle. The thick layer of muscle that forms the walls of the heart is called the myocardium. Contractions of the myocardium pump blood through the circulatory system.

The heart is divided into right and left halves by a wall called the septum. Each half of the heart has two chambers, for a total of four chambers. The upper two chambers, or atria (singular: atrium), receive blood entering the heart. The lower two chambers, or ventricles, pump blood out of the heart. The right side of the heart pumps blood from the heart to the lungs. This pathway is the pulmonary circulation. The left side of the heart pumps blood to the rest of the body. This pathway is the systemic circulation. Flaps of connective tissue, called valves, between chambers prevent blood from flowing backward in the heart.

Each heart contraction begins in a small group of cardiac muscle cells called the pacemaker. From the pacemaker, the impulse travels through the rest of the heart, causing the heart to contract.

When blood leaves the heart for the body, it passes into a large blood vessel called the aorta. As blood flows through the rest of the circulatory system, it moves through three types of vessels: arteries, capillaries, and veins. Arteries are large vessels that carry blood away from the heart. From arteries, blood flows into capillaries, the smallest vessels. Capillaries bring nutrients and oxygen to the cells and absorb carbon dioxide and other wastes. From the capillaries, blood flows into veins and is returned to the heart. Large veins contain valves that keep blood moving toward the heart.

The pumping of the heart produces pressure. The force of the blood on artery walls is called blood pressure. Blood pressure keeps blood flowing through the body. Blood pressure is controlled by the autonomic nervous system and the kidneys.

Diseases of the circulatory system, called cardiovascular diseases, are leading causes of death. Two causes of these diseases are high blood pressure and atherosclerosis, in which fatty deposits build up in arteries. Both high blood pressure and atherosclerosis force the heart to work harder and can lead to heart attack and stroke. Cardiovascular diseases are easier to prevent than cure. Prevention includes exercising regularly, eating a low-fat diet, controlling weight, and not smoking.

37–2 Blood and the Lymphatic System

Blood is a type of connective tissue containing dissolved substances and specialized cells. Blood is almost half cells and just over half fluid. The fluid portion of blood is called plasma. Plasma is mostly water. Proteins in plasma help to clot blood and fight infections.

Cells in blood include red blood cells, white blood cells, and platelets. Red blood cells transport oxygen. A protein called hemoglobin in red blood cells binds to oxygen and carries it throughout the body. White blood cells guard against infection, fight parasites, and attack bacteria. There are many types of white blood cells. White blood cells known as lymphocytes produce antibodies. Antibodies are proteins that help fight infection. Platelets—along with plasma proteins—make blood clotting possible. Platelets cluster around a wound and release proteins called clotting factors, leading to the formation of a clot.

As blood circulates, some fluid leaks from the blood into surrounding tissues. This fluid is called lymph. The lymphatic system consists of a network of vessels, lymph nodes, and organs. This system collects lymph and returns it to the circulatory system. The lymphatic system also helps absorb nutrients and fight infection.

37–3 The Respiratory System

In biology, the word *respiration* is used in two ways. Cellular respiration, as you may recall, is the release of energy from the breakdown of food molecules in the presence of oxygen. The other meaning of respiration is the exchange of gases between an organism and the environment. The human respiratory system brings about the exchange of oxygen and carbon dioxide between the blood, the air, and tissues.

The respiratory system consists of the nose, pharynx, larynx, trachea, bronchi, and lungs. Air from the nose enters the pharynx, a tube in the throat. Air moves from the pharynx into the trachea. At the top of the trachea is the larynx, which contains the vocal cords. From the trachea, air passes into two large passageways in the chest called bronchi (singular: bronchus). Each bronchus leads into one of the lungs. Within

each lung, the bronchus subdivides into smaller passageways, called bronchioles. The bronchioles continue to subdivide until they reach millions of tiny air sacs called alveoli (singular: alveolus). Each alveolus is surrounded by capillaries. Oxygen crosses the thin capillary walls from the alveolus into the blood. Carbon dioxide in the blood crosses in the opposite direction into the alveolus.

Breathing is the movement of air into and out of the lungs. At the bottom of the chest cavity is a muscle called the diaphragm. When the diaphragm contracts, the chest cavity becomes larger. This creates a partial vacuum in the chest. Air pressure causes air to rush in and fill the lungs. When the diaphragm relaxes, the chest cavity becomes smaller. Increased pressure inside the chest forces air back out of the lungs.

The rate of breathing is controlled by the level of carbon dioxide in the blood. This level is monitored by the medulla oblongata in the brain. As the carbon dioxide level rises, the medulla oblongata sends nerve impulses to the diaphragm, causing it to contract. This results in breathing.

Tobacco smoke harms the respiratory system. Three of the most dangerous substances in tobacco smoke are nicotine, carbon monoxide, and tar. Nicotine is a stimulant that increases heart rate and blood pressure. Carbon monoxide is a poisonous gas that blocks the transport of oxygen by blood. Tar contains substances that cause cancer. Smoking can cause emphysema, which is loss of elasticity in the tissues of the lungs. Smoking can also cause lung cancer and heart disease. Passive smoking means inhaling the smoke of others. Passive smoking is damaging to nonsmokers, especially young children. Quitting smoking can improve a smoker's health. The best solution, however, is not to begin smoking.

Section 37–1 The Circulatory System (pages 943–950)

Key Concepts
- What are the structures of the circulatory system?
- What are the three types of blood vessels in the circulatory system?

Functions of the Circulatory System (page 943)

1. Why do large organisms require a circulatory system? _____

_____

_____

_____

2. What is a closed circulatory system? _____

_____

3. List the three components of the circulatory system.

a. _____   b. _____   c. _____

The Heart (pages 944–946)

4. Is the following sentence true or false? The heart is composed almost entirely of muscle.

_____

Match each heart structure with its description.

	Structure	Description
_____	5. pericardium	a. Thick layer of muscle in the walls of the heart
_____	6. myocardium	b. Sac of tissue that encloses and protects the heart
_____	7. atrium	c. Upper chamber of the heart
_____	8. ventricle	d. Lower chamber of the heart

9. Dividing the right side of the heart from the left side is a wall called a(an) _____.

10. Is the following sentence true or false? The heart functions as four separate

pumps. _____

11. Complete the table about the circulatory system.

THE CIRCULATORY SYSTEM

Name of Circulatory Pathway	Side of Heart Involved	Route Blood Follows
Pulmonary circulation		From heart to lungs
	Left side	

12. What happens to blood when it reaches the lungs? _____

_____

13. Why is the blood that enters the heart from the systemic circulation oxygen-poor?

_____

_____

_____

14. Circle the letter of each sentence that is true about blood flow through the heart.

   a. Blood enters the heart through the right and left atria.

   b. Blood enters the heart through the right and left ventricles.

   c. Blood flows from the ventricles to the atria.

   d. Blood flows out of the heart through the right and left atria.

15. Flaps of connective tissue called _____ prevent blood from flowing backward in the heart.

16. Each heart contraction begins in a small group of cardiac muscle cells called the _____ node.

17. Cells that "set the pace" for the beating of the heart as a whole are also called the

_____.

Blood Vessels (pages 946–947)

18. Complete the concept map.

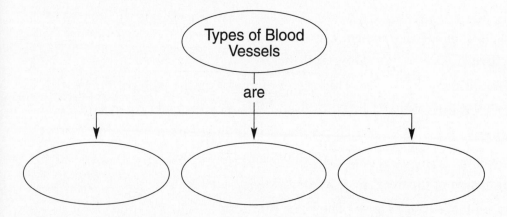

19. Circle the letter of each sentence that is true about arteries.

   a. Most carry oxygen-poor blood.   **c.** They have thin walls.

   b. They can expand under pressure.   **d.** The largest is the aorta.

20. The smallest blood vessels found in the body are the _____.

21. What work is done in the capillaries? _____

_____

22. What keeps blood flowing toward the heart in the largest veins? _____

_____

© Pearson Education, Inc., publishing as Pearson Prentice Hall.

Blood Pressure (pages 948–949)

23. The force of blood on the walls of arteries is known as _____.

24. Is the following sentence true or false? Blood pressure increases when the heart relaxes. _____

Match each type of blood pressure with the force it measures.

	Type of Pressure	Force It Measures
_____	25. systolic	a. Force of the blood when the ventricles relax
_____	26. diastolic	b. Force of the blood when the ventricles contract

27. A typical blood pressure reading for a healthy person is _____.

28. How does the autonomic nervous system regulate blood pressure?

_____

_____

_____

29. How do the kidneys regulate blood pressure? _____

_____

_____

Diseases of the Circulatory System (pages 949–950)

30. A condition in which fatty deposits build up on the walls of arteries is called

_____.

31. High blood pressure also is called _____.

32. Is the following sentence true or false? High blood pressure increases the risk of heart attack and stroke. _____

33. Circle the letter of each sentence that is true about heart attack.

  a. It is caused by atherosclerosis in the coronary arteries.

  b. It occurs when part of the heart muscle begins to die.

  c. Its symptoms include nausea and chest pain.

  d. It requires immediate medical attention.

34. Is the following sentence true or false? A stroke may be caused by a clot in a blood vessel leading to the brain. _____

35. List three ways of avoiding cardiovascular diseases.

  a. _____

  b. _____

  c. _____

Section 37–2 Blood and the Lymphatic System
(pages 951–955)

Key Concepts
- What is the function of each type of blood cell?
- What is the function of the lymphatic system?

Blood Plasma (page 951)

1. The straw-colored fluid portion of blood is called _____.

2. Plasma is about 90 percent water and 10 percent _____

_____

Match each type of plasma protein with its function.

	Type of Protein	Function
_____	**3.** albumin	**a.** Helps blood clot
_____	**4.** globulin	**b.** Regulates osmotic pressure and blood volume
_____	**5.** fibrinogen	**c.** Fights viral and bacterial infections

Blood Cells (pages 952–954)

6. List the three components of the cellular portion of blood.

   a. _____ b. _____ c. _____

7. What is the role of red blood cells? _____

8. What is hemoglobin? _____

_____

9. Is the following sentence true or false? Mature red blood cells have two nuclei.

   _____

10. Circle the letter of each sentence that is true about white blood cells.

    a. They contain nuclei.

    b. They attack foreign substances.

    c. They contain hemoglobin.

    d. They are also called leukocytes.

11. Is the following sentence true or false? Most white blood cells live for an average of 120 days. _____

12. White blood cells that engulf and digest foreign cells are called _____.

13. What does a sudden increase in the number of white cells tell a physician?

_____

14. List the two components of blood that make clotting possible.

a. _____ b. _____

15. Number the drawings below to show the correct sequence in which a blood clot forms when a blood vessel is injured.

   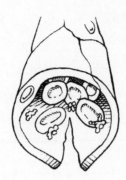   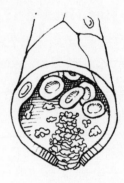

_____   _____   _____

16. A genetic disorder that results from a defective protein in the clotting pathway is

_____ .

The Lymphatic System (pages 954–955)

17. What is the lymphatic system? _____

_____

_____

18. The fluid lost by blood is called _____ .

19. What is the function of lymph nodes? _____

_____

Reading Skill Practice

When you read a section with difficult material, writing a summary can help you identify and remember the main ideas and supporting details. Write a concise paragraph summing up the material under each heading in Section 37–2. Each of your paragraphs should be much shorter than the text under that heading in your book. Include each of the highlighted, boldface vocabulary terms in your summary. Do your work on a separate sheet of paper.

Section 37–3 The Respiratory System (pages 956–963)

⊂▭⊃ **Key Concepts**
- What is the function of the respiratory system?
- How does smoking affect the respiratory system?

What Is Respiration? (page 956)

1. The process by which oxygen and carbon dioxide are exchanged between the lungs and the environment is known as _____.

The Human Respiratory System (pages 956–958)

2. What is the basic function performed by the human respiratory system? _____

_____

_____

3. Label each of the following structures in the drawing of the human respiratory system: nose, pharynx, larynx, trachea, bronchus, and lung.

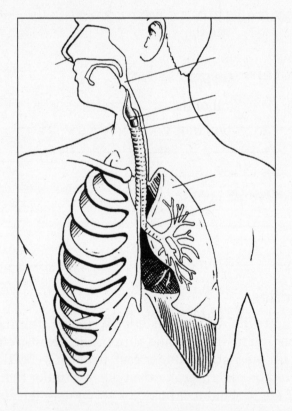

4. Circle the letter of the choice that lists the respiratory structures from largest to smallest.

   a. Alveoli, bronchioles, bronchi   c. Bronchi, bronchioles, alveoli

   b. Bronchioles, bronchi, alveoli   d. Bronchi, alveoli, bronchioles

5. What prevents food from entering your trachea? _____

_____

_____

© Pearson Education, Inc., publishing as Pearson Prentice Hall.

Match each structure of the respiratory system with its description.

	Structure	Description
_____	**6.** pharynx	**a.** Tiny air sacs where gas exchange occurs
_____	**7.** trachea	**b.** Tiny projections that sweep trapped particles and mucus away from the lungs
_____	**8.** cilia	
_____	**9.** larynx	**c.** Tube that serves as a passageway for both air and food
_____	**10.** bronchi	**d.** Large passageways in the chest that lead to the lungs
_____	**11.** alveoli	**e.** Structure at the top of the trachea that contains the vocal cords
		f. Passageway between the pharynx and bronchi

Gas Exchange (page 958)

12. Gas exchange occurs in the _____.

13. Describe the process of gas exchange. _____

_____

_____

_____

14. Circle the letter of each sentence that is true about gas exchange.

 a. It is a very efficient process.

 b. Exhaled air usually contains no oxygen.

 c. The lungs remove about half of the oxygen of inhaled air.

 d. The lungs increase the carbon dioxide content of inhaled air by a factor of 100.

15. Why is hemoglobin needed? _____

_____

_____

Breathing (pages 959–960)

16. The movement of air into and out of the lungs is called _____.

17. The large, flat muscle at the bottom of the chest cavity is the _____.

18. Is the following sentence true or false? The force that drives air into the lungs comes from air pressure. _____

19. What happens when you inhale? _____

_____

_____

20. What happens when pressure in the chest cavity becomes greater than atmospheric pressure? _____

How Breathing Is Controlled (pages 960–961)

21. The part of the brain that controls breathing is the _____.

22. Is the following sentence true or false? Cells in the breathing center monitor the amount of oxygen in the blood. _____

23. Why do airplane passengers in emergency situations often have to be told to begin breathing pressurized oxygen? _____

_____

_____

Tobacco and the Respiratory System (pages 961–963)

24. List three of the most dangerous substances in tobacco smoke.

    a. _____

    b. _____

    c. _____

25. Is the following sentence true or false? Nicotine is a stimulant drug that increases pulse rate and blood pressure. _____

26. Why is carbon monoxide dangerous? _____

_____

_____

27. List three respiratory diseases caused by smoking.

    a. _____

    b. _____

    c. _____

28. Circle the letter of each sentence that is true about chronic bronchitis.

    a. It is characterized by swollen bronchi.

    b. It occurs only in heavy smokers.

    c. It can make stair climbing and similar activities difficult.

    d. It is unrelated to smoking.

29. What is emphysema? _____

30. Circle the letter of each sentence that is true about lung cancer.

    a. Its most important cause is smoking.

    b. It is often deadly.

    c. It cannot spread to other parts of the body.

    d. It is usually detected early enough for a cure.

31. Circle the letter of each way that smoking affects the cardiovascular system.

  a. It constricts the blood vessels.

  b. It causes blood pressure to rise.

  c. It makes the heart work harder.

  d. It causes heart disease.

32. Inhaling the smoke of others is called _____.

33. Why is passive smoking particularly harmful to young children? _____

_____

34. Why is it so hard to quit smoking? _____

_____

35. What is the best solution for dealing with tobacco? _____

_____

Reading Skill Practice

When you read a section with many details, writing an outline may help you organize and remember the material. Outline Section 37–3 by first writing the section headings as major topics in the order in which they appear in the book. Then, beneath each major topic, list important details about it. Title your outline *The Respiratory System.* Do your work on a separate sheet of paper.

Chapter 37   Circulatory and Respiratory Systems

Vocabulary Review

Matching   *In the space provided, write the letter of the definition that best matches each term.*

_____ **1.** pulmonary circulation

_____ **2.** systemic circulation

_____ **3.** aorta

_____ **4.** capillary

_____ **5.** atherosclerosis

_____ **6.** plasma

_____ **7.** hemoglobin

_____ **8.** platelet

_____ **9.** pharynx

_____ **10.** larynx

_____ **11.** artery

_____ **12.** vein

_____ **13.** lymph

a. path of blood from heart to body

b. fluid part of blood

c. cell fragment that helps blood to clot

d. path of blood from heart to lungs

e. smallest type of blood vessel

f. protein in blood that carries oxygen

g. structure containing vocal cords

h. buildup of fat deposits on artery walls

i. tube in throat through which air passes

j. largest artery

k. fluid that is lost by the blood

l. blood vessel that carries blood away from the heart

m. blood vessel that carries blood toward the heart

True or False   *Determine whether each statement is true or false. If it is true, write* true *in the space provided. If the statement is false, change the underlined word or words to make the statement true.*

_____ **14.** Air moves from the pharynx into the <u>bronchus</u>.

_____ **15.** The tiny sacs where gas exchange takes place are the <u>lymphocytes</u>.

_____ **16.** The <u>diaphragm</u> is a muscle that enables breathing.

_____ **17.** Loss of elasticity in the lungs is called <u>lung cancer</u>.

_____ **18.** The stimulant drug in tobacco smoke is known as <u>tar</u>.

Writing Descriptions   *In the space provided, describe each structure of the heart.*

19. myocardium _____

_____

20. atrium _____

_____

21. ventricle _____

_____

22. valve _____

_____

23. pacemaker _____

_____

Summary

38–1 Food and Nutrition

Cells use the chemical energy stored in food to meet their energy needs. The amount of energy in food is measured in calories. Scientists refer to the energy stored in food as dietary Calories with a capital C. The number of Calories you need each day depends on your size and level of activity.

Nutrients are substances in food that supply the energy and raw materials the body uses for growth, repair, and maintenance. Nutrients include water, carbohydrates, fats, proteins, vitamins, and minerals.

Every cell in the human body needs water, because many of the body's processes take place in water. Simple and complex carbohydrates are the main source of energy for the body. Carbohydrates include sugars, starches, and fiber. Fats are formed from fatty acids. The body needs fatty acids to make cell membranes and certain hormones. Deposits of fat protect body organs and insulate the body. Proteins are formed from amino acids. Proteins supply raw materials for growth and repair of the body. In addition, many hormones are proteins. Vitamins are organic molecules that help regulate body processes. They include water-soluble vitamins and fat-soluble vitamins. A diet lacking certain vitamins can have serious consequences. Minerals are inorganic nutrients that the body needs, usually in small amounts. Examples of minerals are calcium and iron.

The Food Guide Pyramid can help people select a balanced diet. The pyramid classifies foods into six groups. It also indicates how many servings from each group should be eaten every day to maintain a healthy diet. Foods at the base of the pyramid should make up the major portion of the diet. Foods at the top of the pyramid should be used in small amounts.

38–2 The Process of Digestion

The function of the digestive system is to break down food into simpler molecules that can be absorbed and used by the cells. The human digestive system is a one-way tube that includes the mouth, pharynx, esophagus, stomach, small intestine, and large intestine. Other structures—including the salivary glands, pancreas, and liver—add secretions to the digestive system.

Digestion starts in the mouth. The teeth tear and crush food. This begins the process of mechanical digestion. Mechanical digestion is the physical breakdown of large pieces of food into smaller pieces. Salivary glands in the mouth secrete saliva, which contains the enzyme amylase. Amylase breaks down starches into sugars. This begins the process of chemical digestion. Chemical digestion is the breakdown of large food molecules into smaller molecules.

The chewed clump of food that is swallowed is called a bolus. It passes through the pharynx and into the esophagus. The esophagus is a tube that connects the throat with the stomach. Muscle contractions, called peristalsis, squeeze the food through the esophagus.

Food from the esophagus empties into the stomach. The stomach is a large muscular sac. Both chemical and mechanical digestion take place in the stomach. Glands in the lining of the stomach produce an acid and the enzyme pepsin. The acid and pepsin work together to begin the chemical digestion of protein. Stomach muscles also contract to churn and mix the stomach contents. This mechanical digestion produces a liquid mixture called chyme.

From the stomach, chyme passes into the small intestine. Most of the chemical digestion and absorption of food occurs in the small intestine. Enzymes from the pancreas help digest starch, protein, and fat. A liquid called bile from the liver dissolves and breaks up fat droplets. The lining of the small intestine also produces several enzymes that help break down carbohydrates and proteins. Nutrients are absorbed by cells lining the surface of the small intestine.

The surface area is greatly increased by tiny fingerlike projections called villi (singular: villus). By the time chyme reaches the end of the small intestine, virtually all the nutrients have been absorbed.

Chyme next enters the large intestine. The primary function of the large intestine is to remove water from the undigested material. After most of the water has been removed, the remaining waste passes out of the body.

Digestive system disorders include peptic ulcers, diarrhea, and constipation. Peptic ulcers are caused by bacteria. Diarrhea occurs when too little water is removed from waste in the large intestine. Constipation occurs when too much water is removed.

38–3 The Excretory System

During normal metabolism, cells produce wastes such as carbon dioxide and urea. Excretion is the process by which the body eliminates these wastes. The main organs of excretion are the kidneys. The kidneys play an important role in homeostasis. They remove waste products from blood, maintain blood pH, and control water content of blood.

The two kidneys are located in the lower back. Blood containing wastes enters the kidneys. The kidneys remove urea, excess water, and other substances from the blood.

Some of the substances are later returned to the blood. The wastes are excreted. The purified blood leaves the kidneys and returns to circulation. The basic unit of function of a kidney is the nephron. Each nephron is a small independent processing unit.

Blood goes through two separate processes in a nephron: filtration and reabsorption. Filtration removes wastes from the blood. It occurs in a structure of the nephron known as the glomerulus. The glomerulus is enclosed within another structure called Bowman's capsule. Reabsorption returns some of the filtered materials back to the blood. These materials include food molecules and water.

The fluid that remains is called urine. Urine contains urea, excess salts, and other substances. Some of the water is removed from the urine in a structure called the loop of Henle. A tube called the ureter leaves each kidney and carries urine to the urinary bladder. The urinary bladder is a saclike organ that stores urine until it can be released from the body. Urine passes from the body through a tube called the urethra.

The kidneys are controlled by hormones and by the composition of the blood. If the blood becomes too concentrated, the kidneys return more water to the blood. If the blood becomes too diluted, the kidneys return less water to the blood.

A person can survive with only one kidney. If both kidneys fail, the person must receive a kidney transplant or undergo dialysis in order to survive. Dialysis purifies the blood by passing it through a filtering machine.

Section 38–1 Food and Nutrition (pages 971–977)

⊂⊃ **Key Concepts**
- What are the nutrients your body needs?
- Why is water such an important nutrient?

Food and Energy (page 971)

1. Cells convert the chemical energy in glucose and other molecules into

   _____ .

2. The energy stored in food is measured in units called _____ .

3. Is the following sentence true or false? Your body can extract energy from almost any
   type of food. _____

4. Besides supplying fuel, what are other important functions of food? _____

   _____

   _____

   _____

   _____

5. What is the study of nutrition? _____

   _____

   _____

   _____

Nutrients (pages 972–975)

6. Substances in food that supply the energy and raw materials your body uses for

   growth, repair, and maintenance are called _____ .

7. List the six nutrients that the body needs.

   a. _____   d. _____

   b. _____   e. _____

   c. _____   f. _____

8. Circle the letter of each sentence that is true about water as a nutrient.

   a. Water is the most important of all nutrients.

   b. Every cell in the human body needs water.

   c. Many of the body's processes take place in water.

   d. Water makes up the bulk of bodily fluids, including blood.

Name_____ Class_____ Date _____

9. How is water lost from the body? _____

_____

10. If enough water is not taken in to replace what is lost, _____
can result.

11. Complete the concept map.

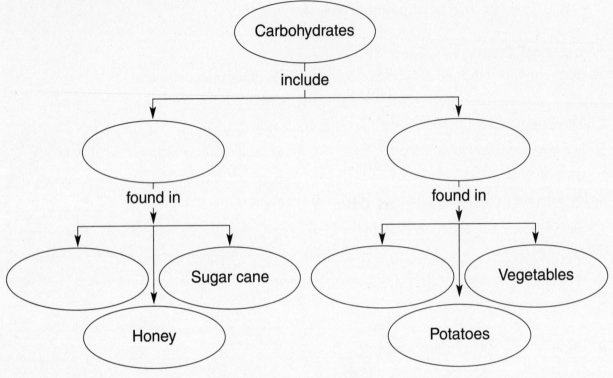

12. Why do you need fiber in your diet? _____

_____

13. Circle the letter of each choice that is a function of fat.

   a. Protecting body organs   **c.** Storing energy

   b. Insulating the body   **d.** Transporting oxygen

14. List four increased health risks associated with a diet high in fat.

   a. _____   **c.** _____

   b. _____   **d.** _____

15. Circle the letter of each choice that is a function of protein.

   a. Supplying raw materials for growth and repair

   b. Making up enzymes

   c. Helping the body absorb certain vitamins

   d. Producing cell membranes

16. The eight amino acids that the body is unable to produce are called

   _____ amino acids.

Match each vitamin with its function.

	Vitamin	Function
_____	**17.** A	**a.** Preventing cellular damage
_____	**18.** D	**b.** Promoting bone growth
_____	**19.** E	**c.** Repairing tissues and healing wounds
_____	**20.** C	**d.** Promoting growth of skin cells

Match each mineral with a food that supplies it.

	Mineral	Food
_____	**21.** calcium	**a.** Table salt
_____	**22.** zinc	**b.** Dairy products
_____	**23.** chlorine	**c.** Eggs
_____	**24.** iron	**d.** Seafood

Nutrition and a Balanced Diet (pages 976–977)

25. Label the missing food groups in the Food Guide Pyramid.

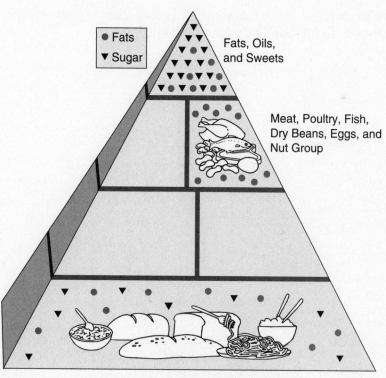

Section 38–2 The Process of Digestion
(pages 978–984)

⬤ **Key Concepts**
- What are the organs of the digestive system?
- What is the function of the digestive system?

Introduction **(page 978)**

1. What is the function of the organs of the digestive system? _____

_____

_____

_____

The Mouth **(pages 978–979)**

2. The physical breakdown of large pieces of food into smaller pieces is referred to as

_____ digestion.

3. The breakdown of large food molecules into smaller molecules that can be absorbed

into the bloodstream is called _____ digestion.

4. Label the drawing of the digestive system with the following structures: mouth, esophagus, stomach, liver, small intestine, and large intestine.

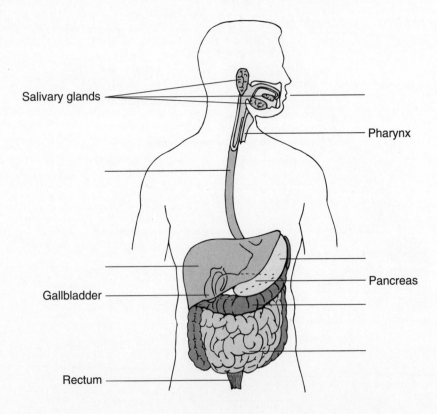

Salivary glands

Pharynx

Pancreas

Gallbladder

Rectum

5. What is the role of teeth in digestion? _____

_____

_____

_____

The Esophagus (page 980)

Match each term with its definition.

	Term	Definition
_____	**6.** bolus	**a.** Contractions of smooth muscle that aid in swallowing
_____	**7.** esophagus	**b.** Clump of chewed food
_____	**8.** peristalsis	**c.** Food tube connecting the mouth and stomach

9. Is the following sentence true or false? The pyloric valve prevents the contents of the stomach from moving back up into the esophagus. _____

The Stomach (pages 980–981)

10. Circle the letter of each sentence that is true about the stomach.

   a. It produces hydrochloric acid.

   b. It produces trypsin.

   c. It helps in the mechanical digestion of food.

   d. It produces amylase.

11. Is the following sentence true or false? Pepsin cannot work under the acidic conditions present in the stomach. _____

12. A mixture of stomach fluids and food is referred to as _____.

The Small Intestine (pages 981–982)

13. Where does most chemical digestion take place? _____

_____

_____

14. Circle the letter of each sentence that is true about the pancreas.

   a. It produces amylase.

   b. It produces sodium bicarbonate.

   c. Its enzymes help break down lipids and nucleic acids.

   d. It produces lactase.

15. What role does the liver play in digestion? _____

_____

_____

_____

16. Bile is stored in a small pouchlike organ called the _____.

Use the table to answer the questions.

Digestive Enzymes			
Enzyme	**Site of Action**	**Site of Production**	**Nutrient Digested**
Amylase	Mouth	Salivary glands	Carbohydrate
Pepsin	Stomach	Lining of stomach	Protein
Lipase	Small intestine	Pancreas	Fat
Amylase	Small intestine	Pancreas	Carbohydrate
Trypsin	Small intestine	Pancreas	Protein
Lactase	Small intestine	Lining of small intestine	Carbohydrate
Maltase	Small intestine	Lining of small intestine	Carbohydrate
Sucrase	Small intestine	Lining of small intestine	Carbohydrate
Peptidase	Small intestine	Lining of small intestine	Protein

17. Where are the majority of digestive enzymes active? _____

_____

18. Which organ or gland produces the greatest number of different digestive enzymes?

_____

19. Which digestive enzyme has more than one site of action and production? _____

_____

20. Which digestive enzymes are active at a site different from the site where they are

produced? _____

21. Which nutrient is digested by more enyzmes than any other nutrient? _____

_____

Absorption in the Small Intestine (pages 982–983)

22. Name the two parts of the small intestine where nutrients are absorbed.

a. _____

b. _____

23. Projections that cover the folds of the small intestine are called _____.

24. Is the following sentence true or false? Molecules of undigested fat and some fatty

acids are absorbed by lymph vessels called lacteals. _____

25. Is the following sentence true or false? The appendix plays an important role in human

digestion. _____

The Large Intestine (page 984)

26. What is the primary job of the large intestine? _____

_____

_____

_____

Digestive System Disorders (page 984)

27. A hole in the stomach wall is known as a(an) _____.

28. When something happens that interferes with the removal of water by the large intestine, a condition known as _____ results.

Reading Skill Practice

When you read about a complex process, representing the process with a flowchart can help you better understand and remember it. Make a flowchart to show how food travels through the digestive system and is broken down into simpler molecules that the body can use. For more information on flowcharts, see Appendix A of your textbook. Do your work on a separate sheet of paper.

Section 38–3 The Excretory System (pages 985–989)

Key Concepts
- What are the functions of the kidneys?
- How is blood filtered?

Functions of the Excretory System (page 985)

1. The process by which metabolic wastes are eliminated is called _____.

2. List four organs that are used for excretion.

   a. _____   c. _____

   b. _____   d. _____

3. List three ways that the kidneys help maintain homeostasis.

   a. _____

   b. _____

   c. _____

The Kidneys (pages 986–988)

4. Circle the letter of each sentence that is true about the kidneys.

   a. They are the main organs of the excretory system.

   b. They are located on either side of the spinal column.

   c. They remove excess water and waste products from the urine.

   d. They receive blood through the renal vein.

Match each term with its definition.

Term	Definition
_____ 5. ureter	a. Saclike organ where urine is stored
_____ 6. urinary bladder	b. Functional unit of the kidney
_____ 7. renal medulla	c. Outer part of the kidney
_____ 8. renal cortex	d. Tube that carries urine from the kidney to the urinary bladder
_____ 9. nephron	e. Inner part of the kidney

10. Is the following sentence true or false? Nephrons are located in the renal medulla.

    _____

11. What ends up in the collecting duct? _____

    _____

12. List the two processes involved in blood purification.

    a. _____   b. _____

13. The small network of capillaries in the upper end of the nephron is referred to as the

    _____.

14. The glomerulus is enclosed by a cup-shaped structure called the _____.

15. Complete the Venn diagram.

Filtration   Reabsorption

Processes that take
place in the nephron

16. The materials that are filtered from the blood are collectively called the

_____.

17. List six materials that are filtered from blood.

a. _____   c. _____   e. _____

b. _____   d. _____   f. _____

18. Which substances are removed from the filtrate and reabsorbed by the capillaries?

_____

_____

19. What happens during the process of secretion? _____

_____

_____

20. Circle the letter of each sentence that is true about urine.

a. It is the material that remains after reabsorption.

b. It contains only urea and water.

c. It is concentrated in the loop of Henle.

d. It is released from the body through the urethra.

Control of Kidney Function (page 988)

21. How are the activities of the kidneys controlled? _____

_____

_____

22. Is the following sentence true or false? As the amount of water in the blood increases, the rate of water reabsorption in the kidneys increases. _____

Homeostasis by Machine (pages 988–989)

23. Is the following sentence true or false? Humans cannot survive with only one kidney.

_____

24. The removal of wastes from blood using a machine is called _____.

Vocabulary Review

Completion *Fill in the blanks with terms from Chapter 38.*

1. The main source of energy for the body comes from _____.

2. Nutrients that are formed from fatty acids and glycerol are _____.

3. _____ are needed for growth and repair of structures such as skin and muscle.

4. Saliva contains the enzyme _____ that breaks the chemical bonds in starches.

5. The contractions that push food through the esophagus into the stomach are called _____.

6. Organic molecules that help regulate body processes are called _____.

7. The tube that connects the throat with the stomach is the _____.

8. The organ that produces bile is the _____.

9. The mixture of partly digested food that leaves the stomach is called _____.

10. The lining of the small intestine is covered with fingerlike projections called _____.

11. The primary organ of excretion is the _____.

12. The functional units of the kidney are called _____.

13. The process of filtration takes place in a structure called the _____.

14. The saclike organ that stores urine is the _____.

15. Urine leaves the body through a tube called the _____.

16. The cuplike structure that encases the glomerulus is called _____.

17. Urea is primarily concentrated in the _____.

Chapter 39 Endocrine and Reproductive Systems

Summary

39–1 The Endocrine System

The endocrine system consists of glands that release secretions into the bloodstream. The secretions are called hormones. Hormones are chemicals released in one part of the body that travel throughout the body and affect cells elsewhere. Hormones bind to specific chemical receptors on cells called target cells. In addition to endocrine glands, there are exocrine glands, such as sweat glands. Exocrine glands release their secretions through ducts directly to tissues and organs.

There are two types of hormones. Steroid hormones can cross cell membranes of target cells, enter the nucleus, and turn genes on or off. Nonsteroid hormones cannot cross cell membranes. Compounds called secondary messengers carry the messages of nonsteroid hormones inside target cells. A wide range of cells also produce hormonelike substances called prostaglandins that affect only nearby cells.

The endocrine system is regulated by feedback mechanisms that help maintain homeostasis. For example, the level of a hormone in the blood may be the feedback that signals a gland to produce more or less of the hormone. Two hormones with opposite effects may work together to maintain homeostasis. This is called complementary hormone action.

39–2 Human Endocrine Glands

Human endocrine glands include the pituitary gland, hypothalamus, thyroid gland, parathyroid glands, adrenal glands, pancreas, and reproductive glands.

The nine pituitary hormones either directly regulate body functions or control the actions of other endocrine glands.

Hormones from the hypothalamus control the pituitary gland. The thyroid gland regulates metabolism. Hormones produced in the parathyroid gland help regulate calcium levels in the blood. The adrenal gland produces hormones that help the body deal with stress. The pancreas secretes insulin and glucagon. Insulin and glucagon keep the level of sugar in the blood stable. If the pancreas fails to produce, or properly use, insulin, diabetes mellitus occurs. Reproductive glands, or gonads, produce gametes. Gonads also secrete sex hormones that produce male and female physical characteristics.

39–3 The Reproductive System

Sex hormones produced by the gonads of an embryo cause the embryo to develop into either a female or a male. Sex hormones also cause puberty to occur. Puberty is a period of rapid growth and sexual maturation that usually begins between ages 9 and 15. At the end of puberty, the male and female reproductive organs are fully developed and able to function.

The main function of the male reproductive system is to produce and deliver sperm. The main organs of the male reproductive system are the testes, which are held in a sac called the scrotum. In the testes, sperm are produced in tiny tubes called seminiferous tubules. Sperm then mature in a structure known as the epididymis. They leave the epididymis through a tube called the vas deferens, which merges with the urethra. The urethra is the tube in the penis that leads to the outside. Sperm are ejected from the penis by contractions. This is called ejaculation.

The main function of the female reproductive system is to produce eggs and prepare the female body to nourish an embryo. The main organs of the female reproductive system are the ovaries. Each ovary contains thousands of follicles. A follicle is a cluster of cells surrounding a single egg. The follicle helps the egg mature. About once a month, an egg matures and is released from the ovary. The egg moves through the Fallopian tube, where it can be fertilized if sperm are present.

After a few days, the egg reaches the uterus. The uterus is connected to the outside of the body by a canal called the vagina.

One egg develops each month during the menstrual cycle. The cycle is controlled by hormones. It has four phases: follicular phase, ovulation, luteal phase, and menstruation. During the follicular phase, an egg matures in its follicle and the uterus is prepared to receive a fertilized egg. Then, the egg is released from the ovary. This is called ovulation. The luteal phase follows. During the luteal phase, the follicle turns into a structure called the corpus luteum. If the egg has been fertilized, it implants in the lining of the uterus. If the egg has not been fertilized, it passes through the uterus without implanting, and menstruation occurs. During menstruation, the lining of the uterus falls away and leaves the body through the vagina.

Diseases that are spread during sexual contact are called sexually transmitted diseases (STDs). STDs can be caused by bacteria and viruses. Common STDs include chlamydia, syphilis, gonorrhea, and AIDS. Abstinence is the only sure way to avoid being infected with STDs.

39–4 Fertilization and Development

Fertilization is the process of a sperm joining an egg. A fertilized egg is called a zygote. The zygote undergoes repeated mitosis and soon develops into a hollow ball of cells called a blastocyst. About a week after fertilization, the blastocyst embeds itself in the lining of the uterus. This is called implantation.

The cells of the blastocyst begin to specialize in a process called differentiation. Some cells migrate to form three cell layers. This process is called gastrulation. The three layers eventually develop into the different organs of the embryo. Researchers are just beginning to understand what controls the development of specialized cells and organs. Gastrulation is followed by neurulation, or the development of the nervous system. As the embryo develops, membranes also form to protect and nourish it. One of these membranes develops into the placenta. The mother and embryo exchange gases, food, and waste products across the placenta.

After eight weeks of development, the embryo is called a fetus. By the end of three months, most of the major organs are fully formed. During the remaining six months before birth, the organ systems mature, and the fetus grows in size and mass.

Childbirth occurs when hormones stimulate the mother's uterus to contract. The contractions push the baby from the uterus and out through the vagina. Twins are born if more than one egg was fertilized or if one zygote split into two embryos during early development.

Growth and development continue throughout infancy and childhood. Adolescence begins with puberty and ends with adulthood. Development continues during adulthood. The first signs of aging usually appear in the thirties.

Chapter 39 Endocrine and Reproductive Systems

Section 39–1 The Endocrine System (pages 997–1002)

🔑 **Key Concepts**
- What is the function of the endocrine system?
- How does the endocrine system maintain homeostasis?

Introduction (page 997)

1. What makes up the endocrine system? _____

_____

_____

2. What do the products of the endocrine system do? _____

_____

_____

Hormones (page 997)

3. Chemicals released in one part of the body that travel through the bloodstream and affect the activities of cells in other parts of the body are called _____.

4. How do hormones affect the activities of other cells? _____

_____

5. Cells that have receptors for a particular hormone are referred to as _____.

6. Is the following sentence true or false? Cells without receptors are not affected by hormones. _____

7. Is the following sentence true or false? Generally, the body's responses to hormones are quicker and shorter lasting than the responses to nerve impulses. _____

Glands (page 998)

8. An organ that produces and releases a substance, or secretion, is called a(an)

_____.

9. What is an exocrine gland? _____

_____

10. Glands that release sweat, tears, and digestive juices are considered _____ glands.

11. What is the function of the parathyroid glands? _____

_____

_____

Match the endocrine gland with the hormone it produces.

	Endocrine Gland	**Hormone It Produces**
_____	**12.** Pineal	**a.** Glucagon
_____	**13.** Thyroid	**b.** Melatonin
_____	**14.** Pancreas	**c.** Epinephrine
_____	**15.** Thymus	**d.** Thyroxine
_____	**16.** Adrenal	**e.** Thymosin
_____	**17.** Ovary	**f.** Testosterone
_____	**18.** Testis	**g.** Estrogen

19. The hormone that regulates metabolism is _____.

Hormone Action (page 999)

20. List the two general groups into which hormones may be classified.

  a. _____

  b. _____

21. Circle the letter of each sentence that is true about steroid hormones.

  a. They are lipids.

  b. They cannot cross cell membranes.

  c. They help regulate gene expression.

  d. They can enter the nucleus.

22. Is the following sentence true or false? Steroid hormones are produced from cholesterol. _____

23. Circle the letter of each sentence that is true about nonsteroid hormones.

  a. They are proteins, small peptides, or modified amino acids.

  b. They can cross cell membranes.

  c. They rely on secondary messengers.

  d. They cannot enter the nucleus.

24. Is the following sentence true or false? Secondary messengers may include calcium ions, cAMP, nucleotides, and fatty acids. _____

Prostaglandins (page 1000)

25. Hormonelike substances produced by other kinds of cells and tissues are called

_____.

26. Why are prostaglandins known as "local hormones"? _____

_____

27. Is the following sentence true or false? Some prostaglandins cause smooth muscles to

contract. _____

Control of the Endocrine System (pages 1000–1001)

28. When does feedback inhibition occur? _____

_____

29. Fill in the missing labels in the diagram to show how the thyroid gland is regulated by feedback controls.

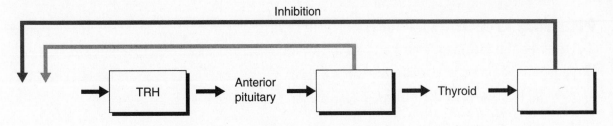

30. Circle the letter of each event that occurs when core body temperature begins to drop.

a. The hypothalamus produces less TRH.

b. More TSH is released.

c. Less thyroxine is released.

d. Metabolic activity increases.

31. Is the following sentence true or false? As you lose water, the concentration of

dissolved materials in the blood falls. _____

Complementary Hormone Action (page 1002)

32. What is complementary hormone action? _____

_____

33. Is the following sentence true or false? Calcitonin increases the concentration of

calcium in the blood. _____

34. If calcium levels drop too low, the parathyroid glands release _____.

35. How does PTH increase calcium levels? _____

_____

_____

36. Why is the regulation of calcium levels so important? _____

_____

_____

Section 39–2 Human Endocrine Glands (pages 1003–1008)

👄 Key Concept
- What are the functions of the major endocrine glands?

Introduction (page 1003)

1. List seven major glands of the endocrine system.

a. _____   e. _____

b. _____   f. _____

c. _____   g. _____

d. _____

Pituitary Gland (page 1003)

2. Describe the pituitary gland and its location. _____

_____

3. List the two parts of the pituitary gland.

a. _____   b. _____

4. In general, what is the role of pituitary gland hormones? _____

_____

Hypothalamus (page 1004)

5. Is the following sentence true or false? The hypothalamus controls the secretions of the

pituitary gland. _____

6. What influences the activity of the hypothalamus? _____

_____

_____

7. In what way is the posterior pituitary an extension of the hypothalamus?

_____

_____

8. Is the following sentence true or false? The hypothalamus has direct control of the

anterior pituitary. _____

Match each pituitary hormone with its action.

	Hormone	Action
_____	**9.** ADH	**a.** Stimulates ovaries and testes
_____	**10.** FSH	**b.** Stimulates production of eggs and sperm
_____	**11.** LH	**c.** Stimulates release of hormones from adrenal cortex
_____	**12.** GH	**d.** Stimulates protein synthesis and growth in cells
_____	**13.** ACTH	**e.** Stimulates the kidneys to reabsorb water

14. What are releasing hormones, and what do they do? _____

_____

_____

_____

Thyroid Gland (page 1005)

15. Where is the thyroid gland located? _____

_____

_____

16. Is the following sentence true or false? The thyroid gland regulates reproduction.

_____

17. List the two hormones produced by the thyroid.

a. _____ b. _____

18. What does thyroxine do in the body? _____

_____

19. Production of too much thyroxine leads to a condition called

_____.

20. An enlargement of the thyroid gland is called a(an) _____.

21. Infants who lack enough iodine to produce normal amounts of thyroxine suffer from

a condition called _____.

22. How can cretinism usually be prevented? _____

_____

_____

Parathyroid Glands (page 1005)

23. How does parathyroid hormone regulate calcium levels in the blood? _____

_____

_____

Adrenal Glands (page 1006)

24. What is the general role of the adrenal glands? _____

_____

_____

25. The outer part of the adrenal gland is called the _____, and

the inner part is called the _____.

26. Is the following sentence true or false? The release of hormones from the adrenal

medulla is regulated by the sympathetic nervous system. _____

27. Complete the table about adrenal gland hormones.

HORMONES OF THE ADRENAL GLAND

Part of Adrenal Gland	Hormones It Produces	Role of the Hormones
	Corticosteroids	Regulating minerals, metabolism
Adrenal medulla		

Pancreas (pages 1007–1008)

28. Is the following sentence true or false? The pancreas is both an endocrine gland and an exocrine gland. _____

29. What is the role of insulin and glucagon? _____

_____

_____

30. When the pancreas fails to produce or properly use insulin, a condition known as

_____ occurs.

31. _____ is an autoimmune disorder that usually develops in people before the age of 15.

32. People with what type of diabetes produce low to normal amounts

of insulin? _____

Reproductive Glands (page 1008)

33. List the two important functions served by the gonads.

a. _____ b. _____

34. The female gonads are the _____, and the male gonads are the

_____.

Reading Skill Practice

Taking notes can help you identify and remember the most important information in a section. Take notes on Section 39–2 by writing the main headings and under each heading listing the most important points. Do your work on a separate sheet of paper.

Section 39–3 The Reproductive System (pages 1009–1015)

🔑 **Key Concepts**

- What are the main functions of the male and female reproductive systems?
- What are the four phases of the menstrual cycle?

Sexual Development (page 1009)

1. Circle the letter of each sentence that is true about sexual development before birth.

   a. Testes and ovaries begin to develop during the first six weeks.

   b. Male and female reproductive organs develop from the same tissues in the embryo.

   c. The testes produce testosterone, and the ovaries produce estrogen.

   d. Hormones determine whether the embryo will develop into a male or a female.

2. What is puberty? _____

   _____

   _____

   _____

3. How does the hypothalamus begin puberty? _____

   _____

   _____

   _____

The Male Reproductive System (pages 1010–1011)

4. Is the following sentence true or false? The release of FSH and LH stimulates cells in the testes to produce testosterone. _____

5. Circle the letter of each term that refers to a structure of the male reproductive system.

   a. testes

   b. Fallopian tube

   c. vas deferens

   d. urethra

6. The testes are contained in a sac called the _____.

7. Why do the testes remain outside the body cavity? _____

   _____

   _____

   _____

8. Is the following sentence true or false? Sperm are produced in the vas deferens.

   _____

9. The structure in which sperm fully mature and are stored is the _____.

10. The tube that leads to the outside of the body through the penis is the

   _____.

11. Label the drawing of a sperm with the following structures: head, nucleus, midpiece, and tail.

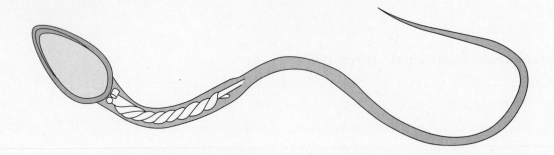

12. A nutrient-rich fluid called seminal fluid, when combined with sperm, forms

_____.

The Female Reproductive System (pages 1011–1012)

13. Circle the letter of each choice that is a structure of the female reproductive system.

a. ovary   **c.** uterus

b. epididymis   **d.** vagina

14. Is the following sentence true or false? The ovaries usually produce only one mature

ovum each month. _____

15. Clusters of cells surrounding a single egg are called primary _____.

16. The hormone that stimulates a follicle to grow and mature each month is

_____.

17. Is the following sentence true or false? Fertilization takes place in the uterus.

_____

The Menstrual Cycle (pages 1013–1014)

18. Circle the letter of each sentence that is true about the menstrual cycle.

a. It lasts an average of 3 to 7 days.

b. It is controlled by hormones.

c. It prepares the uterus to receive an egg.

d. It has four phases.

19. Is the following sentence true or false? The level of estrogen falls at the start of the

follicular phase of the menstrual cycle. _____

20. During the luteal phase, the follicle turns yellow and is now known as the

_____.

© Pearson Education, Inc., publishing as Pearson Prentice Hall.

21. Is the following sentence true or false? The chances that an egg will be fertilized are the greatest during the first two days of the luteal phase. _____

Match each phase of the menstrual cycle with the event that occurs then.

Menstrual Phase	Event
_____ **22.** Follicular phase	**a.** Egg travels through Fallopian tube.
_____ **23.** Ovulation	**b.** Follicle develops.
_____ **24.** Luteal phase	**c.** Lining of uterus is shed.
_____ **25.** Menstruation	**d.** Egg is released from ovary.

26. What triggers menstruation to occur? _____

_____

27. Is the following sentence true or false? A new cycle begins with the last day of menstruation. _____

Sexually Trasmitted Diseases (page 1015)

28. Diseases spread from one person to another during sexual contact are known as

_____.

29. Is the following sentence true or false? Viral infections can be treated with antibiotics.

_____.

30. The most common STD is _____.

Reading Skill Practice

When you read a section, taking notes can help you organize and remember the information. As you read or review Section 39–3, take notes by writing each heading and listing the main points under each heading. Do your work on a separate sheet of paper.

Name_____ Class_____ Date _____

Section 39–4 Fertilization and Development
(pages 1016–1024)

Key Concepts
- What is fertilization?
- What are the stages of early development?
- What is the function of the placenta?

Fertilization (pages 1016–1017)

1. The process of a sperm joining an egg is called _____.

2. Is the following sentence true or false? A fertilized egg is known as a zygote. _____

Early Development (pages 1017–1020)

Match each term with its definition.

	Term	Definition
_____ 3.	Morula	**a.** Organ that nourishes the embryo
_____ 4.	Blastocyst	**b.** Name of embryo when it is a solid ball of about 64 cells
_____ 5.	Implantation	**c.** Name of morula when it is a hollow ball of cells
_____ 6.	Gastrulation	**d.** Membrane that surrounds and protects the embryo
_____ 7.	Amnion	**e.** Process in which the blastocyst attaches to the wall of the uterus
_____ 8.	Placenta	**f.** Process of cell migration that produces three cell layers

9. Is the following sentence true or false? The first few cell divisions take place in the Fallopian tube. _____

10. After eight weeks of development, the embryo is called a(an) _____.

11. Is the following sentence true or false? Most of the major organs and tissues are fully formed by the end of three months of development. _____

Control of Development (page 1020)

12. Is the following sentence true or false? The fates of many cells in the early embryo are not fixed. _____

Later Development (page 1021)

13. What changes occur during the last three months of fetal development? _____
_____
_____

Childbirth (pages 1022–1023)

14. Is the following sentence true or false? The process of childbirth begins when the hormone calcitonin is released from the posterior pituitary gland. _____

© Pearson Education, Inc., publishing as Pearson Prentice Hall.

15. The series of rhythmic contractions of the uterine wall that force the baby out through the vagina is known as _____.

16. What stimulates the production of milk in the breast tissues of the mother? _____
_____
_____

Multiple Births (page 1023)

17. If two eggs are released and fertilized by two different sperm, _____ twins result.

18. If a single zygote splits apart to produce two embryos, _____ twins result.

Early Years (pages 1023–1024)

19. Is the following sentence true or false? A baby's birth weight generally triples within 12 months of birth. _____

20. Is the following sentence true or false? Infancy refers to the first year of life.
_____

21. Circle the letter of each development that occurs during infancy.

a. Crawling   c. Appearance of first teeth

b. Walking   d. First use of language

22. Childhood lasts from infancy until the onset of _____.

23. Is the following sentence true or false? Reasoning skills are not developed until adolescence. _____

24. Adolescence begins with puberty and ends with _____.

25. What produces the growth spurt that starts at puberty? _____
_____
_____

Adulthood (page 1024)

26. Is the following sentence true or false? Adults reach their highest levels of physical strength and development between the ages of 25 and 35. _____

27. When do the first signs of physiological aging appear in most individuals?
_____

© Pearson Education, Inc., publishing as Pearson Prentice Hall.

Chapter 39   Endocrine and Reproductive Systems

Vocabulary Review

Labeling Diagrams   *Fill in each blank with the correct name of the structure from the list.*

penis   urethra   epididymis
scrotum   testis   vas deferens

1. _____

2. _____

3. _____

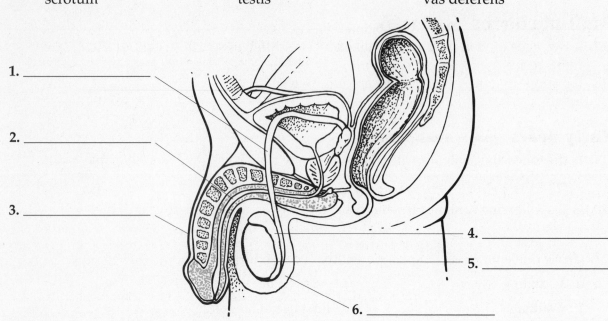

4. _____

5. _____

6. _____

Completion   *Fill in the blanks with terms from Chapter 39.*

7. Secretions of endocrine glands are called _____.

8. Cells that have receptors for a particular hormone are known as _____ cells.

9. The nine hormones produced by the _____ gland regulate body functions or control other endocrine glands.

10. Female gonads are referred to as _____.

11. The reproductive system matures during a period of rapid growth and development called _____.

12. In the ovary, eggs mature in a group of cells known as a(an) _____.

13. An egg is released from the ovary in the process of _____.

14. The _____ is a canal that leads from the uterus to the outside of the body.

15. After an egg is fertilized, it is called a(an) _____.

16. During _____, cells migrate to form three cell layers that later develop into the different organs of the embryo.

17. The mother and embryo exchange gases, food, and waste products across the _____.

18. After eight weeks of development, the embryo is called a(an) _____.

Summary

40–1 Infectious Disease

A disease is any change, other than an injury, that disrupts the normal functions of the body. Diseases are produced by agents such as bacteria, materials in the environment such as cigarette smoke, or inherited conditions. Disease-causing agents are called pathogens. Diseases caused by pathogens are called infectious diseases.

In the 1800s, scientists concluded that infectious diseases are caused by microorganisms, or germs. This idea is now known as the germ theory of disease. A scientist named Robert Koch developed rules to identify the microorganism that causes a specific disease. These rules, known as Koch's postulates, are still used.

Pathogens cause disease by destroying cells, releasing toxins, or disrupting body functions. Types of pathogens include viruses, bacteria, protists, worms, and fungi. Infectious diseases can be transmitted in several ways. Many are spread from one person to another through coughing, sneezing, or physical contact. Some are spread through contaminated water or food. Others are spread by infected animals. Vectors are animals that carry pathogens from person to person.

Antibiotics are drugs that kill bacteria without harming the cells of the host. Antiviral drugs fight certain viral diseases. The best treatment for most infections includes rest, a balanced diet, and fluids.

40–2 The Immune System

The immune system is the body's main defense against pathogens. It produces cells that recognize, attack, destroy, and "remember" each type of pathogen that enters the body. This process is called immunity. The immune system has both nonspecific and specific defenses.

The skin is the most important nonspecific defense. It forms a barrier that few pathogens can get through. Mucus, saliva, and tears trap pathogens and contain an enzyme that kills bacteria. If pathogens manage to enter the body, other nonspecific defenses go to work. The inflammatory response occurs when tissue is damaged by injury or infection. Blood vessels near the site expand, and white blood cells enter the tissues to fight infection. The immune system also releases chemicals that cause a fever. The higher body temperature slows the growth of many pathogens. In addition, cells infected with a virus may produce proteins called interferons, which interfere with the growth of the virus.

If a pathogen is able to get past the nonspecific defenses, the immune system reacts with specific defenses against that particular pathogen. This is called the immune response. A substance that triggers the immune response is known as an antigen. Pathogens may serve as antigens.

There are two types of immune response: humoral immunity and cell-mediated immunity. In humoral immunity, white blood cells, called B cells, produce antibodies that travel through the bloodstream and attack pathogens in the blood. Antibodies are proteins that recognize and bind to specific antigens. In cell-mediated immunity, white blood cells, called T cells, track down and destroy abnormal or infected cells. T cells also attack the cells of transplanted organs. This is called rejection. It can be prevented with drugs. After a pathogen is destroyed, certain B cells or T cells, called memory cells, remain in the body. Memory cells can quickly respond to the same pathogen if it enters the body again. This greatly reduces the chance that the disease develops again.

Besides having a disease, immunity can be acquired in other ways. Vaccination is the injection of a weakened or mild form of a pathogen to produce immunity. This type of immunity is called active immunity. Active immunity appears after exposure to an antigen. Another type of immunity is called passive immunity. It is produced when antibodies enter the body. Antibodies may be injected to fight an infection. Antibodies also pass from mother to fetus. Passive immunity lasts only as long as the antibodies remain in the body.

40–3 Immune System Disorders

There are three types of immune system disorders: allergies, autoimmune diseases, and immunodeficiency diseases. Allergies are overreactions of the immune system to antigens such as pollen. Antigens that cause allergic reactions are called allergens. In response to allergens, the body produces chemicals called histamines, which cause symptoms such as sneezing and watery eyes. Some allergic reactions lead to asthma. Asthma is a chronic respiratory disease in which the air passages become narrower than normal. This may cause coughing and difficulty breathing.

Autoimmune diseases occur when the immune system attacks the body's own cells. For example, in Type I diabetes, the immune system attacks cells of the pancreas that make insulin. Other examples of autoimmune diseases are rheumatoid arthritis, myasthenia gravis, and multiple sclerosis (MS).

Immunodeficiency diseases occur when the normal immune response breaks down. The most common immunodeficiency disease is AIDS. It is caused by the human immunodeficiency virus (HIV). HIV can be transmitted through the exchange of body fluids such as blood. The only no-risk behavior with respect to HIV and AIDS is abstinence. At present, there is no cure or vaccine for AIDS.

40–4 The Environment and Your Health

Anything that increases the chance of disease or injury is a risk factor. Risk factors in the environment include poor air quality and solar radiation. Air quality refers to the number and types of dangerous gases and particles in the air. Water, like air, can carry dangerous substances. For example, human or animal wastes can pollute water with bacteria. Bioterrorism is a new health threat. Bioterrorism is the intentional use of biological agents, such as viruses, to disable or kill people.

Cancer is a life-threatening disease in which cells multiply uncontrollably and destroy healthy tissue. Cancer may cause a tumor. A tumor is a mass of cells growing out of control. Some tumors are not cancerous. All forms of cancer are ultimately caused by harmful mutations. Mutations may be inherited or caused by viruses, chemicals, or radiation. Chemicals that cause cancer are called carcinogens. Sources of potentially harmful radiation include sunlight and radon gas, which is found in rocks and can leak into buildings. Protecting the body from radiation and carcinogens can help prevent cancer. Other ways of maintaining health include eating a healthful diet, getting plenty of exercise and rest, abstaining from harmful activities, and having regular checkups.

Chapter 40 The Immune System and Disease

Section 40–1 Infectious Disease (pages 1031–1035)

Key Concepts
- What causes disease?
- How are infectious diseases transmitted?

Introduction (page 1031)

1. Any change, other than an injury, that disrupts the normal functions of the body, is a(an) _____.

2. What are three ways diseases can come about? _____
_____
_____

3. Disease-causing agents are called _____.

The Germ Theory of Disease (pages 1031–1032)

4. State the germ theory of disease. _____
_____

5. Circle the letter of each scientist whose work led to the germ theory of disease.
   a. Koch   b. Steere   c. Pasteur   d. Burgdorfer

6. Is the following sentence true or false? Lyme disease is caused by bacteria. _____

7. Circle the letter of the type of organism that spreads Lyme disease.
   a. mosquito   b. deer tick   c. deer fly   d. horse fly

Koch's Postulates (page 1032)

8. What are scientists trying to identify when they use Koch's postulates? _____
_____
_____

9. Number the steps in the flowchart below so they show how to apply Koch's postulates.

| Pathogen identified | Pathogen injected into healthy lab mouse | Pathogen grown in pure culture | Healthy mouse becomes sick | Pathogen identified |

____   _____   _____   ____   ____

Agents of Disease (pages 1033–1034)

10. Is the following sentence true or false? Most of the bacteria and yeast that are found in the body are harmful and cause disease. _____

11. List two ways that bacteria can produce illness.

   a. _____ **b.** _____

Match each type of pathogen with a disease caused by that type.

	Type of Pathogen	**Disease**
_____	**12.** Virus	**a.** Athlete's foot
_____	**13.** Bacterium	**b.** Anthrax
_____	**14.** Protist	**c.** Tapeworm
_____	**15.** Worm	**d.** Influenza
_____	**16.** Fungus	**e.** Malaria

How Diseases Are Spread (page 1034)

17. List three ways that infectious diseases are spread.

   a. _____

   b. _____

   c. _____

18. Animals that carry pathogens from person to person are called _____.

19. Is the following sentence true or false? Thorough hand washing does not help prevent the spread of many pathogens. _____

Fighting Infectious Diseases (page 1035)

20. Compounds that kill bacteria without harming the cells of humans or animals are called _____.

21. Circle the letter of each sentence that is true about antibiotics.

   a. They work by interfering with the cellular processes of microorganisms.

   b. Many of them are produced by living organisms.

   c. They were first discovered in the 1940s.

   d. They are effective against viruses.

22. How do antiviral drugs fight viral diseases? _____

_____

_____

Name_____ Class_____ Date_____

Section 40–2 The Immune System
(pages 1036–1042)

Key Concepts
- What is the function of the immune system?
- What are the body's nonspecific defenses against invading pathogens?

Introduction (page 1036)

1. The body's main defense against pathogens is the _____.

Match the type of defense with its role in the body.

	Defense	Role
_____	**2.** Nonspecific	**a.** Destroying harmful pathogens that enter the body
_____	**3.** Specific	**b.** Preventing pathogens from entering the body

Nonspecific Defenses (pages 1036–1038)

4. What is the job of the body's first line of defense? _____
_____
_____

5. List the four components of the body's first line of defense.

   a. _____   c. _____

   b. _____   d. _____

6. Is the following sentence true or false? The body's most important nonspecific defense is the skin. _____

7. How does mucus help protect the body from disease? _____
_____

8. Body secretions contain an enzyme, called _____, that kills bacteria.

9. When does the body's second line of defense come into play? _____
_____
_____

10. Is the following sentence true or false? The inflammatory response is a nonspecific reaction to tissue damage caused by injury or infection. _____

11. White blood cells called _____ engulf and destroy bacteria.

12. Why does an increase in the number of white blood cells indicate that the body is dealing with a serious infection? _____
_____
_____

13. An elevated body temperature is called a(an) _____.

14. Circle the letter of each sentence that is true about elevated body temperature.

    a. It kills many pathogens.

    b. It speeds up the action of white blood cells.

    c. It decreases heart rate.

    d. It slows down chemical reactions.

15. Is the following sentence true or false? Interferon is a protein that helps fight bacterial

infections. _____

Specific Defenses (pages 1038–1040)

16. What is the immune response? _____

_____

_____

17. A substance that triggers the immune response is known as a(an) _____.

18. What are some examples of antigens? _____

_____

_____

19. List the two different immune responses.

    a. _____   **b.** _____

20. Circle the letter of each sentence that is true about humoral immunity.

    a. It is a response to pathogens in body fluids.

    b. It depends on lymphocytes.

    c. It involves antibodies.

    d. It involves plasma cells.

21. A protein that helps destroy pathogens is called a(an) _____.

22. Is the following sentence true or false? Antibodies can fight viruses but not bacteria.

_____

23. Label the antigen-binding sites in the drawing below.

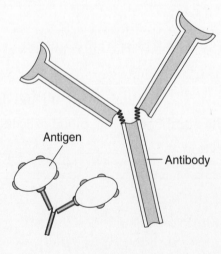

Antigen

Antibody

© Pearson Education, Inc., publishing as Pearson Prentice Hall.

24. Is the following sentence true or false? Plasma cells are specialized B cells.

_____

25. What happens once the body has been exposed to a pathogen? _____

_____

_____

26. Circle the letter of each sentence that is true about cell-mediated immunity.

    a. It is a defense against the body's own cells.

    b. It involves killer T cells.

    c. It involves antibodies.

    d. It causes pathogen cells to rupture and die.

27. Is the following sentence true or false? Cell-mediated immunity is particularly important for diseases caused by prokaryotic pathogens. _____

Acquired Immunity (pages 1041–1042)

28. What is vaccination? _____

_____

_____

29. How do vaccines work? _____

_____

_____

30. Complete the Venn diagram by labeling the two types of immunity.

_____   _____

Is due to antigens
Lasts for life

Can result from vaccination

Is due to antibiotics
Lasts for a short time

Section 40–3 Immune System Disorders
(pages 1043–1047)

Key Concepts
- What is an autoimmune disease?
- How can AIDS be prevented?

Allergies (page 1043)

1. An overreaction of the immune system caused by antigens is called a(an)

   _____.

2. Circle the letter of each choice that is a result of allergens binding to mast cells.

   a. The mast cells release chemicals known as histamines.

   b. There is increased flow of blood and fluids to the surrounding area.

   c. Sneezing, runny nose, watery eyes, and other symptoms occur.

   d. Antihistamines are released by the mast cells.

Asthma (page 1044)

3. A chronic respiratory disease in which air passages become narrower than normal is

   called _____.

Autoimmune Diseases (page 1044)

4. What produces an autoimmune disease? _____

   _____

   _____

   _____

5. Complete the table about autoimmune diseases.

AUTOIMMUNE DISEASES

Autoimmune Disease	Organ or Tissue That Is Attacked
Rheumatoid arthritis	
Type I diabetes	
Myasthenia gravis	
Multiple sclerosis	

AIDS, an Immunodeficiency Disease (pages 1045–1047)

6. Is the following sentence true or false? AIDS is a type of disease in which the immune

   system is weakened by infection. _____

7. What does AIDS stand for? _____

8. List some of the diseases that may be symptoms of AIDS.

   a. _____

   b. _____

9. Circle the letter of the choice that refers to the cells that are attacked by HIV.

   a. Helper T cells   **c.** Red blood cells

   b. Killer T cells   **d.** Helper B cells

10. Is the following sentence true or false? The body does not produce antibodies against HIV. _____

11. Circle the letter of each choice that is true about the spread of HIV.

   a. It is usually spread by casual contact.

   b. It is spread only by sexual contact.

   c. It can be spread by sharing needles.

   d. It is spread only by contact with infected blood or other body fluids.

12. Is the following sentence true or false? Any sexual contact carries some risk of contracting HIV. _____

Reading Skill Practice

When you read about new or difficult concepts, making a concept map can help you better understand and remember the ideas. Make a concept map that shows how immune system disorders are classified, based on the material in Section 40–3. For more information about concept maps, see Appendix A of your text. Do your work on a separate sheet of paper.

Section 40–4 The Environment and Your Health
(pages 1049–1054)

🔑 Key Concepts
- What environmental factors affect your health?
- How can you maintain your health?

Introduction (page 1049)

1. A _____ is anything that increases the chance of disease or injury.

2. Is the following sentence true or false? Both heredity and environmental factors can affect your health. _____

Air Quality (pages 1049–1050)

3. Circle the letter of each factor that is part of air quality.
   a. number and concentrations of gases
   b. amount of sunlight
   c. nature and amount of tiny particles

4. Why can overexposure to carbon monoxide be fatal? _____

_____

_____

5. _____ is a highly reactive form of oxygen that is produced by vehicle exhaust and factory emissions.

6. Allergic reactions can be triggered by _____ .

Water Quality (pages 1050–1051)

7. What has probably been the single most important factor in nearly doubling human life expectancy over the last century or so? _____

8. Circle the letter of each of the following that can be a water pollutant.
   a. human and animal wastes
   b. carbon monoxide
   c. chemicals
   d. dust mites

Bioterrorism (page 1051)

9. The intentional use of biological agents to disable or kill individuals is called

_____ .

10. Why could the release of smallpox virus cause serious problems? _____

_____

_____

Cancer (pages 1052–1053)

11. Circle the letter of each sentence that is true about cancer.

   a. It is generally a life-threatening disease.

   b. It is characterized by cells multiplying uncontrollably and destroying healthy tissue.

   c. It is caused by foreign cells invading the body.

   d. It is easy to treat and to understand.

12. When do cancers begin? _____

   _____

   _____

13. A mass of growing tissue is known as a(an) _____.

14. Is the following sentence true or false? All tumors are cancerous. _____

Match the type of tumor with its description.

Tumor Type	Description
_____ **15.** Benign	**a.** Does not spread to surrounding healthy tissue or to other parts of the body
_____ **16.** Malignant	**b.** Can invade and destroy surrounding healthy tissue

17. List three ways that cancer cells cause illness as they spread.

   a. _____

   b. _____

   c. _____

18. Complete the concept map.

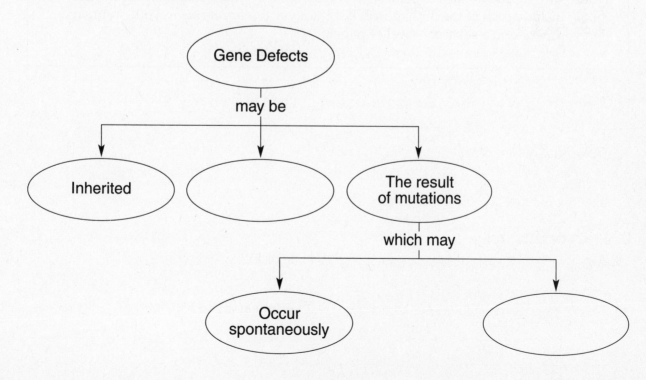

19. Chemical compounds that are known to cause cancer are called

_____ .

20. Why is it important to detect cancer early? _____

_____

Maintaining Health (page 1054)

21. Give three reasons it is important to eat a healthful diet. _____

_____

_____

_____

22. For most people, adequate rest means getting about _____ hours of sleep each night.

23. _____ can cause a variety of respiratory conditions as well as cancers of the lung, mouth, and throat.

24. Is the following sentence true or false? Discovering a disease early does not make it easier to treat._____

Reading Skill Practice

When you read a section with difficult material, writing a summary can help you identify and remember the main ideas and supporting details. Write a concise paragraph summing up the material under each heading in Section 40–4. Each of your paragraphs should be much shorter than the text under that heading in your book. Include each of the highlighted, boldface vocabulary terms in your summary. Do your work on a separate sheet of paper.

Chapter 40   The Immune System and Disease

Vocabulary Review

Matching   *In the space provided, write the letter of the definition that best matches each term.*

_____ **1.** disease

_____ **2.** pathogen

_____ **3.** antibiotic

_____ **4.** immunity

_____ **5.** inflammatory response

_____ **6.** antigen

_____ **7.** vaccination

_____ **8.** allergy

_____ **9.** histamine

_____ **10.** asthma

_____ **11.** risk factor

_____ **12.** vector

a. process in which the immune system produces cells that destroy pathogens or make them harmless

b. substance that triggers the immune response

c. overreaction of the immune system to antigens such as pollen

d. any change, other than an injury, that disrupts the normal functions of the body

e. chemical the body produces in response to allergens

f. drug that kills bacteria without harming the cells of the host

g. disease-causing agent

h. injection of a weakened or mild form of a pathogen to produce immunity

i. animal that carries pathogens from person to person

j. anything that increases the chance of disease or injury

k. response in which blood vessels expand and white blood cells enter infected tissues to fight infection

l. chronic respiratory disease in which the air passages become narrower than normal

Multiple Choice   *In the space provided, write the letter of the answer that best completes each sentence.*

_____ **13.** Koch's postulates are rules for
  a. identifying the microorganism that causes a specific disease.
  b. keeping the environment safe for human health.
  c. determining which vector spreads a disease.
  d. protecting the skin from sunlight.

_____ **14.** Nonspecific defenses include
  a. fever.
  b. interferon.
  c. the skin.
  d. all of the above.

_____ **15.** The type of immunity that results when antibodies are passed from mother to fetus is called
  a. active immunity.
  b. passive immunity.
  c. permanent immunity.
  d. inherited immunity.

_____ **16.** The type of immunity in which T cells attack abnormal or infected cells is known as
  a. humoral immunity.
  b. passive immunity.
  c. cell-mediated immunity.
  d. T cell immunity.

_____ **17.** An example of an autoimmune disease is
  a. Type I diabetes.
  b. AIDS.
  c. asthma.
  d. allergy to pollen.